Annual Reports
on Fermentation Processes

VOLUME 2

Academic Press Rapid Manuscript Reproduction

Annual Reports
on Fermentation Processes

VOLUME 2

EDITED BY

D. PERLMAN

School of Pharmacy
University of Wisconsin
Madison, Wisconsin

ASSOCIATE EDITOR

GEORGE T. TSAO

Laboratory of Renewable Resources Engineering
Purdue University
West Lafayette, Indiana

ACADEMIC PRESS   New York   San Francisco   London   1978
A Subsidiary of Harcourt Brace Jovanovich, Publishers

ACADEMIC PRESS, INC.
111 Fifth Avenue, New York, New York 10003

United Kingdom Edition published by
ACADEMIC PRESS, INC. (LONDON) LTD.
24/28 Oval Road, London NW1 7DX

ISBN 0-12-040302-1

PRINTED IN THE UNITED STATES OF AMERICA

Contents

List of Contributors

Numbers in parentheses indicate the pages on which authors' contributions begin.

BERNARD J. ABBOTT (91), The Lilly Research Laboratories, Eli Lilly and Company, Indianapolis, Indiana

A. ASZALOS (305), Frederick Cancer Research Center, National Cancer Institute, Frederick, Maryland

K. AUNSTRUP (125), Novo Industri A/S, Novo Allé, Bagsvaerd, Denmark

J. BÉRDY (305), Research Institute for Pharmaceutical Chemistry, Budapest, Hungary

TERRY CHOU (1), Laboratory of Renewable Resources Engineering, Purdue University, West Lafayette, Indiana

BRUCE DALE (1), Laboratory of Renewable Resources Engineering, Purdue University, West Lafayette, Indiana

MICHAEL C. FLICKINGER (23), Laboratory of Renewable Resources Engineering, Purdue University, West Lafayette, Indiana

M. GORMAN (203), The Lilly Research Laboratories, Eli Lilly and Company, Indianapolis, Indiana

Y. HIROSE (155), Central Research Laboratories, Ajinomoto Company, Inc., Kawasaki, Japan

TEH AN HSU (1), Laboratory of Renewable Resources Engineering, Purdue University, West Lafayette, Indiana

F. M. HUBER (203), The Lilly Research Laboratories, Eli Lilly and Company, Indianapolis, Indiana

CHRISTINE LADISCH (1), Laboratory of Renewable Resources Engineering, Purdue University, West Lafayette, Indiana

MICHAEL LADISCH (1), Laboratory of Renewable Resources Engineering, Purdue University, West Lafayette, Indiana

TAKASHI NARA (223), Tokyo Research Laboratory, Kyowa Hakko Kogyo, Co., Ltd., Tokyo, Japan

H. J. PEPPLER (191), Whitefish Bay, Wisconsin

K. SANO (155), Central Research Laboratories, Ajinomoto Company, Inc., Kawasaki, Japan

H. SHIBAI (155), Central Research Laboratories, Ajinomoto Company, Inc., Kawasaki, Japan

M. SHIBATA (267), Faculty of Pharmaceutical Sciences, Kumamoto University, Kumamoto, Japan

ROBERT D. TANNER (73), Chemical Engineering Department, Vanderbilt University, Nashville, Tennessee

GEORGE T. TSAO (1, 23), Laboratory of Renewable Resources Engineering, Purdue University, West Lafayette, Indiana

M. UYEDA (267), Faculty of Pharmaceutical Sciences, Kumamoto University, Kumamoto, Japan

WILLIAM A. WEIGAND (43), School of Chemical Engineering, Purdue University, West Lafayette, Indiana

Preface

ANNUAL REPORTS ON FERMENTATION PROCESSES is intended to furnish readers with a critical account of significant developments published during the past few years concerning fermentation processes. Only published materials are included, and the main value of this series is to assist the reader to keep current with developments in areas of fermentation research and development where he may have only peripheral or limited interest. The authors of the chapters of this volume were asked to answer the question "What are the *major* developments in the field that were published this past year?" and have done so admirably.

Many persons are involved in decisions in launching and sustaining a new series focusing on current developments, and we are indebted to them for assisting in this process. The officers, past and present, of the Division of Microbial and Biochemical Technology of the American Chemical Society have been very helpful and supportive of this project. We hope that the volumes will meet the readers' needs, and we look forward to receiving suggestions of modifications for future volumes.

D. Perlman, Chairman

July 20, 1978

Division of Microbial
and Biochemical Technology,
American Chemical Society,
c/o School of Pharmacy
University of Wisconsin
Madison, Wisconsin

CHAPTER 1

FERMENTATION SUBSTRATES FROM CELLULOSIC
MATERIALS: PRODUCTION OF FERMENTABLE
SUGARS FROM CELLULOSIC MATERIALS

George T. Tsao
Michael Ladisch
Christine Ladisch
Teh An Hsu
Bruce Dale
Terry Chou

Laboratory of Renewable Resources Engineering
Purdue University
West Lafayette, Indiana

*In this chapter, the availability and the economy of utiliza-
tion of cellulosic wastes as an alternative natural resource are
first compared to those of petroleum crude oil which is the major
raw material source of current chemical industries. Next, the
technical background of the related subject is described in considerable details from which two factors, (1) highly ordered cellulose structure and (2) lignin seal surrounding cellulose fibers,
will emerge as the major obstacles of hydrolysis of cellulose
contained in cellulose materials. The main subject matter of
this chapter will then be introduced, namely the use of selective
solvent extraction to fractionate cellulosic wastes into three
individual components: cellulose, hemicellulose, and lignin.
Once cellulose is dissolved in a solution, it is no longer pro-
tected by a crystalline structure nor lignin seal. Experimental
results indicate that the re-precipitated cellulose can be easily hydrolyzed by either acids or enzymes to give high yield of
glucose.*

I. THE POTENTIAL AND THE ECONOMY OF CELLULOSIC WASTES AS
    ALTERNATIVE NATURAL RESOURCE

Through photosynthesis, solar energy is absorbed, converted
and stored in the biomass of farm crops, trees, bush plants,
algae, and other vegetations. Crops, trees, and many other green
plants are now produced for various economical reasons. These
is, however, always a large amount of cellulosic wastes that is
currently not utilized. According to Bellamy (1), such wastes
are available in the U.S. at about one billion tons per year.
Estimates by other authors are of the same order of magnitude.
For instance, Reed (2) gives a figure of 588 million tons per
year for "collectible biomass" in the United States. Stephens
and Heichel (3) have an estimate of 730 million tons per year of
animal manures and agricultural crop wastes but not including
forest wastes. Stone (4), Sloneker (5), and Cooper (6) set the
cellulosic wastes from forest and pulp industries, agricultural
crops and animal feedlots, and food and vegetable processing
industries at 200, 812, and 2 million tons, respectively, making
a total of 1,034 million tons per year. All the figures cited
are on the basis of dry matters.

Being in a solid form and being usually scattered over large
land surfaces, the cellulosic wastes require large expenses for
their collection and transportation to central processing plants.
On the other hand, one should not overlook the equally large
expenses of exploration, well drilling, pumping, transportation,
and so on, needed for producing petroleum. Particularly, most
rich and easily accessible oil fields have already been explored,
and for new sources of petroleum such as those of North Sea and
Alaska Northern Slope, the costs are also high. In any case, the
supply of crude oil is limited and can last about 50 more years
at the present rate of consumption. Cellulosic wastes are an
annually renewable resource.

Perhaps a more realistic and meaningful assessment can be
made for cellulosic wastes as a potential alternative source of
chemicals by the following analysis. Suppose we take an area of
25 miles radius in one of the major farm states such as Indiana.
Corn is the main crop here and currently a rate of about 120
bushels of corn (weighing about 7,000 pounds) per acre per year
can be produced. For every pound of corn (i.e. corn kernels)
harvested, there is also produced one pound of solid wastes including cobs, stalks, husks, leaves, and roots (7,8). These
wastes are currently plowed under in the field and are of value
to the soil as a physical conditioner as well as a source of
fertilizer value. Approximately for every ton of wastes taken
away from the field, one has to spend about 5 dollars worth of
fertilizer to replace its fertilizer value (5,7). Depending on
the grade of the land, one can take anywhere from 25% to 100% of
the crop residues from the field without causing deterioration of
the soil condition (8). Suppose that, on the average, 50% of the

residues is collected. Also, assume that there are 500 acres of
farm per square mile. We can potentially collect about 1.5
million tons of crop waste per year from an area of 25 mile
radius. The "25 mile" figure is chosen because it is a reasonable distance for a 10-ton truck to make two round trips per day
to collect and deliver 20 tons of cellulosic waste to a central
processing plant. The cost of collecting and transporting the
20 tons of waste is estimated to be $300 including the costs of
the truck, gasoline and the driver. Therefore, the cellulosic
wastes from corn can be made available at a delivered cost of $30
per ton ($5 to replace the fertilizer value, $10 extra payment to
the farmer as an inducement and for his extra expense, and $15
for extra expenses) at a rate of 1.5 million tons per year.

Cellulosic wastes from many other sources can be made available at an even lower cost than corn crop residue. For instance,
wood chips at some locations are sold at $8 per ton. Animal
feedlot wastes are another source of cellulose which has in fact
a negative value. Bagasse, the fibrous residue after removal of
sugar juice from cane, is available at sugar mills. Wet bagasse
is currently burned for heating value. Because of the high moisture content, the heat from a ton of bagasse can be replaced by
that of $7.50 worth of coal. This list can go on and on to show
that the sources of cellulosic wastes are widespread. Furthermore, additional cellulosic materials such as grass, hay, etc.,
can be purposely raised on land of marginal quality that is not
suitable for production of human food and/or animal feed.
Through successful plant breeding, fast-growing trees can also
become a major source of cellulosic raw materials in the not-very-
distant future.

II. GENERAL BACKGROUND

Most cellulosic solids contain three major components: cellulose, hemicellulose, and lignin, in ratios of roughly 4:3:3
(9-11). These are only approximate figures. For instance,
softwood contains typically 42, 25 and 28% cellulose, hemicellulose, and lignin, respectively, while corncobs contain about
40, 36 and 16%. Cellulose is a homogeneous polymer of glucose,
while hemicellulose molecules are often polymers of pentoses
(xylose and arabinose), hexoses (mannose) and a number of sugar
acids. Lignin is a polyphenolic macromolecule (12-14).

Vanillin is a well known chemical derived from lignin on an
industrial scale. If lignin is made available in large quantities in a fairly dry state, it can be burned as a fuel. Lignin
is relatively higher in C- and H- and lower in O-content than
cellulose and hemicellulose, and is the most valuable of the
three with regard to heating value (15). At least, direct burning can be the means of utilizing lignin before other more

valuable large-volume applications can be developed. As shown
later, direct burning will make the overall process of production
of fermentable sugars from cellulosic materials more than energy
self-sufficient.

Hydrolysis of hemicellulose to mono- and oligo-saccharides
is comparatively an easy matter (16-18) which can be accomplished
with either acids or enzyme under moderate conditions. Utilization of hemicellulose hydrolysates as a fermentation carbon
source will be fully discussed in the next chapter.

Unlike hemicellulose, cellulose is strongly resistant to
hydrolysis. In recent years, cellulose utilization has been the
subject of many active research projects. Recent renewed interest in cellulose as an alternative source of fuels and chemicals
resulted in much expanded research activities on cellulose
hydrolysis. There have been numerous papers published on this
subject and a complete list of pertinent literature is too long
to compile. There are the following conference proceedings and
books published in recent years on cellulose utilization, each
of which in turn contains a large number of articles and references (19-24).

   (1) Proceedings of the Seventh Cellulose Conference, edited
       by E. C. Jahn, Interscience (1971).
   (2) Proceedings of the Eighth Cellulose Conference, edited
       by T. E. Timell, Interscience (1976).
   (3) Cellulose Technology Research, ACS Symposium Series,
       edited by A. F. Turbak, ACS (1975).
   (4) Symposium on Enzymatic Hydrolysis of Cellulose, edited
       by M. Bailey, T. M. Enari and M. Linko, published by
       the Finnish National Fund for Research and Development
       (1975).
   (5) Cellulose as a Chemical and Energy Resource, edited by
       C. R. Wilke, Biotech. Bioeng. Symposium Series No. 5,
       Interscience (1975).
   (6) Enzymatic Conversion of Cellulosic Materials: Technology
       and Applications, Biotech. Bioeng. Symposium Series No. 6,
       edited by E. L. Gaden, M. H. Mandels and L. A. Spano,
       Interscience (1976).

III.   MAJOR OBSTACLES TO CELLULOSE HYDROLYSIS

Cellulose is a linear homopolymer of anhydroglucose units
linked together with 1,4-beta-glucosidic linkages. Generally
speaking, cellulose is difficult to hydrolysis due to two reasons:
(1) its highly ordered crystalline structure and (2) a lignin
seal surrounding cellulose fiber as a physical barrier. From a
process engineering viewpoint, the 1,4-beta-glucosidic linkage in
cellulose is no more difficult to break than the 1,4-alpha-
glucosidic linkage in starch if the cellulose molecules are fully

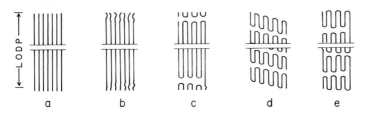

FIGURE 1. *Molecular arrangements in the protofibril: (a)*
(a) Full extension and complete crystalline model. (b) Fibrilized
fringe micellar model. (c) Fibrillized model of Ellefsen.
(d) Manley's planar zig-zag model. (e) Chain-folding model with
fold length much smaller than LODP.

hydrated and exposed and are free from hindrance by the lignin
seal and crystalline structure. In other words, the difficulty
in obtaining fast and complete hydrolysis of cellulose is due to
not the primary linkage of the cellulosic polymeric chain but
rather the secondary and tertiary structures of cellulosic
materials.

Individual linear polymeric cellulose molecules are linked
together to form elementary fibrils. Depending upon its source,
the degree of polymerization DP, or the number of anhydroglucose
units per molecule of cellulose, ranges from about 1,000 (cellulose in newsprint) to as high as 10,000 (in cotton). In hydrolysis with acids, DP drops quickly and levels off at a more or less
constant value of 100 to 200 (known as "LODP" for *leveling off*
degree of polymerization) corresponding to a length of 500 to
1,000 Å. The easily hydrolyzable portion of cellulose is often
referred to as the "amorphous" region of cellulose, and the
resistant residue the crystalline cellulose. On the average,
cellulose is 15% amorphous and 85% crystalline. In order to
hydrolyze crystalline cellulose, a strong acid at a high temperature is needed, which makes chemical and equipment costs prohibitively high. The strongly acidic conditions also cause decomposition of the glucose product into undesirable degradation
by-products.

Once the amorphous cellulose is removed, rod-shaped particles
of crystalline cellulose can be obtained. In the case of cotton,
the particles are about 400 Å long and 100 Å wide. Further hydrolysis of the rod shaped particles with strong acid can reduce
particle weight by as much as 80% and yet the particles remain
unaltered in a number of their properties including molecular
chain length (25-27) and water sorption (26,27), reflecting the
strong crystalline order in such particles.

The crystalline structure of cellulose is still a subject of considerable controversy. Two major schools of thought exist. Based on the observation of chain folding in linear synthetic polymers, models of cellulose fibrils involving folded chains have been suggested. On the other hand, structure models based on extended cellulose molecules are also found in the literature. Recently, Chang (28) summarized various molecular arrangements of cellulose and showed several such models in Figure 1.

If cellulose molecules are fully extended, the length of the protofibril (also known as elementary fibril) is expected to be much longer than 500 to 1,000 Å measured from those of wood and cotton cellulose. Consequently, Chang was able to rule out models (a) and (b) if Figure 1. The fact that the length of fully extended molecules of the LODP agrees well with those of crystalline cellulose after the "amorphous" region was removed by acid hydrolysis suggests that the remaining cellulose chains are no longer folded. Consequently, models (d) and (e) are also considered unlikely. Chang (28) believes that model (c) is the one that agrees with most of the known evidence. In summary, the fine structure of cellulose fibril is as follows (Figure 2):

(1) A cellulose molecule folds back and forth on itself within a plane with a fold length corresponding to that of a LODP unit. This structure is called a "Platellite."

(2) A platellite has the approximate dimensions of LODP x 38 Å x 6 Å, and is the smallest structure unit of cellulose.

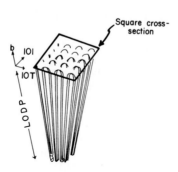

FIGURE 2. *Perspective view of a cellulose crystalline according to the Chang model.*

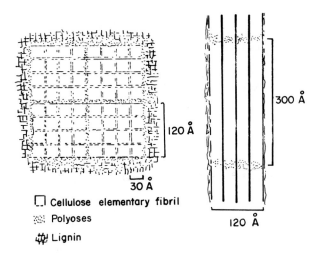

FIGURE 3. Model of the ultrastructural organization of the
cell wall components in wood; cross section on the left, longi-
tudinal section on the right.

    (3) Several platellites are packed to make up the crystal-
lite or protofibril of cellulose.
    Chang's model can then be incorporated into a high-level
structure shown in Figure 3.
    (4) In addition to elementary or protofibril, there are two
further fibrillar elements, namely fibrils of about 120 Å and
fibrils of about 250 Å. The latter are called microfibrils.
    (5) If a systematic structure is assumed, the 120 Å fibrils
consist of 16 elementary fibrils and the microfibrils should
consist of four 120 Å fibrils.
    The anhydroglucose units are linked together through 1,4-
beta-glucoside bonds. Most of these bonds in cellulose exist in
a configuration known as Herman's form. Through repeated beta-
linkages, linear polymeric cellulose molecules can be built up.
Chang (28) indicated the existence of another beta-bond which
involves a deflection of approximately 60° from the normal
Herman's form. With two or three such successive deflected beta-
bonds, a loop can be formed in a cellulose polymer to produce a
180° U-turn which is essential for chain folding. It is further
postulated based upon thermodynamic considerations that these
exposed, deflected beta-linkages are more susceptible to hydrolytic cleavage. Therefore, the so-called "amophous" regions in a
cellulose fibril could be zones rich in loop-bonds containing

many deflected beta-glucosidic linkages. After hydrolysis by a
dilute acid that removes "amorphous" regions, cellulose left is
of an increased "crystallinity" and is very resistant to further
acid hydrolysis.

Native cellulose fibers exist in the cell wals of trees and
other vegetative materials. The cell wall architecture is
schematically depicted in Figure 4, which suggests the cementing
role of lignin and the hindrance it creates to cellulose hydrolysis.

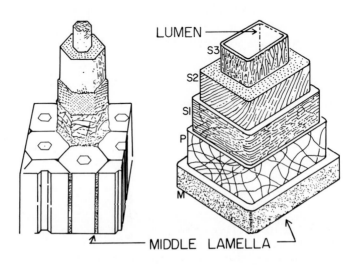

FIGURE 4.   Cell-wall architecture.

Surrounding the fiber, and heavily lignified and stiff is the middle lamella (M in Figure 4), shared by adjacent fibers. The outermost layer of the fiber is called the primary wall (P) which was formed on cell division. The secondary wall, formed during the growth and maturation of the cell, is subdivided into the transition lamella (S1), the main secondary wall (S2) and the inner secondary wall (S3). The middle lamella which is heavy on lignin is about 1 to 2μ thick. It is amorphous and generally porous. The primary wall is usually very thin of only 300 Å corresponding to three layers of cellulose elementary fibrils. The secondary wall (S1, S2 and S3) which thickens during cell growth contains the majority of cellulose. It is anywhere from 1 to 10μ thick consisting of cellulose microfibrils in helical arrangement (9).

With the fwo factors, (1) strong crystalline structure and (2) lignin barrier, fully described, we are now in a position to understand the difficulties faced by many researchers working with cellulose hydrolysis by either acids or enzymes. Acids are nonspecific catalysts; they can attack cellulose as well as lignin. For instance, sulfurous acid can de-ligninate (9) and also act as a catalyst for cellulose hydrolysis (not very effective because of being a very weak acid). Unfortunately, due to the strong crystallinity, only very strong acids can hydrolyze cellulose to a high conversion level. When strong acids are used, the chemical costs (including the cost of alkali for subsequent neutralization) are high. And as unspecific catalysts strong acids also promote the degradation of glucose and reduce its yield. Therefore, acid hydrolysis has not been a useful method for cellulose hydrolysis even though it was used occasionally under special circumstances (during the Second World War, for instance).

Enzymes are specific catalysts, cellulases can convert cellulose into glucose with little by-products. Unfortunately, being highly specific, cellulase has no direct hydrolytic effect on lignin. Being macromolecular (molecular weight of 38,000 to 75,000), cellulase enzymes cannot easily penetrate through the lignin seal surrounding the cellulose fibers. Thus, the problem here is the nonaccessibility of cellulose to the enzymes. To overcome the lignin barrier hindrance, cellulosic materials have been ball-milled to sizes of 300 mesh or less (29,30). By then, indeed the cellulosic material becomes readily hydrolyzable by cellulase enzymes. However, the cost of milling cellulosic materials to a very small size is prohibitively high (31). Therefore, like acidic hydrolysis, enzymatic hydrolysis of cellulose has not been a commercial success.

IV. CELLULOSE HYDROLYSIS AFTER PRETREATMENT BY SOLVENT

    To remove the two obstacles of cellulose hydrolysis due to
(1) lignin barrier and (2) cellulose structure, the use of a solvent to selectively extract cellulose from solid wastes has been
tried. Once dissolved, cellulose can be hydrolyzed free from the
two obstacles. Early experiments in our laboratory at Purdue
University have shown that a solvent known as Cadoxen (32) (its
composition to be given later) can readily dissolve cellulose.
Cadoxen is actually a solution of alkaline pH containing ethylene
diamine and water. When excess water is added to a cellulose-
cadoxen solution, cellulose will reprecipitate in a soft floc.
Upon standing, cellulose can recrystallize and become again resistant to hydrolytic attack. When the cellulose is still in the
form of a soft floc, it can be easily hydrolyzed with either
cellulase enzymes or acids to give high yield of glucose. *Tricoderma viride* cellulases were tested and found to be active in the
presence of the Cadoxen-water solution. Acid hydrolysis was also
tried. Excess acid was added to neutralize first the basic solvent whereupon cellulose reprecipitated and then bring the pH
down to an acidic level. Upon standing, the cellulose was hydro-
lized and redissolved into the acidic solution. These preliminary
results thus suggested a highly promising process of cellulose
isolation and hydrolysis. The overall process of conversion of
cellulosic materials including a solvent pretreatment is shown in
Figures 5 and 6. Solvent A is essentially for removal of hemicellulose. It can be a warm alkaline or dilute acid solution.
Such a treatment also helps to remove other extractable materials
and reduce the degree of polymerization of cellulose.
    This review will describe three solvents (Solvent B in Figures
5 and 6) that have been successfully used in pretreatment of cellulose to achieve high levels of glucose production. Other solvents are also being examined in our laboratory for such applications.

A. *Cadoxen as a Cellulose Solvent*

    After hemicellulose is removed (Figure 5), cellulose and lig-
nin are left in a wet state. Since Cadoxen is an alkaline liquid,
the wet residue should be washed with water to remove residual
acid if acid were used for hemicellulose selective extraction.
If the hemicellulose extraction were done with NaOH to begin with,
the washing would not be critical. In fact, addition of NaOH to
Cadoxen can increase the solubility of cellulose in Cadoxen by
several percent (33).
    Cadoxen or tris (ethylenediamine) cadmium hydroxide, first
introduced by Jayne and Neushaffer in 1957 (32), is a clear,
colorless, nearly odorless liquid, is stable for an almost

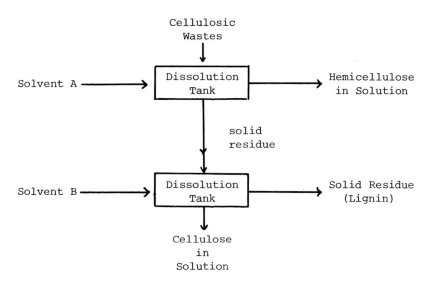

FIGURE 5. *Flowsheet of process of selective solvent separation of hemicellulose, cellulose and lignin.*

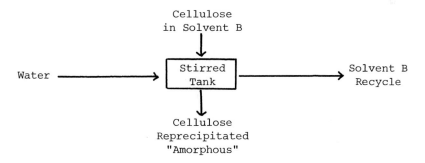

FIGURE 6. *Reprecipitation of cellulose.*

unlimited time, causes little degradation of cellulose and is relatively easy to prepare. Its composition includes 25 to 30% ethylenediamine in water and 4.5 to 5.2% cadmium (added as oxide or hydroxide) based upon the total liquid weight. Cadoxen is considered a useful solvent in cellulose hydrolysis for several reasons.

(1) It contains 70 to 75% water in its formulation. This is a very important point. All cellulosic wastes when harvested and collected contain considerable amounts of moisture. Cadoxen requires no predrying, which avoids an otherwise costly operation.

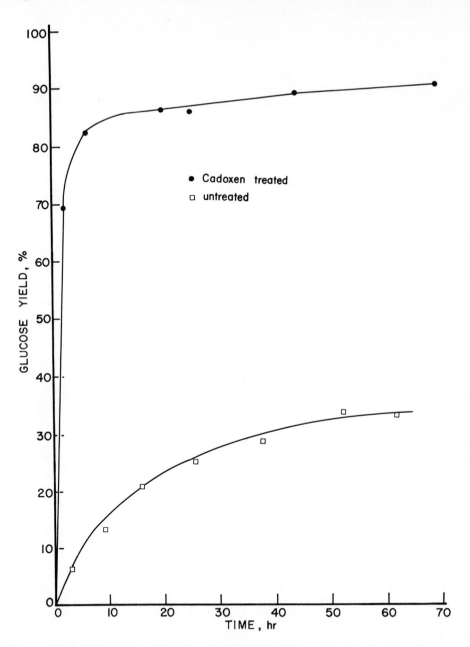

FIGURE 7. Hydrolysis rates of pretreated vs untreated
cellulose (Avicel containing 8% moisture).

For some other cellulose solvents, even trace amounts of water can reduce cellulose solubility in the solvents drastically. Such solvents should be almost automatically excluded from further consideration for the proposed application.

(2) Cadoxen can dissolve some ten percent by weight of cellulose at room temperature which is reasonably high.

(3) Cadoxen-cellulose solution is stable at room temperature.

(4) The components of Cadoxen including ethylenediamine and cadmium are apparently nontoxic to cellulase enzymes. As soon as the solution is neutralized to pH 5 (whereupon the dissolved cellulose will reprecipitate), cellulase can be added into the mixture (if desired) and hydrolyze the cellulose floc to yield glucose.

Figure 7 gives a comparison of the rate and the yield of hydrolysis of a microcrystalline cellulose (Avicel of FMC Corporation) between those with and without a pretreatment of Cadoxen. The hydrolysis was catalyzed by a commercial enzyme preparation from *Tricoderma viride*. Similar comparisons are given in Figure 8 for corn crop residue and for bagasse.

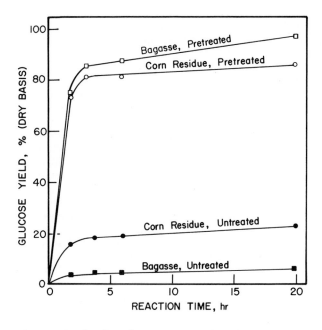

FIGURE 8. *Hydrolysis timecourses of cadoxen pretreated residues.*

B. CMCS as a Cellulose Solvent

CMCS is a solvent which, unlike cadoxen, is made of components on the GRAS ("Generally Recognized as Safe") list. Hence this solvent is less toxic than cadoxen and therefore easier to handle.

1. Solvent Composition. CMCS is an aqueous solution of 17% sodium tartrate, 6.6% ferric chloride, 7.8% caustic, and 6.2% sodium sulfite.

The solvent can be made both in liquid and dry forms. The powder is obtained by treating the liquid CMCS as described previously with approximately 0.5 volume methanol per volume CMCS. A fine green powder is formed which when dissolved in 7.8% caustic gives a solvent with properties similar to those of the original (liquid) CMCS. The significance of solid CMCS is that it opens the possibility of manufacturing the "solvent" in a central plant. Thus, the solvent could be shipped dry to individual plants utilizing cellulosic materials. The result would be an overall savings in capital and operating costs due to economies of scale since individual plants would not need to invest in the equipment required to produce the powder.

2. Dissolution of the Powder. Both liquid CMCS and powdered CMCS dissolved in 7.8% caustic readily dissolve up to 4% Avicell at room conditions.

3. Reprecipitation of Cellulose. The cellulose dissolved in CMCS is reprecipitated upon addition of methanol or water.

4. Recovery of Solvent. When Avicell is dissolved and then reprecipitated the solvent can be readily washed from the cellulose. As shown in Figure 9, approximately 3 volumes wash water per volume CMCS results in essentially complete recovery of solvent.

The CMCS, which is now diluted with water, can be concentrated to its original strength by evaporation under partial vacuum.

5. Enzyme Hydrolysis of CMCS Treated Corn Residue. Corn residue was mixed with CMCS in a 5:5:1 solvent:residue ratio (by weight). After standing 6 hours, the cellulose was precipitated in situ and the solvent was washed from the residue. The residue was then mixed with buffer (pH 5) and cellulose enzyme and incubated at 45°C. The rate of glucose formation was monitored using a Beckman glucose analyzer.

At the enzyme:cellulose ratio used in this experiment (7,600 IU/lb cellulose), 70% yields of glucose were obtained in 20 hours (see Figure 10). Further incubation increased the glucose yield to 90%.

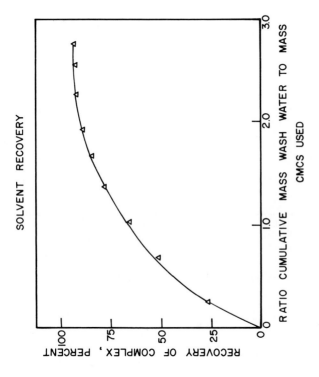

FIGURE 9. *Recovery of CMCS.*

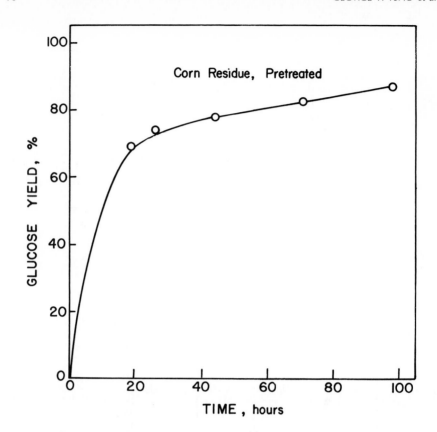

FIGURE 10.   Hydrolysis timecourse of CMCS pretreated corn
residue.

C.   Concentrated Sulfuric Acid as a Cellulose Solvent

Sulfuric acid is a swelling and a solvation agent for cellulose. At 55% acid concentration swelling occurs and at 75% acid
solvation.

When Avicel was mixed with sulfuric acid at acid concentrations of up to 60%, swelling occurred. At concentrations between
60 and 70% the mixture became translucent. The Avicel was recovered by adding water to the cellulose/acid solutions to dilute
the acid followed by centrifugation to spin down the cellulose.
At a 70% acid level approximately 8% of the cellulose initially
added to the acid was not recovered. The Avicel which was

recovered, however, when hydrolyzed with an enzyme preparation at
pH 5 gave 90% conversion to glucose in one hour. Cellulose swollen with 50% acid gave 50% conversion when hydrolyzed with the
same enzyme preparation.

If, instead of water, an organic solvent such as methanol is
added as a diluant to the cellulose/acid solutions, cellulose
will also be reprecipitated. In this case, less than 1% of the
cellulose initially added to the acid was not recovered. The
reprecipitated cellulose when hydrolyzed with enzyme at pH 5 gave
90% conversion to glucose in about one hour.

The sulfuric acid treatment was applied to cornstover as both
a solvent and a catalyst for hydrolysis. A dilute acid is first
used to remove hemicellulose. The solid residue is filtered and
dried to about 10% moisture. Seventy percent sulfuric acid is
added to wet the solid residue with strong mixing and tumbling.
Methanol is then added to dilute the mixture. After filtration,
water is added and the solid residue is hydrolyzed to yield glucose. The filtrate which contains sulfuric acid and methanol is
treated for recycling. Laboratory results have shown that reprecipitated cellulose can be hydrolyzed to 90% plus conversion
to glucose with the dilute sulfuric acid without the use of cellulase enzymes.

V. PROCESS DESCRIPTION

Two major obstacles to cellulose hydrolysis are: (1) strong
crystalline structure of cellulose, and (2) protective lignin
seal surrounding cellulose fibers. By selectively dissolving
cellulose in a solvent, one should be able to remove both obstacles in one treatment. The flowsheets in Figures 5 and 6 give an
outline of this processing concept.

The reprecipitated cellulose can be readily hydrolyzed to a
high yield of glucose by either a dilute acid and/or cellulase
enzymes.

A more detailed flowsheet of a process using sulfuric acid is
shown in Figure 11. In this case, sulfuric acid is employed both
as a catalyst for hydrolysis and as a solvent. Besides the acid
and the cellulosic raw material, only lime and an organic solvent
such as methanol is needed. A preliminary acid hydrolysis of the
raw material removes hemicellulose and a small portion of cellulose. This hydrolysate also contains those constituents in the
raw material that are extractable by a dilute acid. The solvent
treated cellulose together with lignin is hydrolyzed again with a
dilute acid to give a hydrolysate stream containing mostly glucose. The residual lignin can be a raw material for chemical
processing or it can be burned for heat.

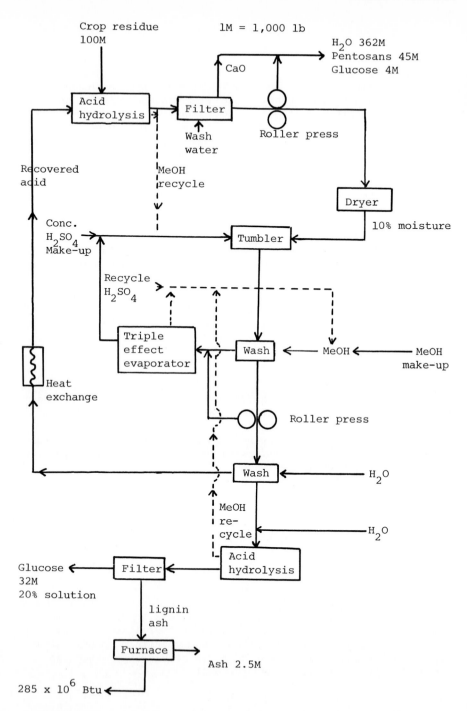

FIGURE 11. Sulfuric acid process flowsheet 50 tons crop residue/day.

The composition of cellulosic materials varies widely from plant species to species. It also varies due to different harvesting and storage conditions. A selected average composition for farm crop residues is given below (on dry weight percent).

Cellulose	34.3%
Hemicellulose	39.6%
Lignin	19.9%
Protein and others	4.6%
Ash	2.5%

The flowsheet in Figure 11 is based upon a feed of 100,000 pounds of cellulosic raw material. A crude cost analysis is given (Table I) showing the fermentable sugars can be made at a cost of about 1.6 cents per pound. The cost analysis is not complete for it does not include such items as labor, depreciation, interest, and tax. A more comprehensive cost analysis can be made after the completion of a pilot plant study.

TABLE I. Cost Analysis

Item	Quantity	Unit price	Cost
Crop residue	100,000 lb	$0.015/lb	$1,500
H_2SO_4	7,460 lb	$0.020/lb	$ 149
MeOH	1,800 lb	$0.064/lb	$ 115
Heat	78×10^6 Btu	$2.500/$10^6$ Btu	$ 195
CaO	3,620 lb	$0.015/lb	$ 54
Total raw materials and major utility cost			$2,013

Credit for recoverable heat from burning residual
lignin $(285 \times 10^6$ Btu) ($2.50/$10^6$ Btu) $ 713
Cost after lignin credit $1,300
Available fermentable sugars:
(1) Glucose   32,010 lb
(2) Pentosan stream   48,900 lb
                                                     80,910 lb
Unit cost of fermentable sugar from $30/ton crop residue

$$= \frac{\$1,300}{80,910 \text{ lb}} = 1.6 \text{ cents/lb}$$

REFERENCES

1. Bellamy, W. D., *Biotech. Bioeng. 16,* 869 (1974).
2. Reed, T. B., "Biomass Energy Refinery for Production of Fuel
    and Fertilizer," *in* "Proceedings of the Eighth Cellulose
    Conference" (T. E. Timell, ed.), p. 1.   Interscience (1976).
3. Stephens, G. R. and Heichel, G. H., "Agricultural and Forest
    Products as Sources of Cellulose," *in* "Cellulose as Chemical
    and Energy Resource" (C. R. Wilke, ed.), Biotech. Bioeng.
    Symposium Series No. 5, p. 27.   Interscience (1975).
4. Stone, R. N., "Timber, Wood Residues, and Wood Pulp as
    Sources of Cellulose," *in* "Enzyme Conversion of Cellulosic
    Materials: Technology and Application" (E. L. Gaden et al.,
    eds.), Biotech. Bioeng. Symposium Series No. 6 (1976).
5. Sloneker, J. H. "Agricultural Residues, Including Feedlot
    Wastes" (E. L. Gaden et al., eds.), Biotech. Bioeng. Sympo-
    sium Series No. 6, p. 235 (1976).
6. Cooper, J. L., "The Potential of Food Processing Solid
    Wastes as a Source of Cellulose for Enzymatic Conversion"
    (E. L. Gaden et al, eds.), Biotech. Bioeng. Symposium Series
    No. 6, p. 251 (1976).
7. Ladisch, M. R., Gong, C. S., and Tsao, G. T., "Utilization
    of Corn Crop Residues as a Potential Source for Single Cell
    Protein" *in* Proceedings of Society Ind. Microbiology Annual
    Meeting 1976 (in press).
8. Petriz, D. C., Smith, W. H., Lectenberg, V. L., and Parsons,
    S. D. Publication ID 104 (1975). Cooperation Extension
    Service, Purdue University, West Lafayette, Indiana.
9. Rydholm, S. A., "Pulping Processes." Interscience (1965).
10. Otto, E., Spurlin, H. M., and Grafflin, M. W., "Cellulose
    and Cellulose Derivates, Parts 1-3," 2nd Ed., Vol. 5, of
    Book Series on High Polymers. John Wiley (1954-55).
11. Bikales, N. M. and Segal, L., "Cellulose and Cellulose
    Derivatives, Parts 4 and 5" as Vol. 5 of Book Series of High
    Polymers. John Wiley (1971).
12. Brauns, F. E., "The Chemistry of Lignin." Academic Press
    (1952).
13. Brauns, F. E. and Brauns, D. A., "The Chemistry of Lignin,
    Supplement Volume." Academic Press (1960).
14. "Lignins: Occurrence, Formation, Structure and Reactions"
    (K. V. Sarkanen and C. H. Ludwig, eds.). Wiley-Interscience
    (1971).
15. Falkehag, S. I., "Lignin in Materials" *in* Proceedings of
    the Eighth Cellulose Conference (T. E. Timell, ed.), p. 247.
    Interscience (1976).
16. BeMiller, J. N., *Advances Carbohyd. Chem. 22,* 25 (1967).
17. Pigman, W. and Moschera, J., Adv. Chem. Series, No. 117,
    Am. Chem. Soc. (1971).

18. Browning, B. L., "Methods of Wood Chemistry," Vol. 2, Chapter 26. Interscience (1967).

19. "Proceedings of the Seventh Cellulose Conference" (E. C. Jahn, ed.). Interscience (1971).

20. "Proceedings of the Eighth Cellulose Conference (T. E. Timell, ed.). Interscience (1976).

21. Turbak, A. F., Cellulose Technology Research, ACS Symposium Series, *Am. Chem. Soc.* (1975).

22. Symposium on Enzymatic Hydrolysis of Cellulose (M. Bailey, T. M. Enari, and M. Linke, eds.). The Finnish National Fund for Research and Development (1975).

23. "Cellulose as a Chemical and Energy Resource" (C. R. Wilke, ed.). Biotech. Bioeng. Symposium Series No. 5. Interscience (1975).

24. "Enzymatic Conversion of Cellulosic Materials: Technology and Applications" (E. L. Gaden, M. H. Mandels, and L. A. Spano, eds.). Biotech. Bioeng. Symposium Series No. 6. Interscience (1976).

25. Daruwalla, E. H. and Shet, R. T., *Textile Res. J. 32,* 942 (1962).

26. Millett, M. A., Moore, W. E., and Saeman, J. F., *Ind. Eng. Chem. 46,* 1493 (1954).

27. Achwal, W. B. and Nabar, G. M., *Textile Res. J. 30,* 872 (1960).

28. Chang, M., *Polymer Science, Part C 36,* 343 (1971).

29. Wilke, C. R., "Glucose from Cellulose in Municipal Wastes," paper presented at the Am. Inst. Chem. Eng. Annual Meeting, Philadelphia (Dec. 1973).

30. Wilke, C. R. and Mitra, G., "Process Development Studies on Enzymatic Hydrolysis of Cellulose." Biotech. Bioeng. Symposium Series No. 5, p. 253. Interscience (1975).

31. Nystrom, J., "Discussion of Pretreatment to Enhance Enzymatic and Microbiological Attack of Cellulosic Materials." Biotech. Bioeng. Symposium Series No. 5, p. 221. Interscience (1975).

32. Jayme, G. and Neuschaffer, K., *Die Makro. Chemie 28,* 71 (1957).

33. Donetzhuber, A., *Svensk Papperstidning 63,* 447 (1960).

CHAPTER 2

FERMENTATION SUBSTRATES FROM CELLULOSIC
MATERIALS: FERMENTATION PRODUCTS
FROM CELLULOSIC MATERIALS

Michael C. Flickinger
George T. Tsao

Laboratory of Renewable Resources Engineering
Purdue University
Wesy Lafayette, Indiana

I. A CARBOHYDRATE BASED CHEMICAL INDUSTRY - MYTH OR REALITY

It is naive to suggest a magical, abrupt displacement of
basic petrochemical industries by fermentation processes based on
cellulosic raw materials. A more realistic examination of the
chemical industry, however, will reveal that substitution of fermentation derived fuels, chemical feedstocks, and protein supplements for those currently derived from nonrenewable resources is
now possible due to the low cost quantitative recovery of hexoses
and pentoses from any cellulosic material. Despite opinions to
the contrary (1), cellulose will remain our largest renewable resource and most logical raw material upon which to base our future chemical needs.

This review will discuss the potential for cellulosic-derived
fermentation substrates for those industrial fermentations which
benefit the most from such an inexpensive renewable substrate
source. Fermentation products solely derived from microbial
metabolism, such as the enzyme and antibiotic industries, will
gain little advantage. However, those fermentation products
which directly compete with a current synthetic process based on
a nonrenewable raw material will definitely gain an advantage by
switching to a cellulose-derived substrate.

The solvent pretreatment cellulose process may not immediately
solve, but will significantly alleviate, the fossil-fuel dependency of the chemical industry. There will be petrochemical processes for key industrial feedstocks that the fermentation industry cannot compete with, such as production of large-volume

aromatics (benzene, *p*-xylene) and propylene derivatives. However, as the supply and depletion rates of oil, gas, and coal reserves are more precisely defined in the future (2,3), a new fermentation industry utilizing inexpensive cellulose-derived sugar
syrups will gain prominence. The fermentation industry today is
presented with the economic and technological challenge of producing large-volume, low mark-up products. The solvent pretreatment cellulose process may now allow this industry to firmly progress from dependence on molasses, and formerly inexpensive hydro-
carbon substrates, to cellulosics.

A.   *The Outlook for Cellulosics*

Two recent developments suggest that a carbohydrate-based
chemical industry may be on the verge of becoming a reality. The
first is the current state of the U.S. and western European chemical industries. Petrochemical outlook analysts appear to agree
that the industry will suffer in two areas through the 1980's
(4-7). First is the increasing level of unused capacity in the
basic chemical feedstocks and fibers (8). The decreasing capacity use of ethylene (88%), propylene (76%), butadiene (91%), benzene (81%), and *p*-xylene (79%) underlies product pricing and
eventual industry expansion. The outlook of these basic industrial feedstocks (Figure 1) forecasts the direction of the petrochemical industry. The second factor is that the petrochemical
industry faces an inevitable future increase in the cost of their
basic raw material due to increased costs of exploration and exploitation of fossil-fuel reserves. With capacity in basic chemicals leveling off at 80%, and the cost of petroleum and natural
gas bound only to increase, the petrochemical industry will find
increasing raw material costs harder to cover and new expansion
more difficult to justify.

The long-term prospects for a carbohydrate based industry
have been suddenly and dramatically improved by the cellulose-
solvent pretreatment process. The doubling of the quantity of
glucose recoverable from cellulose from the previous 50% (acid
hydrolysis) yield to 100% yield has immediately doubled the yield
of all previously reported fermentation-derived fuels and feedstocks from cellulose. In addition, chemical (9,10) and microbial
utilization of pentoses from hemicellulose and the potential for
useful chemical and combustible fuel by-product credits from lignin (11,12,48) greatly improves the economics of renewable resources in competition with petrochemicals (discussed in Section
B).

One of the more important aspects of the solvent pretreatment
breakthrough, with regards to economic implications, is the general nature of the process. Previously, only the microbial conversion of grain and molasses (commodities subject to widely varying
price) to ethanol, acetone, and butanol, had been tried in the

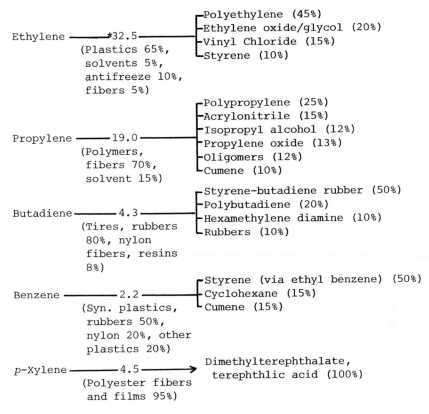

FIGURE 1.   Major petrochemical feedstocks *[annual production first quarter 1978 (8) in billions of pounds].

U.S.   These conversions met with limited success (13,14) except in times of commodity surpluses or when counted as a by-product credit in waste treatment (15-17).   However, due to the pretreatment process, now *any* cellulose containing material can serve as a raw material.   This fact, coupled with a variety of hexose and pentose fermentations, may now allow for the economic production of valuable fuels, chemical feedstocks, and protein supplements, even though the chemical routes from glucose may be more complex than from ethylene.   When the price of one cellulosic raw material fluctuates, other sources can be substituted and different products produced from the same fermentation facility.   This is not always true of chemical plants with limited versatility which rely on one raw material and are designed to produce only a limited number of products.   In essence, a combined fermentation facility using cellulosic substrates, integrated with complementary chemical processes, is no longer dependent upon one raw

material source, nor is it solely dependent on the economics of
one product. This factor alone should stimulate future invest-
ment in fermentation-derived chemicals from cellulosics.

B. Failure of Previous Schemes

The literature contains many varied routes from cellulose to
industrial chemical intermediates (10,18-20,48). The potential
uses for cellulosics are so diverse that no single product will
dominate future technology. The previous schemes of Becher (19)
and Wilke (22) have failed to realize that the economics of hexose
production from cellulose hinges on the value of hemicellulose,
lignin, and stillage disposal. The cellulosic material can contain as much as 15% to 35% hemicellulose and 6-20% by weight lignin (11,22). Goldstein (9,11,12) and Edwards (10) have suggested
the high yield (75%) conversion of xylose to furfural (54¢/lb)
(23) for production of a valuable chemical by-product from soft-
wood-derived hemicellulose.

Our own laboratory is currently investigating the potential
of 2,3-butanediol production from pentoses using strains of the
Klebseilla (24) and *Aeromonas genera* (25). Economic microbial
conversion of hemicellulose-derived pentose mixtures to 2,3-
butanediol or ethanol as chemical feedstocks (26) or liquid fuels
could potentially improve the overall cost of hexose production
from cellulose.

The utilization of lignin is equally important in the overall
process economics. Lignin obtained in a purified form from the
solvent pretreatment process has high fuel value for direct com-
bustion, or for gasification (11,000 Btu/lb) (27). The Brazil-
lians have developed schemes for coke production from lignin, a
valuable resource for a country without coal reserves (48). In
addition, lignin's potential for chemical or microbial degradation
to catechols, monomeric phenols, cresylic acid and benzene (11)
forecasts a large area for industrial exploitation as a readily
renewable chemical and energy source.

C. Production of Key Intermediates by Fermentation

It may be much more economically feasible for the fermentation
industry to focus its latest technology and process development
efforts on production of several large-volume key chemical intermediates rather than on many diverse end products. An integrated
scheme of intensive cellulose production, substrate treatment,
fermentation, chemical processing and product recovery is essential. In the example given by Hayes (28), neither raw material
costs (12) nor biosynthetic optimization (29) alone can solve the
problem of economic operation. The scheme proposed in Figure 2
would utilize fermentation for the high-volume conversion of the

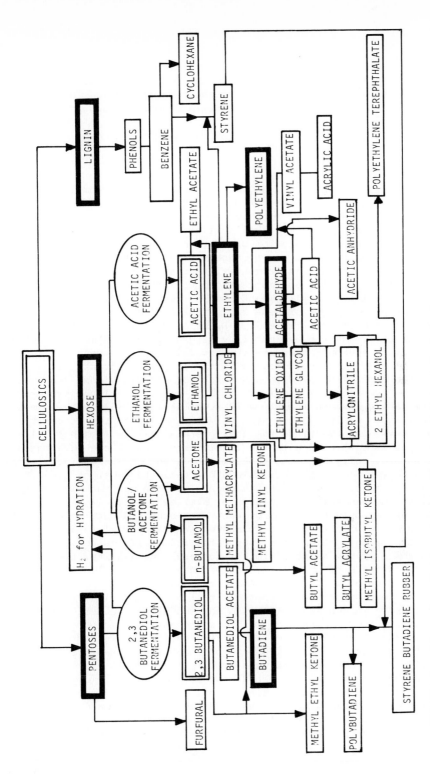

FIGURE 2. The role of fermentation in production of feedstocks.

primary components of cellulose (glucose, pentoses) into basic
key industry chemicals: ethanol, acetic acid, acetone, n-butanol,
or 2,3-butanediol, and possibly phenols (aromatics).   These could
serve as building blocks for an entire chemical industry (30,31).

II.   SUGAR SYRUPS FROM THE SOLVENT PRETREATMENT CELLULOSE PROCESS

Numerous authors (32-36,48) have reviewed and compared
molasses, sucrose, and starch with possible cellulosic-derived
fermentation substrates with agreement on three important factors
for choice of substrate: availability, quality, and cost.   For
the high output fermentation products needed for industrial intermediates, raw material and product recovery costs may be the most
important components in fermentation production (21,37).
     Current process estimates from our laboratory suggest that
the availability, quality, and cost of glucose derived from the
solvent pretreatment process may compare favorably with glucose
derived from starch (Table I).   Since a variety of cellulosics
can be utilized, the availability of glucose syrups may not be as
subject to seasonal harvests or crop failures.   Present estimates
predict a 20% glucose stream with the following advantages:
(1) few hemicellulose components (polyuronides, xylans, arabans)
will be present; (2) lignin is separated in the solvent process
eliminating its consideration in sugar streams; (3) by the use of
immobilized cellulase (or eventual elimination of the necessity
for enzyme treatment) no residual protein will be present; (4) ash
present is separated with the lignin fraction.   These advantages
effectively eliminate the problems predicted by Seeley (32).   This
glucose syrup will be available at an estimated cost of 1.6-2.5¢/
lb (dry basis) (this price includes a $30/ton raw material cost)
which compares well with starch of similar quality (4-12¢/lb).
This price would be an improvement over beet and cane molasses
(3-10¢/lb), which must also compete with the animal feeds market.
     The major problem with substrates from cellulosics is the fer-
mentation of the hemicellulose fraction.   The quality, availability, and price of this fermentable sugar stream will depend on the
composition of various cellulosic residues.
     Protein present in corn-stalk residues (approximately 7% for
corn grown in Indiana) will also be removed by the hemicellulose
extraction and may be a desirable component for either isolation
as a protein supplement or as a fermentation nutrient.   Our laboratory is currently studying possible pentosan streams from various
residues for fermentation into useful liquid fuels and chemical
feedstocks.   With an estimated cost also of 1.6¢/lb (dry basis),
although this mixture may be complex, its price and quality will
compare favorably with cane and beet molasses (37) and whey (36)
as a fermentation substrate.   Some cellulosic residues, such as
corncobs, may produce a hemicellulose fraction of predominately

TABLE I. Carbohydrate or Carbohydrate-Derived Fermentation Substrates

Substrate	Major components	Approximate %	Reproducibility	Price	Competing market
Molasses-cane	Sucrose Dextrose Fructose Other carbohydrates Protein	30-40 4-9 5-12 2-5 2-5	Fair	3-10¢/lb (dry basis)	Animal feed
Molasses-beet	Sucrose Raffinose Invert sugar Glutamic acid Other organics Protein	51 1 1 3 10 5	Fair	3-10¢/lb (dry basis)	Animal feed
Invert syrup	Sucrose Invert sugar	3 67	Good	5-22¢/lb	Food
Raw sugar	Sucrose Invert sugar	97 1	Good	5-10¢/lb	Animal feed
Glucose (corn-starch derived)	Glucose Maltose, isomaltose, trimers	95 5	Good	5-25¢/lb	Corn as food, animal feed, isomerase
Glucose (cellulose derived)	Glucose	95	Good	1.6-2.5¢/lb	Solid fuel, animal feed
Pentoses (Hemicellulose derived)	Xylose, mannose, arabinose Glucose Protein	90 0-8 3-7	Fair (depending on cellulose source)	1.6-2.5¢/lb	Furfural, xylitol, solid fuel
Ethanol (Fermentation)	Ethanol	95-100	Excellent	9-16¢/lb (less if captive)	Industrial solvent, chemical feedstock, liquid fuel

one component (90% xylose) which would greatly simplify its industrial development and expand its potential for chemical (furfural,
xylitol) (51) as well as for microbial uses.

III.   POTENTIAL LARGE-VOLUME FERMENTATION PRODUCTS FROM CELLULOSICS

A. *INDUSTRIAL ALCOHOL*

   The potential for production of ethanol from renewable resources as an industrial solvent and chemical intermediate is
greater than that as a liquid fuel. A detailed cost analysis of
the advantages of the cellulose solvent pretreatment process for
alcohol production is not possible before additional information
on the by-product credits of the hemicellulose stream, lignin,
and fermentation stillage is available.
   The literature contains many cost estimates of the production
of ethanol. Cysewski and Wilke (21) estimate the cost of ethanol
production, including single-cell protein production credits, to
be $1.05/gal ($12.35/MM Btu). They suggest that every ¢/lb for
sugar adds 14¢/gal to the ethanol production cost. The basic
fermentation charges from their process are 20-30¢/gal. Lipinsky
(49) suggests a cost of $1.14/gal for sugar-cane derived ferment-
able sugars, with existing technology ($13.36/MM Btu). This esti-
mate is on the basis of of 6¢/lb sugar (dry basis) requiring 15
lbs of fermentable solids per gallon of alcohol (35). The raw
material costs comprise $0.76/gal with the remaining $0.38/gal
production costs including taxes, profits, and capital charges.
   Current estimates based on the solvent pretreatment process
indicate a fermentable sugar cost of 1.6¢/lb-2.5¢/lb (including
labor). Adding on the same $0.38/gal production cost, ethanol
produced with this new technology could be produced at $0.62-
$0.76/gal ($7.29-$9.00/MM Btu). As speculative as these cost
estimates may be, they do demonstrate the magnitude of potential
economic advantages of the solvent pretreatment and pentose
credits, and also that the industrial alcohol produced by fermentation with this new technology is competitive with synthetic
ethanol from ethylene, whose cost is $1.12/gal (24). Pilot plant
studies on this new technology should verify these predictions.
   Even though ethanol from cellulosics is competitive with synthetic alcohol, the future of fermentation alcohol may lie in the
development of new, large domestic markets as either a basic
chemical intermediate or as a liquid fuel. The investor who
views the current 200 million gal/year U.S. synthetic alcohol
production at 65% capacity (8), with a decreasing acetaldehyde
derivative market and little future in any overseas markets (39),
may not be impressed simply with the competitive price of fermentation alcohol. The current forecast for "traditional" synthetic
alcohol markets is a growth of only 2-3%/year up to 264 million
gallons by 1981.

Alcohol/gasoline blends as motor fuels have a long history and will continue to stir interest in regions where it is looked on not so much as a fuel from renewable resources, but more as a means of development of an additional market for farm commodities. The idea of blended fuels, even though complicated by the necessity of strict elimination of water from alcohol, has survived and co-existed with petrochemical motor fuels in the past in South Africa (28) and in Brazil, where it continues to gain importance. Distillation facilities for 320 thousand liters/day capacity are being planned for Brazil with an annual capacity of 20 billion liters by the year 1981 to cover 20% of the gasoline consumed in the country (40). A 10% blend of alcohol with gasoline in the U.S. would mean a 10 billion gallon/year market based on the 1975 consumption of 300 million gallons/day (41).

Additional liquid motor fuel markets may be realized for cellulosics by a combination of fermentation alcohol production with zeolite catalytic processes for the conversion of alcohols directly to gasoline, now proposed as part of the direct utilization of coal for motor fuels (42,43). Proponents of this new process state that economics are not favorable for gasoline production now; however, as crude oil prices continue to increase, cellulosics may find themselves eventually competing directly with coal for the liquid fuel market (43). Estimates suggest that the zeolite processes, when starting from coal, will add 40¢-50¢/gallon to the current price of gasoline. This may not be able to compete with the stated 5¢-10¢/gallon added cost of the conversion/gallon of gasoline when starting from alcohol.

B. Chemical Feedstocks

Whether or not new industrial alcohol markets can be developed for fermentation alcohol, even with the more favorable technology, may not be as critical to the establishment of a carbohydrate-based chemical industry as the point at which it becomes economically viable for dehydration of ethanol to ethylene. Miller (44,45), Finn (46), Heitz (47) and Sheppard and Lipinsky (49) have attempted to analyze the complexities of determining the price at which dehydration of ethanol will become feasible. Sheppard and Lipinsky suggest that the cost of petroleum would have to triple in order for ethanol produced from sugars to become economically competitive (49). Davies (43) predicts that coal will be the more economical feedstock for ethylene until the price of oil soars to $30/bbl (1974 dollars). By following the calculations of Heitz (47), with the current ethylene price of 12.5¢/lb and a 2¢/lb dehydration cost, ethanol would be competitive at 40¢/gallon (4.70/MM Btu). The true economics of this critical point are determined by numerous noneconomic considerations such as the complexities of marketing, distribution, facility amortization, regional employment (49), as well as our foreign

balance of payments. The calculations of Miller (45), Perrone
(48), and Davis (17) showing the effect of ethylene cost on ethanol cost have attempted to predict how far in the future ethanol
dehydration is. Remember that the price of ethylene from petroleum was relatively stable at 3.0¢ to 3.5¢/lb until 1972. In
less than six years the price has risen to over 12¢/lb.

As critical as ethanol dehydration is for supplying the key
chemical intermediates of ethylene, polyethylene, and acetaldehyde, Figure 2 proposes additional fermentations as sources of
chemical feedstocks and liquid fuels: the acetic acid, n-butanol
fermentations from glucose and the production of 2.3-butanol from
pentoses. Both of the latter fermentations, as the technology
exists today, suffer from low final concentration of the desired
product (butanol/acetone 1.5%-3.5% (51,52), 2,3-butanediol 5%-10%
(53), and low yields of sugar consumed (butanol-acetone 0.3 gm/
gm, 2,3-butanediol 0.2-0.4 gm/gm depending upon carbohydrate
source). Ongoing biochemical, genetic, and isolation engineering
studies under the auspices of the U.S. Department of Energy's
Fuels from Biomass program should lead to improved yields and
less energy intensive product recovery methods.

Both n-butanol and acetone are valuable feedstocks and may
also have potential as liquid fuels [butanol 15,000 Btu/lb, acetone 13,000 Btu/lb (10)]. Acetone is an important intermediate
in methylmethacrylate used in plexiglas, acrylic plastics and
latex paints. Methyl isobutyl ketone, methyl isobutyl carbinol,
and isophorone are additional valuable derivatives of acetone.
Butanol is a versatile feedstock not only as a solvent but for
production of butyl acetate, butyl acrylate, glycol esters and
plasticizers.

There are currently four synthetic processes for acetone or
butanol production from petrochemicals (31). The economics of
the production of these two feedstocks, from cane juice at 6¢/lb,
has been analyzed by Sheppard and Lipinsky (35). With ethylene
at 12¢/lb and propylene at 8.4¢/lb, it would be economical to
produce n-butanol and acetone from sucrose when the price of
petroleum reaches $17/bbl (assuming a 30% marketing cost). This
estimate suggests that with the less expensive cellulose-derived
glucose and additional improvement in the yield and final concentration, the acetone-butanol fermentation may be economically
useful for feedstock production.

The fourth fermentation for chemical feedstocks (Figure 2) is
the production of 2,3-butanediol from pentoses. This diol may
prove to be a more versatile chemical with higher-valued derivatives than either n-butanol or acetone. Butadiene (23¢/lb) can
be produced with existing technology from this diol. The current
market for butadiene in styrene-butadiene rubber and polybuta-
diene is large (3 million lbs/year). Even though the unsaturated
compound can be produced from ethanol (54), it may be more feasible to produce it directly from the diol (via butanediol acetate)
as a feedstock credit for pentosan utilization as previously

mentioned.   In addition, 2,3-butanediol has several other large
volume derivatives such as methyl ethyl ketone, methyl vinyl ketone, and methyl vinyl carbinol as well as numerous useful smaller
volume derivatives (55), and as a liquid fuel (11,700 Btu/lb).
     Co-production of hydrogen from both of these fermentations
will be useful for captive use in hydrogenation, but may not be
economical for distribution as a gaseous fuel due to its low
heating value of 275-325 Btu/st cu ft in comparison with methane,
1,000 Btu/std cu ft, and natural gas, 900-1,200 Btu/std cu ft
(10).
     Comparison of the key petrochemical feedstocks from Figure 1
with those of Figure 2 shows that there are intermediates where
microbial products cannot be substituted. Propylene-derived feedstocks are noticeably absent from Figure 2. Large-volume aromatics are suggested to be derived from lignin, but this technology
is nonexistent today. Perhaps some of these chemicals could be
derived from a return to the "Reppe chemistry" of the 1950's with
fermentation ethanol or acetylene (from carbide) as the nucleus
(56). Current investigation of microbial acrylic acid production
(57) may help to develop a renewable resource base for these intermediates. The Mobil process for conversion of alcohols to hydrocarbons could be exploited as a source of aromatic feedstocks
(78,79).

C. *Microbial Polysaccharide*

     The market for cellulose-derived carbohydrates in microbial
polysaccharides production is large because in these fermentations, substrate costs are critical in determining polysaccharide
costs. In order to compete for this market, fermentable sugar
streams from renewable resources must be able to compete in quality and price with existing abundant glucose and sucrose sources.
All industrial polysaccharide-producing fermentations utilize
either glucose or sucrose as substrates (60) (Table II) and will
continue to rely on these readily available carbon sources. Even
though microbial polysaccharides can be produced from five carbon
sugars (58), the mixed pentose fermentable sugar stream from
cellulosics may be of little value in biopolymer production.
Polysaccharides produced from this substrate would be of undeter-
mined composition with inconsistent properties--totally unsuitable
in the industry today where medium composition must be precisely
defined to produce polysaccharides with exacting properties (59).
     In the immediate future, the major markets for microbial poly-
saccharides derived from cellulosics are in bentonite drilling
mud lubrication polymers and enhanced oil recovery (EOR) applications. Cellulose-derived glucose syrups may provide a cost advantage in the competition between microbial polysaccharides
(xanthan gum) and partially hydrolyzed polyacrylamides.
     As the price of microbial polysaccharides increases, users of
this polymer for bentonite drilling mud lubrication are substi-
tuting other less expensive cellulose derivatives, such as

TABLE II. Microbial Polysaccharides of Commercial Importance (60)

Name	Organism	Type of Process	Substrate	Component Sugar of Polymer
Dextran	Leuconostoc mesenteroides	cell-free enzyme	glucose (sucrose)	glucose
Xanthan gum	Xanthomonas campestris	bacterial	glucose, glucose syrup	glucose (acetate), glucuronic acid, mannose (pyruvate)
Pullulan	Aureobasidium pullans	fungal	glucose syrup	glucose
Erwinia Exopolysaccharide	Erwinia tahitica	bacterial	glucose?, glucose syrup?	glucose, galactose, fucose, uronic acid (acetyl)
Scleroglucan	Sclerotium glucanicum	fungal	glucose	glucose
Microbial alginate	Azotobacter vinelandii	bacterial	sucrose	mannuronic acid, guluronic acid (acetate)
Bakers Yeast Glycan	Saccharomyces cerevisiae	yeast	glucose	glucose, mannose
Curdlan	Agrobacterium sp Alcaligenes faecalis	bacterial	glucose	glucose

carboxymethyl cellulose, which are less effective. Improvements
in the production cost of xanthan gum would increase the potential for this polymer in the drilling muds market which is estimated to be at 3,000 tons per year by 1980 (61).

In polymer flooding (secondary oil recovery) and micellar-
polymer flooding (tertiary oil recovery), mobility control polymers are used to reduce the mobility of injected water. Polymers
can reduce mobility by decreasing effective rock permeability and
by increasing effective fluid viscosity (62). At present, partially hydrolyzed polyacrylamides dominate the technology. Use of
xanthan gum in polymer flooding has been supplanted by the less
expensive polyacrylamides.

However, xanthan gum has been demonstrated in laboratory and
field tests to be superior to polyacrylamides in salt compatibil-
ity, mobility reduction, polymer retention, and resistance to
mechanical degradation. What appears to be limiting future large-
scale use of xanthan is increased polymer quality (removal of
cellular debris to prevent plugging) and cost of production (62).

There is little doubt that use of microbial polysaccharides
in surfactant flooding (tertiary oil recovery) will be one of the
largest future markets. Polymer demand for this application has
been estimated by Wells (61) to be between 138-248 thousand pounds
per day by 1986 starting at 7,300 to 18,300 pounds daily by 1979.
This estimate is based on utilization of 50% polysaccharide and
50% polyacrylamide. Current pricing has placed the price of polysaccharide for EOR at $2.25 ± 0.20/lb and that for polyacrylamide
at $1.30 ± 0.30/lb (61). A cheaper glucose syrup may effectively
close this price gap, resulting in an even larger biopolymer
annual market than the 200-250 million pounds predicted.

D. *Protein Supplements*

Carbohydrates hold the greatest potential for future single-
cell protein development because they are renewable. Alternative
fuel uses and animal feed demands will determine the economic
availability of cellulose-derived fermentable sugar substrates.
Current high costs for sugar (18¢/lb), dextrose (16¢/lb), and
corn syrups (12¢/lb) indicate that commercial prospects for a
feed grade SCP from these carbohydrate sources is unlikely (63).
Utilization of carbohydrate wastes or unrefined carbohydrate
syrups will become the future renewable resource base for SCP
production.

Waste streams such as whey, sulfite waste liquor, potato
wastes, and alkali-treated bagasse (64) have all been successfully utilized for SCP substrates (65). Molasses will probably
not significantly compete as an SCP source as it will bring a
higher price in the animal feeds market (63).

The slim profit margins of SCP production from alkanes of the
1960's has been completely eliminated by the increasing price of
crude oil and the adequate world supply of soy protein. In the

long term, as competing food demands begin to limit protein feed
sources, soy protein prices will rise. During this same period,
petroleum-based SCP production costs from ethanol (ethylene) and
methanol (methane) will also increase in spite of improvements in
fermentation technology. When this occurs, production of SCP
supplements for animal feeds from carbohydrates will become more
widespread in order to meet the demands of the animal feeds industry. Future SCP production from cellulosics will offer defi-
nite competitive advantages over those processes which now utilize methanol or synthetic ethanol as substrates.

     Fermentation ethanol may have the best future as a substrate
for SCP production (36,66). The advantages of ethanol have been
summarized in Table III (66). Many microorganisms have been reported to utilize ethanol as a sole source of carbon and energy
(66) as well as an important co-substrate (36) (Table IV). The

TABLE III. *Advantages of Ethanol as a Substrate for SCP (66)*

* Purity
* Acceptability
* Ease of storage and handling
* Nontoxicity
* Versatility as a substrate or co-substrate
* Miscibility with water
* Relatively low O_2 demand
* Relatively low heat produced
* High cell yields on per-gram basis
* Metabolized by numerous bacteria and yeast as a sole source
    of carbon and energy

TABLE IV. *Some Bacterial and Yeast Genera Reported as
            Candidates for SCP Production on Ethanol (66)*

Bacteria	Yeasts
Acetobacter	Candida
Acinetobacter	Debaromyces
Arthrobacter	Endomycopsis
Bacillus	Hansenula
Brevibacterium	Mycoderma
Corynebacterium	Pichia
Hyphomicrobium	Rhodoturula
Nocardia	Saccharomyces
Pseudomonas	

primary disadvantage of ethanol as an SCP source has been cost.
However, because of the low cost of fermentation ethanol made
possible by the improved cellulose hydrolysis process, this industrial alcohol can now compete with ethylene-derived ethanol as
an SCP substrate. Nonfood-grade cellulosic wastes can be used
for ethanol production. Ethanol as a pure product would then be
suitable for converting into SCP supplements destined for human
consumption, such as torula yeast. In this way, ethanol as a key
chemical intermediate may find additional uses as an SCP source
for two reasons: first, because of the ability to produce it at
a given standard of purity, and secondly, because of its ease of
transportation and storage which allows for control over SCP substrate supply.

The demand for protein in human diets will continue to in
crease drastically as a result of population growth and rising
standards of living in all countries of the world. Improved recovery of hexoses and pentoses from cellulose may accelerate
efforts toward eventual replacement of hydrocarbon-derived SCP
processes and effectively compete with soybean meal and fish meal
prices for these expanding markets.

IV. AREAS WHERE FUNDAMENTAL RESEARCH IS NEEDED

Industrial development of SCP processes as one of the first
high-volume/low-cost fermentation products has been responsible
for the rapid development of continuous fermentation technology,
innovative fermenter design, and interest in low-capital cost
fermentation facilities (19). Development of high-volume chemical feedstocks from carbohydrate fermentation may require a complementary era of intensive research in fermentation technology.
The primary disadvantage for production of liquid fuels and feedstocks by fermentation is product concentration. The economics
of any of the large-volume fermentation products mentioned could
be dramtcially improved with as little as a 2-5-fold increase in
concentration in the final fermentation broth. Product yields
and productivity may be improved by cell recycle and multistage
continuous systems. Concentration, however, may require less
emphasis on sophisticated computer coupled process control, and
more emphasis on fundamental biochemical and genetic studies concerning the biochemistry of product inhibition and enzyme regulation. Various investigators have begun the study of product inhibition in ethanol production (67-70), methods for increasing
the final alcohol concentration (71), as well as low-pressure
ethanol recovery (72-74). These studies should be extended to
other potential feedstock-producing fermentations.

Because of the varied composition of hemicellulose, complete
microbial utilization of cellulose presents another area where
fundamental research is required. Few studies of batch utilization of multiple substrates have appeared in the literature.

Continuous culture and modeling studies (74-77) have contributed
to our understanding of adaptive enzyme systems and microbial
growth in the presence of more than one substrate. However, the
majority of commercially important fermentations today are batch
processes. Efficient utilization of the mixed pentose stream
from hemicellulose, by either a batch or continuous process, may
be vital for improvement of overall cellulose utilization process
economics.

Successful establishment of large-volume renewable resource-
based fermentations, particularly in developing countries, will
necessitate development of low technology or "village-level"
processes. The physical nature of cellulosic residues and the
economics of their harvesting and transport will favor smaller
fermentation plants. Decreasing capital intensity in fermentation technology, coupled with a network of small plants built
near the source of cellulosics and designed to serve a small distribution system, may give additional economic advantage to renewable resource based chemicals over large scale, capital intensive oil- or coal-based chemical plants (43). Integration of
these facilities with both food and materials processing plants
will offer added advantages (49).

Numerous biochemical advantages of defined mixed cultures,
noted for SCP production (65), should be exploited in efforts to
obtain stable nonaseptic microbial systems for low technology
feedstock production. Even though carbohydrates do not offer
the selective advantages as a substrate that hydrocarbons have,
defined mixed cultures or genetically improved strains may exhibit increased stability to resist contamination.

Changes in technology and philosophy will be required in
order to establish a renewable resource base for the chemical
industry. Utilizing cellulosics as this basis, we are tapping
the earth's most abundant and readily renewable resource, while
providing our industries with relatively inexpensive, and reliable, raw materials.

REFERENCES

1. Moore, C. A., *Chem. Technol. 6*, 762 (1976).
2. Povitch, M. J., *Chem. Technol. 6*, 434 (1976).
3. Klass, D. L., *Chem. Technol. 4*, 161 (1974).
4. "World Chemical Outlook '78," *Chem. Eng. News 55 (51)*, 30
    (1977).
5. "Petrochemical Outlook-Marketing and Chemical Engineering,"
    Chem. Eng. Progress 73 (7), 26-45, *73 (8)*, 11-16, *73 (9)*,
    25-32, *73 (10)*, 25-35, *73 (11)*, 25-45 (1977).
6. Greek, B. F. and Fallwell, W. F., *Chem. Eng. News 55 (49)*,
    10 (1977).
7. Greek, B. F. and Fallwell, W. F., *Chem. Eng. News 56 (2)* 10
    (1978).

8. "Capacity Use Still Slides in Basic Chemicals," *Chem. Engr. News 56 (10)* 9 (1978).
9. Goldstein, I. S., *Science 189 (4206)* 847 (1975).
10. Edwards, V. H., *in* "Cellulose as a Chemical and Energy Resource" (C. R. Wilke, ed.), Biotechnol. Bioeng. Symp. No. 5, p. 321. John Wiley & Sons, New York (1975).
11. Goldstein, I. S., *in* "Enzymatic Conversion of Cellulose Materials: Technology and Applications" (E. L. Gaden, M. H. Mandels, E. T. Reese, and L. A. Spano, eds.), Biotechnol. Bioeng. Symp. No. 6, p. 293. John Wiley & Sons, New York (1976).
12. Goldstein, I. S., *Chem. Eng. News 54 (50),* 4 (1976).
13. Startz, W. H., *in* "Industrial Fermentations" (L. A. Underkofler and R. J. Hickey, eds.), Vol. 1, p. 17. Chemical Publishing Co., New York (1954).
14. Hodge, H. M. and Hildebrandt, F. M. *in* "Industrial Fermentations" (L. A. Underkofler and R. J. Hickey, eds.), Vol. 1, p. 73. Chemical Publishing Co., New York (1954).
15. McCarthy, J. L., *in* "Industrial Fermentations" (L. A. Underkofler and R. J. Hickey, eds.), Vol. 1, p. 95. Chemical Publishing Co., New York (1954).
16. Saeman, J. F. and Andreasen, A. A., *in* "Industrial Fermentations" (L. A. Underkofler and R. J. Hickey, eds.), Vol. 1, p. 136. Chemical Publishing Co., New York (1954).
17. Davis, H. G., *in* "Industrial Fermentations" (L. A. Underkofler and R. J. Hickey, eds.), Vol. 1, p. 339. Chemical Publishing Co., New York (1954).
18. Becher, P., *Chem. Eng. News 54 (16),* 12 (1976).
19. Williams, R., *in* "Sucrochemistry" (J. L. Hickson, ed.), American Chemical Society Symposium, Vol. 41, p. 274. American Chemical Society, Washington, D.C. (1977).
20. Finn, R. K., *in* "Cellulose as a Chemical and Energy Resource" (C. R. Wilke, ed.), Biotechnol. Bioeng. Symp. No. 5, p. 279. John Wiley & Sons, New York (1975).
21. Cysewski, G. R. and Wilke, C. R., *Biotech. Bioeng. 28,* 1287 (1976).
22. Stone, R. N., *in* "Enzymatic Conversion of Cellulose Materials: Technology and Applications" (E. L. Gaden, M. H. Mandels, E. T. Reese, and L. A. Spano, eds.), Biotechnol. Bioeng. Symp. No. 6, p. 223.
23. *Chem. Market Reporter 213 (9)* (1978).
24. Wood, W. A. and Mortlock, R. P., *J. Bact. 88 (4),* 838 (1964).
25. Stanier, R. Y. and Adams, G. A., *Canad. J. Res. 38,* 168 (1944).
26. Ledinghan, G. A. and Neish, A. C., *in* "Industrial Fermentations" (L. A. Underkofler and R. J. Hickey, eds.), Vol. 2, p. 27. Chemical Publishing Co., New York (1954).
27. Goheen, D. W., Glennie, D. W., and Hoyt, C. H., *in* "Kirk-Othmer Encyclopedia of Chemical Technology" 2nd Ed., Vol. 12, p. 363. John Wiley & Sons (1967).

28. Hayes, F. W., *in* "Sucrochemistry" (J. L. Hickson, ed.),
     American Chemical Society Symposium, Vol. 41, p. 313.
     American Chemical Society, Washington, D.C. (1977).

29. Nyiri, L. K. and Charles, M., *in* "Annual Reports on Fermen-
     tation Processes" (D. Perlman and G. T. Tsao, eds.), Vol. 1,
     p. 365. Academic Press, New York (1977).

30. "Basic Organic Chemistry Part 5: Industrial Products"
     (J. M. Tedder, A. Nechvatal, and A. H. Jubb, eds.). John
     Wiley & Sons, New York (1975).

31. "Faith, Keyes, and Clark's Industrial Chemicals," Fourth
     Ed. (F. A. Lowenheimer and M. K. Moran, eds.). Wiley-
     Interscience, New York (1975).

32. Seeley, D., *in* Cellulose as a Chemical and Energy Resource"
     (C. R. Wilke, ed.), Biotechnol. Bioeng. Symp. No. 5, p. 343.
     John Wiley & Sons, New York (1975).

33. Selby, K., *in* "Industrial Aspects of Biochemistry" (B.
     Spencer, ed.), p. 787. FEBS North-Holland/American Else-
     vier (1974).

34. Elder, A. L., *in* "Enzymatic Conversion of Cellulose Mater-
     ials: Technology and Applications" (E. L. Gaden, M. H.
     Mandels, E. T. Reese, and L. A. Spano, eds.), Biotechnol.
     Bioeng. Symp. No. 6, p. 275. John Wiley & Sons, New York
     (1976).

35. Sheppard, W. J. and Lipinsky, E. S. *in* "Sucrochemistry"
     (J. L. Hickson, ed.), American Chemical Society Symposium,
     Vol. 41, p. 336. American Chemical Society, Washington,
     D.C. (1977).

36. Ratledge, C., *in* "Annual Reports on Fermentation Processes"
     (D. Perlman and G. T. Tsao, eds.), Vol. 1, p. 49. Academic
     Press, New York (1977).

37. Meyna, J., "Utilization of Sugar in Industrial Fermentation,"
     ISRF Study No. 312, 1971-72, Unpublished.

38. Cysewski, G. R. and Wilke, C. R., *Biotech. Bioeng. 19,* 1125
     (1977).

39. Anderson, E. V., *Chem. Eng. News 55 (2),* 12 (1977).

40. "Palm Nuts: Raw Materials for the Production of Alcohol and
     Coal," Brazillian Office of Industry and Commerce, Secretary
     of Industrial Technology, Brazilia, July (1977).

41. "Statistical Abstract of U.S. 1977," U. S. Dept. of Commerce,
     Bureau of Census, September (1977).

42. "Mobil Proves Gasoline-from-Methanol Process," *Chem. Eng.
     News 56 (5),* 26 (1978).

43. Davis, D. S., *Chem. Eng. News 56 (10),* 22 (1978).

44. Miller, D. L., *in* "Cellulose as a Chemical and Energy Re-
     source" (C. R. Wilke, ed.), Biotechnol. Bioeng. Symp. No. 5,
     p. 345. John Wiley & Sons, New York (1975).

45. Miller, D. L., *in* "Enzymatic Conversion of Cellulose Mater-
     ials: Technology and Applications" (E. L. Gaden, M. H.
     Mandels, E. T. Reese, and L. A. Spano, eds.), Biotechnical
     Bioeng. Symp. No. 6, p. 307. John Wiley & Sons, New York
     (1976).

46. Finn, R. F., *in* "Cellulose as a Chemical and Energy Resource" (C. R. Wilke, ed.), Biotechnol. Bioeng. Symp. No. 5, p. 353. John Wiley & Sons, New York (1975).

47. Heitz, R. G., *in* "Cellulose as a Chemical and Energy Resource" (C. R. Wilke, ed.), Biotechnol. Bioeng. Symp. No. 5, p. 357. John Wiley & Sons, New York (1975).

48. Perrone, J. C., "The Hydrolytic Processes in the Utilization of Renewable Resources," Nat. Inst. Tech. Brazillian Office of Ind. and Commerce, Sec. Ind. Tech., Rio de Janeiro, Nov. (1976).

49. Lipinsky, E. S., *Science 199,* 644 (1978).

50. Jaffee, G. M., Szkrybalo, W., and Weimert, W., U.S. Pat. 3,627,636, Dec. 14, 1971.

51. Hongo, M., U.S. Pat. 2,945,786, July 19, 1960.

52. McCutchan, W. N. and Hickey, R. J., *in* "Industrial Fermentations" (L. A. Underkofler and R. J. Hickey, eds.), Vol. 1, p. 347. Chemical Publishing Co., New York (1954).

53. Olson, B. H. and Johnson, M. J., *J. Bact. 55,* 209 (1948).

54. Waddons, L. A., "Chemicals from Petroleum," 3rd Ed., p. 80. John Wiley & Sons, New York (1973).

55. Ledingham, G. A. and Neish, A. C., *in* "Industrial Fermentations" (L. A. Underkofler and R. J. Hickey, eds.), Vol. 2, p. 33. Chemical Publishing Co., New York (1954).

56. "Basic Organic Chemistry Part 5: Industrial Products" (J. M. Tedder, A. Nechvatal, and A. H. Jubb, eds.), p. 76. John Wiley & Sons, New York (1975).

57. Sinskey, A., Dept. of Energy, Division of Solar Energy Research, Fuels from Biomass Newsletter (H. R. Bungay and T. J. Walsh, eds.). February (1978).

58. Sutherland, I. W., *in* "Extracellular Microbial Polysaccharides" (P. A. Sanford and A. Laskin, eds.), ACS Symp. Ser. 45, p. 40. American Chemical Society, Washington, D.C. (1977).

59. McNeeley, W. H., *in* "Microbial Technology" (H. J. Peppler, ed.), p. 381. Reinhold, New York (1968).

60. Lawson, C. J., *in* "Sucrochemistry" (J. L. Hickson, ed.), American Chemical Society Symposium, Vol. 41, p. 282. American Chemical Society, Washington, D.C. (1977).

61. Wells, J., *in* "Extracellular Microbial Polysaccharides" (P. A. Sanford and A. Laskin, eds.), ACS Symp. Ser. 45, p. 299. American Chemical Society, Washington, D.C. (1977).

62. Sandvik, E. I. and Maerker, J. M. *in* "Extracellular Microbial Polysaccharides" (P. A. Sanford and A. Laskin, eds.), ACS Symp. Ser. 45, p. 242. American Chemical Society, Washington, D.C. (1977).

63. Wells, J., *in* "Sucrochemistry" (J. L. Hickson, ed.), American Chemical Society Symposium, Vol. 41, p. 297. American Chemical Society, Washington, D.C. (1977).

64. Callihan, C. D. and Dunlap, C. E., Report SW-24C Federal Solid Waste Management Program Contract No. PH 86-68-152, U.S. Environmental Protection Agency (1971).

65. Laskin, A. I., *in* "Annual Reports on Fermentation Processes" (D. Perlman and G. T. Tsao, eds.), Vol. 1, p. 151. Academic Press, New York (1977).
66. Laskin, A. I., *in* "Single Cell Protein from Renewable and Non-renewable Resources" (E. L. Gaden and A. E. Humphrey, eds.), Biotech. Bioeng. Symp. No. 7, p. 91. John Wiley & Sons, New York (1977).
67. Bazua, C. D. and Wilke, C. R., *in* "Single Cell Protein from Renewable and Non-renewable Resources" (E. L. Gaden and A. E. Humphrey, eds.), Biotech. Bioeng. Symp. No. 7, p. 105. John Wiley & Sons, New York (1977).
68. Zines, D. O. and Rogers, P. L., *Biotech. Bioeng. 13*, 293 (1971).
69. Aiba, S., Shoda, M., and Nagatani, M., *Biotech. Bioeng. 10*, 845 (1968).
70. Holtzberg, I., Finn, R. K., and Steinkrous, K. H., *Biotech. Bioeng. 9*, 413 (1967).
71. Nagodawithana, T. W., Casiellano, C., and Steinkraus, K. E., *Appl. Microbiol. 28 (3)*, 383 (1974).
72. Ramalingham, A. and Finn, R. F., *Biotech. Bioeng. 19 (4)*, 583 (1977).
73. Cysewski, G. R. and Wilke, C. R., *Biotech. Bioeng. 19*, 1125 (1977).
74. Edwards, V. H., *Biotech. Bioeng. 11 (1)*, 99 (1969).
75. VanDedem, G. and Moo-Young, M., *Biotech. Bioeng. 17*, 1301 (1975).
76. Bader, F. C., Meyer, J. S., Fredrickson, A. G., and Tsuchiya, H. M., *Biotech. Bioeng. 17*, 279 (1975).
77. Harder, W. and Dijkhuizen, L., *in* "Continuous Culture 6 Applications and New Fields" (A. C. R. Dean, D. C. Ellwood, C. G. T. Evans, and J. Melling, eds.), p. 297. Ellis Horwood, Chichester (1976).
78. Yurchak, S., Wise, J. J., Silvestri, A. J., and Chang, C. D., Mobil Process for the Conversion of Methanol to Hydrocarbons. Symposium on "Organic Chemical Feedstocks of the Future." 11th Middle Atlantic Regional Meeting, Am. Chem. Society, April 20-23 (1977).
79. Chang, C. D. and Silvestri, A. J., *J. Catalysis 47(2)*, 249 (1977).

CHAPTER 3

COMPUTER APPLICATIONS
TO FERMENTATION PROCESSES

William A. Weigand

School of Chemical Engineering
Purdue University
West Lafayette, Indiana

The use of computers for monitoring, operating and controlling fermentation processes has been on a rapid increase in the last 10 years. The expanded use of the computer for the off-line and on-line optimization of fermentations, and possibly entire plants, is probably in the not-too-distant future. The importance of this subject to industry, because of the economic and product quality benefits, and the importance to academic types because of the many very interesting problems to be solved, both from the fundamental and applied areas of biochemical engineering, justifies a review of this subject area for the second consecutive year in this publication.

Last year's review by D. D. Dobry and J. L. Jost (1) was an excellent account of this subject. Their emphasis was from the viewpoint of the use of the computer to assist in the operation of industrial fermentation operations, e.g. production. Also, they emphasized the published developments five years prior to their writing. Further, they reported on the eleven existing computer-controlled fermentation systems reported in the literature up to that time. Their report also discussed the choices in the design of a computer-coupled system, and the requirements a system must satisfy, both from the point of view of industrial production. Further, they reported on modeling, control and optimization for computer-controlled fermentors. They concluded, among other things, that the models and/or correlations needed for advanced control are not presently available and that the future challenge in fermentation process control is the on-line optimization of the process.

This report will build upon and hopefully complement theirs by emphasizing both modeling, control and parameter estimation for computer-coupled fermentors and, in particular, will examine the area of fermentation optimization. Although this review will, in most instances, concentrate on developments from the last five years, it will, when necessary for clarity and comprehensiveness, dip below their five-year constraint. Also, this review attempts not to discuss references already covered by Dobry and Jost except in certain cases where it is deemed necessary for cohesiveness or in other cases where we wish to emphasize additional points on a particular reference.

In addition, a brief mention of five additional computer-coupled systems will be given. Also, using the Purdue system as an example, a description of the important features of computer-coupled fermentors for use in academic and institutional environments, where usually more fundamental engineering questions are examined, will be presented. Of course, this type of computer-fermentor system might also be useful for the more fundamental engineering studies pursued by industry.

Of course, because of the nature of this subject, much of the detailed published work in these areas of computer-coupled system descriptions, modeling and control developments, and optimization developments are from either academic or institutional settings. Therefore, working under this understandable constraint, the following report is a second review of this important subject, the intention being to collect and examine information relating to computer-coupled fermentation processes of present or potential industrial interest.

I.   COMPUTER-COUPLED FERMENTATION SYSTEMS FOR RESEARCH PURPOSES

The report by Dobry and Jost elaborated on the choices in design and system requirements of a computer-coupled fermentation system emphasizing features needed for industrial purposes. Similar feelings on this topic have been expressed by Jefferis (2,3). Also, much information on the efforts at standardizing the software and hardware interfaces for computer control can be found in the annual reports of workshops held by the Purdue Laboratory for Applied Industrial Control (PLAIC) headed by T. J. Williams (4). It would not be useful to elaborate on the accounts given on this subject since the review of last year did a thorough job. Instead, this review will examine these topics from the point of a system for research purposes. This would be useful not only for academic or institutional situations, but might also be useful for the more basic research studies performed in industry.

Last year's review also listed the published accounts of eleven existent computer-controlled fermentation systems. Of the eleven, only two were from industrial fermentations and both of these were from European companies. The nine others were either in an academic or institutional setting (see Table I of Dobry and Jost). However, they report that, although not published, at least six American pharmaceutical companies appear to be applying computers to fermentation control.

In addition to these reported eleven systems, there are at least five additional academic institutions with computer-coupled systems, four in the United States and one in the Soviet Union. They are at Lehigh (Nyiri and Charles), Maryland (Hatch and Cadmen), Rutgers (Constantinides) and Purdue (Weigand and Lim) in the U.S. and at the Kazan S. M. Kirov Institute for Chemical Technology (Yenikeyev) in the U.S.S.R. Only the installation at Purdue will be discussed in this report since the author of this review is most familiar with its details and philosophy. It is simply used as an example of what points to consider when the primary use is fundamental engineering studies.

The current system at Purdue was designed to permit considerable flexibility and accuracy with relative ease of operation. Currently a single fermentor with either a 7 or 14ℓ jar is employed and operation is in the batch, fed batch or continuous mode. Also, it employs a mixture of set point control and computer cascaded set point control, depending on the variables in question. A schematic of the fermentor is shown in Figure 1. In particular, the variables of temperature, pH, agitator speed, airflow rate, liquid volume and substrate feed rate are under set point control, where the set point of the analog controller can be prescribed either by a signal from the computer, or from a control panel at the site of the fermentor (see Table I). These six variables are then under control whether or not the computer is operating. In addition, it gives one the ability to control some of these variables by computer and some by the local mode.

TABLE I.

Setpoint controlled variables	Computer-analog cascaded controlled variables
Temperature (T) pH Air flow rate (AF) Agitator speed (AS) Inlet volumetric flow (VF) Liquid volume (V)	Dissolved oxygen (DO) Optical transmittance (OT) Carbon dioxide in fermentor off-gas Oxygen in fermentor off-gas Variables calculated from dissolved oxygen and/or off-gas, e.g. RQ, etc.

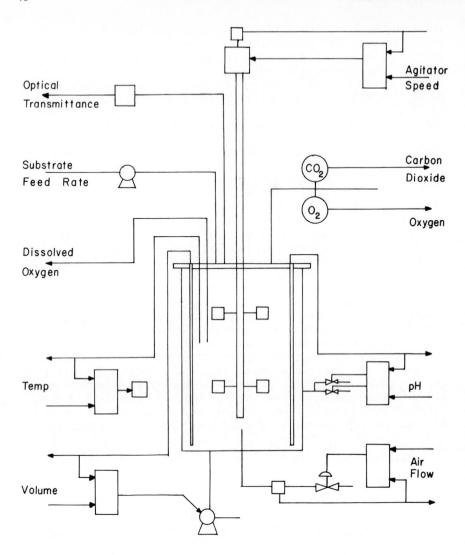

FIGURE 1.   Fermentor vessel and associated instrumentation.

In addition, the variables dissolved oxygen, optical transmittance and the carbon dioxide and oxygen in the fermentor off-
gas are measured. They, in turn, can be controlled by sending
these signals to the computer, employing software control algo-
rhythms, and then sending voltages back to the set points of the
analog controllers. For example, dissolved oxygen is controlled
by either the agitator speed, the air flow rate, or a combination
of both. This is an example of cascaded set point control (see
Table I). The optical transmittance (which is used for cell density) is controlled by the substrate feed rate if operating in
the continuous or fed batch modes. The off gas CO_2, or respiration coefficient (RQ), or some other calculated off gas variable,
is also controlled by the substrate feed rate, as is the usual
case (10,16). However, the system as designed can manipulate one
of the other set point controlled variables to control these
measured variables. For example, cell concentration might be
altered by manipulating the temperature, or pH, or agitation
speed, or airflow rate, or any combination of these if it were
desired to do this. In a similar way, the RQ might be altered
by changing the temperature or pH, etc. This ability then gives
the researcher considerable flexibility to utilize the normal
means to control the variables of D.O., O.D., CO_2, O_2, RQ, etc.,
or to investigate some less usual means of control. This is a
very desirable feature in an academic research environment. For
example, calculated optimal fed batch policies, such as inlet
substrate flow rate and pH profiles designed to maximize penicillin production (51) could be experimentally tested while other
variables such as temperature and dissolved oxygen are held at
constant values. Then for example, with the termination of the
above run, experiments with a methanol utilizer for SCP production (with substrate inhibited growth) using continuous culture,
maintaining a desired cell concentration (either at an open loop
stable or open loop unstable value) by running as a turbudostat
(5), could be carried out by simply calling a different program
from the disc.

An example of some experimental data showing the behavior of
both manipulated and dependent variables for a batch run with a
methanol utilizing bacteria is shown in Figure 2. In this run
the temperature was increased in a linear fashion from 20°C to
40°C over a period of 12 hours. The dissolved oxygen concentration started near 97% saturation with the agitator speed at 150
rpm and the air flow at 2 l/min and dropped to the desired level
of 70% as the cell concentration increased. When the 70% level
was reached, the agitation speed increased to maintain DO constant. This continued until the upper limit of agitator speed of
1000 rpm was reached (at about 12.6 hours), at which time the air
flow quickly increased to almost 5 l/min. Note that the DO is
barely affected when this occurs, but remains at 70% saturation.
At the end of this period, the substrate was completely used up
at about 13.4 hours. When this occurred, the DO rose quickly
from 70% to 84% and then slowly increased to about 93% after the

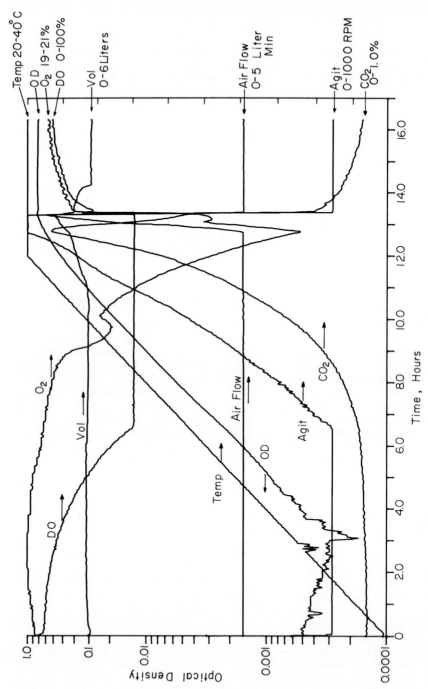

FIGURE 2. Batch fermentation.

time of substrate exhaustion. Note that the agitator speed and
air flow immediately dropped back to their original values of
150 rpm and 2 l/min, respectively. The pH was maintained constant at a value of 7.0 during the entire batch. Of course, this
batch run could have had time varying profiles of temperature,
pH and DO if this were desired. The ability to have this degree
of flexibility is desirable for fermentor optimization and control studies, but it is also useful for studies of growth and
product formation kinetics and their dependence on either constant or time functions of important manipulated variables.

A system should not only have a high degree of flexibility
but should also be relatively convenient to use and monitor for
the experimentor located at the site of the fermentor. In our
case this was accomplished by a control panel located immediately
adjacent to the fermentor. The panel is pictured schematically
in Figure 3. The control panel contains the analog circuit cards
which perform the functions of signal conditioning, transmission
to and from the computer, and analog control. These are located
in the chassis at the bottom of the panel. In addition, all
measurements and setpoints are displayed on a digital panel meter
(DPM). The DPM is a 3 3/4 digit dual slope integrating meter.
With it, the experimentor has the ability to observe all process
measurements, set all local setpoints if a manipulated variable
is not on computer set point control (the six adjusting pots for
local set points are located near the bottom of the panel), or
observe current setpoints if they are being sent from the computer. Currently, there are sixteen measurements and set points
displayed on the single panel meter as shown in Figure 3. Rather
than a rotary switch, pushbuttons (located at the top of the
panel), digital logic and CMOS analog multiplexers are used for
selecting the desired signal which is then displayed on the DPM
in engineering units. The digital logic also sets the decimal
point automatically, and causes signal lockout once a variable
has been selected for display. The panel has the room to expand
to 24 analog signals for future needs. In addition, a teletype
is at the fermentor site if communication with the computer is
required.

All of the signal measurement, conditioning and transmission
loops and the hardware analog control loops are completely electronic, employing the latest solid state integrated circuit technology. In addition, all nonlinearities in measurement loops
were removed by using internal electronic feedback. This is required for the DPM, but then also provides for convenience when
programming the control software, e.g. RPM of 0 to 1000 corresponds linearly with 0 to 10 volts at the A/D converters. Also,
the design and component selection was such that the generated
noise levels are below the resolution of the A/D converters on
the computer, i.e. below 5 mV.

All of the above discussions on the highly instrumented fermentor with its particular controlled and measured variables, the
control panel, and the analog circuits for signal conditioning,

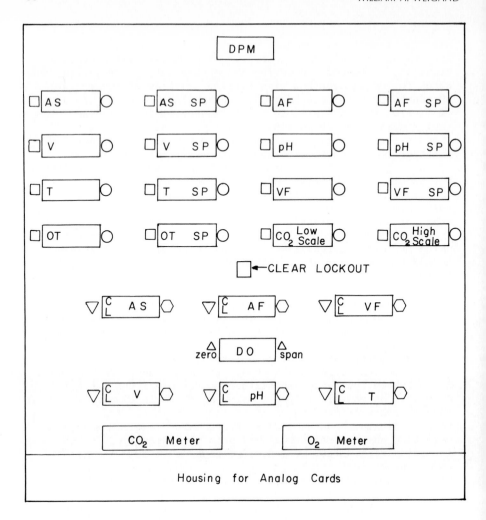

FIGURE 3.   Control panel.   □ = button; O = light;
▽ = toggle switch; ⬡ = pots for local SP; C = computer; L =
local; SP = set point;   △ = pots for DO calibration. See
Table I for other abbreviations.

transmission and analog control described as our system was designed and constructed by two graduate students at Purdue as part
of their thesis research; Robert Mohler for the Ph.D. and Paul
Hennigan for the M.S. A more detailed account of these and other
aspects of this computer-coupled fermentor system is given by
Mohler *et al.* (6).

The current computer system being used at Purdue is a Data
General Nova 840. It has 32K of memory, a moving head disc,
32 A/D, 8 D/A, digital I/O, teletypes, paper tape reader, cas-
sette, and alphanumeric (main console) and graphical CRT's.
Fortran with a real time disc operating system (RDOS) is employed.
This system is partially used for undergraduate education at the
present time in the transfer operations laboratory and in the
near future it will be used in the process control course. In
order to overcome the conflicts between research and undergraduate
education, another computer system is currently being brought
on-line and will take over the research tasks in September or
October of 1978. This new computer is a PDP 11-34 with dual
moving head discs, 48 K of memory and an alphanumeric CRT as main
console. There are 16 A/D, 8 D/A and 16 bits of digital I/O.
The main advantages of this system are its expandability and the
RXS-11M operating system which permits independent multi-user
operation. This operating system will permit several interfaced
fermentors to be operated simultaneously and independently (if
enough core memory is available) while yet other users develop
software or perform data analysis. Because of this system's
flexibility, the initial stages of design for another highly
instrumented fermentor (14ℓ) with all DDC control, is in progress.
It is hoped to complete its development and construction by the
summer of 1979. This second fermentor will permit comparisons
between set point computer control (often called supervisory control) and the more versatile direct digital control, the purpuse
being engineering studies of control strategies and fermentor optimization policies. It will also permit a two-staged fermentation system to be considered. In addition, 3 or 4 small (1ℓ)
fermentors currently used for growth kinetics studies or turbidostat control studies are planned to be interfaced to the computer
for DO, pH, OD and temperature control. These small fermentors
are used in either the batch or continuous mode. This will permit more reliable data to be obtained and recorded without the
expense of purchasing the commercially available analog controllers for these variables. Interfacing to some of these small
fermentors is hoped to be finished sometime in the late fall or
winter of 1978.

The above discussion on the current computer coupled system
at Purdue, and changes currently being made and planned for the
near future, was presented with the purpose of describing a concrete example of a versatile, useful system for the fundamental
engineering studies which take place at academic institutions, or
for that matter, useful in any situation where flexibility,

transmission and analog control described a system designed and
constructed by two graduate students at Purdue as part of their
research. A more detailed account of these and other aspects of
this computer-coupled system is given by Mohler *et al*. (6).

II.   MODELS AND METHODS FOR COMPUTER CONTROL OF FERMENTORS

     In the article by Dobry and Jost, this topic was discussed by
classifying the control method on the basis of the model that was
used. The three types of model classification and the literature
references used by them as examples were 1) physical models where,
for example, the effects of things like air flow and/or agitator
speed upon mass transfer are used to control the dissolved oxygen
(7), 2) biochemical models where control decisions are based upon
some measured variable which is related to the biochemical physiological) state of the system, for example respiration quotient,
RQ, may be maintained at some value to achieve the desired performance of the fermentor by manipulating the inlet flow rate of
limiting substrate (8), and 3) system models where knowledge of
mass and heat transfer is combined with biochemical kinetics to
form a more general picture of the fermentation (9,10). An example is the use of material balance with gas measurements and
the ammonia addition rate to estimate other important variables,
e.g. cell mass.
     Classification along the lines of physical, biochemical and
system models appears to be a useful concept; however, there may
be cases where the choice of class for some of the published work
appears to be somewhat arbitrary. In any case, the brief discussion which follows uses this same grouping system, but will be
confined to a discussion of only the biochemical and system model
types.

A.   *Biochemical Models*

     A means to optimize a batch fermentation for nonbiomass prod-
ucts is proposed by Humphrey and Jefferis (11). They present an
optimal feeding policy for the case where the specific product
formation rate has a maximum with respect to the specific growth
rate, i.e. it is both growth associated and nongrowth associated.
The approach is to operate in the semi-batch mode with repeated
drawoff. The feeding policy is such that the specific growth
rate is maintained at the value where the specific product formation rate is maximum. In addition, the cell concentration is
kept at the maximum value just below the choke-out point due to
oxygen transfer limitations. The net result is that the volumetric product formation rate is at its maximum value. The rate of
substrate addition is the manipulated variable used to control

the fermentor system. They propose to do this by determining the
oxygen uptake rate from the inlet and outlet gas streams in order
to estimate the growth rate and cell mass densities by a model
with a computer.

In a related paper, Ryu and Humphrey (12) present an example
of how computer process control would be used to maintain certain
key parameters at optimum levels for maximum penicillin production. The variables of oxygen transfer rate, oxygen uptake rate,
specific growth rate and carbohydrate uptake rate are determined
on-line with the computer and continuously controlled at their
optimum values by manipulating the feed rate of substrate and the
oxygen supply and demand. This latter variable is affected by
the apparent viscosity, the power input and the superficial air
velocity.

In another example of control by a biochemical model, the
process analysis and optimization of the growth of *Candida utilis*
on molasses was discussed by Nyiri and Krishnaswami (13). The
effect of carbon to nitrogen ratio (C/N) on cell protein synthesis and ethanol formation was determined by pulsing the system
while the culture was in the early logarithmic phase. The C/N
was related to the respiratory quotient (RQ), which in turn is
related to the physiological condition of the cells. In subsequent experiments, cascaded metabolic control was performed, that
is, the previously defined optimum C/N ratio of 2.0 was maintained
by the computer by maintaining the RQ at its corresponding value
of 1.0. This approach is essentially the same as the one presented by Krishnaswami and Parmenter (14) as described by Dobry and
Jost.

The question of a relation between RQ and the physiological
condition of cells during batch growth was given a further examination by Nyiri, Toth and Charles (15). The transition stages
during growth of *C. utilis* were found to be correlated with the
RQ, and relations between RQ and 1) nucleic acid, 2) protein and
3) alcohol syntheses were reported.

An example of the use of RQ as the measured variable, which
can be used to manipulate the substrate feed rate to avoid the
glucose effect in the production of bakers yeast, is given by
Aiba, Nagai and Nishizawa (16). The feed rate was changed in a
stepwise manner, without the benefit of automatic control, to
maintain the RQ in the range 1.0 to 1.2 and the specific growth
rate and yield were maintained constant at optimal yield conditions throughout the period of the fed batch operation for fermentations with both glucose and molasses. It was also shown
that the total oxygen consumption rate could be used as the
measured variable. One notable difference here from some papers
dealing with fed batch is that the change in volume associated
with fed batch operation was taken into account when the material

balance equations were developed. This paper is obviously closely
related to the paper by Nagi, Nishizawa and Yamagato (8) discussed
by Dobry and Jost.

An example of the on-line computer adjustment to manipulate
the dilution rate (D) until the cell productivity (DX) was maxi-
mized is given by Whaite and Gray (17) for a continuous fermentation. Dynamic delays between the response of cell concentration
(X) and the change in dillution rate caused problems of cycling.
This was overcome by accounting for the rate of change of X before
D was altered and by restricting the permissible step size change
of D.

B. *System Models*

The modeling approach of Cooney, Wang and Wang (9,10) was discussed by Dobry and Jost as an example of a system model. The indirect measurement of cell density was accomplished by material
balance for carbon, hydrogen, oxygen and nitrogen and the measurement of the oxygen uptake, carbon dioxide production, gas flow
rate, and ammonia addition. The system was a fed batch fermentation of bakers yeast and the objective was to maximize the yield.
It does not appear that the change in volume was accounted for in
the material balances or was done by Aiba *et al.* (16), even though
initial volumes of 6 liters and final volumes of 10 or 11 liters
were indicated (10). However, accurate estimates of cell mass
were achieved on-line with a computer.

The idea for control with a system model would be to use the
model with several measured variables, to determine several quantities which are not directly measurable and then to make use of
this more detailed knowledge to improve fermentor performance by
manipulating several variables if this were required. However,
as correctly pointed out by Dobry and Jost, even though this more
complex model was utilized (10), the control scheme is essentially
the same as the one used in the biochemical model scheme (16),
that is, the substrate feed rate was manipulated to maintain the
RQ near a value of 1.0. However, this does not indicate that this
approach is not useful, or that it was used inappropriately, but
possibly only that for the system studied, and the desired control
objective, a control scheme of equivalent simplicity to the one
of the biochemical approach resulted. For example, if a single
control objective such as maximize cell yield by minimizing ethanol production is desired and it is found by the biochemical model
approach that the relatively simple control scheme of maintaining
RQ between 1.0 and 1.2 accomplished the task very well, then one
would not expect that a more complex model, which yields more information, would indicate that the simple procedure of RQ constan-
cy is inappropriate, and therefore it may not be surprising that
the complex system model resulted in the same control strategy.
If, however, a more demanding set of control objectives were

imposed upon the system, that is, not only maximize cell yield, but also maintain some other system output (s) [or input (s)] at some optimal value (s), then it would appear that the more complex system model has a better chance of success.

The question of model complexity and control schemes to be used is then related to both the system complexity and the desired control objectives. Therefore, as more involved control objectives are sought, then more complex models and control schemes will need to be developed in the future.

An alternate approach to indirect measurement of the important state variable cell density has been developed by Zabriskie and Humphrey (18). This approach differs from the previous approach of Cooney *et al.* in that only one chemical component, molecular oxygen, is balanced and then used with a model for cell density estimation. Correlations relating biomass concentration and growth rate with molecular oxygen uptake rate and carbon dioxide evolution rate data were developed. The correlations were based on a balance model for molecular oxygen which contained yield and maintenance terms. Accurate estimates of biomass concentration and growth rate were achieved for two of the three fermentations tested. The third fermentation, bakers yeast, required metabolic dependent adjustments to the yield and the maintenance terms in order to produce the desired accuracy of estimation. These adjustments were effective and produced accurate estimates in real-time with a computer.

A thorough account of the application of the method of quasilinearization to fermentor modeling is given by Reuss, Jefferis and Lehmann (19). Examples included parameter identification in a growth model for a batch fermentation and both parameter and state estimation in a column fermentor. For the batch reactor, coefficients for specific growth rate and cell maintenance were determined by using measurement of the oxygen uptake rate along with periodic measurements of the cell density. Predictions of cell density and growth rate were made for the entire course of the fermentation and excellent agreement with experiment for cell density was shown. The example for the column reactor involved estimation of the unknown parameters, the Stanton number and the Peclet number, which occur in the distributed parameter model of the process. This was done by measuring the oxygen content of the liquid at different positions in the column, and agreement with experimental results for dissolved oxygen profile along the column reactor for an extended batch fermentation are shown. The computer system for the column fermentor consisted of a time shared machine in the background which performed the model parameter identification, interacting with a process control machine in the foreground which performed the on-line predictions of the dissolved oxygen profiles.

In yet a different mode of approach, Svrcek, Elliott and Zajic (20) demonstrate the use of the extended Kalman filter to dampen the variance in measurable states and to track parameter values of the nonlinear equations. The demonstration is

accomplished by computer simulation of a temperature dependent
endogenous metabolism model. Control was produced by standard
feedforward and proportional-integral modes. Dillution rate was
manipulated to maintain cell concentration constant in the light
of load disturbances introduced by variations of inlet substrate
concentration. The improvement produced by the Kalman filter was
illustrated by imposing noise on the simulated fermentor variables.

III. OPTIMIZATION OF FERMENTATION

     Optimization based upon mathematical schemes are discussed in
this section. The other method of intuitively developing an optimal control scheme once a model for the system has been found
was discussed in terms of modeling in Section II.
     First, a brief account of mathematical optimization techniques
which have been, or could be, applied to fermentation systems will
be made prior to examining their applications. Many of these
standard techniques may not be familiar to a majority of biochemical engineers, and therefore a brief account, with some references containing more detailed information, is useful if a more
complete picture is to be given when fermentation optimization
applications are discussed. In this way any potential uses may
be more accurately assessed. The application discussion which
then follows is organized along the lines of the type of fermentor considered, that is, batch, fed batch or continuous.

A. *Optimization Techniques*

     Mathematical optimization techniques may be put into two
broad classes: point optimization techniques and path (or function) optimization techniques. Point optimization is needed for
processses or plants operating at the steady state condition, that
is points, or to a process which is not at steady state, but which
is influenced by inputs which are not functions of time, e.g.
batch fermentors with manipulated variables held constant. On the
other hand, path or function optimization is required for processes which are being operated with inputs that are functions of
time, e.g. batch fermentation with a time varying temperature
profile, or fed-batch fermentations, or continuous fermentors
during transient periods.
     The standard methods for point optimization include: 1) dif-
ferential calculus for systems which can be described by algebraic
or differential expressions, 2) systematic search techniques based
on the principle of differential calculus such as the methods of
steep decent, Fibonacci search, etc., based on the gradient concept (21), and 3) systematic programming techniques such as

linear programming (22), nonlinear programming (22), and geometric programming (23), etc. Some useful illustrations of the application of many of these techniques can be found in a book by W. H. Ray and J. Szekely (24). Their applications are metallurgy and chemical engineering examples; however, they are useful since they put these optimization concepts into concrete terms of engineering relevance.

The standard methods of path or function optimization include: 1) variational methods, most useful when the manipulated input variables and state variables are not constrained (25), 2) a more general formulation of function optimization based on the variational approach, called the maximum (or minimum) principle of Pontryagin, particularly useful when the manipulated input variables and/or state variables are constrained (26), and 3) various other related techniques such as optimization of a two-state variable system by Green's theorem (27), the approach (or viewpoint) of functional analysis (28) useful for certain types of systems (29-31), although not yet applied to fermentor optimization, and approaches to produce an optimal estimate and control of measured variables in the presence of noise (32). Alternate approaches such as given in (27) and (28) often have the feature of avoiding the two-point boundary value problem resulting from the maximum principle.

Useful illustrations of some of the above techniques for function optimization applied to chemical processes are given by R. S. Schechter (33) and M. M. Denn (34). Examples of optimal control schemes based on the path optimizing techniques also are quite available in the literature (35,36).

B. Fermentation Optimization Applications

Most of the point and path optimizing techniques briefly reviewed above have been applied to a variety of fermentation systems, at least in terms of analysis and simulation. However, there have not been too many cases of published experimental verifications with the actual fermentation systems upon which the system models were based. These applications are discussed below.

C. Point Optimization

The point optimization technique of linear programming has had some application to fermentation systems. A particular example is given by Jefferis (37) when he discusses the application of the computer for SCP production. He states that large-scale SCP production will require the application of the computer to the overall operation of the complete production process, that is, the principle process subdivisions of medium preparation, fermentation, recovery and product handling. This last phase of

product handling is discussed in terms of blending the SCP with
other protein sources such as fish meal, soya beans, etc. The
problem then is to blend these materials to achieve a desired
dietary balance while minimizing the product cost. He presents
a simple example of the use of linear programming, with a cost
function which must be minimized while satisfying protein, tryp-
tophane and nucleic acid constraints.

A more complex example of the application of a point optimization technique is given by Okabe, Aiba and Okada (38). They
apply a modification of the complex method of Box (39) to determine the conditions of aeration and agitation such that the annual
expenditure (cost of the process) is minimized while producing
some fixed annual fermentation production. The method is illustrated by an example of a penicillin fermentation by using a correlation between penicillin yield and the volumetric coefficient
of oxygen transfer. The coefficients of oxygen transfer and
aeration rate were the independent (manipulated) variables which
are constrained, as was the number of batch cycles, and an optimal solution was obtained rapidly (i.e. in terms of computation
time) with their modifications to Box's method. In essence, the
complex method of Box is an approximation for the gradient needed
for the steep descent method when it is inconvenient to obtain
analytical expressions for the derivatives of the objective function (in this case annual cost). Their modifications assure that
the global optimum point will be found and also cause the computer calculation time to be shortened.

This modified method of Box was used by Okabe and Aiba (40,
41) to optimize the entire process of fermentation and isolation
as described by Dobry and Jost. As they point out, the aspect of
optimizing with respect to cost makes the formulation of Okabe
and Aiba more pertinent to industrial fermentation. However, it
seems that it would be even more useful to formulate the optimization to maximize the difference between income and cost, i.e.
the profit, whenever possible. Minimum cost, in general, is not
necessarily equivalent to maximum profit.

Using the method of the discrete maximum principle, Blanch
and Rogers (42) evaluate optimal policies for the production of
gramicilin S in multistage continuous culture. An economic objective function was developed which accounts for the number and
size of the fermentors, the costs of antibiotic extraction, substrate costs, and the variability of the selling price of the
gramicilin S. The state variables were the cell, substrate and
antibiotic concentrations and the decision variables were the
temperature, pH and number of stages. The optimal pH, temperature and number of stages were determined to be 7.24, 28.3°C and
3, respectively, as was the point where the selling price of
antibiotic made production no longer profitable.

D.   Path Optimization

The published accounts of the application of function (path) optimization techniques are more numerous than those of point optimization.   This may be due to the fact that most fermentations, being batch or fed batch, are often ideally suited to formulation as a path optimization problem.   Another factor may be that most of the published work is from the academic area, and these researchers, by the nature of their experimental capabilities and the constraints of the usual academic framework (particularly in the U.S.) are not as concerned with the entire plant as the system to be optimized as would the industrial researcher in this field.   The above points are somewhat obvious, but are repeated here because many industrial people often seem disappointed that the published academic work does not come closer to solving problems of more immediate relevance to them.   A closer working relationship between academic institutions and industry, as in Japan, would narrow the gap.   In any case, the discussion of function optimization application is divided along the lines of the type of fermentor which was considered as the system for optimization, that is, the batch, fed batch, and continuous fermentor.

E.   Batch Fermentors

Most of the published work on path optimization for batch fermentors is concerned with finding optimal temperature or pH profiles.   The first application seems to be that of Constantinides, Spencer and Gaden (43) where optimal temperature profiles for batch penicillin fermentation were obtained by methods based on the continous maximum principle and the calculus of variations. As a prerequisite to this work, models were developed by Constantinides, Spencer and Gaden (44) which represented the growth rate of cells and synthesis rate of penicillin (the state equations) to be functions of the temperature only.   This restriction is a major limitation of these models for both the pH and nutrient concentrations affect the state variables.   Of course, pH can be held constant, but nutrient concentration varies if none is added to the batch.   However, this simplification was necessary in order to establish a basis for optimizing the fermentation, that is, in order to formulate an optimization problem which is reasonable to solve.   Even with this assumption, the problem was not simple since the parameters in the state equations were found to be complex functions of temperature.   In addition, another complexity arose since cell concentration was constrained to be a nondecreasing function (a condition caused by the temperature function found) and therefore a procedure to handle this state variable constraint aspect of the problem developed by Bryson, Denham and Dreyfus (45) had to be employed.   This in turn placed constraints on the manipulated variable, the temperature.   The objective was to maximize penicillin production for a fixed batch processing time. The resulting formulation was complex and the resulting necessary conditions for optimality required the solution of a difficult numerical problem. However, the resulting optimal temperature profiles indicated that penicillin yield could be improved by about 15% over the best yields obtained with a constant temperature of 25°C. In addition, the optimum temperature profiles were simple functions of time, and since temperature is a variable which is not difficult to manipulate, a reasonable approximation to these optimum profiles can be expected. For example, one of the resulting optimal profiles had the initial temperature at 27.1°C for the first 56 hours of the fermentation followed by a linear drop in temperature to 18.7°C from the 56th to the 84th hour, the temperature was then held at 18.7 until the 184th hour when it is then shifted back to 27.1°C for the last 24 hours of the fermentation.

In a later paper, King, Aragona, and Constantinides (46) present a method of solution to the same penicillin problem but where the temperature profile is restricted to be only on upper or lower values, that is, no linear decrease is allowed. The idea behind this being that this sub-optimal case would be easier to implement in practice since the temperature is either on the upper or lower constraint with one switch. The formulation of this sub-optimal problem now becomes one of parameter identification for the chosen sub-optimal control policy, and it is achieved through numerical computations using a second-order gradient technique. Their results indicate only a 2% decrease in yield from the optimal solution given previously (43). However, in order to achieve the sub-optimal solution, a number of assumptions were made. These were that (i) the process temperature can be instantaneously changed and (ii) the temperature dependent coefficients in the state equations are also instantaneous functions of temperature. But also, they required the optimal solution developed previously as a basis for comparison and they further assume that the optimal policy given there is sufficiently more difficult to implement so that the sub-optimal approach is justified. This last assumption is doubtful if one has a computer-coupled fermentor. All of these assumptions are concerned with solutions which show a 2% difference in yield, i.e. optimal *vs* sub-optimal; however, since optimization results based on the maximum principle are often highly dependent on the model used, a final answer as to whether the optimal *vs* sub-optimal policy *vs* even the constant temperature policy is best cannot be given until actual experimental comparisons for these policies are made.

In a pair of related papers, Rai and Constantinides (47) and Constantinides and Rai (48) examine the optimization of the batch gluconic acid fermentation. In this problem, two important extensions over the previous penicillin fermentation optimizations were made. The first was that both the temperature and pH were chosen as the manipulated control variables. The second change was that the model included four state variables, the cell, glucose, lactose and gluconic acid concentrations. Therefore, changes in nutrient concentration are accounted for. The parameters in the state equations were then experimentally determined as functions of both pH and temperature. The minimization problem was then formulated using the maximum principle along the lines of the previous work (43) and again resulted in a complex numerical problem. The objective was to maximize the gluconic acid yield for a fixed batch time of 8 hours, and the control variables were constrained to lie between 25.0°C and 35.4°C for the temperature and 5.4 and 7.0 for the pH. The resulting optimal temperature and pH profiles were found not to change over a significant range and so constant values of 34.2°C and 7.0 pH were found to give results which were essentially the same as the optimal profiles (47). This situation might seem strange since it appears that the result was essentially a point optimization, even though a path optimization technique was used. Simulation with these constant optimal values indicated a 15.4% higher gluconic acid yield in 20% less time than experiments conducted at 30°C and pH 5.8 by Koga *et al.* (49). An experiment conducted at 33.7°C and pH 7.0, conditions close to optimum, resulted in an 84.5% yield in less than 4 hours (48), a time saving of 60% over the other experimentally reported results of Koga *et al.* where an 84.5% yield was obtained in 10 hours.

Although not a fermentation, there is another reported batch optimization by Lim and Emigholz (50) which is closely related to this work. This concerns the optimal operation of a batch reactor for the isomerization of D-glucose to D-fructose. Both the isothermal as well as nonisothermal operations of a batch isomerization are considered using whole cells which contain intracellular glucose isomerase. The model involves a reversible Briggs Haldane reaction with dual inactivation mechanisms for the enzyme, and the three state variables are the enzyme, glucose, and protease concentrations. The elementary rate constants are found as temperature functions of the Arrhenius type and the model is capable of predicting the time course of the reaction over a wide range of 40-80°C. The decision variables considered for optimization are (1) the time of reaction t_f, (2) the amount of whole cells (or free enzyme) to be added, W_o, and (3) the temperature, T, which could be held constant or varied throughout the course of the reaction. Under the condition of a fixed (desired) final fructose concentration, typically 47% for the examples given, it is found that only two of the three decision variables are independent for isothermal runs, while all three can be varied for the non-isothermal runs. That is, for isothermal operation, if the operation is optimized with respect to t_f and T, then W_o is automatically fixed at some value sufficient to give a 47% conversion; while for non-isothermal operation the problem is to determine the optimal temperature profile $T(t)$, for given values of W_o and t_f while still satisfying the constraint of 47% conversion.

For the isothermal case, this is basically a point optimization problem of the calculus type for the system described by the
three state equations with the constraint that the fructose concentration at the end corresponds to 47% conversion. This can
best be solved numerically. The solution is then obtained for
four performance indices: (1) minimization of the initial cell
concentration, W_o, (2) maximization of residual enzyme activity,
$E(t_f)/E$, (3) minimization of the consumption of enzyme activity,
$W_o[1-E(t_f)/E_o]$, and (4) minimization of annual costs.

For the non-isothermal reactor operation, the problem becomes
one of path (or function) optimization. The problem is formulated
by the maximum principle and a steep descent method is used to
find the optimal temperature profile. The numerical computation
is somewhat costly (computer time) and involved. For this case
only the last 3 performances indices mentioned above were considered. The advantage of operating the reactor using a programmed temperature profile is shown by comparing with the optimal
isothermal operation. Programmed temperature improved $E(t_f)/E_o$
up to 30%, up to 12% for $W_o[1-E(T_f)/E_o]$ and improvements for
annual cost are also found over the isothermal case but the magnitude depends on the relative cost of the reactor to cells (enzyme). This improvement occurs because non-isothermal operations
provide an additional degree of freedom in that the initial cell
concentration, the reaction time and the temperature can all be
manipulated to give the optimal policy, but at the expense of
more involved and time-consuming computations. Also, in certain
situations the optimal temperature profile can turn out to be
isothermal. Thus, what would be desirable to have is prior criteria which can be used to judge the merit of non-isothermal
operation before committing the time and effort to perform the
path optimization calculations. Cases where the less complicated
and faster point optimization problem is indicated would be desirable if these optimizations are to be performed on-line for
computer control.

F.   Fed Batch Fermentors

In the fermentation industry there are some types of operations which are neither batch nor continuous. One of these is
the semibatch or fed batch process where the feed rate of limiting substrate can be a constant or some general function of time.
The published accounts of optimization for these processes, based
on the mathematical techniques for function (or path) optimization are not great in number.

A brief description of optimization for fed batch is given at
the end of a paper by Andreyeva and Biryukov (51). This paper is
concerned, for the most part, with models for the effect of pH on
the specific formation rate of cells and metabolite. The specific growth rate of cells of *P. chrysogenum* is shown to be
described by an equation based on a combination of substrate

ionization and competitive inhibition while the specific formation rate of antibiotic is described by a second-order polynomial.
They indicate that the case where an optimal pH profile, rather
than constant pH, is needed is when the optimum pH for specific
growth rate for cells (μ) and metabolite (q_A) are different, or
as they put it "sharp maxima for μ and q_A without coincidence of
the pH extremes." They then present the results for the optimization of a fed batch fermentation where both the feeding policy
for limiting substrate and the pH time profile are optimized
simultaneously to produce the objective of maximizing metabolite
concentration for a fixed processing time while constraining the
total amount of substrate consumed. The mathematical analysis is
not presented, but the structure of the optimal policies derived
from the maximum principle is given in a figure, along with a description of its meaning. The form of the solution indicates por-
tions which contain singular control inputs, and therefore the
analysis may be somewhat complex. Their last paragraph then indicates that optimal calculations performed for penicillin biosynthesis gave good agreement with an experimentally found pH
changing program. The system is modeled with four state equations, that is, for biomass, substrate, inhibiting metabolite,
and antiobiotic concentrations, and two control variables, feed
rate of limiting substrate and pH. In addition, they consider
the mean culture age in the antibiotic equation (52). The form
of their equation is a particular type of fed batch operation
where the change in volume is negligible. This will be true for
the cases where the inlet substrate stream is very concentrated;
however, it is not the most general formulation.

In a related and informative paper, Fishman and Biryukov (53)
go more into the detail of the problem formulation of optimal fed
batch fermentation for metabolite production. In this case only
the limiting substrate feed rate is the control variable but
similar state equations, including the use of mean culture age in
the antibiotic equation, are used. The mean culture age is experimentally determined and fit to a second-order polynomial. In
addition, another state variable, the integral of the cell concentration, is added to make the equation for antibiotic growth
autonomous and independent of previous history. They then have
five state equations and one controlling input. In addition to
the integral constraint on the total glucose supplied, the instantaneous rate of glucose addition is constrained between 0 and
an upper bound of U_{max}. The objective then is to find u(t) to
produce maximum penicillin production at the end of the process.
The optimal function, u(t), is shown to be one which rapidly
fills and then lets the vessel sit in batch while the cells grow
and age to the optimum for the greatest rate of antibiotic production. The control input then follows a singular arc to maintain this optimal antibiotic growth rate until the integral constraint on total glucose addition is reached, and then u(t) is
zero (i.e. batch) again until the penicillin concentration

reaches its maximum. The optimal input function for u(t) is
compared with a constant feeding policy and it is shown to be an
improvement. It is apparent that this work had originally been
completed before the paper described earlier (51), where both
u(t) and pH(t) were the controlling inputs.

Another case of fed batch optimization is given by Ohno,
Nakanishi and Takamatsu (54). In their formulation they choose
to maximize the rate of product formation by manipulating the
volumetric flow rate into the fermentor, which was constrained
by upper and lower bounds. They used a method developed by Miele
(27) based on the use of Green's theorem. The fed batch model
they consider has four state variables and it considers not only
the cell, substrate and product equations, but also the volume
balance equation. In this sense, their model is more general
than those considered previously (51,53); however, the optimization method they consider is much more restrictive. In order to
use the Green's theorem approach the system model must contain
only two state variables and both final states must be specified.
In essence, the method of Miele transforms the performance index
to be optimized to a line integral and then Green's theorem is
used to transform the line integral to a surface integral. The
path which then minimizes this surface integral can then be found
by examining the state space plot of possible paths for the two-
dimensional system. In this way, use of the maximum principle,
and the difficulties which may arise with singular arcs, are
avoided. The solution to the fed batch fermentation problem then
involved several modifications to transform their problem to one
suitable for this method. The first step was to reduce the
4-dimensional state variable model to 2 state variable by developing an algebraic relationship between 3 of the state variables (S, V, and X) and then by fortunately being able to represent the objective function to be optimized as the integral of
the other state variable. Then after the application of two
theorems which related their performance index to a line integral
and also provided a means to compensate for the fact that one of
their remaining state variables was not fixed at the final time,
a solution was provided. The method was illustrated with curve
fit growth models for a lysine fermentation. The example, shown
for the special case of no upper limit on volumetric flow rate,
indicated that the type of optimal feed trajectory obtained depended on the ratio of the final to initial fermentor volume.
Three different types of solution trajectories, corresponding to
3 different regions of reactor volume ratios, were shown, and
for one a solution very similar to that of Fishman and Biryukov
(53) resulted.

In a more recent paper, Ohno, Nakanishi and Takamatsu (55)
once again consider optimal operation for a fermentation whose
product is not cell mass but some metabolite. The state variables are as in their previous article but no upper bound is
placed on volumetric flow. However, in this paper they genera-
lize the volume balance equation by considering that outflow from

the fermentor is possible, i.e. $\dot{V} = F_1 - F_2$, where F_2 is the outflow. This change then makes it possible to consider the optimal
mode of fermentor operation one step further, i.e. with $F_2 = 0$
the possibilities are batch ($F_1 = 0$) or fed batch; however, when
$F_2 \neq 0$ the possibility of continuous operation arises (i.e. when
$F_1 = F_2 \neq 0$). The objective in this paper is to maximize the
amount of desired product (yield) in a fixed operating time.
This differs from the objective of their previous paper (54)
where they maximize the rate of desired product formation. Optimal solutions are generated by using a transformation developed
by Kelley (56). This transformation reduces the dimensionality
of the state equations to two, and in the process the singular
problem which is common for fermentor path optimization is eliminated so that the maximum principle is more easily applied. The
results produced by application to the lysene fermentation indicate the mode of fermentor operation is dependent upon both the
ratio of the final to initial fermentor volumes and the length of
the operating time. For the lysine example, it is shown that for
long operating time continuous operation eventually occurs, i.e.
batch to continuous or fed batch to batch to continuous, while
for large capacity fermentors the fed batch operation becomes
important.

A simplified procedure for optimization of a fed batch fermentor was given by Yamane' *et al.* (57). They consider two objective functions, the yield and the rate of production of the
desired metabolite, which, along with various combinations of
free and fixed final conditions lead to four different optimization problems. They start with the same state equations as used
by Ohno *et al.* (54) but proceed, through various manipulations,
to reduce the problem to one which requires only the cell balance
and product balance equations to be considered. They then develop a simplified method based on the maximum principle. However, these manipulations remove the actual manipulated control
variable, the inlet volumetric feed rate, from the remaining
state equations and cause control of the state variables to occur
by manipulating the trajectory of the specific growth rate of
cell mass. The optimal trajectory of specific growth rate then
leads to the corresponding optimal volumetric flow rate by using
a relationship developed during the state equation reduction
process. Unfortunately, this procedure leads to optimal flow
trajectories which are often not physically realizable. In particular, this occurs when the optimal policy indicates a negative
feed rate. They then develop a suboptimal policy for these por-
tions of the trajectory by simply setting the feed rate to zero,
that is, batch operation. This strange situation of negative
optimal feed rate is a consequence of the unconventional method
they use to simplify the problem. An example is presented which
uses a specific metabolite production expression which apparently
describes certain amino acid and enzyme fermentations. Their example shows that the suboptimal policy is required in three of

the four optimization problems they considered. Unfortunately,
they did not choose to compare their method with other more conventional ones, say by using the example from the previous work
of Ohno *et al.* (54).

G. *Continous Fermentors*

Continous fermentation has not been extensively used in the
fermentation industries. Only a few products such as bakers
yeast and vinegar have been produced continuously. However, the
future may find a greater use of continuous operation. For example, if large quantities of chemicals or fuels are produced
from renewable resources, continous operation might become in-
creasingly popular.

Some of the first applications of function optimization techniques to continous fermentation appear to be a series of three
papers by D'Ans, Kototovic and Gottlieb (58-60). In all three
papers optimization was achieved by the Green's theorem method
originally developed by Miele (27). This method was also later
used in other fermentation optomizations (54,62). In the first
paper by D'Ans *et al.* (58), the problem considered was the change
of the fermentor from some initial state to some desired state in
the minimum time by varying the dilution rate within some admissible range, that is, $0 \leq D \leq M$. The system equations consisted
of the cell and substrate balance with Monod growth. The set of
reachable states and admissible trajectories are determined from
the inspection of the phase plane of the state variables and a
simple feedback control law is determined where the dilution rate
is either at the upper or lower boundary, depending upon the
value of a function of the state variables. Of course, the feedback control law assumes one can measure the cell and substrate
concentrations on-line. Also, the Monod growth model does not
generally describe the dynamic changes in most continous cultures.
No specific system is used as an example either by simulation or
experiment.

Their second paper (59) considers the optimization problem of
removing the maximum amount of nutrient during the transient
change from some initial state to the optimum steady state operating point. The intention is to improve the start-up and operation in waste treatment. Once again the Monod growth model is
used with the cell and substrate state equations. An example of
the simulation of continuous anerobic digestion shows that their
optimal trajectories would remove much greater amounts of substrate during transient periods. Again, the model and example
are the weak points; however, their approach does produce a solution for the nonlinear state regulator problem with possibly less
effort than use of the maximum principle due to the singular arc
in the optimal trajectories.

In their third paper in this area (60), they consider maximum cell production during the transient approach to the optimal steady state. They consider the substrate inhibition model proposed by Andrews (61). They obtain an optimal policy in terms of a feedback controller and report agreement between simulated results and experiments performed by them with *E. Coli* which involve switching from batch to continuous culture, i.e. start-up.

In an excellent article, Takamatsu *et al.* (62) present the solution for time optimal start-up of a fermentor to a desired optimal steady state continuous condition for an amino-acid fermentation. The state variables are the cell, substrate and product concentrations and the controlling function, dillution rate, is constrained between upper and lower bounds. The optimization problem is formulated in terms of the maximum principle and the optimal trajectories, which include singular arcs, are verified to be optimal by using Green's theorem. The authors also clearly point out that the initial state, as well as the final state, must satisfy the stoichiometric relation as a requirement for time optimal start-up. They also present the solution for maximum product production during a dynamic operating period. In fact, this can be considered as an alternate start-up procedure to the time optimal case. Again, the form of the solution is obtained by the maximum principle with Green's theorem used to obtain the actual switching policy. The optimal control for this second start-up method consists of singular arcs for the general case where the initial conditions do not satisfy the stoichiometric relation, but it is shown that when they do the singular arc disappears and the optimal policy is simply a single switch of the dilution rate between its minimum and maximum permitted values. Experimental results which show good agreement with this last optimal policy are also presented.

An article by Muzychenko *et al.* (63) presents an outline for the optimal operation of continuous fermentations with the objective of maximum biomass production. The article suggests the use of a simple growth model, in particular Monod or Monod-Ierusalimskii, consider cell and substrate concentration as the state variables and dilution rate as the control variable. The paper then describes the process of model coefficient identification during start-up in the batch mode followed by determination of the optimal steady state conditions using these estimates. The data collected during the transient to this first estimate of the optimal steady state operating point is then used to update the model coefficients. A new optimal operating point is then calculated and a time optimal control policy is used to change to this state. The fermentor would then be operated at this optimal steady state and the model parameters would be updated periodically using certain properties of the turbidostat or chemostat operation. New optimal conditions, and the minimum time policy, would then be calculated and implemented to improve fermentor performance whenever significant parameter changes were detected.

Some elaboration is made of this scheme, but for the most part no
detail is given. Operation in the above mode would be an excellent objective to pursue; however, the actual achievement of this
scheme for most fermentations could be a complex and time-consuming process.

IV. FUTURE DIRECTIONS

    The future direction in computer control of fermentation pro-
cesses should move toward the goal of optimal operation, using
whatever tool, technique, or insight is most appropriate for the
problem considered. From an academic viewpoint, a somewhat fundamental engineering approach, where a model system is used for
experimental work (say a bacterium on methanol or bakers yeast
on glucose) seems to be a way to proceed if results which are
more understandable and extendable are desired. Also, this
approach may permit the optimization policies developed by the
more rigorous mathematical techniques to be demonstrated by experiment. Then progress toward more complex industrial situations would be made by adding complexities one at a time, if
possible, until the goal of reaching a system of reasonable use
to industry would be reached. This is usually not a task rapidly
achieved, and prolonged fundamental research efforts of several
years will probably be involved. Even then it should not be expected that all of the most advanced concepts of point or path
optimization will be utilized to solve many of the problems of
industrial complexity. The papers of Foss (64) and Lee and Weekman (65) indicate how great the gap between advanced optimization
and control research from academia, and actual practice in the
chemical process industries has been. A tendency has been to
attempt to demonstrate more advanced mathematical optimization
schemes at the expense of the relevance of the system model, that
is, complex methods are often only successful when applied to
simple systems. If this happens, then one can produce a series
of elegant solutions, but the search to match it with a relevant
problem rarely is successful. It is disappointing to some to
find that the optimal control of a simple chemical process
(achieved with much labor) produces results which are about the
same as with conventional proportional integral control action
which is properly tuned and has an adequate sampling frequency.
Of course, the results from one industry's experience does not
necessarily mean that the same thing will happen in another. For
example, the use of the more advanced concepts of optimization
and adaptive control have apparently had a greater success rate
with aerospace systems than in the chemical process industries.
The fermentation industry certainly has complex problems, as do
the chemical process industries, but perhaps the nature of the
processes (i.e. batch or fed batch) will lend themselves more
readily, after some effort, to path optimization schemes. The

fact that some of these optimization schemes indicate feeding policies that resemble policies that have been found through experience gives one a reason to have optimism.

The alternate approach of using intuitive control and optimization schemes, after a biochemical or systems model for the fermentation has been developed, also has positive and negative aspects. If one is determined to immediately work on a system closer in complexity to that found in industry, rather than progressively add complexity, then the hope of finding the actual key state variables and a model which relates them, being able to measure a sufficient number of these so that the other unmeasurable ones can be accurately estimated, and then implementing calculated optimal policies, all in one relatively short time period, makes success by the more mathematically rigorous optimization techniques less likely. In this case it seems that many problems will have to be approached almost on a system-by-system basis using the more intuitive approach, but without as great an expectation of producing techniques more generally applicable to a broad class of fermentations.

It is possible that the way to proceed is some compromise between these two approaches, i.e. the optimization methods which require fairly accurate state variable models, such as the maximum principle, and the approach which produces good control for a particular system, such as maximum yield for yeast fermentation by maintaining $RQ = 1.0$. A dual approach such as this may produce results of interest and use to industry. Hopefully, the results of each approach will complement the other, leading to sounder solutions of more complex problems.

V. CONCLUSIONS

The computer control and optimization of fermentation processes is of great economic interest to industry and also has generated a substantial effort in academic institutions. This review article has attempted to complement the one of the previous year written by members of the industrial community by examining the same subject areas considered to be important, but from the view of a member of the academic community. The topics of a computer-coupled system for fundamental engineering research, models and methods for computer control, and, in particular, the area of optimization as applied to fermentation, were discussed with the hope of generating information of present or potential industrial interest.

The use of modeling and optimization for on-line computer control will continue to be of interest in industry as long as it is economically justified, in spite of what is done in the academic field. Hopefully, though, its progress and quality will be influenced in a positive way by academic contributions to this important and interesting field.

REFERENCES

1. Dobry, D. and Jost, J., "Annual Reports on Fermentation
    Processes" (D. Perlman, ed.), Vol. 1, Chapter 5. Academic
    Press, New York (1977).
2. Jefferis, R. P., *Process Biochemistry*, April, 10 (1975).
3. Jefferis, R. P., Abstracts, 5th International Fermentation
    Symposium. Berlin (1976).
4. Williams, T. J., minutes of "International Purdue Workshop
    on Industrial Computer Systems," sponsored by Purdue Labora-
    tory for Applied Industrial Control (PLAIC), Spring and Fall
    (1969-1978).
5. DiBiasio, D., Lim, H. C., Weigand, W. A., and Tsao, G. T.,
    AIChE J (1978).
6. Mohler, R., Hennigan, P., Lim, H. C., Tsao, G. T., and
    Weigand, W. A., 2nd International Conference on Computer
    Applications in Fermentation Techniques. Philadelphia,
    Pennsylvania (1978).
7. Jefferis, R. P. III, Biela, J. A., and Nyiri, L. K., Ab-
    stracts, 75th National AIChE Meeting. Detroit, Michigan
    (1973).
8. Nagia, S., Nishizawa, Y., and Yamagata, T., Abstracts, 5th
    International Fermentation Symposium. Berlin (1976).
9. Cooney, C. L., Wang, H. Y., and Wang, D. I. C., *Biotechnol.
    and Bioeng. 19*, 55 (1977).
10. Wang, H. Y., Cooney, C. L., and Wang, D. I. C., *Biotechnol.
    and Bioeng. 19*, 69 (1977).
11. Humphrey, A. E. and Jefferis, R. P. III, IVth Giam Meeting,
    San Paulo, Brazil, July (1973).
12. Ryu, D. Y. and Humphrey, A. E., *J. of Applied Chemistry and
    Biotechnol. 23*, 283 (1973).
13. Nyiri, L. K. and Krishnaswami, C. S., paper presented at the
    Meeting of American Society for Microbiology, Chicago,
    Illinois, May (1974).
14. Krishnaswami, C. S. and Paramenter, Abstracts, 168th ACS
    Meeting, Atlantic City, NJ, September (1974).
15. Nyiri, L. K., Toth, G. M., and Charles, M., *Biotechnol. and
    Bioeng. 17*, 1663 (1975).
16. Aiba, S., Nagai, S., and Nishizawa, Y., *Biotechnol. and
    Bioeng. 17*, 1001 (1976).
17. Whaite, P. and Gray, P. P., *Biotechnol. and Bioeng. 19*, 575
    (1977).
18. Zabriskie, D. W. and Humphrey, A. E., *AIChE J. 24*, 138
    (1978).
19. Reuss, M., Jefferis, R. P. III, and Lehmann, J., Gesell-
    schaft fur Biotechnologische Forschung mbH., Workshop at
    Braunschwerg - Stockheim, GFR, July 5 (1976).

20. Svrcek, W. Y., Elliott, R. F., and Zajic, J. E., *Biotechnol. and Bioeng. 16*, 827 (1974).

21. Beveridge, G. S. G. and Schechter, R. S., "Optimization: Theory and Practice." McGraw-Hill, New York (1970).

22. Hadley, G., "Nonlinear and Dynamic Programming." Addison-Wesley, Inc., Reading, Massachusetts (1964).

23. Duffin, R. J., Peterson, E. L., and Zener, C., "Geometric Programming." John Wiley & Sons, Inc., New York (1967).

24. Ray, W. H. and Szekely, J., "Process Optimization." John Wiley & Sons, Inc., New York (1973).

25. Bliss, G. A., "Lectures on the Calculus of Variations." The University of Chicago Press, Chicago (1946).

26. Pontryagin, L. S., Boltyanskii, V. G., Gamkrelidze, R. V., and Mishchenko, E. F., "The Mathematical Theory of Optimal Processes." John Wiley & Sons, Inc., New York (1962).

27. Miele, A., "Optimization Techniques" (G. Leitman, ed.). Academic Press, New York (1962).

28. Vainberg, M. M., "Variational Methods for the Study of Non-linear Operations." Holden-Day, Inc., San Francisco (1964).

29. Weigand, W. A. and D'Souza, A. F., *J. of Basic Eng. 91D*, 161 (1969).

30. Weigand, W. A., *I & EC Fundamentals 69*, 641 (1970).

31. Turrie, B. D., Clinton, J. H., and Weigand, W. A., *Chem. Eng. Commun. 2*, 5 (1975).

32. Kalman, R. E. and Bucy, R. S., *ASME Trans. 82D*, 95 (1961).

33. Schechter, R. S., "The Variational Method in Engineering." McGraw-Hill, New York (1967).

34. Denn, M. M., "Optimization by Variational Methods." McGraw Hill, New York (1969).

35. Athans, M. and Falb, P., "Optimal Control." McGraw-Hill, New York (1966).

36. Lapidus, L. and Luus, R., "Optimal Control of Engineering Processes." Blaisdall Pub. Co., Waltham, Massachusetts (1967).

37. Jefferis, R. P. III, Gesellschaft fur Biotechnologische Forschung mbH, SCP Symposium Braunschweig-Stockheim, March (1975).

38. Okabe, M., Aiba, S., and Okada, M., *J. of Ferment. Tech. 51*, 594 (1973).

39. Box, M. J., *Computer J. 8*, 42 (1965).

40. Okabe, M. and Aiba, S., *J. Ferment. Technol. 52*, 279 (1974).

41. Aiba, S. and Okabe, M., Proc. of 1st International Congress of IAMS, p. 137. Tokyo (1974).

42. Blanch, H. W. and Rogers, P. L., *Biotechnol. and Bioeng. 14*, 151 (1972).

43. Constantinides, A., Spencer, J. L., and Gaden, E. L., *Biotechnol. and Bioeng. 12*, 1081 (1970).

44. Constantinides, A., Spencer, J. L., and Gaden, E. L., *Biotechnol. and Bioeng. 12*, 803 (1970).

45. Bryson, A. E., Denham, W. F., and Dreyfus, S. E., *AIAA J. 1*, 2544 (1963).
46. King, R. E., Aragona, J., and Constantinides, A., *Int. J. Cont. 20*, 869 (1974).
47. Rai, V. R. and Constantinides, A., *AIChE. Symp. Ser. 132*, 114 (1973).
48. Constantinides, A. and Rai, V. R., *Biotechnol. and Bioeng. Symp. 7*, 613 (1974).
49. Koga, S., Burg, C. R., and Humphrey, A. E., *Appl. Microb. 15*, 683 (1967).
50. Lim, H. C. and Emigholz, K. F., Proc. Enzyme Eng. Conf., Portland, Oregon, August (1975).
51. Andreyeva, L. N. and Biryukov, V. V., *Biotechnol. and Bioeng. Symp. 4*, 61 (1973).
52. Aiba, S., Humphrey, A. E., and Mills, N. F., "Biochemical Engineering," 1st Edition. Academic Press, New York (1965).
53. Fishman, V. M. and Biryukov, V. V., *Biotechnol. and Bioeng. Symp. 4*, 647 (1974).
54. Ohno, H., Nakanishi, E., and Takamatsu, T., *Biotechnol. and Bioeng. 18*, 847 (1976).
55. Ohno, H., Nakanishi, E., and Takamatsu, T., *Biotechnol. and Bioeng. 20*, 625 (1978).
56. Kelley, J. H., *J. SIAM Control 2*, 234 (1965).
57. Yamané, T., Kume, T., Sada, E., and Takamatsu, T., *J. Ferment. Technol. 55*, 587 (1977).
58. D'Ans, G., Kokotovic, P., and Gottlieb, D., *J. Optim. Theory Applic. 7*, 61 (1971).
59. D'Ans, G., Kokotovic, P., and Gottlieb, D., *IEEE Trans. Auto Cont. AC-16*, 341 (1971).
60. D'Ans, G., Gottlieb, D., and Kokotovic, P., *Automatica 8*, 729 (1972).
61. Andrews, J. F., *Biotechnol. and Bioeng. 10*, 707 (1968).
62. Takamatsu, T., Hashimoto, I., Shioya, S., Mizuhara, K., Koike, T., and Ohno, H., *Automatica 11*, 141 (1975).
63. Muzychenko, L. A., Mascheva, L. A., and Yakovleva, G. V., *Biotechnol. and Bioeng. Sym. 4*, 629 (1974).
64. Foss, A. S., *AIChE J. 19*, 209 (1973).
65. Lee, Y. and Weekman, V. W., *AIChE J. 22*, 27 (1976).

CHAPTER 4

KINETIC HYSTERESIS IN ENZYME
AND FERMENTATION SYSTEMS

Robert D. Tanner

Chemical Engineering Department
Vanderbilt University
Nashville, Tennessee

I. HYSTERESIS IN PHYSICAL SYSTEMS

Hysteresis is defined (1) in physics as "the failure of a property that has been changed by an external agent to return to its original value when the cause of the change is removed." The word comes from the Greek *husterēsis*, a shortcoming. In magnets it is often exhibited as "the failure of the magnetization in that body to return to its original value when the external field is reduced" (1). A typical simulation study of this phenomena is illustrated in reference (2) by a phenomenological model describing ferromagnetic hysteresis.

In practice, hysteresis has been generalized to refer to deviations from, not just an original or starting point, but from any point along a hysteresis trajectory. When the trajectory of ascent differs from the trajectory of descent of a process (even though the starting and finishing point are the same), that phenomenon also is referred to as hysteresis.

Numerous examples of the more generalized definition of hysteresis or "shortcoming" are found in the scientific literature. In a chapter of the book, *The Solid Gas Interface*, Everett (3) cites many illustrations of adsorption hysteresis. One example, the adsorption of benzene by polyvinylidene char, illustrates a counterclockwise hysteresis adsorption curve for large particle size char-pellets, but no discernible hysteresis area for very fine particle size pellets. Clearly, then, adsorption hysteresis curves can be used to infer at least one length dimension of an adsorbing particle. Ruckenstein and Prieve (4) have suggested that the differences in adsorption and desorption rates, due to such factors as the particle size, can be exploited to develop a new separation technique which they call potential-barrier chromatography.

Hysteresis has also been described in dynamic fluids, as apparent surface tension hysteresis (5), and in the transition between two flow states of stirred vessels (6). In materials with memory, the underlying mathematical description of time-reversal and thermodynamic symmetry can be posed in terms of entropy production (7). Reference has also been made to possible application in neuroscience by relating hysteresis to the molecular memory record (8).

The aggregation behavior of synthetic polypeptides, such as poly-α-L-glutamic acid, can lend insight into the tertiary or quaternary structure as the polypeptide in solution passes between two states. A hysteresis cycle of the optical rotation describes one such transition, caused by temperature changes, which is also affected by changes in pH (9). Several different polypeptides also show hysteresis in their thermomechanical behavior when their rigidity is measured as a function of temperature. Such experiments are even appropriate for undergraduate research projects (10).

A particularly topical hysteresis curve can be observed in the data describing the stomatal resistance as a function of light intensity for corn leaves. Stomatal resistance hysteresis may be caused by water stress, by carbon dioxide, by diffusion through the stomate, by temperature, and by aging and hormonal control (11). Models describing the hysteresis phenomena have direct application to the agricultural problems of water conservation and crop production (11).

With these agricultural, polypeptide, fluid, mechanical, adsorption, and ferromagnetic examples as background, each illustrating the widespread phenomena of hysteresis in nature, we focus on one particular hysteresis system that is found in dynamic fermentation systems. These fermentation dynamic hysteresis functions, in turn, often can be understood by relating them to their underlying enzyme behavior, hence the initial development of enzymatic hysteresis in this review.

II. HYSTERESIS IN ENZYME SYSTEMS

It has been suggested that "the hysteresis concept in enzymatic systems is likely to be of general importance, at any rate in complex, interlocking metabolic pathways, and it will no doubt be widely used to explain the inexplicable" (12). The same reference in *Nature* suggests that "the concept of enzymatic hysteresis may unify much of the biochemical properties of enzymatic behavior, such as cooperativity, allosterism, and induced-fit in

complex enzymes." Citing Frieden (12), the concept of hysteresis
may in the end "simplify, rather than complicate, the interpreta-
tion of metabolic regulation." One example in which hysteresis
may be a factor is the aspartate utilization scheme for *E. coli*.
Here "the feedback inhibition of homoserine dehydrogenase activity by threonine also blocks the production of methionine, and
therefore normal growth." Other hysteresis examples are found in
the feedback inhibition of threonine deaminase by isoleucine, the
hydride transfer step from ethanol in the liver alcohol dehydro-
genase-NADH system, as reported by Shore and Gutfreund (12), and
the behavior of the glucose-6-phosphate dehydrogenase reaction
configuration (13).

Bistability in the recent book by Bailey and Ollis (14) is
illustrated by hysteresis of insolubilized peroxidase in an open
reaction system (15). The hysteresis of this enzyme system is
attributed to the interactive effects of both molecular reaction
and diffusion.

In the study of cell longevity, due to chemical changes
caused by aging, recent work has shown that the ability to degrade proteins and to affect reproduction and thymus activity has
been linked biochemically to aging (16). "As cells age they
apparently lose their ability to degrade specific enzymes as well
as proteins, in general," and "enzymes such as catalase, aldolase,
isocitrate lipase, and superoxide dismutase lose from 30 to 70%
of their activity in animals between the time an animal is born
and the time it dies." Taking the example of the aging of man's
thymus immunity system to demonstrate correlations of age with
disease states, it can be shown that a counterclockwise hysteresis curve relates thymus-dependent immunity with the concentration of the polypeptide, thymosin (16). This thymus study fits
the subject of this article when it is noted that the immunity
hysteresis curve area is considerably reduced due to aging. The
immunity reduction during aging over the course of polypeptide
changes may therefore be correlated with the hysteresis curve
area. This effect is similar to that of fermentation hysteresis
curves, to be discussed. In the latter case, the area can be related to the rate of enzyme induction during the course of a
batch process.

It should be mentioned that the degradation of drugs in mam-
mals also provides another, albeit more complex, hysteresis system in which enzymes such as those in liver microsomes (17) play
a major role. For example, in the study of the degradation of
the tranquilizer chlordiazepoxide·HCl in the dog, Kaplan *et al.*
(18) have measured simultaneously the time courses of the lead
compound and two of its decomposition products. These trajectories were then used to build kinetic models for developing drug
regimen therapies. Since body enzyme levels may be useful in
estimating their corresponding drug (substrate) requirement to
achieve a given level of drug in the body (19), cross plots of
the enzyme degradation product concentration against the inter-

mediate degradation compound concentration may lead, via hysteresis curve analysis, to further information about the drug's metabolism with degradation enzymes. In turn, such estimates of enzyme levels could result in better strategies for administering the drug. In particular, a cross plot of the rate of the second chlordiazepoxide·HCl decomposition product, demoxypam, against the first decomposition product, n-demethyl chlordiazepoxide, led to clockwise hysteresis curves for each of two dogs used in the study (20). From the direction of the curve, it was postulated that, in addition to the main decomposition pathway of the drug, a new parallel pathway also contributes to degradation. Such a pathway could lead to more rapid drug action if the second decomposition product were pharmacologically more active then the preceding moieties (20).

Other pharmaceutical systems described by hysteresis curves, which in turn may be the result of enzymatic (or protein) action, include the excretion rate of sodium ion as a clockwise hysteresis function of the diuretic chlorothiazide (21), and the counterclockwise hysteresis curve relating the reduction in physiological performance as a function of the dosage of the drug, D-lysergic acid diethylamide (22).

III. MODELING KINETIC HYSTERESIS IN ENZYME SYSTEMS

The word "kinetic" is used to invoke the usual connotation of time varying trajectories found in chemical systems. As in physics and control theory applications, kinetic hysteresis curves have time only as an implicit variable, since they represent cross plots of concentrations or rates at common time points. To make this description more concrete, we examine the counterclockwise curve of malachite green formation, $d(P)/dt$, as a function of the product of horseradish peroxidase enzyme-hydrogen peroxide complex, (ES), and leucomalachite green, (S_2), in Figure 1. The data used for this cross plot are those taken by B. Chance (23) in an early stopped-flow study of the peroxidase system. This cross plot, connecting the implicit common time points which originally appeared in reference (24), illustrates that the early time points (initial transient trajectory) lie below the later time points (stationary-state trajectory). This example of a kinetic enzyme hysteresis curve demonstrates what type of information can be inferred from the trajectory's direction and shape.

The primary effect, easily discernible and not readily confounded by experimental error (because of the many experimental points involved), is that of direction. The direction of the curve in Figure 1 is counterclockwise. At first glance, it would seem that whatever would cause a change in direction would be due to some nonlinear effect, since the curve is not linear. Invoking nonlinearity, in fact, was shown to be unnecessary (24) from a simulation of the linear kinetic network of:

A→B→C→D

which led to a counterclockwise hysteresis curve when d(D)/dt was
plotted as a function of (B).   Here, parentheses indicate concentrations, and t, time.   The chemical species are denoted by the

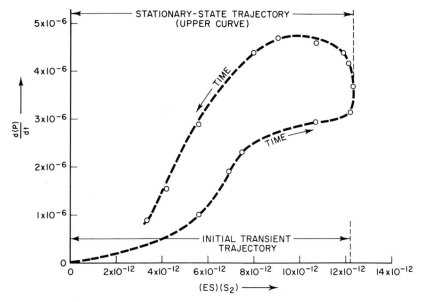

FIGURE 1.   Rate of malachite green formation as a function
of (ES) (S_2).   B. Chances' classical peroxidase reaction data
(1943).   Reprinted from reference (24), Figure 6.   (With permission of the publisher, The American Institute of Chemical
Engineers.)

A→B→C→D

which led to a counterclockwise hysteresis curve when d(D)/dt was
plotted as a function of (B).   Here, parentheses indicate concentrations, and t, time.   The chemical species are denoted by the
letters.   As expected from the law of mass action and the assumption of elementary kinetic reactions, a cross plot of d(D)/dt
against (C) leads to a linear curve, with a slope equal to the
rate constant of the step C to D.
    It is seen from the above simple analysis that a tool is
available to discriminate between two models: one, A→B→D and the
other A→B→C→D, when d(D)/dt is plotted against (B).   If that plot
is linear, (C) is in negligible concentration if it exists at all,
but if nonlinear, (C) is significant to the system.   Returning to
the peroxidase example shown in Figure 1, the original model proposed by Chance in 1943 postulated that only one intermediate
state, ES, was present.   The graphical consequence of the presence

of only one intermediate in the proposed model is that a cross plot of the data would be linear. In Figure 1, $(ES)(S_2)$ is plotted on the abscissa rather than (ES) alone, in order to take into consideration the two substrate, nonlinear system. Since the curve in Figure 1 is distinctly a counterclockwise hysteresis function, however, analysis implies that more than one intermediate enzyme-substrate complex must exist. This implication was verified independently of the hysteresis analysis when Chance later postulated and subsequently measured, in 1952, two enzyme-substrate complexes along with a free radical intermediate state (25).

A more subtle and less rigorous inference from Figure 1 perhaps may be drawn from the change in convexity of the lower curve. Clearly, such a change is within experimental error for smoothed and differenced product data. Nevertheless, it still may be useful to see if the ramifications of convexity reversal can offer clues to determine which variables may be important in model building, and subsequent experimental studies. To better elucidate the change in convexity of a hysteresis curve, the phenomena of clockwise versus counterclockwise hysteresis is first examined, again using linear models. The motivation for understanding clockwise hysteresis curves originally came from studying the clockwise hysteresis curve observed for the chlorothiazide drug (21), previously referenced.

After developing many linear and nonlinear models, it was established (26) that clockwise hysteresis between the rate of formation of product E and a precursor such as C came about because of a shunting step around C, such as:

$$A \rightarrow B \rightarrow C \rightarrow D \rightarrow E$$

One such simulation of this model is shown as curve 3 in Figure 2. When the rate constant defining the shunting step from B to E in the model (k_6 in Figure 2) was reduced to half the value, keeping the other rate constants constant, the circumscribing curve collapsed. This "figure eight" collapsed curve is depicted by curve 2 in Figure 2. Finally, when k_6 became negligible (zero in Figure 2), the previously established counterclockwise curve was simulated, as expected. This latter curve is shown for comparison as curve 1, also in Figure 2.

To return to Figure 1, where there is a reversal in curvature on the lower branch of the hysteresis curve, the problem of description seems then to be one of combining the notion of overall counterclockwise hysteresis (that is, a primary sequential pathway) with the contribution of a weaker shunting pathway effective primarily during the initial transient (26). When such a scheme was simulated, as shown by curve 1 in Figure 3, the convexity change occurred too early on the transient trajectory (at the small (C) values). One way to shift the convexity change to higher (C) values was accomplished by modifying the last step of

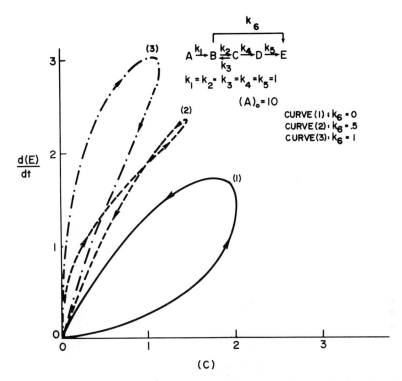

FIGURE 2. *Effect of shunting on hysteresis. Reprinted (with permission of the publisher, Elsevier Sequoia) from reference (26), Figure 4.*

the model: by relating the product to its immediate chemical precursor in nonlinear fashion, as shown by curve 2 in Figure 3. In this case, a quadratic last step of 2E→F shifted the convexity change so that the shape of the latter curve more closely mimicked Figure 1. Physical counterparts for both the quadratic step (2 free radicals combine to form the product) and shunting (a possibility with many enzyme-substrate species) seem to fit this peroxidase example, to strengthen the case for such hysteresis model building (26). With the background of clockwise and counterclockwise hysteresis curves developed in terms of parallel and sequential pathways, we now turn to the more complex fermentation systems, consisting of not only the enzyme catalyzed pathways, but also the biochemical cell machinery network.

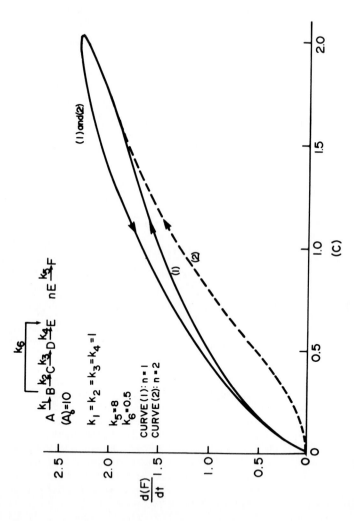

FIGURE 3. Effect of the terminal step on a counterclockwise hysteresis curve. Reprinted (with permission of the publisher, Elsevier Sequoia) from Reference (26), Figure 5.

IV.   HYSTERESIS IN FERMENTATION SYSTEMS

Hysterisis in a batch fermentation system was perhaps first considered by Burg, in his master's thesis, as one description of the rate of formation of gluconic acid as a function of its precursor, gluconolactone. His data were subsequently published in 1967, as part of a modeling study, co-authored with Koga and his advisor, Humphrey (27). The fermentation studied was that of the *Pseudomonas ovalis* system for synthesis of the acid from glucose. A cross plot of the data was subsequently graphed independently as a counterclockwise hysteresis curve, in a publication three years later (28).

Kinetic hysteresis in an open (or continuous) fermentation process was proposed even earlier, in a paper by Perret in 1960 (29). Experimental verification of Perret's prediction of a counterclockwise hysteresis curve, relating specific growth rate to substrate concentration during feed substrate step changes, was later provided by Storer and Gaudy in 1969 (30). As described in reference (26), Storer and Gaudy observed this effect in the response of heterogeneous microbial populations, obtained from municipal sewage, to a diet of glucose serving as the growth limiting nutrient. Another physical model for open system hysteresis was developed by Lee, Jackman, and Schroeder (31) in terms of dispersed and flocculated microbial growth, using Monod growth terms to describe the hysteresis trajectory reported by Gaudy and Storer.

It also seems appropriate to mention hysteresis between two steady-state operating points in the α-galactosidase system (produced by a mold) discussed in the book by Bailey and Ollis (14). This phenomenon of multiple steady states due to diauxie, synchrony, or multiple species effects in continuous fermentation systems has only recently been studied (32,33), and further investigation seems to be timely for clarifying hysteresis relationships between states.

V.   MODELING KINETIC HYSTERESIS IN FERMENTATION SYSTEMS

In batch fermentation systems kinetic hysteresis generally refers to the changing relationship between the ascending (or initial time) trajectory of a product rate, and the descending rate curve (describing the stationary-state), each as a function of the same intermediate chemical specie. The ascending curve often depicts the product rate behavior coincident with the cell lag phase, while the descending rate often occurs, physically, when the cells are in their growth and stationary phases. What seems to be the fundamental difference between the product rate versus intermediate concentration kinetic hysteresis curve for an enzyme system which was discussed previously, and that for a

fermentation system, is the difference between the catalyzing enzyme trajectories. In the enzyme system case, the sum of free and
bound enzyme, or total enzyme level, is fixed throughout the reaction. On the other hand, in the fermentation case the "total" enzyme level changes during the course of the fermentation, as the
enzymes are synthesized and then degraded by the microbial cell.

An example is now given to illustrate the kinetic fermentation
system. We note in Figures 4 and 5, taken from reference (34) and
originally developed from the data of Rai and Constantinides (35),
that such curves could be either counterclockwise or clockwise.
In this particular case, the rate of formation of gluconic acid as
a function of gluconolactone, the direction of the hysteresis trajectory is temperature dependent. Figure 4 is for the 25°C case
and Figure 5, the 33.7^{O}C study. At the intermediate temperature
of 30°C and also at pH 5.8, the hysteresis curve developed from
Rai and Constantinides' data has the same counterclockwise trajectory as Figure 4, but with a smaller inscribed area (34). This
latter curve was also developed earlier using Burg's data (27) and
reported in reference (28).

To better understand the meaning of a fermentation kinetic
hysteresis curve, we will start by examining a curve of the form
of Figure 4. It was originally surmised that the counterclockwise hysteresis describing the gluconic acid system came about as
a result of the presence of an enzyme, gluconolactonase, not previously associated with the bacteria, *Pseudomonas ovalis* (28).
If the presence of the enzyme were verified experimentally, then
a hysteresis curve of this type could be used in general to predict the existence of an unrecognized enzyme. The reason for
postulating the enzyme contribution to the gluconolactone-gluconic
acid system is that if gluconic acid, G, came (mechanistically)
solely from the lactone, L, by chemical hydrolysis, then the rate
curve shown in Figure 4 would be linear. Since the points in
Figure 4 seem to be ordered in time, in a nonrandom fashion, the
probability of such a curve resulting from scatter in the data
about a line would be extremely small, and hence, the linear correlation would be tenuous at best (28). Proposing that an enzyme
would also convert L to G led to a reasonable explanation for the
hysteresis response curve. Biochemical validity of such an enzyme
being present seems to be possible, considering the fact that
lactonase is found in other microbial systems (35).

In the first computer experiment of the gluconic acid fermentation system, using a model describing cell growth and enzymatic
(as well as chemical), hydrolytic conversion of gluconolactone to
gluconic acid, the level of lactonase was kept constant. This
computer experiment was the analog of the enzyme kinetic hysteresis case, discussed earlier, because of the constant total enzyme
level. As might have been expected, the counterclockwise trajectory of d(G)/dt versus (L) was so close to a straight line that
such a curve could not legitimately be discriminated from that of
a line, taking experimental error into consideration. A subsequent simulation, with the lactonase enzyme being generated within

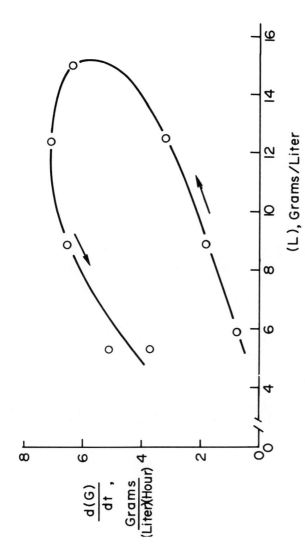

FIGURE 4. Experimental data of rate of formation of gluconic acid as a function of glucono-lactone concentration. pH = 5.8 and T = 25°C. Counterclockwise hysteresis. Reprinted by permission of the Society of Fermentation Technology, Japan, from reference (34), Figure 1.

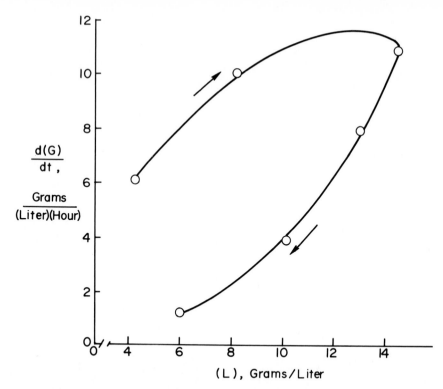

FIGURE 5. *Experimental data of rate of formation of gluconic acid as a function of gluconolactone concentration. pH = 5.8 and T = 33.7°C. Clockwise hysteresis. Reprinted by permission of the Society of Fermentation Technology, Japan, from reference (34), Figure 1.*

the system (in an inductive manner for convenience), demonstrated that the upper and lower branches of the hysteresis trajectory could easily be separated (24). A smooth counterclockwise hysteresis curve of approximately the shape of that shown in Figure 4 was generated. This computer study, therefore, indicated that enzyme synthesis could provide a reasonable explanation for a counterclockwise hysteresis curve in keeping with known biochemical constructs.

Since the counterclockwise hysteresis curve (28), obtained from the data in reference (27), seemed to come to a point or a cusp, the question was raised as to whether such behavior had particular physical meaning. This question was addressed in a computer simulation study (36), even though it was recognized that such a cusp on a hysteresis curve, obtained by differencing data, would lie well within experimental error. The idea behind such a

computer study was to see if meaningful leads about fermentation
mechanisms could be obtained even if the original premise of cusp
formation was tentative. Experimental verification could then
follow up any promising computer predictions.

One biochemical mechanism which could cause the shape of a
fermentation hysteresis curve to change is that of a protease
attacking the enzyme responsible for the original hysteresis
curve. For example, if that protease (needed for the conservation of material within the microbial cell by causing the turnover of amino acids) degraded the enzyme faster than it was synthesized, the direction of the hysteresis curve could change. In
other words, the catalytic rate of reaction would be smaller late
in the reaction than in the early stages, since the enzyme catalyst would be in smaller total concentration. That was, in fact,
the result predicted by a computer simulation of the gluconic
acid system, when the lactonase was degraded faster than it was
produced (36). Details of the simulated fermentation model are
provided in references (28) and (37). The computer   study also
indicated, by the simulation of cusp formation, that the protease
model could cause the cusp on the hysteresis curve as was surmised. After some computer experimentation, it turned out that a
rate of protease degradation could be developed such that both
the cusp and the counterclockwise characteristics of the hysteresis curve could be obtained together (36). Based on the simulation, it then was decided that a cusp was most likely the result
of the tradeoff between the formation and degradation rates of
the key enzyme. When these two rates equalized, the cusp resulted.

The phenomena of equal rates of formation and degradation of
proteins in nature is not unreasonable. A fascinating study of
hibernating animals at the Mayo Clinic Farms (38) reported recently that:

> "As sleep begins in a bear during hibernation, the bio-
> chemical mechanisms become delicately balanced. Normally,
> the bear, like other animals, manufactures and breaks
> down proteins at a constant rate in a process called
> 'protein turnover'."

Presumably, the overall rate of protein degradation is normally
greater than that of synthesis, because of the continuing need
for intake of "critical" amino acids. In the Mayo Farms study,
however:

> "The researchers found that protein turnover speeds up
> five times during hibernation without increasing the
> amount of protein in the body at one time. This con-
> servation program provides the bear with as much pro-
> tein at the end as at the beginning of the winter
> sleep. The process is so efficient that the bear
> does not form excess amounts of urea, the waste pro-
> duct of protein breakdown, which is excreted in urine
> and which becomes toxic when large quantities build
> up."

Returning to the change in direction of the fermentation hysteresis curves shown in Figures 4 and 5 due to temperature changes, a simulation study was performed trying to explain this phenomenon in terms of enzyme formation and protease degradation mechanisms. Since the previous simulation study undertaken to understand cusp formation led to a change of direction of the hysteresis curve when the protease action was large relative to enzyme formation, that study inferred that since protease activity is a function of temperature, such changes could result from changes in the temperature of the system.

When the pH 5.8 data of Rai and Constantinides were graphed as a sequence of temperature dependent hysteresis curves, an interesting oscillatory effect was observed (34). At the lowest temperature of 25°C (Figure 4), a counterclockwise curve described the rate of formation of gluconic acid as a function of gluconolactone in the *Pseudomonas ovalis* fermentation system. When the fermentation was repeated at the slightly higher temperature of 28°C, the direction of the hysteresis curve changed to clockwise. The oscillation in direction continued when it was observed that the 30°C run led again to a counterclockwise curve, which also held for the next run at 32°C. Again, when the experiment was repeated at the slightly higher temperature of 33.7°C (Figure 5), the curve changed direction to clockwise. An intermediate hysteresis curve (that is, one with no discernible area or direction) resulted at the highest temperature experiment of 35.4°C. Possibly, a higher temperature would lead again to a clockwise trajectory.

One possible explanation for this oscillatory hysteresis effect is that the system, probably comprised of a lactonase and its countering protease, was effected by the differential temperature sensitivities of these two enzymes (34). If these two enzymes have noncongruent, horseshoe-shaped, negative convexity activity versus temperature curves, it would be possible to construct a scheme in which the protease would be negligible at 25°C.

The activity curves would be such that the relative protease strength at 28°C would then increase, followed by stronger relative lactonase activity at 30°C and up to 32°C. At 33.7°C, the two enzymes would be evenly matched on these activity curves. Reference (34) proposed one scheme in which two rate constants were affected by temperature in such a way to generate the sequence of hysteresis trajectories.

For the sake of completeness, two more topics at least should be mentioned. First, the relationship between the shunting on enzyme systems and those changes affecting enzyme generation in a fermentation system. Superficially, the protease attack of the primary catalytic enzyme can be viewed as a parallel effect, much like shunting in the enzyme system, but the relationship between shunting and enzyme generation needs further clarification. The question of what happens when an enzyme system with parallel pathways each of which is differently affected by outside forces,

such as temperature and protease effects, is still unanswered.
One beginning, however, has been made as to how parallel pathways
in a fermentation system would behave under different pH conditions. When the rate of acid formation data of Luedeking and
Piret (39), for the batch lactic acid fermentation, were plotted
against time, a "shoulder" occurred at a pH of 4.5, which was
shortened at a pH of 4.8, and then became imperceptible at a pH
of 5.2. The postulate of a parallel pathway provided a reasonable explanation for this effect (40). It appears that extension
of the analysis of parallel pathways, in terms of kinetic hysteresis, to fermentation also would prove to be worthwhile.

The second topic in need of further study is that of growth
rate hysteresis in open fermentation systems, previously cited in
references (29) through (31). It turns out that this system can
be analyzed using the notions of series and parallel flow steps
when the flow enters a sequence of stirred reactors (26). Further
analysis of such systems may provide useful insight into the behavior of chemostats and other continuous fermentation systems.

VI. CONCLUSIONS

It has been shown that kinetic hysteresis can be a useful tool
in elucidating mechanisms in both enzyme and fermentation systems.
Hysteresis may be particularly helpful in suggesting the presence
of an enzyme not previously suspected in a fermentation system.
As a tool for discrimination between models, hysteresis can be
used to imply the presence of parallel pathways, of additional
intermediate states, and of proteases countering the primary enzyme systems. Hysteresis may even be used to infer rates of enzyme induction, possibly suggesting constitutive and induced
mechanisms. Used cautiously, in keeping with the limitations of
the data, hysteresis curve analysis appears to aid in experimental
design by reducing the number of experiments needed for the elucidation of fermentation mechanisms. As a gestalt, the entire kinetic hysteresis trajectory provides a graphical picture which
apparently offers more than the sum of the ascending and descending branches.

REFERENCES

1. Morris, W., ed., "The American Heritage Dictionary of the
    English Language," pp. 650 and 784. American Heritage Pub-
    lishing Company, Inc., and Houghton Mifflin Company, Boston
    (1969).
2. Davis, A. M., *Simulation*, 153, November (1975).
3. Everett, D. H., Chapter 36, "Adsorption Hysteresis," *in* "The
    Solid-Gas Interface" (E. A. Flood, ed.), Vol. 2, p. 1055.
    Marcel Dekker, Inc., New York (1967).

4.   Ruckenstein, E. and Prieve, D. C., *A.I.Ch.E. Journal 22*, 276
     (1976).
5.   Horn, L. W. and Davis, S. H., *J. Colloid Interface Sci. 51*,
     459 (1975).
6.   Ando, K. Hara, H., and Endoh, K., *Intern. Chem. Eng. 11*, 735
     (1971) and first published in *Kagaku Kōgaku (Chem. Eng.
     Japan) 35*, 466 (1971).
7.   Gurtin, M. E., *Arch. Rational Mech. Anal. 44*, 387 (1972).
8.   Katchalsky, A. and Neumann, E., *Int. J. Neuroscience 3*, 175
     (1972).
9.   Schuster, T. M., Jennings, B. R., and Spach. G., *in* "Symmetry
     and Function of Biological Systems at the Macromolecular
     Level" (A. Engström and B. Strandberg, eds.), p. 213. Wiley,
     New York (1969).
10. Krug, R., *A.I.Ch.E. Student Members Bulletin 14*, 16 (1973).
11. Lemon, E., Stewart, D. W., and Shawcroft, R. W., *Science 174*,
     371 (1971).
12. "Enzymes--and Now Hysteresis," *Nature 229*, 155 (1971).
13. Robbins, J. E., Jucera, C., and Wall, K., Paper Number 61,
     Biochemistry Section, 26th ACS Northwest Regional Meeting,
     Bozeman, Montana (June 1971).
14. Bailey, J. E. and Ollis, D. F., "Biochemical Engineering
     Fundamentals." McGraw-Hill Book Company, New York (1977).
15. Degn, H., *Nature 217*, 1047 (1968).
16. "Chemical Changes Caused by Aging Discovered," *C & E News 55*,
     16 (1977).
17. Fingl, E. and Woodbury, D. M., *in* "The Pharmacological Basis
     of Therapeutics" (L. S. Goodman and A. Gilman, eds.), 4th
     Ed., p. 13. The MacMillian Co., New York (1970).
18. Kaplan, S. A., Lewis, M., Schwartz, M. A., Postma, E.,
     Cotler, S., Abruzzo, C. W., Lee, T. L., and Weinfeld, R. E.,
     J. Pharm. Sci. 59, 1569 (1970).
19. Tanner, R. D. and Wilhelm, D. E., *A.I.Ch.E. Symposium Series*,
     74, 172, 53 (1978).
20. Tanner, R. D. and Wilhelm, D. E., *A.I.Ch.E. Symposium Series*,
     74, 172, 64 (1978).
21. Loo, J. C. K., Tanner, R. D., and Bondi, J. V., "The Role of
     Hysteresis in Selecting a Model to Describe the Elimination
     of Body Sodium by a Diuretic," paper presented at the A.I.Ch.
     E. Meeting, Detroit, June (1973).
22. Levy, G., Gilbaldi, M., and Jusko, J. W., *J. Pharm. Sci. 58*,
     422 (1969).
23. Chance, B., *J. Biol. Chem. 151*, 553 (1943).
24. Tanner, R.D., *A.I.Ch.E. J. 18*, 385 (1972).
25. Chance, B., *Arch. Biochem. and Biophys. 41*, 416 (1952).
26. Tanner, R. D. and DeAngelis, L. H.,*Chem. Eng. J., 8*, 113
     (1974).
27. Koga, S., Burg, C. R., and Humphrey, A. E., *Applied Micro.
     15*, 683 (1967).
28. Tanner, R. D., *Biotech. Bioeng. 12*, 831 (1970).

29. Perret, C. J., *J. Gen. Microbiol. 22*, 589 (1960).
30. Storer, F. F. and Gaudy, A. F., Jr., *Envir. Sci. Tech. 3*, 143 (1969).
31. Lee, S. S., Jackman, A. P., and Schroeder, E. D., *Water Res. 9*, 491 (1975).
32. Aris, R. and Humphrey, A. E., *Biotech. Bioeng. 19*, 1375 (1977).
33. Russell, R. M. and Tanner, R. D., *Ind. Eng. Chem. Proc. Des. Dev. 17*, 157 (1978).
34. Tanner, R. D. and Yunker, J. M., *J. Ferm. Tech. 55*, 143 (1977).
35. Rai, V. R. and Constantinides, A., *A.I.Ch.E. Symp. Series 69*, 132, 114 (1973).
36. Tanner, R. D., *Chem. Eng. Sci. 29*, 169 (1974).
37. Tanner, R. D., Loo, A. C., Shisler, J. L., Reed, M. W., Rowlett, R. D., Morris, J. W., Schlossnagle, G. W., and Overley, J. R., *A.I.Ch.E. Symp. Series, 73*, 167, 55 (1977).
38. Altman, L. K. (originally reported in *The New York Times*), *The Tennessean 34* (Dec. 8, 1977).
39. Luedeking, R. and Piret, E. L., *J. Biochem. Microbial. Technol. Eng. 1*, 393 (1959).
40. Tanner, R. D. and Overley, J. R., *Biotech. Bioeng. 16*, 485 (1974).

CHAPTER 5

IMMOBILIZED CELLS

Bernard J. Abbott

The Lilly Research Laboratories
Eli Lilly and Company
Indianapolis, Indiana

I. INTRODUCTION

The scope and organization of this review is similar to that used in the first part of this series (1). The primary emphasis is on processes that utilize immobilized microorganisms for the production or degradation of compounds. Analytical devices that employ immobilized cells (2-5) and systems based on immobilized mammalian cells (6-13) or organelles (14-17) are not included. Most of the work summarized in this report was published during the past year; however, some pertinent pre-1977 papers that were omitted from the first survey also are included. Citations to processes that were discussed in the first review (1) are limited to more recent reports that provide additional information on the processes.

Two reviews on immobilized cells were published during the past year (18,19). Jack and Zajic's (19) excellent overview categorized immobilized cell processes by the type of immobilization method used. Their report also discussed the immobilization of mammalian cells and the chromatographic separation of microorganisms. A review by Chibata and Tosa (18) summarized their excellent work on immobilized cell systems that utilize polyacrylamide gel entrapment. The pioneering work of Chibata's group at the Tanabe Seiyaku Co. provided the impetus for the resurgence of interest in immobilized cell technology and also resulted in the development of two commercial processes (18).

A working definition of immobilized cells, a listing of their potential advantages/disadvantages, and a brief historical perspective were presented previously (1).

II. IMMOBILIZATION METHODS

A. *New Methods*

   Most of the new immobilization methods reported in last year's
patent and scientific literature were minor variations of previously described procedures. Among the exceptions was a report
by Fukui and coworkers on the entrapment of cells in photohardening resins (16,21). A suspension of *Proteus vulgaris* cells in
phosphate buffer was mixed with dimethacrylate, polyethylene glycol (mol. wt. 1000), and benzoin methylether. The mixture was
cast on a polyester film and then irradiated for 3 min with a
2 Kw high-pressure mercury lamp to initiate a free radical polymerization reaction that entrapped the cells in a nonionic hydrophilic resin. Resins were also prepared as a urethanized adduct
from a mixture of a polyisocyanate, polyethyleneglycol and 2-hy-
droxyethyl(meth)acrylate. Another report describes the entrapment of cells in photohardening resins that contain ionic substituents (20). These initial studies (20,21) did not describe
the effects of resin entrapment on the catalytic activity of
cells; but at the 4th Enzyme Engineering Conference (September
1977), Fukui *et al.* (16) reported that resin-entrapped cells of
Hansenula jadinii retained the ability to synthesize CDP-choline
or CDP-ethanolamine from CMP and choline or ethanolamine. The
activity of the cells in the resin was found to be greater than
the activity of a comparable cell preparation entrapped in polyacrylamide gel.
   Abstracts from the 4th Enzyme Engineering Conference describe
two other new cell immobilization methods: entrapment in cellulose beads (22) and entrapment in carrageenan (23). Cellulose
beads were prepared by dissolving cellulose in a mixture of N-
ethylpyridinium chloride and DMF. Dried cells of *Actinoplanes
missouriensis* were added to the solution and beads were formed
by passing the mixture through an orifice into water. The beads,
after further treatment with glutaraldehyde, were used for the
isomerization of glucose (22). Chibata (23) and coworkers, in
attempting to develop an alternative to their highly successful
polyacrylamide gel entrapment procedure, evaluated a variety of
polymeric materials as entrapment matrices. Comparisons of agar,
alginate, collagen, starch, and carrageenan, indicated that carrageenan had the best overall characteristics for cell immobilization. Entrapment was accomplished by mixing a cell suspension at
45–50°C with a solution of carrageenan at a similar temperature.
A gel was formed by cooling the mixture and/or contacting it with
gelation agents such as cations, amines, or solvents. The newly
formed gel was granulated and then hardened by treatment with a
bifunctional reagent (e.g., glutaraldehyde). The glucose isomerase activity of *Streptomyces phaeochromogenes* had a half-life
of 289 days in the carrageenan matrix (23). The half-life of the

aspartase activity of *E. coli* cells in carrageenan was 686 days
(23)! In polyacrylamide gel, *E. coli* aspartase displays a half-
life of 120 days (25).

The interaction of concanavalin A (Con A) with cell wall constituents provides the basis for another new immobilization method
(24). Con A binds to mannans in yeast cell walls and to α-D-
glucopyranosyl residues of bacteria. Cells were immobilized by
adsorbing Con A to magnetite and mixing the resultant complex
with a suspension of cells. *Candida utilis, Lactobacillus plan-
tarum, Streptococcus faecalis,* and *Bacillus subtilis* NCIB 10263
were immobilized by this procedure (24). *B. subtilis* ATCC 23029,
which has β-D-glucopyranosyl residues substituted on its teichoic
acids, was not bound by the magnetite-Con A complex. The capacity
of magnetite for Con A was about 10.5 mg/g. This low capacity
severely limits the amount of cells that can be bound and thus
renders the method unattractive from a processing viewpoint. The
flocculation of yeast and bacteria by magnetite-Con A may be useful as an agglutination test (24). Ionizing irradiation has been
used to immobilize microorganisms in a two-step process that involves adsorption of cells to a solid support followed by entrapment of the support/cell complex in a polymer matrix (26-28).
The adsorbing matrix may be any of a variety of materials such as
woodchips, silica gel, activated carbon, synthetic fibers, and
ceramics (26). Insoluble salts of acetates, carbonates, sul-
phates, and oxalates were also used as supporting matrices (27).
After the cells are adsorbed to the support, they are mixed with
a monomer such as 2-hydroxyethyl methacrylate which is then polymerized at -78°C by ^{60}Co irradiation. Although embedding the
support complex in the polymer prevents the loss of cells from
the support by desorption, the advantages of this immobilization
method over simple entrapment of free cells in the polymeric
matrix is unclear. Comparisons were not made of the activity and
stability of cells immobilized by the two-step process and those
immobilized by direct entrapment in the polymer. The adsorption/
polymerization method also was employed with cell-free enzymes
(26). Soluble enzymes may be more advantageously immobilized in
the two-step process as demonstrated by Tosa and coworkers (29).
They found that cell-free aspartase was more stable when adsorbed
to a solid matrix and entrapped in polyacrylamide gel than when
the free enzyme was entrapped without the prior adsorption step.
Nevertheless, the stability of the adsorbed/entrapped enzyme was
significantly less than the stability of intracellular aspart se
of polyacrylamide entrapped cells.

A modified polymer entrapment procedure was developed in
which granular aggregates of *Lactobacillus bulgaricus* were coated
with a thin film of acetylcellulose (30). The granules were prepared by lyophilizing the cells and treating them with acetone.
The granules (1-5 mm) were then dipped into a mixture of acetylcellulose, formamide and acetone, washed with water, and air
dried. The lactase activity of these cells was not inactivated
by the procedure (30).

The report on immobilized cells in Volume I of this series (1)
pointed out that "at the present time there are no good methods
for covalently binding cells to solid matrices." Good covalent
coupling methods should have an advantage over adsorption methods
by eliminating the problem of release or desorption of cells from
the support. Covalently immobilized cells also lack the additional diffusion barrier posed by the polymeric matrix surrounding entrapped cells. Jack and Zajic (31) recently succeeded in
covalently linking cells of *Micrococcus luteus* to carbodiimide
activated carboxymethylcellulose. The immobilized cells retained
>75% of their initial histidine ammonia lyase activity and con-
verted histidine to urocanic acid during 16 days of continuous
operation with no loss of activity. Immobilization was achieved
by activating carboxyl groups on polymeric support materials with
1-ethyl-3-(3'-dimethylaminopropyl)-carbodiimide·HCl (EDAC). EDAC
activates carboxyl groups by forming an O-acylisourea intermediate
that can react with nucleophilic groups on the cell surface to
form a covalent bond. Cell immobilization did not occur when EDAC
was eliminated rrom the coupling reaction indicating that immobilization probably occurred covalently and not by adsorption.
Studies with surfactants suggested that the covalent coupling
procedure did not destroy or alter the permeability of the cell
membrane. The general utility of this immobilization procedure
may be limited. The coupling reagent EDAC is expensive and some
microorganisms could not be linked to one or more of the carboxy-
late polymers tested. In addition, the dry weight of cells bound
per gram of dry support, which was not determined in these studies, may be substantially less than that reported for adsorption
and entrapment systems.

B.   *Related Studies*

During the past year a number of papers were published on the
interaction of microorganisms with solid surfaces, the characteristics of microbial aggregates and films, and the effect of bifunctional reagents on microbial cells. Although the objective
of these papers was not to design cell immobilization systems for
specific biochemical processes, they will be briefly discussed
because they provide information that may be useful for developing
and understanding immobilized cell systems.

In a study of the factors that influence the flocculation of
microorganisms by bentonite (32,33), the presence of divalent
cation Mg^{++} (0.02M) was found to be much more effective than Na^+
in promoting flocculation. Flocculation in the presence of Mg^{++}
was essentially independent of pH but flocculation in deionized
water or solutions containing sodium ions was pH dependent (33).
No correlation was observed between the gram reaction of the cells
and their flocculation behavior (31). Electrophoretic mobilities
indicated that both the cells and bentonite were negatively

charged during flocculation. The formation of the following
flocculation complex was proposed to account for these results:
bacteria$^{\delta-}$...$(Mg^{++})_n$...$^{-\delta}$bentonite (33).

The presence of montmorillonite (.25%) in cultures of various
Streptomyces, Micromonospora, and *Nocardia* species markedly accelerated the growth rate of the microorganisms (34). The montmorillonite also appeared to increase the proportion of glucose consumption that was channeled to biomass synthesis. Powdered $CaCO_3$,
Na_2SiO_3, and Ca-exchange resins had no effect. When montmorillonite was confined to dialysis tubing, it retained most of its
capability to stimulate growth (34). The changes associated with
the presence of the solid matrix (montmorillonite) were probably
due to adsorption of toxic metabolic products.

The attachment of bacteria to aluminum surfaces was studied
with mixed cultures in a chemostat (35). Attachment was much
greater when the cultures were under carbon-limiting conditions
than with a nitrogen limitation. These results were unexpected
because the nitrogen limitation increased the production of extracellular polysaccharide which was thought to act as an adhesive
for cell attachment. An alternative mechanism for cell attachment
was proposed in which glucose binds as a molecular film to aluminum and acts as a bridge to bind glucose receptor sites on the
cell surface (35).

Four factors were identified that influenced the adsorption
of a marine pseudomonad to polystyrene: culture concentration,
amount of time allowed for attachment, culture age, and temperature (36). The effect of culture age was attributed to either
changes in the motility of the cells or the amount of surface
polysaccharide they contain. The most interesting aspect of the
results is that adsorption could be described by a Langmuir adsorption isotherm:

$$[x]_s = \frac{[x]_s [x]_{ads}}{K'} + \frac{R}{K}$$

where $[x]_s$ is the culture concentration, $[x]_{ads}$ is the number of
cells adsorbed, R is the rate of adsorption, and K' and K are
constants (36).

A study of the effect of polyethyleneimine (PEI) on the flocculation of *E. coli* concluded that the primary mechanism of flocculation was not polymer bridging, but adsorption coagulation
(37). Large PEI molecules adsorb to the cell surface neutraliz-
ing some of the negative charge and creating a charge reversal
(positive charge) on areas of the cell where excess polymer ad-
sorbs. As a result, patches (mosaics) of differing charges develop on the cell surface. The alignment of positive patches with
negative patches on approaching cells leads to an electrostatic
attraction which is responsible for coagulation (37).

Ashby and Bull (38) described a laboratory scale fermentor
that is useful for studying the growth of microorganisms on particulate surfaces in suspension. The vessel is a modified air-
lift fermentor containing a sedimenting effluent tube that enables
it to be operated continuously. The use of "air lift" eliminated
the problems of abrasive particles penetrating seals and bearings,
and accelerating the wear on recirculating pumps.

A variety of mathematical models have been developed to predict the behavior of biological waste treatment systems. These
models are frequently based on the fact that microorganisms in
waste treatment systems exist primarily in flocs and/or films.
These modeling approaches may also apply to more structured immobilized cell systems that are used for producing cell metabolites.
Two models, reported recently, were based on nutrient diffusion
into microbial aggregates (39) and substrate removal by microbial
films (40). The substrate removal model was in good agreement
with experimental data except at high hydraulic (flow) rates and
high substrate concentrations (39). The relatively simple diffusion model predicted oxygen limitations would occur with small
rapidly metabolizing aggregates and with more slowly metabolizing
large aggregates (40).

The multiple reuse of mycelial pellets is one of the simplest
forms of cell immobilization and one that has found commercial
utility. A recent review article on the growth of molds in
pellets describes the types of pellets formed and the factors
that influence pellet formation (41). This paper also discusses
mathematical models of pellet growth and models for nutrient diffusion into pellets.

A review on the biological uses of glutaraldehyde describes
the chemistry of the compound and its interactions with biological materials (42). Although the use of glutaraldehyde for cell
immobilization was not reviewed, an excellent overview is presented on the interaction of glutaraldehyde with various structural components of microorganisms.

C. *Dialysis, Filtration, and Sedimentation*

Enzymes are frequently immobilized by containment with semi-
permeable membranes using devices such as hollow fiber modules
and ultrafiltration cells. Microorganisms can, and have been,
immobilized in a similar fashion to facilitate their multiple
reuse, or extended continuous use, without cell loss (Table I).
The use of membranes or filters in fermentation vessels predates
the recent emergence of interest in cell immobilization. In 1969
Schultz and Gerhardt (43) published an extensive review on the
design, theory and experimental evaluation of dialysis culture of
microorganisms. Since that time, additional studies on dialysis
and related cultivation methods have appeared, although interest
in the area has been rather limited.

   In the past, dialysis fermentation methods were not identified
with immobilized cell technology. Dialysis constitutes a form of
cell immobilization because it provides for nondestructive physical confinement or localization of freely suspended microorganisms. The lack of association of dialysis culture with cell immobilization may be attributed in part to the fact that dialysis
cultivation has little or no potential for economical large-scale
use. The importance of the dialysis cultivation is that it demonstrates that dramatic improvements can be made in fermentation
processes when an ample supply of nutrients is provided and toxic
products are removed. Furthermore, the limited practical utility
of dialysis may be circumvented by the application of more economical methodology that achieves the same objectives. For example,
dialysis could be replaced by ultrafiltration; or settling devices
and filtration equipment could be incorporated into fermentation
vessels to enable cells to be reused.
   A listing of examples of the use of dialysis and ultrafiltration as cell immobilization methods is presented in Table I. The
table and accompanying discussion are limited to the publications
that appeared after the review by Schultz and Gerhardt (43).
   End products of fermentation processes frequently inhibit
their own synthesis. Dialysis cultivation can be used to prevent
this inhibition by maintaining product concentrations in the culture broth below inhibitory levels. Kominek used this approach
to produce cycloheximide, an antifungal antibiotic produced by
Streptomyces nourse (44-47). Initial experiments demonstrated
that a linear decline occurred in the rate of cycloheximide synthesis as the cycloheximide concentration increased (46). Complete inhibition of synthesis occurred at 1 mg/ml of antibiotic.
The dialysis system consisted of a small fermentor (3L medium)
with dialysis tubing 50 cm^2 surface area) fastened to the baffles
(44,47). In conventional dialysis, the fermentor contents are
dialyzed against a large uninoculated reservoir of medium.
Kominek replaced the medium reservoir with a small volume of
methylene chloride. The dialysate was bubbled through methylene
chloride which extracted cycloheximide from the aqueous phase.
The extracted dialysate then was aerated to remove traces of solvent and recycled through the fermentor via the tubing. In the
nondialysis control fermentation, the rate of cycloheximide production began to decline 3 to 4 days after inoculation and maximum product concentration was obtained by the seventh day (46).
The use of dialysis extended the linear portion of the cycloheximide production curve and by day 10 of the process the product
yield was twice that of the nondialyzed fermentation (44,47).
The solids content of the solvent reservoir was 82% cycloheximide.
Dialysis/extraction, in addition to increasing product yield,
concentrated and partially purified the antibiotic.
   Abbott and Gerhardt used dialysis fermentation to increase
the production of salicylic acid from naphthalene by *Pseudomonas
fluorescens* (48,49). The cultivation vessel contained an upper

TABLE I.   Cell Immobilization by Containment with
           Semipermeable Membranes

Product	Substrate	Microorganism	Immobilization method
Cycloheximide	Glucose	Streptomyces griseus	Dialysis tubing in a fermentor. Dialysate extracted to recover product
S. faecalis cells	Glucose	Streptococcus faecalis	Rotating microfiltration unit incorporated into a fermentor
----	COD	Activated sludge	Sludge retained in reactor by ultrafiltration
Proteases or amylase	----	Bacillus polymyxa Serratia marcescens Streptococcus thermophilus Clostridium acetobutylicum	Cells and enzymes retained in dialysis tubing in fermentation vessel
Microbial slime	Several nutrient media	A variety of cultures were tested	Microorganisms cultivated on cellophane placed on agar plates
Salicylic acid	Naphthalene	Pseudomonas fluorescens	Cultivation and reservoir chambers separated by dialysis membrane
Threonine	Sorbitol	Escherichia coli	Cultivation and reservoir chambers separated by dialysis membrane
Ammonium lactate	Whey	Lactobacillus bulgaricus	Culture dialyzed against water
Proteases	Peptone, casamino acids	Clostridium histolyticum	Cultivation in ultrafiltration device
Lactic acid	Glucose	Lactobacillus delbrueckii	Fermentor dialyzed against a nutrient reservoir
E. coli cells	Glucose	E. coli	Fermentor dialyzed against nutrient reservoir

Remarks	Company of Institution	Reference
Product yield increased two-fold by dialysis	Upjohn Company	44,47
Biomass concentration was increased 45-fold over conventional batch fermentation	University of California	57
Biomass concentrations of 20-40 g/L were obtained with 97-99% COD removal	Rensselaer Polytechnic Institute	52
5-22 fold increases in enzyme concentrations were achieved	University College, Dublin	51
----	Toho University	67
----	Michigan State University	48,49
Dialytic removal of threonine did not increase threonine yields	Michigan State	50
Continuous dialysis culture maintained for 94 days	Michigan State	53,54
Enzyme production increased ≈4-fold	MIT	68
Dialysis increased the specific rate of lactic acid production	Columbia University	69
150 g/L dry cell weight obtained	Karolinska Institute	55,56

culture chamber that was separated from a lower reservoir chamber by a dialysis membrane. Aeration and mixing were provided by mounting the vessel on a rotary shaker (48). In the nondialysis control fermentation, salicylic acid concentration reaches a maximum of 10-12 mg/ml 48-72 hr after inoculation. Dialysis fermentation was initiated by filling the reservoir chamber with sterile medium 72 hr after the culture chamber was inoculated. Diffusion of salicylic acid into the reservoir chamber maintained the product concentration in the culture chamber below inhibitory levels. As a result, both growth and salicylic acid production continued for an extended time period (48). The continuation of growth and the accumulation of biomass resulted in more rapid rates of product synthesis as the process continued (49). Periodically the reservoir chamber was drained and replaced with fresh medium because the salicylic acid concentration was too high to maintain a favorable concentration gradient for removal of additional product from the culture chamber. The continuous dialytic removal of salicylic acid enabled product production to continue at an ever-increasing rate for 15 days. The process was halted on day 15 only because of a rupture in the dialysis membrane. Overall, the use of dialysis changed the fermentation from one that accumulated 10-12 mg/ml of product in 2-3 days to one that produced 206 mg/ml (based on inoculated volume) in 15 days.

Dialysis cultivation also was attempted as a means to increase threonine production by an auxotrophic mutant of *E. coli* (50). The use of dialysis resulted in a doubling of the cell concentration but no increase in threonine production was observed. Subsequent experiments established that in this fermentation threonine was not inhibiting its own synthesis (50).

The production of extracellular proteases and amylase in dialysis culture was examined by Fogarty and Griffin (51). *Bacillus polymyxa, Serratia marcescens, Streptococcus thermophilus,* and *Clostridium acetobutylicum* were cultivated in dialysis tubing which was suspended in a fermentor that served as a nutrient reservoir. The concentration of the enzymes in the dialysis tubing was 5.5- to 22.7-fold greater than in the nondialyzed control fermentation (51). However, the total amount of enzyme produced in the tubing was less than what would have been produced without dialysis if both culture and reservoir medium were inoculated. Thus, the only advantage of dialysis in these fermentations was to concentrate the enzymes in the relatively small volume inside the tubing.

The use of high concentrations of microorganisms (20-50 g/L) in activated sludge systems leads to a significant increase in the rate of BOD removal. The practical use of dense cell populations is hampered by the poor settling characteristics of the sludge. Hardt and coworkers (52) explored the possibility of using ultrafiltration as a separation technique for concentrated sludge systems. Turbulent flow (≈ 3 ft/sec) was maintained across the membranes to prevent sludge accumulation at the membrane surface. The ultrafiltration units were operated at 35-75 psig and an average ultrafiltrate flux rate of 4.5 gal/day/ft^2 was obtained. The high solids activated sludge ultrafiltration system consistently removed 97-99% of the COD in the influent waste stream. Soluble organic compounds with a molecular weight greater than 800 accumulated in the reactor and biomass concentration declined (presumably by lysis) from 30 g/L to 20 g/L during the ultrafiltration experiment. Even though a reduction in biomass concentration occurred, the authors concluded that ultrafiltration was a highly effective way of separating microbial solids from effluent and that the method enabled better control of the nutrient/cell mass ratio and sludge wasting rate (52).

Gerhardt *et al.* (53,54) utilized a combination of continuous culture and dialysis to convert cheese whey into ammonium lactate. The whey medium, which contained 230 mg/ml of lactose, was inoculated with a culture of *Lactobacillus bulgaricus* and fermented nonaseptically at pH 5.3 and 44°C. The fermentor contents were dialyzed against water and the process was operated continuously for 94 days. When the fermentor was operated at a hydraulic dilution rate of .053 hr^{-1} (19 hr retention time), 97% of the lactose was metabolized. The ammonium lactate in the fermentor dialysate was more highly purified and somewhat less concentrated than the ammonium lactate produced in conventional batch or continuous cultures. Dialysis cultivation also permitted the use of more concentrated whey solutions and more rapidly converted lactose to lactic acid.

Extremely high concentrations of microorganisms can be obtained by supplying adequate nutrients to the culture and removing the toxic metabolites that accumulate. Landwall and Holme (55,56) dialyzed cultures of *E. coli* B using a 1/11 culture/reservoir volume ratio and obtained biomass concentrations of 140-150 g dry wt ℓ^{-1}. The cessation of growth in the nondialyzed cultures was attributed to the accumulation of a mixture of low molecular weight volatile fatty acids. At high biomass concentrations in the dialysis culture, the rate of production of these acids exceeded their rate of removal by dialysis. Thus, the acids also reached inhibitory levels during dialysis, preventing the attainment of still higher cell concentrations.

A nondialysis fermentor that achieves essentially the same objectives as dialysis cultivation was developed by Sortland and Wilke (57). The fermentor contained a built-in rotating cylindrical microfilter (Millipore WH membrane, 0.45μ) that permitted the continuous removal of a cell-free effluent. The continuous removal of inhibitory metabolites by the filter fermentor enabled *Streptococcus faecalis* to be grown anaerobically to a population density 45 times greater than that obtained by simple batch culture.

A similar filtration-based fermentation device, called a rotofermentor, was used by Margaritis (58) to produce ethanol from glucose by anaerobic fermentation with *Saccharomyces*

cerevisiae. A yeast concentration of 30.7 g dry wt 1^{-1} accumulated 42-47 g/L ethanol. The rotofermentor achieved an ethanol
productivity of 27 g/L/hr, which greatly exceeds the rate of
2.65 g/L/hr obtained from the same amount of glucose in a conventional continuous fermentor.

     In another approach to high productivity ethanol production,
Cysewski and Wilke (59) coupled cell recycle with vacuum fermentation. Cell recycle (immobilization) was accomplished with a
settling device which maintained a high cell population. Operating the fermentor under vacuum enabled the inhibitory product
(ethanol) to boil away at temperatures compatible with yeast
metabolism. Without vacuum, a recycle fermentation receiving a
10% glucose feed supported 50g dry wt 1^{-1} of biomass and produced
ethanol at a rate of 29 g/L/hr. When the fermentor was operated
with vacuum and no cell recycle, a 33.4% glucose feed led to an
ethanol productivity of 40 g/L/hr. Coupling both cell recycle
and vacuum fermentation, the rate of ethanol production reached
the astonishing value of 82 g/L/hr (59).

III. IMMOBILIZED CELL PROCESSES

A. *Glucose Isomerase*

     The amount of high fructose syrup (HFS) produced by enzymatic
isomerization of glucose obtained from starch is estimated, by
1980, to reach 7-8 billion pounds annually in the United States
alone (60). The rapid growth of this industry and the immense
economic importance of HFS technology provide the impetus for the
continued efforts to develop more efficient (competitive) processes. With one possible exception, no major advances in immobilized cell HFS processes are evident from literature published
during the past year (Table II). The exception is the carrageenan
entrapment system (23) discussed on page 92.   The extremely
long half-life afforded by carrageenan matrix may enable processing costs to be substantially reduced.

     Casey (61) recently presented an historical perspective on
the development of HFS technology. His report provides an interesting insight into the economic and technological factors that
shaped the chain of events leading to the new technology.

     New studies were published on the isolation of glucose
isomerase-producing microorganisms (62). Comparative studies
were made on the amount of glucose isomerase activity produced
by various microorganisms (62,63) and procedures were described
for increasing isomerase production (63). Kinetic analyses and
process engineering studies were made on three immobilized cell
HFS processes (64-66). Ryu *et al.* (64) optimized the performance
of a column reactor that contained heat-treated cells of
Streptomyces phaeochromogenes. The cells were retained in the

TABLE II. Glucose Isomerization by Immobilized Cells

Product	Substrate	Microorganism	Immobilization Method	Remarks	Company or Institution	Reference
Fructose	Glucose	Streptomyces phaeochromogenes	Heat treated cells used in column reactor	Reactor half life of 94 hours	Korea Advanced Institute of Science	64
Fructose	Glucose	Bacillus coagulans	Homogenized and axially extruded cell paste cross-linked with glutaraldehyde	Reactor half life of 500 hours. Industrial production planned	Novo Industri A/S	66
Fructose	Glucose	Streptomyces phaeochromogenes	Cells mixed with "high porous polymer" and packed in a column	34% of the glucose in a 55% glucose solution was isomerized	Sanyu Engineering	70
Fructose	Glucose	Streptomyces sp.	Cells aggregated with chitosan and treated with a 10% citrate solution	No activity lost during 7 days continuous operation	National Food Research Institute	72
Fructose	Glucose	Arthrobacter sp.	Flocculation by a polyelectrolyte	---	R. J. Reynolds Co.	71
Fructose	Glucose	Streptomyces venezuelae and Bacillus sp.	Cells complexed with collagen	Engineering and economic aspects of process described	Rutgers University	65
Fructose	Glucose	Streptomyces olivaceus	Cells crosslinked with glutaraldehyde	Half life in a column reactor was 60 days	Miles Laboratories	73

column by a Millipore membrane mounted at the bottom. The kinetic
studies demonstrated the effect of enzyme loading, substrate concentration, reaction time, and enzyme inactivation rate on reactor
productivity. The utility of this particular process seems to be
limited by the relatively short half-life (~94 hr) of the enzyme.

Vieth and Venkatsubramanian (65) reviewed their work on the
development of an HFS process that employes collagen complexation
for cell immobilization. Design parameters for a commercial scale
HFS plant were outlined and the process engineering aspects of the
proposed plant were described. The design calculations were based
on experimental data from laboratory scale reactors. A preliminary economic analysis indicated that the process would be economically viable. The half-life of the enzyme in this process was
estimated to be 75 days (65).

Poulsen and Zittan (66), at Novi Industries in Copenhagen, developed an immobilized cell HFS process that is expected to be in
commercial operation this year. An "atypical" strain of *Bacillus
coagulans* was immobilized by extruding wetted spray-dried cells
through an axial extruder (700 μm). The extruded pellets were
treated with glutaraldehyde, washed with water, and dried. The
dried crosslinked pellets retained 20-30% of the initial glucose
isomerase activity and were used in column reactors in sizes up
to 60 L. The isomerase activity of the pellets exhibited a half-
life of about 21 days in continuous operation. This relatively
short half-life, compared to some other HFS processes, would seem
to render this system uncompetitive from an economic standpoint.
However, the disadvantage of a short half-life could be offset by
factors such as higher productivities and lower costs for cell
production and immobilization.

B. *Amino Acids*

The most notable development in the use of immobilized cells
for the production of amino acids is in the report by Chibata on
the entrapment of aspartase-containing *E. coli* cells in a carrageenan matrix (23). The 628 day half-life of aspartase in the
cell/carrageenan matrix is over 5-fold greater than that obtained
with polyacrylamide entrapment of *E. coli*. If other operational
characteristics of the carrageenan process compare favorably to
the polyacrylamide system, the former should replace the latter
for the commercial production of aspartic acid.

A study was conducted to determine why aspartase activity in
cells entrapped in polyacrylamide gel is much more stable than
cell-free soluble aspartase entrapped in polyacrylamide gel (29).
The results indicated that the greater stability of intracellular
aspartase is due to binding of the enzyme to cell particles or
membrane fragments. Isolation of the enzyme from the cell dis-
rupts its association with the particulate fraction and greatly
reduces stability. Although good stability can be restored by

attaching the soluble enzyme to a support susch as Sepharose,
whole cell entrapment eliminates both the need for such supports
and the additional steps of enzyme isolation and purification.

Nelson (74) immobilized cells of *Rhodotorula gracilis* by covalent attachment to a glycidyl methacrylate polymer (Table III).
Covalent bonds presumably were formed by the reaction of amino
groups on the cell surface with epoxy substituents on the polymer.
The immobilized cells retained 49% of their initial phenylalanine
ammonia-lyase activity. In a 30 ml reaction mixture containing
14.7g wet immobilized cells, 2.25g of trans cinnamic acid were
converted in 18 hr to L-phenylalanine in 90% yield. The cell complex retained 77% of its initial activity after one batch reaction. Similar results were obtained when the microorganism was
immobilized by copolymerization with glycidyl methacrylate and
methylenebisacrylamide (94).

Bacterium cadaveris also was immobilized by covalent attachment to a glycidyl methacrylate polymer (74). The cells were
crosslinked with glutaraldehyde prior to immobilization to mini-
mize enzyme losses. The immobilized cell complex was used to
synthesize aspartic acid from fumaric acid. Product yields were
not reported and the stability of the complex was not assessed.

C. *Antibiotics*

Nelson (74) used the covalent coupling methods and copolymerization methods described above to immobilize cells of *Proteus
rettgeri* that produce penicillin acylase (Table III). Crosslinked
cells attached to a glycidyl methacrylate polymer retained 65% of
their initial acylase activity. The immobilized cell complex was
used in a series of 20 batch reactions to produce 6-aminopenicil-
lanic acid (6-APA) from penicillin G. Initial product yield was
only 75% and the complex lost 50% of its activity during the 20
reactions.

D. *Carbohydrate Transformations*

Carbohydrate transformations, other than glucose isomerization, have been operated commercially with immobilized enzymes
and cells. Mycelia pellets have been used to hydrolyze raffinose
in beet molasses, and cellulose acetate entrapped lactase (β-
galactosidase) has been used to produce low lactose milk. New
raffinose processes have not been reported recently, but two new
immobilized cell processes for lactose hydrolysis were described
(Table IV). In one process, cells of *Lactobacillus bulgaricus*
were entrapped in agar pellets and used in a column reactor (82).
The other process used the same microorganism but immobilization
was achieved by coating lyophilized cell aggregates (granules)
with a cellulose acetate film (30).

TABLE III. Preparation of Amino Acids and Antibiotics by Immobilized Cells

Product	Substrate	Microorganism	Immobilization Method	Remarks	Company or Institution	Reference
			Amino Acids			
L-Methionine	N-Acetyl-DL-methionine	Aspergillus ochraceus	Crosslinking with glutaraldehyde in the presence of ovalbumin	Crosslinked pellets displayed less thermal stability than untreated pellets	Amano Pharmaceutical	76,85
L-Aspartate	Ammonium fumarate	E. coli	Entrapment in polyacrylamide gel	Stabilities of immobilized cells and enzyme were studied	Tanabe Seiyaku Co.	29,75
Tyrosine	---	Erwinia herbicola	Cells treated with soluble collagen and entrapped in cellulose acetate	Cellulose acetate membranes were made	Research Institute for Production Development	77
Tyrosine	---	Erwinia herbicola	Cells treated with soluble collagen and complexed with N-polyacrylate	---	Research Institute for Production Development	78
L-Amino	N-Acyl-DL-amino acids	---	Treatment with gelatin and cross-linking with glutaraldehyde	---	Kyowa Yuka Co.	79

Amino Acids

Product	Substrate	Microorganism	Immobilization Method	Remarks	Company or Institution	Reference
L-Aspartic acid	Fumaric acid	Bacterium cadaveris	Cells treated with glutaraldehyde and bound to a glycidyl methacrylate polymer	---	Pfizer Inc.	74
L-Phenyl-alanine	Trans cin-namic acid and NH_3	Rhodotorula gracilis	Cells bound to glycicyl meth-acrylate polymer	Immobilized cells retained 49% of initial phenylalanine ammonia lyase activity	Pfizer Inc.	74
6-Aminopeni-cillanic acid	Penicillin G	Proteus rettgeri	Cells treated with glutaral-dehyde and re-acted with a glycicyl meth-acrylate polymer	50% of initial activity re-mained after 20 reactions	Pfizer Inc.	74
6-Aminopeni-cillanic acid	Penicillin G or Peni-cillin V	E. coli, Streptomyces griseus, Nocardia gardneri	Cells entrapped in polyacryl-amide gel	E. coli immo-bilized cell column lost no activity after 168 hours of continuous operation	Tanabe Seiyaku Co.	80,81

TABLE IV. *Transformations of Carbohydrates by Immobilized Cells*

Product	Substrate	Microorganism	Immobilization Method	Remarks	Company or Institution	Reference
Glucose and Galactose	Lactose (milk)	Lactobacillus bulgaris	Entrapment in agar	Agar pellets used in column reactor	Snow Brand Milk Products	82
Glucose and Galactose	Lactose (milk)	Lactobacillus bulgaris	Cell paste shaped into granules, lyophilized, and covered with acetyl cellulose film	Lactase was not denatured by immobilization procedure	Snow Brand Milk Products	30
Ketoses	Alditols	Acetobacter suboxydans	Entrapment in polyacrylamide gel	Treating cells with glutaraldehyde did not result in intercellular crosslinking	Queens University	83
Gluconic acid	Glucose	Aspergillus niger	Cells treated with glutaraldehyde and reacted with a glycidyl methacrylate polymer	Cells also immobilized by copolymerization and by bonding to reactive monomer followed by monomer polymerization	Pfizer Inc.	74

Product	Substrate	Microorganism	Immobilization Method	Remarks	Company or Institution	Reference
Gluconic acid	Glucose	Aspergillus sp.	Cell-free glucose oxidase bound to mycelia pellets with glutaral-dehyde	95% of glucose oxidase activity remained after immobilization	Tokyo Institute of Technology	84
Reducing sugars	Inulin	Kluyveromyces marxianus	Entrapment in alginate gel	Entrapped cell had half-life of 350 hours	Tate and Lyle Co.	17

Acetobacter suboxydans was immobilized by entrapment in polyacrylamide gel and by crosslinking with glutaraldehyde (83). The
immobilized cells catalyzed the oxidation of polyhydric alcohols
(alditols) to ketoses. Oxidation rates with the immobilized cells
were much lower than rates measured with untreated cells.

Mycelia pellets of an *Aspergillus sp.* were treated with glutaraldehyde in the presence of albumin and used in a column to
oxidize glucose (84). Treatment with the bifunctional reagent
restricted the loss of enzyme activity from the pellets. A similar procedure was employed to retain aminoacylase activity in
pellets of *Aspergillus ochraceus* (85). The ovalbumin minimizes
the leakage of enzyme from the pellets presumably by forming a
crosslinked protein network on the pellet surface.

E. *Organic Acids*

New reports on the production of organic acids by immobilized
cells are listed in Table V. The process for producing urocanic
acid from histidine was discussed in the section on "New Immobilization Methods."

Chibata and his coworkers (86) recently described how they
developed and optimized their immobilized cell process for producing L-malic acid from fumaric acid. An initial comparison of malic acid production by various microorganisms indicated that highest production rates were achieved with *Brevibacterium ammoniagenes*. The organism was immobilized by entrapment in polyacrylamide gel and studies were initiated to optimize malic acid synthesis. Malic acid production by *B. ammoniagenes* was accompanied
by the production of an unwanted side product, succinic acid.
The loss of substrate to succinic acid biosynthesis and the problems this side product created in the isolation of malic acid required that its synthesis be inhibited to establish a commercially
viable process. Succinic acid synthesis was suppressed by treating the entrapped cells with acetone, bile acids, deoxcholic acid,
or bile extract. Bile extract was the most effective and economical treatment. Bile extract treatment also brought about a 15-
fold increase in the rate of malic acid synthesis by the entrapped
cells. Other surfactants caused similar rate increases without
inhibiting succinic acid formation. The higher rate of malic acid
synthesis was attributed to an increase in cell membrane permeability caused by the surfactants. The mechanism by which bile
acids suppressed succinic acid formation is not known, but it
probably involves the inhibition or loss of the enzyme cofactor
needed for the reduction of fumarate to succinate.

A column packed with polyacrylamide gel granules containing
B. ammoniagenes cells was operated at a flow rate of 0.23 ml/ml
bed vol/hr with a 1M sodium fumarate solution. Malic acid was
produced in 70% overall yield and the column half-life during
continuous operation was 52.5 days (86). This process has been
operated commercially by the Tanabe Co. in Japan since 1974.

TABLE V. Production of Organic Acids by Immobilized Cells

Product	Substrate	Microorganism	Immobilization Method	Remarks	Company or Institution	Reference
Urocanic acid	L-Histidine	Micrococcus luteus	Cells covalently bonded to carbo-diimide-activated carboxymethyl cellulose	75% of histi-dine ammonia lyase activity remained after immobilization	University of Toronto and University of West Ontario	31
L-Malic acid	Fumaric acid	Brevibac-terium ammoniagenes	Entrapment in polyacrylamide gel	Kinetic analy-sis performed on column reactor	Tanabe Seiyaku Co.	86,87
Erythorbic acid	---	Penicillium cyaneofulvum	Entrapment in polyacrylamide gel	---	Meiji University	88
Lactic acid	Glucose	Lactobacil-lus del-bruckii	Entrapment in polyacrylamide gel	---	Inst. Univ. Technol. Le Montet	89
Citric acid	Sucrose	Aspergillus niger	Complexation with collagen	48% activity retained	Rutgers University	14,15

F. Degradation

Cells of *Lactobacillus casei* entrapped in polyacrylamide gel were used continuously for 9 months to degrade malic acid (Table VI). A 150 ml reactor containing 50 ml of gel particles metabolized the substrate at a rate of 1.9 g/L/hr (90). Manometric measurements of CO_2 evolution indicated that the rate of malic acid metabolism increased about 5-fold during the 9-month study. A similar activation phenomenon was observed by Larsson *et al.* with gel-entrapped cells of *Corynebacterium simplex* that produced prednisolone from cortisol (91). These activity increases are probably due to growth of the microorganism in the gels. The gel-entrapped *L. casei* cells may be useful for removing malic acid from wine (89).

Nitrate removal was accomplished by immobilized cells of *Pseudomonas aeruginosa* or a *Hyphomicrobium* species entrapped in polyacrylamide gel (89). A 150 ml stirred reactor containing 5 ml of *P. aeruginosa* gel granules was operated continuously at a flow rate of 48 ml/hr with a 2 g/L KNO_3 solution. No nitrate was detected in the reactor effluent after 7 or 15 days of continuous operation. Gel granules containing the *Hyphomicrobium* species were used in a 250 ml reactor that was operated continuously for 2 months at a flow rate of 40 ml/hr. From the 3 g/L of KNO_3 in the influent stream, the reactor reduced NO_3^- at a rate of 20 mg/L/hr.

Microbial cells adsorbed to inorganic matrices are used in some large waste treatment plants for nitrate removal (92). At the East Hyde Sewage Works in England, waste water is forced up through a sand bed on which a microbial flora was allowed to develop. The sand bed is maintained anaerobically and methanol is added to the waste stream to support the growth of *Hyphomicrobium sp.* and other nitrate-reducing microorganisms. Another plant at Rye Meads processes 81,000 cubic meters per day and uses a similar system except that it does not require the addition of methanol. Nitrate reductions of 50 to 90% are achieved at these plants (92).

G. Other Products

Among the more novel uses of immobilized cells are the conversion of milk to "yogurt" and the production of electricity with a biochemical fuel cell (Table VII). Divies (89) entrapped a mixed culture of *Lactobacillus bulgaricus* and *Streptococcus thermophilus* in polyacrylamide gel and produced yogurt in a continuous reactor that operated for 10 days. The palatability of the product was not reported. The biochemical fuel cell contained cells of *Clostridium butyricum* entrapped in polyacrylamide (94). The gel/cell suspension was polymerized on a platinum black electrode so that one side was coated (0.1 cm thick) with the gel. The electrode was immersed in a glucose-phosphate buffer solution that

TABLE VI. Degradation Reactions Catalyzed by Immobilized Cells

Substrate	Microorganism	Immobilization Method	Remarks	Company or Institution	Reference
Phenol	Pseudomonas sp.	Adsorption to anthracite coal particles	2 liter fluidized bed removed up to 10g phenol per day	Oak Ridge National Laboratory	27
Nitrate	Mixed culture growing on methanol	Adsorption to sand	90% nitrate removal under anaerobic conditions	Water Research Center	92
Diacetyl	Fleischmann's yeast	Yeast contained by dialysis tubing	Yeast autolyzed during the reaction	Oregon State University	93
Diacetyl	Fleischmann's yeast or Saccharomyces carlsbergensis	Yeast trapped in diatomaceous earth filter bed	---	Oregon State University	93
Nitrate	Pseudomonas aeruginosa	Entrapment in polyacrylamide gel	Nitrate removed from 2g/L solution	Inst. Univ. Technol. Le Montet	89
Nitrate	Hyphomicrobium sp.	Entrapment in polyacrylamide gel	Reactor operated 2 mo. and removed 20 mg NO_3/L/hr	Inst. Univ. Technol. Le Montet	89
Malic acid	Lactobacillus casei	Entrapment in polyacrylamide gel	Malic acid decarboxylase activity retained for 9 mo. continuous operation	Inst. Univ. Technol. Le Montet	89,90
Benzoic acid	Pseudomonas putida	Entrapment in polyacrylamide gel	---	Shell Biosciences Lab.	104

TABLE VII. Other Products Produced by Immobilized Cells

Product	Substrate	Microorganism	Immobilization Method	Remarks	Company or Institution	Reference
Ethanol	Glucose	Saccharomyces cerevisiae	Entrapment in aliginate gel	Column with 10 hr residence time produced 2-4% ethanol solutions for 13 days	Tate & Lyle Ltd.	17
Ethanol	Glucose	Saccharomyces carlsbergen- sis	Yeast trapped in a diatomaceous earth filter bed	5% ethanol solutions pro- duced during 100 hr contin- uous operation	Carlton and United Brewer- ies Ltd.	95
Ethanol	Glucose	Saccharomyces cerevisiae	Cells recycled back to fermentor with a settling device	Using cell re- cycle and vacuum fermen- tation, 82 g/L/ hr of ethanol produced	University of California	59
Ethanol	Molasses	Saccharomyces cerevisiae	Entrapment in polyacrylamide gel	70 ml of gel particles in 250 ml reactor produced 320 mM/L/hr of ethanol	Inst. Univ. Technol. Le Montet	89
Ethylene	Acetylene	Azotobacter vinelandii	Adsorption to anion exchange resin	Model system for nitrogen fixation	University of Virginia	97

Product	Substrate	Microorganism	Immobilization Method	Remarks	Company or Institution	Reference
Pyridoxal phosphate	Pyridoxine phosphate	Pseudomonas polycolor and Kloeckera sp.	Entrapment in polyacrylamide gel	Kloeckera sp. entrapped to destroy H_2O_2 produced by P. polycolor pyridoxine phosphate oxidase	Kyoto University	98
Androstra-dienedione	Progesterone	Fusarium solani	Spores recovered and re-used	Ten re-uses of spores without loss of activity	Cairo University	102
Δ^4-Cholestenone	Cholesterol	Mycobacterium rhodochrous	Complexation with collagen	---	Rutgers University	14,15
Ammonia	Nitrate	Anacystis nidulans	Complexation with collagen	Immobilized algal cells	Rutgers University	14,15
Oxygen	Water	Anacystis nidulans	Complexation with collagen	27% of initial activity retained	Rutgers University	14,15
Yogurt	Milk	Lactobacillus bulgaricus and Streptococcus thermophilus	Entrapment in polyacrylamide gel	---	Inst. Univ. Technol. Le Montet	89
Coenzyme A	ATP and pantothenic acid	Sarcina lutea	Entrapment in polyacrylamide gel	No activity lost after 5 batch reactions	Tanabe Seiyaku Co.	103
CDP-Choline or CDP-ethanolamine	CMP and choline or ethanolamine	Hansenula jadinii	Entrapment in photo-cross-linked resin	---	Kyoto University	16

Product	Substrate	Microorganism	Immobilization Method	Remarks	Company or Institution	Reference
Candicidin	Glucose	Streptomyces griseus	Complexation with collagen	Immobilized cells retained 14% of the activity of growing cells	Rutgers University	14,15
Electricity	Glucose	Clostridium butyricum	Entrapment in polyacrylamide gel on platinum black electrode	Fuel cell operated continuously for 15 days producing 1.2 mA from 2.7 mmol glucose/day	Tokyo Institute of Technology	94
Wine	Grape juice	Saccharomyces cerevisiae	Entrapment in polyacrylamide gel	Ethanol productivity was 18 g/L/hr	Inst. Univ. Technol. Le Montet	89
Wine	Grape juice	Yeast	Yeast retained by "slant tube" fermentor	25 g/L/hr ethanol produced with 3.1 hr residence time	Western Regional Research Laboratory	96
Prednisolone	Cortisol	Arthrobacter simplex	Entrapment in polyacrylamide gel	Detailed procedures for preparing immobilized cells were described	University of Lund	99
Cortisol	Reichstein's S	Curvularia lunata	Entrapment in polyacrylamide gel	---	University of Lund	99

Product	Substrate	Microorganism	Immobilization Method	Remarks	Company or Institution	Reference
$\Delta^{1,4}$-3-Keto-steroids	Δ^5-3β-hydroxy-, Δ^5-3β-acetoxy-, and Δ^4-3-keto-steroids	Arthrobacter sp., Nocardia sp., or Mycobacterium sp.	Entrapment in polyacrylamide gel	Immobilization limited the production of secondary steroid products	All Union Sci. Res. and Biotech. Inst., USSR	101
--	Hydrocortisone	Mycobacterium globiforme	Entrapment in polyacrylamide gel	Electron microscopic study made of entrapped cells	Acad. Sci., USSR	100

was connected to a cathode chamber with a salt bridge. A carbon electrode served as the cathode. The anode potential of the cell was -0.65V vs a saturated calomel electrode. A constant current of 1.1 to 1.2 mA was obtained during 15 days of operation. The current was generated by the electrochemical oxidation of H_2 and formic acid produced by the entrapped cells. The fuel cell required large amounts of cells to produce a relatively small amount of power: 24 watts/kg dry immobilized cells.

The feasibility of using immobilized cells to produce ethanol, in beverage form or as a raw material or energy source, was explored in several laboratories (59,89,95,96). Wilke and his coworkers (59) developed a vacuum fermentor with cell recycle that enabled them to achieve ethanol productivities of 80 g/L/hr (see Immobilization Methods, p. 102). With these high productivities, fermentation ethanol derived from glucose via starch or cellulose may eventually compete economically with fuels and raw materials derived from petroleum. Kierston and Buck (17) used cells of *Saccharomyces cerevisiae* entrapped in a calcium alginate gel to produce ethanol from glucose in a column reactor. A 10% glucose solution, which passed through the column with a 10-hr residence time, was converted to ethanol in 65-90% of the theoretical yield (i.e., 2 moles ethanol from 1 mole glucose). The half-life for ethanol production was estimated to be 10 days.

S. cerevisiae also was entrapped in a polyacrylamide gel and used to ferment grape juice (89). A two-stage reactor operated in series produced ethanol at a rate of 18 g/L/hr. The reactor was operated continuously for 1 month at a hydraulic dilution rate of 0.32 hr^{-1} (in each stage) with an influent sugar concentration of 126 g/L.

Wick and Popper (96) described a novel fermentor device that immobilizes microorganisms that have good settling properties. The fermentor, which was termed a slant tube, consisted of single tubes or tube bundles wound around an ascending spiral support 4' in diameter and 22' in height. Grape juice, inoculated with yeast culture, was passed through the tube or tube bundle from the bottom to the top where it exited the spiral. Rapid settling of the yeast maintained the biomass in the bottom of the spiral while cell-free fermented juice exited from the top. The reactor was operated under a variety of conditions to optimize the fermentation. At a residence time of 3.1 hr, 90% of an 18% sugar solution was metabolized and ethanol was produced at a rate of 25 g/L/hr.

Grinbergs et al. (95) studied the possibility of producing beer in a fermentation system that consisted of a bed of yeast cells admixed with celite. Glucose solutions were forced upward through the bed under pressure and yeast-free eluate containing ethanol and other fermentation products were obtained. Beer made with this reactor was organoleptically unacceptable because of a high level of α-diketones. Other problems encountered with this process were the release of nitrogenous material from the yeast (presumably lysis) and plugging of the yeast bed.

IV. CONCLUDING REMARKS

Continued interest in the use of immobilized cells as alternatives to conventional fermentation processes or immobilized enzyme systems is evident in the number of entries in the preceding tables. The number and types of metabolic products produced by immobilized cells increased very little during the past year. The prepondence of recent studies has dealt with new cell immobilization methods and optimization of previously developed methods and processes. Among the notable contributions to immobilization methodology are the covalent attachment of cells to a solid matrix (31) and the entrapment of microorganisms within carrageenan (23). The report by Jack and Zajic (31) appears to be the first example of the successful immobilization of a microorganism by covalent binding to a solid support. The immobilized cells retained 75% of their histidine ammonia lyase activity and were stable for 16 days during continuous use. Carrageenan entrapment of whole cells is of particular interest because of the long enzyme half-life afforded by this immobilization method. The general utility of carrageenan entrapment for stabilizing enzymes in microbial cells has not yet been fully assessed. If carrageenan entrapment proves to be a generally effective stabilization method, it may enable the commercial exploitation of immobilized cell processes that presently are not economically feasible. Another aspect of carrageenan entrapment that must be evaluated is its effect on cofactor leakage and/or cofactor regeneration in immobilized cells. Hopefully, this method, or other methods under development, can lessen the problems associated with using cofactor-requiring enzymes in immobilized cell systems.

ACKNOWLEDGMENT

The author gratefully acknowledges Dr. A. Laskin for providing information on the 4th Enzyme Engineering Conference.

REFERENCES

1. Abbott, B. J., *Annu. Reports Ferment. Processes 1*, 205 (1977).
2. Rechnitz, G. A., Riechel, T. L., Kobos, R. K., and Meyerhoff, M. E., *Science 199*, 440 (1978).
3. Rechnitz, G. A., Kobos, R. K., and Gebauer, C. R., *Anal. Chim. Acta 94*, 357 (1977).
4. Karube, I., Mitsuda, S., Matsunaga, T., and Suzuki, S., *J. Ferment. Technol. 55*, 243 (1977).

5. Suzuki, S., Karube, I., and Matsunaga, T., 4th Enzyme Engineering Conf., Bad Neunahr, Ger., Sept. (1977).
6. Evans,, W. H., Mage, M. G., Peterson, E. A., *J. Immunol. 102*, 899 (1969).
7. Wigzell, H. and Anderson, B., *J. Exp. Med. 129*, 23 (1969).
8. Truffi-Bachi, P. and Wofsy, L., *Proc. Nat. Acad. Sci., U.S. 66*, 685 (1970).
9. Zabriskie, D., Ollis, D. F., and Burger, M. M., *Biotechnol. Bioeng. 15*, 981 (1973).
10. Rutishauser, U. and Sachs, L., *J. Cell Biol. 65*, 247 (1975).
11. Kinzel, V., Kubler, D., Richards, J., and Stohr, M., *Science 192*, 487 (1976).
12. Pitra, C., Dreyer, G., and Abel, H., *Studia Biophysica, Berlin 59*, 239 (1976).
13. Anon., *Indust. Res.* 40 (Nov. 1977).
14. Vieth, W. R. and Venkatasubramanian, K., 4th Enzyme Engineering Conf., Bad Neuenahr, Ger., Sept. (1977).
15. Venkat, K., International Biochemical Symposium, Toronto, Oct. (1977).
16. Fukui, S., Tanaka, A., and Gellf, G., 4th Enzyme Engineering Conf., Bad Neuenahr, Ger., Sept. (1977).
17. Kierstan, M. and Bucke, C., *Biotechnol. Bioeng. 19*, 387 (1977).
18. Chibata, I. and Tosa, T., *Adv. Appl. Microbiol. 22*, 1 (1977).
19. Jack, T. R. and Zajic, J. E., *Adv. Biochem. Eng. 5*, 125 (1977).
20. Fukui, S., Yamamoto, T., and Iida, T., German Patent 2,629,693.
21. Fukui, S., Yamamoto, T., and Iida, T., German Patent 2,629,692.
22. Linko, Y., Pohjola, L., Viskari, R., and Linko, P., 4th Enzyme Engineering Conf., Bad Neuenahr, Ger., Sept. (1977).
23. Chibata, I., 4th Enzyme Engineering Conf., Bad Neuenahr, Ger., Sept. (1977).
24. Horisberger, M., *Biotechnol. Bioeng. 18*, 1647 (1976).
25. Sato, T., Mori, T., Tosa, T., Chibata, I., Fukui, M., Yamashita, K., and Sumi, A., *Biotechnol. Bioeng. 17*, 1797 (1975).
26. Japan Atomic Energy Res., Japanese Patent 77,15888 (1977).
27. Japan Atomic Energy Res., Japanese Patent 77,15886 (1977).
28. Japan Atomic Energy Res., Japanese Patent 77,15889 (1977).
29. Tosa, T., Sato, T., Nishida, Y., and Chibata, I., *Biochim. Biophys. Acta 483*, 193 (1977).
30. Miyata, N. and Kikuchi, T., Japanese Patent 76,128477 (1976).
31. Jack, T. R. and Zajic, J. R., *Biotechnol. Bioeng. 19*, 631 (1977).
32. Casey, M., Maeda, Y., and Fazeli, A., *J. Ferment. Technol. 55*, 174 (1977).
33. Alemzadeh, I., Maeda, Y., and Fazeli, A., *J. Ferment. Technol. 55*, 181 (1977).

34. Martin, J. P., Filip, Z., and Haider, K., *Soil Biol. Biochem.* *8*, 409 (1976).
35. Brown, C. M. Ellwood, D. C., and Hunter, J. R., *FEMS Microbiol. Lett. 1*, 163 (1977).
36. Fletcher, M., *Can. J. Microbiol. 23*, 1 (1977).
37. Treweek, G. P. and Morgan, J. J., *J. Colloid Interface Sci. 60*, 258 (1977).
38. Ashby, R. and Bull, A. T., *Lab. Pract. 26*, 327 (1977).
39. Matson, J. V. and Characklis, W. G., *Water Res. 10*, 877 (1976).
40. Harris, N. P. and Hansford, G. S., *Water Res. 10*, 935 (1976).
41. Metz, B. and Kossen, N. W. F., *Biotechnol. Bioeng. 19*, 781 (1977).
42. Russell, A. D. and Hopwood, D., *Prog. Med. Chem. 13*, 271 (1976).
43. Schultz, J. S. and Gerhardt, P., *Bacteriol. Revs. 33*, 1 (1969).
44. Kominek, L., United States Patent 3,915,802 (1975).
45. Kominek, L. A., United States Patent 3,915,803 (1975).
46. Kominek, K. A., *Antimicrob. Ag. Chemotherap. 7*, 856 (1975).
47. Kominek, L., *Antimicrob. Ag. Chemotherap. 7*, 861 (1975).
48. Abbott, B. J. and Gerhardt, P., *Biotechnol. Bioeng. 12*, 577 (1970).
49. Abbott, B. and Gerhardt, P., *Biotechnol. Bioeng. 12*, 591 (1970).
50. Abbott, B. J. and Gerhardt, P., *Biotechnol. Bioeng. 12*, 603 (1970).
51. Fogarty, W. M. and Griffin, P., *J. Appl. Chem. Biotechnol. 23*, 401 (1973).
52. Hardt, F. W., Young, J. C., Clesceri, L. S., and Washington, D. R., *Environ. Sci. Technol. 5*, 345 (1971).
53. Coulman, G. A., Stieber, R. W., and Gerhardt, P., *Appl. Environ. Microbiol. 34*, 725 (1977).
54. Stieber, R. W., Coulman, G. A., and Gerhardt, P., *Appl. Environ. Microbiol. 34*, 733 (1977).
55. Landwall, P. and Holme, T., *J. Gen. Microbiol. 103*, 345 (1977).
56. Landwall, P. and Holme, T., *J. Gen. Microbiol. 103*, 353 (1977).
57. Sortland, L. D. and Wilke, C. R., *Biotechnol. Bioeng. 11*, 305 (1969).
58. Margaritis, A., Doctoral Dissertation, University of California, Berkeley (1974).
59. Cysewski, G. R. and Wilke, C. R., *Biotechnol. Bioeng. 19*, 1125 (1977).
60. Anon., *Chemical Week 117*, 33 (1975).
61. Casey, J. P., *Cereal Foods World 22*, 48 (1977).
62. Joseph, R., Shanthamma, M. S., and Murthy, V. S., *J. Food Sci. Technol. 14*, 73 (1977).

63. Vaheri, M. and Kayppinen, V., *Process Biochem. 5*, July/Aug. (1977).
64. Ryu, D. Y. and Chung, S. H., *Biotechnol. Bioeng. 19*, 159 (1977).
65. Vieth, W. R. and Venkatasubramanian, K., *in* "Methods in Enzymology" (K. Mosbach, ed.), Vol. 44. Academic Press, New York (1976).
66. Poulsen, P. B. and Zittan, L., *in* "Methods in Enzymology" (K. Mosbach, ed.), Vol. 44. Academic Press, New York (1976).
67. Goto, S., Enomoto, S., Takahashi, Y., and Motomatsu, R., *Japan J. Microbiol. 15*, 317 (1971).
68. Wang, D., Sinsky, A., and Butterworth, T., "Membrane Science and Technology" (J. Flynn, ed.). Plenum Press 98, London (1970).
69. Friedman, M. R. and Gaden, E. L., *Biotechnol. Bioeng. 12*, 961 (1970).
70. Kubo, T., Komatsu, T., Kawai, K., Sugihara, T., and Yamada, Y., Japanese Patent 77,61243 (1977).
71. Lee, C. K. and Long, M. E., United States Patent Reissue 29,130 (1977).
72. Tsumura, N. and Kasumi, T., United States Patent 4,001,082 (1977).
73. Lantero, O. J., 4th Enzyme Engineering Conf., Bad Neuenahr, Ger., Sept. (1977).
74. Nelson, R. P., United States Patent 3,957,580 (1976).
75. Chibata, I., Tosa, T., and Sato, T., *in* "Methods in Enzymology" (K. Mosbach, ed.), Vol. 44, p. 739. Academic Press, New York (1976).
76. Suzuki, S., Hirano, K., Hiraga, K., and Takagi, Y., Japanese Patent 77,03891 (1977).
77. Yamada, H., Okamura, S., Kojima, H., Okamoto, Y., and Ito, Y., Japanese Patent 76,144779 (1976).
78. Hino, T., Yamada, H., Okamura, S., Kojima, H., Okamoto, Y., and Ito, Y., Japanese Patent 76,144780 (1976).
79. Suzuki, S., Japanese Patent 77,47983 (1977).
80. Chibata, I., Tosa, T., and Sato, T., United States Patent 3,953,291 (1976).
81. Tanabe Seiyaku Co., British Patent 1,442,282 (1976).
82. Miyata, N. and Kikuchi, T., Japanese Patent 76,133484 (1976).
83. Schnarr, G. W., Szarek, W. A., and Jones, J. K. N., *Appl. Environ. Microbiol. 33*, 782 (1977).
84. Karube, I., Hirano, K., and Suzuki, S., *Biotechnol. Bioeng. 19*, 1233 (1977).
85. Hirano, K., Karube, I., and Suzuki, S., *Biotechnol. Bioeng. 19*, 311 (1977).
86. Yamamoto, K., Tosa, T., Yamashita, K., and Chibata, I., *Europ. J. Appl. Microbiol. 3*, 169 (1976).
87. Yamamoto, K., Tosa, T., Yamashita, K., and Chibata, I., *Biotechnol. Bioeng. 19*, 1101 (1977).
88. Kato, E., *Meiji Daigaku Kagaku Gijutsu Kenkyusao Nempo 16*, 26 (1974).

89. Divies, C., French Patent 844,766 (1977).
90. Divies, C. and Siess, M., *Ann. Microbiol. (Paris) 127B,* 525 (1976).
91. Larsson, P. O., Ohlson, S., and Mosbach, K., *Nature 26,* 796 (1976).
92. Anon., *New Scientist 74,* 401 (1977).
93. Tolls, T., Shovers, J., Sandine, W., and Elliker, P., *Appl. Microbiol. 19,* 649 (1970).
94. Karube, I., Matsunaga, T., Tsuru, S., and Suzuki, S., *Biotechnol. Bioeng. 19,* 1727 (1977).
95. Grinbergs, M., Hildebrand, R., and Clarke, B., *J. Inst. Brew. 83,* 25 (1977).
96. Wick, E. and Popper, K., *Biotechnol. Bioeng. 19,* 235 (1977).
97. Kirwan, D. and Gainer, J., *Enzyme Technol. Renewable Resour., Proc. Grantees-Users Conf. 1976,* 31 (1976).
98. Chu, Y., Tani, Y., Lee, T., and Yu, T., *Hanguk Sikpum Kwahakhoe Chi. 9,* 183 (1977).
99. Larsson, P. and Mosbach, K., *in* "Methods in Enzymology" (K. Mosbach, ed.), Vol. XLIV, p. 187. Academic Press, New York (1976).
100. Koscheenko, K., Gulevskaya, S., Sukhodol'skaya, G., Lusta, K., Fikhte, B., and Skryabin, G., *Dolk. Adak. Nauk. SSSR 223,* 1211 (1977).
101. Voishvillo, N., Kamernitskii, A., Khaikova, A., Leont'ev, G., Paukov, V., and Nakhapetyan, L., *Bull. Acad. Sci. USSR Div. Chem. Sci. 25,* 1303 (1976).
102. Zedan, H. and El-Tayeb, O., *Plant Med. 31,* 163 (1977).
103. Tanabe Seiyaku Co., Japanese Patent 75,126884 (1976).
104. Mason, J. R., Pirt, S. J., and Somerville, H. J., 4th Enzyme Engineering Conf., Bad Neuenahr, Germany, September (1977).

CHAPTER 6

ENZYMES OF INDUSTRIAL INTEREST;
TRADITIONAL PRODUCTS

K. Aunstrup

Novo Industri A/S
Novo Allé
Bagsvaerd, Denmark

The enzyme literature is extensive; it comprises well over 10,000 papers per year. Although less than 50% of these publications are concerned with microbial enzymes and most of these are quickly evaluated as having no industrial interest, still a few thousand papers per year are of potential interest for the industrial development of enzymes. This is in striking contrast to the less than one hundred papers dealing with industrial processes. Furthermore, it is interesting to observe that only a few papers describe the processes of the highest economic importance today. This distribution may not be surprising--research deals with the possibilities of the future and not with the well established processes, but it explains why this report contains so little on the processes used at present in the enzyme industry.

I. PROTEOLYTIC ENZYMES

From an economical point of view, proteases are the most important industrial enzymes (1). The dominating application is the use of the alkaline serine protease of *Bacillus licheniformis* in detergents. The annual world consumption of this enzyme is estimated at about 500t of pure enzyme protein. The second largest application is the use of Mucor proteases in the cheese manufacture, and as number three we have the *Aspergillus* proteases which are used in digestive aids and in baking. The important use of the *Aspergillus* proteases in the manufacture of soy sauce is difficult to quantify since the enzymes are not isolated, but prepared and used directly in the factories. The importance of this application can be estimated from the fact that the yearly production of soy sauce in Japan alone is more than a billion liters.

The protease preparations used today function well in the applications for which they are used, and new commercial products are not to be expected until new applications are found which require new properties of the enzymes.

Research is now concentrated on basic studies of the molecular properties of the proteases and on studies which are important to the microbiological metabolism.

A. *Bacillus Proteases*

1. *Extracellular Enzymes*. The bacitracin producing strain A-5 of *B. licheniformis* also produces extracellular protease. Up to 10% of the bacitracin is bound so firmly to the protease that they are not separated by gel chromatography or by CMC-chromatography. Treatment with $CHCl_3$ separate the complex. Bacitracin inhibits the protease activity, but the complex has antibiotic activity. Only one of the three proteases which can be separated by CMC-chromatography is inhibited by bacitracin (2).

Bacillus sphaericus protease has been purified and crystallized (3). Judging from the inhibition by DFP (diisopropyl fluorophosphate), it is a serine protease, but it differs from the known serine proteases from *Bacillus* in that it is strongly inhibited by EDTA and it is unique among the Bacillus enzymes in having a disulfide linkage. Optimum pH is 9 and the enzyme is stable between pH 5 and 11. The molecular weight (Mw) is 27,000 like that of the subtilisins. The enzyme contains two Ca^{++}, but no Zn; there is no immunological cross reaction with other known *Bacillus* enzymes.

In 1974 a "microprotease" with the extraordinarily low Mw of 2,700 was reported in a special strain of *B. cereus*. The enzyme has now been reinvestigated (4), and it was found that the strain produces a neutral Zn protease of Mw about 30,000, similar to the known *Bacillus* proteases. There was no indication as to the enzyme being an oligomer, and it was suggested that the "microprotease" is an artifact formed by autolysis of the protease during the preparation.

The molecular basis for thermostability has been extensively studied, but no satisfactory explanation has been given.

A new technique was used by Barach and Adams (5). They compared the thermal denaturation of the heat stable metalloprotease Thermolysin and a metalloprotease from a psychrophilic *Pseudomonas sp.* at ultrahigh temperatures. Under these conditions it was shown that the thermal inactivation was comparable for the two enzymes although at lower temperatures Thermolysin was much more

heat stable than the *Pseudomonas* enzyme. It was assumed that the
cause of denaturation at the lower temperature is not heat inactivation, but autolysis followed by heat inactivation.

It is suggested that the ability of these metallo enzymes to
resist extreme temperatures most likely reflects structure flexibility and the interplay of divalent cations in allowing rapid
and accurate enzyme renaturation rather than the maintenance of
native structure during heating.

The formation of neutral, thermostable protease from B. stearothermophilus was studied by Zuber and Siedler (6). Ca is necessary for the stability (20 mg/l), but a much higher concentration
(80 mg/l) is necessary to stabilize the formation of the enzyme.

2. *Intracellular Enzymes*. Proteolytic activity is important
in the sporulation process where a large protein turnover occurs
in the cell, and several serine proteases have been purified from
sporulating cells.

Two genetically different enzymes were isolated from B. *cereus*
(7). Their primary function is believed to be the supply of amino
acids in protein turnover. A similar serine protease was isolated
from B. *thuringiensis* (8). This enzyme requires Ca^{++} for activity
and is completely inhibited by EDTA, Mw 23,000. The enzyme is
different from the extracellular serine protease and it will spe-
cifically hydrolyze the β-subunit of RNA polymerase.

During germination of *Bacillus* spores, two proteins, A and B,
are rapidly hydrolyzed to amino acids. A serine protease specific
for hydrolysis of these proteins has been isolated from B. *megaterium*. The further hydrolysis to amino acids is catalyzed by an
aminopeptidase. The protease is very unstable and disappears
rapidly in the late phases of germination (9).

A protein inhibitor for the intracellular serine protease of
B. *subtilis* (10) is present in the cells during both vegetative
growth and sporulation. This is the first example in procaryotic
cells of such intracellular protease inhibitors which are well
known from eucaryotic cells. The inhibitor is not active on the
extracellular serine protease.

Penicillinase is produced by B. *licheniformis* in a membrane
bound, lipoprotein form which is transformed to an extracellular
enzyme by cleavage of a lipopeptide containing 24 amino acids.
This process is catalyzed by a highly specific serine protease
which only hydrolyzes peptide bonds involving the carboxy groups
of serine and threonine. The reactivity with casein is low, and
the stability is highly dependent on Ca^{++}, Mw 21,000, pH optimum
7-9.5 (11,12).

B. *Aspergillus Proteases*

Takadiastase, which is prepared from *Aspergillus oryzae*, contains acid protease that can be separated in a carbohydrate-free component and a glycoprotein component with 49% carbohydrate, but the same amino acid composition. Takadiastase is made by semi-solid fermentation, but if the same strain is grown in a liquid culture, four protease components can be isolated (13). The properties of these components are identical to the proteases of Takadiastase, both with regard to amino acid composition, specificity, and immunological properties, but their carbohydrate content varies from 19 to 43%, and the heat stability is better for the components with a high carbohydrate content.

The carbohydrate components are glucose, galactose and mannose; no hexosamine was detected. Some of the carbohydrates are present as homopolymers in the form of mannan and galactan. The results indicate that the polysaccharides bound to this protease vary in both chemical and physical properties according to the physiological conditions under which the enzyme is produced.

It has been suggested (14) that although the polysaccharides are tightly bound to the acid protease, this does not involve a covalent bond. The evidence for this assumption is that the polysaccharides obtained after proteolytic digestion contain no detectable amino acids, no hexosamine is present, the carbohydrate could not be separated by procedures which would normally liberate covalently bound bound carbohydrate from proteins, such as treatment with cold trichloroacetic acid, 8M urea, 6M guanidine HCl or alkaline treatment. A complete dissociation was obtained with 50% acetic acid; this was also in disagreement with the behaviour of other glycoproteins.

An acid proteinase may be extracted from growing cells of *A. oryzae* (15); this enzyme is similar to the extracellular enzyme. About 15% of the intracellular enzyme is membrane bound and may be released by treatment with Triton X-100. Two components may be separated; they have hydrophobic properties and precipitate when the surfactant is removed. At least part of the membrane bound protease may be an intermediate in the acid protease secretion.

In the preparation of soy sauce, the formation of a high concentration of amino acids is important. The acid proteases of *A. oryzae* are endoproteases which only liberate small amounts of free amino acids. The formation of free amino acids in the process is due to a combined effect of the acid protease and carboxypeptidases formed by the fungus (16). The development of strains which are hyperproductive for peptidase is therefore of interest in soy sauce manufacture. The selection of mutants may be made by testing the activity on Leu-Gly-Gly. A rapid screening method based on the formation of a yellow zone around the colonies on an agar plate containing leucyl-p-nitroanilide is not useful as this method selects mutants with a high activity of leucine aminopeptidase, an enzyme which will only liberate small amounts of amino acids from protein (17).

A. *oryzae* forms at least seven aminopeptidases, one of which has been purified, viz. leucinaminopeptidase IV. It is uncommon in being a serine enzyme and uninhibited by metal chelators (18).

The specificity of the acid protease from *A. saitoi* (syn. *A. phoenicis*) has been studied; the pure enzyme free of the carboxy peptidase also produced by the fungus will preferentially cleave peptide bonds which have a hydrophobic amino acid such as tyrosine, leucine, isoleucine or phenylalanine in the P_1^1 position [N terminal in the peptide formed during hydrolysis (19)].

C.   *Other Fungal Proteases*

The homology in amino acid sequence between animal proteases such as pepsin and the acid fungal proteases has been discussed by many authors. The molecular structure of acid protease from *Rhizopus chinensis* and *Endothia parasitica* was compared in X-ray analysis (3Å resolution) (20). The two enzymes have similar secondary and tertiary folding; they are bilobal and have a cleft between the lobes. The enzymes show extensive similarities, also with pepsin. A similar homology was found in other studies between the acid protease from *Penicillium roqueforti*, Penicilopepsin, and the acid protease from *E. parasitica* (21). A mechanism of catalysis for penicillopepsin has been proposed, based on the crystal structure of the enzyme (22). The mechanism is in many ways similar to the one previously derived for carboxy peptidase. A review on recent developments in enzyme catalytic mechanisms has been prepared by Fruton (23).

Penicillium caseicolum, which is a frequent surface mold on soft cheese like camembert, produces several acid proteases. Fifteen fungal strains were studied; they all produced the same type of enzyme system consisting of at least two proteases with pH optimum of the mixture at 6 and 9. A protease of minor activity with optimum at pH 5 could be separated by gel chromatography (24). The neutral protease component has Mw 20,000, pH opt. close to 6; EDTA is an inhibitor. The properties of this enzyme are close to those of Protease II of *Penicillium roqueforti* and of Protease II of *Aspergillus oryzae*.

An alkaline protease, which coagulates citrated blood, has been isolated from a *Cephalosporium sp.* (25). The enzyme is dependent on Ca^{++} and it is not a serine enzyme. Blood coagulation required the presence of prothrombin or an unknown factor present in this preparation. It is assumed that the enzyme has a thrombokinase-like activity, but contrary to most microbial proteases it has low activity towards fibrinogen and fibrin.

In the preparation of ontjom in Indonesia, peanut press cake is fermented with *Neurospora sitophila*. This organism secretes lipase and α-galactosidase, and it will also hydrolyze the peanut proteins to peptides and free amino acids. The fungus produces a heat-sensitive (inactivated above 40°) and oxygen-sensitive intracellular protease with pH opt. 6-7. An extracellular protease is also formed, but its properties have not been investigated (26).

In *Neurospora crassa* the extracellular protease synthesis is induced by protein and repressed by ammonium ion (27). Amino acids also repress the protease formation, and repressing amino acids accumulate in the amino acid pool under protein induction.

An extracellular acid carboxypeptidase has been isolated from *Penicillium roqueforti* (28). The enzyme is a serine peptidase and is not inhibited by metal chelators. The specificity is low, and the enzyme releases neutral, alkaline or acid amino acids. The enzyme is similar to other fungal carboxypeptidases.

D. *Yeast Protease*

Candida lipolytica produces extracellular acid, neutral and alkaline protease. The neutral and alkaline proteases were secreted at neutral and alkaline pH respectively, whereas the acid protease was produced at all pH values. The neutral protease is a serine protease which is strongly dependent on Ca^{++} and inhibited by EDTA. Mw 38,000, pH opt. 6.8 (29).

The synthesis of alkaline protease by *C. lipolytica* is stimulated by a poor carbon source (weak catabolite repression), low pool concentrations of cystein and ammonium and by addition of protein to the medium. It is suggested that no single common metabolic signal is responsible for the derepression during carbon, nitrogen or sulfur limitation in *C. lipolytica* (30).

E. *Microbial Proteases in the Dairy Industry*

Sternberg (31) has reviewed the literature on microbial rennets, including methods of production, purification and application of the three commercially used rennet preparations *M. pusillus, M. miehei* and *E. parasitica*). A list of patents for rennet substitutes reveals an extensive interest in the development of new rennet enzymes. Since 1972 reports have been published describing production of milk coagulating enzymes from 6 *Bacillus sp.*, 2 *Streptomyces sp.* and 36 species of fungi. None of these preparations have found significant commercial application.

Mucor pusillus rennet has been purified by iso electric focusing in a sucrose density gradient. The ratio of milk coagulating activity to protease activity of the purified product was 4.5 times that of the crude product (32).

The proteolytic activity of the microorganisms in the cheese is important for flavor development. It is usually difficult to separate the action of rennet, lactic acid bacteria and other microorganisms of the cheese.

The effect was studied in a sterile curd prepared free of rennet by acidifying milk with gluconolactone and adding enzyme solutions in various concentrations. Neutral protease of *Penicillium caseicolum* and acid protease of *Penicillium roqueforti* play a fundamental role in proteolysis by increasing the soluble nitrogen with little formation of amino acids. Intracellular protease from *Streptococcus lactis* led to a large increase in the amounts of amino acids. There is a synergistic effect of the enzymes, and the first 24 h or the ripening period are the most important to the proteolytic action.

It is suggested that the addition of external proteases be used to improve the quality of the cheese and to accelerate cheese ripening (33).

An undesired effect may be caused by *Achromobacter*, a common infection in milk products. This bacterium produces an extracellular protease which hydrolyzes casein to bitter tasting components. The enzyme is heat stable in dairy products and may survive pasteurization (34).

II. AMYLOLYTIC ENZYMES

The large-scale use of amylolytic enzymes in the starch industry, which started in 1960 with glucoamylase, has accelerated rapidly during the last few years (35). This is mainly caused by the introduction of isomerized glucose in fructose syrups (36). In this process four enzymes are used, α-amylase, pullulanase, glucoamylase, and glucose isomerase. The process is a beautiful example of enzyme technology achieving a technically and economically satisfactory solution to a complex chemical problem. A number of new processes are being developed at present, e.g. maltose production, and there is no doubt that the starch industry now is the most enzyme minded industry.

A. Alpha-amylases

The hydrolysis of starch molecules by alpha-amylases has been discussed by several authors, and the difference in action pattern has been explained by two theories, that of multiple attack and that of preferred attack. In the multiple attack theory it is assumed that all bonds in the molecule are equally susceptible to hydrolysis. After a random encounter between enzyme and substrate and after hydrolysis of one bond, only one part of the substrate leaves the enzyme, and the other part of the substrate is retained to undergo a second hydrolytic event at a bond close to the newly exposed reducing group, producing small molecules such as maltose or maltotriose. This repetitive attack may take place a number of times before the ultimate separation between substrate and enzyme. In the theory of preferred attack or multichain attack, a single hydrolytic event is postulated during each encounter between enzyme and substrate. Differences in action patterns are then explained by the assumption that the glucosidic bonds are not equally susceptible to hydrolysis. Especially bonds near the chain ends may be more resistant. A mathematical treatment of the results in the literature shows that only pancreas amylase is capable of multiple attack, other amylases including *Bacillus* and *Aspergillus* amylase act by a multichain mechanism (37). In the hydrolysis of maltose by the saccharifying alpha-amylase of *B. subtilis* there is an initial lag phase and the hydrolysis curve has a sigmoid shape. Furthermore, oligosaccharides are formed during the hydrolysis process. These phenomena may be explained by assuming that hydrolysis of maltose takes place via a combined transglucosylation and hydrolysis, where the primary reaction cyclus is

$$\text{maltotriose} + \text{maltose} \rightarrow \text{maltotetraose} + \text{glucose}$$
$$\text{maltotetraose} \rightarrow \text{maltotriose} + \text{glucose}$$

The lag phase is explained by a slow initial formation of maltotriose; this is supported by the fact that the lag phase is prevented by addition of a small amount of maltotriose to the reaction mixture. It has been possible to simulate the experimental data by a computer model based on this theory (38).

Digestion of starch in the rumen is essential to maximum utilization of feed grain by the ruminant. At present three rumen amylases are known, produced by *Streptococus bovis*, *Clostridium butyricum* and *Bacteroides amylophilus*. The latter organism produces extracellular amylases. Six enzymes were separated by electrophoreses, one of these was purified, and it was shown that its properties were similar to those of other microbial alpha-amylases: pH opt. 6.3, stability range 5.8-7.5, pI 4.6, Mw 92,000. Ca^{++} and Co^{++} were strong activators. The enzyme hydrolyzed raw starch slowly, but hydrolyzed soluble starch readily to give predominantly maltose and maltotriose, but only a trace of glucose. The accumulation of extracellular amylase seemed partly dependent on cell-lysis (39).

In composting materials one often finds *Thermomonospora curvata* which is a cellulolytic thermophile. The organism also secretes an extracellular alpha-amylase which is of importance in the composting of starch containing material. This enzyme has been purified and its properties determined: Mw 62,000, pH opt. 5.5-6, inactivation above 65°C. The enzyme is peculiar in that it hydrolyzes starch to a mixture of maltotetraose and maltopentaose instead of glucose and maltose (40).

B. Glucoamylases

The use of glucoamylase from *Aspergillus niger* for starch hydrolysis has increased rapidly in the last few years because a high dextrose syrup is a necessary intermediate in the manufacture of the new isomerized glucose-fructose syrups. A short review on the applications, properties and reaction kinetics of glucoamylase has been prepared by Cho and Bailey (41).

The molecular basis for the catalytic activity and stability of glucoamylase was studied by several authors.

Photooxidation of proteins in the presence of Rose bengal or methylene blue results in a destruction of tryptophan residues. When applied to glucoamylase I of *A. niger*, the result is a pH dependent loss of activity, which is analogous to the rate of destruction of free l-tryptophan. Maltose protects the tryptophan residues in the molecule and the enzyme activity. It is concluded that the active center of glucoamylase I is a cleft, lined with tryptophanyl residues that participate in the binding of the substrate. One or more carboxylic acid residues are involved in bond cleavage (42).

Thermal inactivation of *Rhizopus* glucoamylase is reduced in the presence of glucose, gluconolactone, lactose or glycerol. The protective effect of glucose or gluconolactone is ascribed to a binding to the active site, whereas it is assumed that the effect of lactose and glycerol primarily is caused by a reduction in the dielectric constant of the solution (43). The binding constant of glucose was calculated from model equations and shown to agree with the expected value.

The carbohydrate structure of the glucoamylases is of practical importance because it is related to the thermostability of the enzyme.

Three glucopeptides are formed by pronase digestion of the *Rh. javanicus* glucoamylase. Two of these contain N-acetylglucosamin bound to asparagin, and the third contains mannose bound to threonine and serine in chains of two mannose molecules linked together by an α-1,3-bond. The peptide apparently contains a row of five threonine residues followed by one serine residue, each coupled to mannose like this (44):

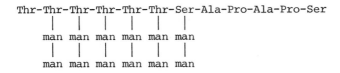

```
Thr-Thr-Thr-Thr-Thr-Thr-Ser-Ala-Pro-Ala-Pro-Ser
 |   |   |   |   |   |
man man man man man man
 |   |   |   |   |   |
man man man man man man
```

In the commercial starch hydrolysis process, dry substance concentrations of about 30% are used. Under these conditions a certain amount of oligosaccharides is unavoidable in the final reaction mixture, primarily isomaltose, panose and nigerose. These saccharides may be formed by reversion reactions catalyzed by the glucoamylase or by transglucosylation reactions catalyzed

by a trace of transglucosylase in the enzyme preparation. A
quantitative study of the reaction of puridied glucoamylase and
transglucosylase from A. *niger* with maltose and glucose has been
made with C^{14} labeled carbohydrates (45). Under the reaction
conditions, glucoamylase converted glucose and maltose into 2.2
and 1.9% oligosaccharides respectively. Transglucosylase formed
under similar conditions 5.7 and 33% oligosaccharides from glucose and maltose. The reaction did not go to equilibrium. Transglucosylase also synthesized oligosaccharides from malto oligosaccharides of higher molecular weights to yield compounds with
α-1,6-linked glucosyl groups at the nonreducing end. No such
activity was detectable with glucoamylase.

Starch granules are attacked by glucoamylases, and it is
possible to obtain up to 90% hydrolysis of the starch by using
alpha-amylase free glucoamylase from A. *niger* or R. *niveus*. The
Rhizopus enzyme attacked more readily the starch granules than
the *Aspergillus* enzyme, and component I of this enzyme was the
most active. It has previously been shown that this component is
more active against glycogen and soluble starch than component
II. By following the degradation of the starch granules by
scanning electron microscopy, it was observed that the different
glucoamylases form individually characteristic surface pictures.
It is suggested that this is due to the differences in debranching effect of the glucoamylases (46).

Amylase preparations from A. *oryzae* possess a weak glucoamylase activity which may be separated into three components (47)
with Mw 76,000, 38,000, and 38,000 respectively. The first component differs from the others in having a high debranching
activity, ability to digest raw starch and a better thermostability. Optimum pH for all three components is 4.5-5.

Penicillium oxalicum glucoamylase may be separated into two
components. They are glycoproteins with a carbohydrate content
of 3.9 and 3.2%. The properties are similar, pH opt. 4.5-5, and
rapid inactivation at 60°C. Soluble starch and its components
are hydrolyzed completely to glucose, and the relative rate of
hydrolysis of maltose is 15% of that of amylopectin. There was
no detectable hydrolysis of isomaltose (48).

Monascus sp. are used in the Orient for coloring food and
beverages red. The amylolytic activity is usually low, but
Monascus keoliang used in the preparation of the Taiwan drink
Kaoliang produces significant amounts of glucoamylase (49). The
enzyme was separated into two components with Mw 48,000 and
68,000 of which the high molecular weight component is the more
stable. The enzymes are rapidly inactivated at 60 and 70°C respectively, pH opt. is 4.5, and soluble starch is hydrolyzed
completely to glucose.

Pioularia oryzae, the plant pathogenic fungus of the rice
blast disease, produces a glucoamylase, but no alpha-amylase or
transglucosylase. The glucoamylase is unique in having pH optimum at 6.5 (50).

Glucoamylase is found in thermophilic fungi such as *Mucor miehei, Humicola lanuginosa,* and *Sporotrichum thermophile* (51). The enzymatic activity obtained was small, and no evaluation of enzyme properties was made.

C. *Alpha-glucosidases*

During recent years several alpha-glucosidases have been found in *Bacillus* species. The enzymes do not appear to have any immediate commercial interest, but they are important to the metabolism of these organisms which are used in the production of other enzymes.

A membrane bound alpha-glucosidase has been found in *B. amyloliquefaciens.* The enzyme is rapidly inactivated at temperatures above 40°C, pH opt. is 6.8, and Mw is 27,000. The relative rate of hydrolysis is: p-nitrophenyl-alpha-glucoside 100, maltose 40, isomaltose 32, maltotriose 32, soluble starch 0, sucrose 140. The enzyme is apparently active in the hydrolysis of low molecular weight dextrins since no other enzyme system for their hydrolysis has been detected in this organism (52).

A thermophilic organism called *Bacillus thermoglucosidius,* which is closely related to *B. stearothermophilus,* secretes alpha-glucosidase in the medium. The enzyme has the following properties: Mw 55,000, pH opt. 5-6, rapid inactivation above 70°C, phenyl-alpha-glucoside and methyl-alpha-glucoside are hydrolyzed, but not maltose, maltotriose or soluble starch (53). The enzyme resembles the isomaltase found in *Saccharomyces cerevisiae.*

A maltose hydrolyzing alpha-glucosidase has been found in a number of thermophilic, amylolytic Bacillus strains. The enzyme is initially intracellular but is released in the medium during sporulation (54).

Alpha-glucosidases have also been found in the mycelium of many fungi. The enzyme from *Mucor racemosus* has the properties: Mw 105,000, pH opt. 4-6, rapid inactivation at 50°C. Phenyl-alpha-glucoside, maltose, isomaltose, maltotriose and soluble starch are hydrolyzed. Maltotriose is a transglucosylation product with maltose. Maltose and isomaltose are strong inhibitors; this has not been observed with other microbial alpha-glucosidases (55).

Mucor rouxii grows aerobically in mycelial form and anaerobically in yeast-like form. During aerobic growth, maltose is hydrolyzed by a cell wall bound maltase which is absent under anaerobic conditions. If the mycelial form is induced under anaerobic conditions by addition of EDTA, the maltase is formed. Its synthesis is therefore not dependent on the presence of oxygen, but on the structure of the cell wall.

Three alpha-glucosidases have been found in *Saccharomyces carlsbergensis.* The enzymes are typical alpha-glucosidases in having high activity towards alpha-phenyl-glucoside. One

hydrolyzes isomaltose, but not maltose, whereas the other two
hydrolyze maltose and not isomaltose (56).

D. Maltogenic and Debranching Amylases

Beta-amylase from plants are usually used for producing maltose, but since these enzymes are expensive and unstable, many
attempts have been made to prepare microbial substitutes.

A process has been developed for production of alpha-amylase-
free beta-amylase from *Bacillus circulans*. The enzyme has the
properties: Mw 60,000, pI 4.6; it is independent of Ca^{++} and not
inhibited by SH reagents. It may be used in starch hydrolysis up
to 60°C. Maltose concentrations up to 58% may be obtained. The
enzyme is extracellular and the organism is cultivated at 45°C
and pH 7-8. The yield is quite small. The strains applied in
the process are mutants in which the ability to produce alpha-
amylase has been removed (57).

Synthesis of beta-amylase by *B. megaterium* has been studied
in batch culture with feeding of the carbon source. The best results are obtained by feeding starch at a modified exponential
rate; overfeeding, as revealed by the presence of reducing sugars
in the broth, reduces yield (58).

When beta-amylase is used to produce high-maltose syrups from
starch, it is necessary to use other means of breaking the alpha-
1,6 bonds of amylopectin. If this is done by acid hydrolysis or
alpha-amylases, a substantial amount of glucose is formed and the
resulting maltose yield is not over 60%. If the branch points of
amylopectin are broken by pullulanase or isoamylase, the yield of
maltose with beta-amylase is increased considerably, so that
80-90% may be achieved.

Both enzymes are formed by a newly isolated strain of *B.
cereus var mycoides*, and an industrial process for making maltose
in high yields from starch based on this organism has been developed (59).

The best yields of both enzymes were obtained when the organism was grown in a medium containing organic nitrogen and starch
hydrolysate as carbon source. A mutant was found which had twenty
times increased beta-amylase yield and was independent of induction by starch or dextrins. It was shown that K^+ in the medium
would increase the beta-amylase yield, whereas Mn increased the
pullulanase yield. No enzyme activity could be found within the
cells (60).

The beta-amylase has the properties: Mw 35,000, pH opt. 7,
temperature opt. 50°C, the thermostability is less than that of
malt beta-amylase, maltose is released on the beta form. The
pullulanase has Mw 110,000, pH opt. 6-6.5, same temperature relationships as the beta-amylase, it is stabilized by Ca^{++}.

Pullulan, beta limit dextrin, amylopectin, and glycogen are hydrolyzed, but not panose, isomaltose or isomaltotriose.   The enzyme has little affinity towards the branches in unhydrolyzed
amylopectin (61).

In starch hydrolysis, the enzymes act together with alpha-
amylase, which is used to liquefy the starch to as low a DE value
as possible, e.g. less than 10.   The beta-amylase and pullulanase
are typically used at 50°C and pH 6 with a reaction time of 100h.
The maximum maltose yield obtained was 95%.   The process offers
interesting possibilities for production of high maltose syrups.
The drawbacks of the process as described now are the low process
temperature which makes it difficult to avoid contamination and
the low enzyme yield which makes the process expensive (59).

A method for isolation of pullulanase or isoamylase producing
organisms has been described (62).   It consists in plating the
organisms on a medium containing amylopectin or waxy maize starch.
When colonies of microorganisms appear, the medium is stained with
iodine, and the amylopectin will turn violet.   Blue zones around
a colony indicate the formation of debranched amylopectin and thus
the formation of debranching amylase by the colony in question.
The method cannot be used with alpha-amylase producing organisms.

Pullulanase of *Klebsiella pneumonia* is found cell-bound and
extracellularly.   It may be released from the cells by detergents
or by proteolytic action.   It is assumed that the extracellular
enzyme has been released by the bacteria's own proteolytic system.
Preparations of pullulanase made by the different methods have a
molecular weight varying between 500,000 and 60,000.   The high
molecular weight enzyme is bound to a lipopolysaccharide and the
low molecular weight preparation has probably been proteolytically
degraded.   An enzyme with Mw 151,000 can be released from the
cells by treatment with a protease component from pronase.   The
specific activity is twice as high as that of the extracellular
enzyme.   It is suggested that the various forms of the enzyme
have the same amino acid backbone, but that various parts of the
molecule are cleaved.   It is furthermore postulated that several
sites of the molecule are of importance to the activity, since
the various degradation products of the enzyme show different
specificity (63).

Enevoldsen has described a method for purification of pullulanase in which Schardinger-alpha-dextrin is bound to Sepharose.
Pullulanase was eluted from the column by Schardinger-beta-dextrin
and was subsequently freed from this by chromatography on Sephadex.
The reasoning behind the method is that pullulanase is inhibited
by both Schardinger dextrins, but the beta-dextrin is a stronger
inhibitor than the alpha-dextrin (64).

The commercial exploitation of debranching enzymes has so far
been concentrated on pullulanase from *Klebsiella pneumoniae*, but
other enzymes are also of interest such as the isoamylase from
Pseudomonas deramosa (65).   This enzyme which was discovered in
1968 debranches amylopectin at a much higher specific rate than

pullulanase. The complete hydrolysis of starch necessary for
metabolism of the organism is effected by intracellular alpha-
amylase and glucanase.

III. OTHER CARBOHYDRASES

A. *Alpha-glucanases and Dextranases*

     Under unfavorable harvesting conditions, *Leuconostoc* infec-
tions may occur in the sugar juice prepared from beet or cane.
The dextran formed increases the viscosity of the juice and causes
manufacturing problems which result in sugar losses. Treatment
with a commercial dextranase from a *Penicillium sp.* solves the
technical problems and reduces the sugar losses considerably. The
enzyme is used at 55°C and pH 5; the best results are obtained if
the juice is treated at low dextran concentration; there is no
sugar loss due to invertase action (66).
     Dental plaques are formed by the bacteria of the mouth; the
plaque consists of alpha-glucans of complex composition containing both alpha-1,3 bonds and alpha-1,6 bonds. Several enzyme
preparations for the hydrolysis of these substances have been
developed in the past, but it appears that a mixture of alpha-
glucanases is necessary to dissolve the plaque. Plaque formation
may also become a problem with dentures, and it has been shown
(67) that a satisfactory cleaning composition can be prepared
from dextranase, mutanase, and protease. It is interesting that
the use of this cleaning agent will reduce the problems of Candida infections of the mouth.
     A new endo-glucanase for the hydrolysis of mutan (the alpha-
1,3-glucan produced by *Streptococcus mutans*) was found in a
Streptomyces sp. The properties of the enzyme are: Mw 70,000,
pH opt. 5.4, rapid inactivation at 60°C. This enzyme alone hydrolyzes mutan to about 40%, but in combination with dextranase
80% hydrolysis can be reached (68).

B. *Hemicellulases*

     The interest in utilization of plant waste materials has also
intensified the study of hemicellulases. An example of a new
application is the addition of *Aspergillus niger* hemicellulase to
a methane fermentation process where soy bean seed coat was the
raw material (69). The fermentation process was accelerated so
as to be completed in half the usual time and the chemical oxygen
demand of the residue was reduced to 7% of the usual level.
     D-xylans are found in the hemicellulose fraction of higher
plant cell walls; they consist of a beta-1,4-linked D-xylopyranose
chain which commonly has side branches of alpha-1,3-linked

arabinofuranose and alpha-1,2-linked D-glucuronopyranose.   The
number and kinds of branch residues are characteristic for different plant groups; in some xylans the xylopyranose residues are
acetylated at carbon 2 and 3.

Xylan hydrolysis is of interest in connection with a utilization of cellulosic materials and especially in the manufacture of
the sweetener xylitol.

Xylanases are found in many fungi and several endo xylanases
have been purified, e.g. from *Aspergillus niger* (Mw about 25,000,
pI 4.2, pH opt. 4, 20% carbohydrate) (70); *Trichoderma pseudo-
koningii* (Mw about 17,000, pI 9.6, pH opt. 5) (71); *Irpex lacteus*
(72), *Trichoderma reesei* and *Aspergillus sp.* (73).

It is characteristic of these pure xylanases that the hydrolysis products predominantly constitute xylobiose and higher polymers; small amounts of free xylose are formed.   Furthermore, the
hydrolysis of xylane is incomplete; the degree of hydrolysis is
usually 20-50%.

Product inhibition influences the reaction and a larger conversion is found when the hydrolysis products are removed.   The
purified xylanase from *Irpex lacteus* also shows endocellulase
activity; the experimental data indicate that both activities are
caused by one enzyme protein.

An xylosidase from *Malbranchea pulchella var sulfurea* is well
suited for hydrolysis of xylobiose; complete hydrolysis is obtained in a concentration as high as 10% without transglucosylase
reactions.   Properties: Mw 26,000, pH opt. 6.2-6.8, Km 3 mM,
V_{max} 35 μmol/mg/min (xylobiose), Ca^{++} stabilizes.   The enzyme will
also hydrolyze xylane, but at a lower rate than xylobiose (74).

Beta-1,4-mannans are found in the hemicellulose fraction of
wood, and the enzymatic hydrolysis of this substance is of general
interest.

Several microorganisms hydrolyze mannan, but there are few
reports on purified enzymes.   An endomannanase was isolated from
a commercial cellulase product made from *A. niger*.   This enzyme
has a remarkable heat stability; it has temperature optimum above
80°C.   Mannans are hydrolyzed to mannose and mannobiose, which is
not attacked by the enzyme (75).

Yeast cell walls contain alpha-mannan, and enzymes for hydrolysis of these substances are therefore of some interest in the
preparation of yeast hydrolyzates.   Alpha-mannanases are found in
several wood rotting fungi; a good source is *Phellinus abietis*
which has been shown to produce at least three enzymes active in
mannan hydrolysis, alpha-mannosidase, exomannanase and endomannanase (76).

C. Beta-glucanases

The enzymatic hydrolysis of the beta-glucans of barley is important in the brewing industry, but there is a large potential area of application in hydrolysis of the glucans present in the cell walls of yeast and many fungi. The composition of these glucans is complex and they are usually difficult to hydrolyze. The many beta glucanases isolated from a number of microorganisms have so far primarily been used as tools in structural carbohydrate studies.

Candida utilis produces an extracellular exo-beta-glucanase which is assumed to hydrolyze both beta-1,3- and beta-1,4-bonds (77). The enzyme is an acid glucoprotein with 68% carbohydrate.

Nagasaki has purified an extracellular exo beta-1,3-glucanase from a "fungi imperfecti" which also produces endo-beta-glucanase (78), and an intracellular exo beta-1,3-glucanase from *Kluyveromyces aestuarii* has been purified and characterized (79). All these enzymes are glucoproteins; they hydrolyze the glucan under formation of glucose, but they have low activity against cell wall glucans.

D. Cellulolytic Enzymes

This area is undoubtedly the most active field of research within the microbial enzymes. The commercial application of cellulase is still insignificant, and it is difficult to see at the moment whether a traditional cellulase preparation will become economical for the use in cellulose hydrolysis. It is perhaps more likely that the cellulase will have to be formed in situ by organisms growing on the cellulose or by direct utilization of the fermentation broth in a process like the one developed by the Natick group (80).

Much progress has been made in both cellulase production, chemistry, and application as can be seen in the extensive reviews prepared by Ghose (81) and by Enari and Markkanen (82). "Proceedings of the Symposium of Bioconversion of Cellulose Substances into Energy Chemicals and Microbial Protein" summarizes all aspects of cellulase production and application (83). Reese has written an excellent article on "Degradation of Polymeric Carbohydrates by Microbial Enzymes" in which he gives a survey of hydrolytic enzymes acting on cellulose, starch, and pectin, and draws parallels between the different enzymes and processes (84).

A theoretical model for the cellulose hydrolysis has been made, including equations for endoglucanase, exoglucanase, cellobiohydrolase, and cellobiase. The model is applicable only to soluble cellulose derivatives (85).

Trichoderma is still the most important source of cellulase and the most popular organism for research. The species *Trichoderma viride* has been renamed *Trichoderma reesei* in honor of the work of Dr. E. T. Reese (86). This new nomenclature will be used here.

Since economy is the greatest barrier to industrial utilization of cellulase, mutants with improved yield are of importance. By using an agar plate technique with acid swollen cellulose, it has been possible to find a mutant of *T. reesei* QM 9414 which gives a five-fold increase in filter paper activity. The mutant is furthermore highly independent of catabolite repression. Because the ratio between cellulolytic enzymes is different in the two strains, a differential control of each enzyme in the cellulose complex is implied (87).

The growth of *T. reesei* was studied in continuous culture on a cellulose, salts medium. Data on the growth kinetics were obtained at three levels of pH, and it was found that a linear relationship exists between minimum specific growth rate μm, endogenous metabolism coefficient K, Michaelis Menten coefficient K_S and the hydrogen ion concentration (88).

Sophorose is known as an inducer for cellulase in *Trichoderma*, but sophorose added to the growth medium is rapidly hydrolyzed to glucose and metabolized. Thus, the inhibitory action of large concentrations of sophorose may be explained as catabolite repression (89).

Several groups are studying the molecular basis of the individual pure cellulases. Gum and Brown purified *T. Reesei* cellobiohydrolase which forms a large part of the extracellular protein of the organism. The amino acid and carbohydrate composition of the molecule was determined. One molecule of enzyme contains the following moles of carbohydrate: glucosamin 3.4, mannose 26.4, glucose 4.8, and galactose 2.4, Mw 48,400. The carbohydrates were found in short chains; a detailed structure was suggested. It is assumed that the carbohydrate composition of the molecule depends on the strain and on growth conditions (90).

A purified endo-cellulase component was treated with *T. reesei* protease and it was found that a number of components could be separated chromatographically from the reaction mixture. Some of the components could be identified with components found in the natural enzyme preparation; it is therefore concluded that some of these components are degradation products formed by proteolysis during the growth of the organism (91).

Cellobiose is a major product of the cellulose hydrolysis by *T. reesei* preparations. In most applications one wishes to hydrolyze this cellobiose, both because it inhibits the cellulase reaction and because glucose is the desired end product.

Gong et al. (92) isolated cellobiase from a commercial *T. reesei* cellulase preparation. Three distinct components could be separated by DEAE chromatography. The components have similar catalytic properties and it is assumed that they are formed from

one component by proteolytic action, Mw is about 76,000. An
equation was made for the hydrolysis reaction, describing the
process over an eight-fold range of substrate concentration and
conversions of up to 90%. Product inhibition is significant; Ki
for glucose is 1-4 mM. Substrate inhibition has previously been
reported, but is of less significance; Ki for cellobiose is about
30.

     In apparent disagreement with this, Maguire found in a similar
study that glucose stimulates the hydrolysis up to initial concentrations of 90 mM (93).

     Since *T. reesei* is a relatively poor producer of cellobiase,
other sources of this enzyme have been sought (94). More than 200
strains of fungi and bacteria were tested for cellobiase activity.
Two *Aspergillus* strains were superior, *A. phoenicis* QM 329 and *A.
niger* QM 877. It was also found that most commercial enzymes prepared from *A. niger* had cellobiase activity.

     The enzyme production in submerged culture was induced by
betaglucosides such as methyl-β-glucoside and the enzyme production could be doubled by the addition of surfactant. The cellobiase from *A. phoenicis* was purified, Km 0.75 mM for cellobiose,
pH opt. 4.3, the enzyme is rapidly inactivated at 70°C, and it is
inhibited at cellobiose concentrations above 10 mM. When the cellobiase was mixed with *T. reesei* cellulase, the rate of hydrolysis
could be doubled.

     The cellulase system of *Fusarium solani* has also been exten-
sively studied. Wood (95) has purified the C_1 component of this
cellulase, and he has found that it is a cellobiohydrolase. He
has furthermore been able to reestablish the hydrolysis rate on
cellulose of the crude preparation by combining this enzyme with
endocellulase.

     Cellulase formation has been studied more or less extensively
in a large number of fungi and bacteria. In most cases the work
has been concentrated on the optimization of growth conditions
and preliminary studies on purified cellulase components. The
species reported as cellulase producers since 1976 are listed
below. Fungi: *Aspergillus clavatus* (96), *A. flavus* (97), *A.
niger* (98), *A. sydowi* (99), *A. tamarii* (100), *Botryodiplodia
theobromae* (101), *Ceratocystis paradoxa* (102), *Chaetomium cellu-
lolyticum* (103), *Fusarium avenaceium* (104), *F. solani* (95),
Fusarium sp. (105), *Irpex lacteus* (106), *Mucor racemosus* (107),
Neurospora crassa (108), *Pellicularia filamentosa* (109), *Penicillium citrinum* (110), *Poria placenta* (111), *Poronia oedipus* (112),
Schizophyllum commune (113), *Trichoderma koningii* (114), *T. pseu-
dokoningii* (114), *T. lignorum* (115). Yeast: *Trichosporon cuta-
neum, Trichosporon pullulans* (116). *Streptomyces: Streptomyces
cellulochryseos* (117). *Bacteria: Aeromonas sp.* (118), *Cellulo-
monas sp.* (119), *Clostridium thermocellum* (120), *Cytophaga sp.*
(121).

     When enzymatic hydrolysis of wood is attempted, the lignin
and hemicellulose components must also be taken into account.
In a study of the relationships between hemicellulose and

cellulose (122), wood chips were delignified with sodium hypo-
chlorite and were treated by xylanase, mannanase and cellulase
purified from commercial enzyme preparations. The enzymes were
applied alone and in combination and the hydrolysis was followed
by column chromatography of the soluble products and the degraded
holocellulose was studied by electron microscopy. It was found
that in the holocellulose xylan can be selectively hydrolyzed by
xylanase, whereas mannan cannot be decomposed by mannanase and
cellulose is only attacked after the xylan has been at least
partly removed. This supports the idea of xylan being deposited
between the cellulose fibrils or even encrusting them.

E. Lactases

     Lactase is now beginning to be commercially accepted as a
means of improving the quality of milk products and for better
utilization of whey. Holsinger and Woychik have reviewed the
applications (123,124). The higher sweetness of lactose hydrolyzed milk, corresponding to 0.9% added sucrose, does not make it
unacceptable to consumers, and it is an advantage in a number of
applications such as cultured milk products and ice cream. The
use of whey and its fractions in food has been studied extensively. Lactose hydrolyzed whey can be used for soft drinks or alcoholic drinks prepared by fermentation with *Kluyveromyces fragilis*.
Lactose hydrolyzed whey permeate has been used in the manufacture
of fruit soft drinks or as an ingredient in frozen desserts, ice
cream or confectionary.
     When milk powder is prepared from lactose hydrolyzed milk, it
is important to maintain a low humidity in the powder in order to
avoid nonenzymatic browning. This milk powder shows a lower water
resorption than normal milk powder at low water activities, but
twice as high a water resorption at high water activities (125).
     Hourigan (126) has studied the kinetics of lactose hydrolysis
in reconstituted skim milk with lactase from *Saccharomyces lactis*
and *Aspergillus niger*. For the *A. niger* lactase at 50°C, apparent
K_i for galactose was 2.44 mM and Km 32.9 mM. For the *S. lactis*
lactase at 35°C, apparent K_i was 8.55 mM and Km 63.7 mM. This
shows the severe competitive product inhibition which becomes a
problem if extensive lactose hydrolysis is desired with these two
enzymes.
     A new lactase has been found in *Arthrobacter simplex* (127).
It has the properties: Mw 500,000, pH opt. 6.3-6.4, Km 10.5 mM,
for lactose, the enzyme is inactive in the absence of monovalent
cations, it is a tetramer and it is inhibited by SH-reagents and
by EDTA.

F. Pectinases

The practical applications of pectinases have been reviewed
by Dürr and Schobinger (128). An interesting newer application
of pectinases is in the preparation of liquid fruit in which a
complete solubilization of the raw material is obtained by a combination of mechanical treatment and enzymatic action. In this
operation both pectinase and cellulase are necessary, but a
degradation of the highly esterified pectin should be avoided.

The use of pectinase in the manufacture of wine offers a number of advantages (129-131), yield improvement, increased color
intensity, and several technological advantages. The treatment
has to be well balanced to avoid reduction in the organoleptic
quality. In some instances it has been found that the aroma of
the wine was improved.

Pectic enzymes are often found in plant pathogenic fungi. An
endopolygalacturonase was purified from *Rhizoctonia fragaria*
which is pathogenic to strawberries. Two isoenzymes could be
separated; the enzymes were glucoproteins, Mw 36,000, pI 6.8 and
7. The properties were similar to other fungal polygalacturoni-
dases (132).

IV. OTHER ENZYMES

A. Lipases

There is a growing interest for microbial lipases in a number
of old and new applications. Lipase containing detergents have
been known since the introduction of enzyme detergents in 1914,
but the performance has not been satisfactory due to low activity
of the lipase. There is a renewed interest in lipase containing
detergents because with the usual laundering process fat stains
are difficult to remove from some fabrics, such as hollow fiber
polyester. Improved presoak preparations have been developed,
and a satisfactory result is obtained by using lipase in combination with synthetic activators such as naphthalene sulfonates
(133).

In some types of cheese, lipolysis is important to the development of the right flavor. In mold ripened cheese, such as the
blue cheese types, the lipase is derived from the fungus. In
other types of cheese, the lipase is traditionally obtained by
coagulating the milk with whole stomachs which also contain some
lipase. This technique is especially used in Italian cheese such
as Fontina and Romano cheese.

A satisfactory lipase action can be obtained with an esterase
from *Mucor miehei*, the fungus used in the production of microbial
rennet. The lipase is prepared free of rennet by filtering the
mycelium at pH 5 and is recovered from the filter cake by adjusting the pH to 10.5. The enzyme is most active on short-chain

triglycerides at pH 5, but it will hydrolyze a number of fats and oils at pH 8. There is no indication of position specificity (134). A review on the use of lipase in the dairy industry has been prepared by Arnold et al (135).

Lipase may also be used to improve the flavor of animal food (pet food) which normally contains up to 16% fat. A process has been developed in which the fat is emulsified with a proteinaceous emulsifier and then treated with lipase and protease (136).

An interesting potential application of lipase is in the synthesis of glycerides, especially cocoa butter which is a triglyceride of stearic, oleic and palmitic acids. As a basis for such synthetic reactions the specificity of pure lipases from *Aspergillus niger, Rhizopus delemar, Geotrichum candidum,* and *Penicillium cyclopium* was studied with triolein and cocoa butter as substrates (137). It was shown that the lipase from *A. niger* and *R. delemar* has a specificity similar to that of pancreas lipase and that they do not attack the 2-position, whereas they show low specificity towards the fatty acid. *G. candidum* and *P. cyclopium* will attack all positions, but the former enzyme showed a preference for oleic and palmitic acids. This is in disagreement with other observations that *G. candidum* lipase preferentially liberates unsaturated fatty acids.

Glyceride synthesis by the four lipases described above was investigated (138) in a reaction mixture containing 80% glycerol and 2% acid; the reaction lasted 16h at 30°C. The lipases from *A. niger* and *R. delemar* synthesized glycerides with a wide range of acids, not only fatty acids, but the acids never entered the 2-position. The highest degree of synthesis (about 70%) was obtained with oleic acid. The lipases from *G. candidum* and *P. cyclopium* only reacted with long-chain fatty acids; these were attached in all positions.

The specificity of *G. candidum* lipase has been studied in more detail by Jensen (139). The enzyme is specific for the acyl group and will hydrolyze glycerides with fatty acids containing cis-9 and cis-9,12 unsaturation. Trans-isomers will as a rule not be hydrolyzed, and it is suggested that the enzyme is used to obtain fractions enriched in these acids from partially hydrogenated food fats.

Phycomyces nitens forms a lipase which is activated by bile salts. Properties: Mw 26,500, pI 5.9, four half cystin groups in the molecule, no carbohydrate or lipid, pH optimum 6-7, rapid inactivation above 40°C. The hydrolysis of triolein is interesting in that diglycerides, but no monoglycerides, accumulate in the reaction mixture. Triolein is hydrolyzed completely which indicates that the enzyme is not position specific (140).

The lipase from *Pseudomonas fluorescens* has been purified and crystallized. The molecule does not contain carbohydrate or lipid; the amino acid composition shows that only one half cystin group is present. The properties are: Mw 33,000, pI 4.5, pH

optimum 7.0, and the enzyme is rapidly inactivated at 70°C. Triglycerides are hydrolyzed completely, the preferred substrate is
tricaproylglycerol, but there is also good activity against tri-
palmitylglycerol (141,142).

Chromobacterium viscosum forms two lipases A and B (143).
The properties are: A: Mw 120,000, pI 4.7, carbohydrate content
14%, no lipid, one half cystin; B: Mw 27,000, pI 6.9, no carbohydrate or lipid. The amino acid composition of both enzymes was
determined and a low content of hydrophobic amino acids was found
contrary to expectations. The lipases were efficiently purified
by adsorption on silicone covered glass beads followed by desorption with nonionic detergent (144).

In a screening program for alkaline lipase, it was observed
that this enzyme was formed by several bacteria, but never by
fungi or yeasts (145). Lipase with optimum pH at 9.5 was found
in two *Pseudomonas* strains. The enzymes were precipitated at pH
4. The *Ps. fragi* lipase had extremely good heat stability and
was active up to 80°C. Both enzymes were cell-bound and were
released by raising the pH to 10; they were inhibited by anionic
detergents and by bile acid.

B. *Ligninase*

Lignin is a complex compound; its degradation requires a mul-
tienzyme system involving oxidizing enzymes. So far no enzyme
system has been isolated, which in vitro will effect a complete
lignin degradation. Several microorganisms are able to solubi-
lize lignin in vivo, but at a slow rate.

A process for biological production of cellulose pulp from
lignified cellulose has been developed (146). Strains of white
rot fungi such as *Peniophora cremea* are inoculated on wood chips
and incubated for a suitable time (about 60 days) at room temperature. Cellulase free mutants of other fungi such as *Sporotrichum pulverulentum* may also be used. Up to 50% of the lignin
could be removed with a cellulose loss of only 2%.

C. *Tannase*

Tannase is an acylhydrolase which will hydrolyze tannin to
gallic acid and carbohydrate. The enzyme is found in several
Aspergillus species (147). *Aspergillus niger* tannase is a glycoprotein with Mw 55,000 and 21% carbohydrate, primarily mannose.
The carbohydrate is probably linked to threonine and serine (148).

V.   RECOVERY PROCESSES

Industrial enzyme recovery is primarily based on methods generally used in the chemical and biochemical industry. Concentration by reverse osmosis or ultrafiltration and preparation of dust-free granules have been the main points of interest during the last few years. Most of the literature on these subjects is not directed towards the enzyme industry and will not be reported here.

A number of processes for production of dust-free enzyme granulates have been published. A typical method (149) consists in mixing enzyme concentrate with a melted nonionic detergent and spraying this into cool air in a cooling tower where the droplets will solidify and form granules.

In a new method (150) for making dust-free, abrasion-resistant granules, the enzyme powder is mixed with a waxy material and cellulose fibers and is granulated in a drum granulator or a similar mechanical granulator. The cellulose fibers cause the granulation process to run smoothly and make the granules resistant to mechanical damage.

In the preparation of intracellular enzymes there are two main problems, breaking the cell wall without damaging the enzyme and separation of the desired enzyme from the other components of the cell.

An extensive review on methods for disruption of microorganisms has been prepared by Coakley, Bater and Lloyd (151); theory and laboratory methods are discussed, but not industrial-scale operations.

Nucleic acid is one of the major problems in the purification of intracellular enzymes, and many methods have been designed for their removal. A new cationic polymer of polyacrylate type carrying a positively charged nitrogen-containing group has been found to selectively precipitate nucleic acids (152).

VI.   TOXICOLOGY

In 1969 some examples of respiratory illness were reported in a factory making enzyme detergents. The reactions were supposedly caused by enzyme allergy due to high levels of enzyme dust in the factory. When this was known, precautions were immediately taken to reduce the dust level by using a liquid slurry of enzyme instead of a powder and by introducing improved dust control, improved ventilation, protective clothing, etc. As a result, detectable respiratory illness has been eliminated. An extensive medical control program of the workers involved in this production was also started and a report on this work has been published (153). The program comprised a medical examination, chest X-ray,

spirometry, skin test, serological tests, and lung function
studies. Furthermore, the dust level and the enzyme content of
the dust were monitored at strategic places in the factory.

It was shown that atopics, i.e. persons with a previous history of allergy, were more likely than normal workers to become
positive to the skin test. Consequently such people were not employed in the factory. A positive skin test is a good indication
of exposure to enzyme dust, but as a rule workers with a positive
skin test had no clinical symptoms, no detectable change in lung
function, and no reaction to working conditions. A positive skin
test is therefore no contraindication to working with these products. In the serological studies, it was interestingly found
that a group of stable boys tested as a control had a higher level
of haemagglutinating antibodies specific to the detergent enzyme
than the factory workers, presumably because they had an occupa-
tional exposure to *B. subtilis*.

VII.   REVIEW ARTICLES AND BOOKS

A.   *Bacillus Enzymes*

Priest has written an extensive review on extracellular enzyme synthesis in the *Genus Bacillus*. All extracellular enzymes
from *Bacillus sp.* are listed and the physiological function,
regulation of synthesis, genetic analysis, and method of secretion are well covered. The review is concentrated more on the
basic information than on the industrial aspects of enzyme synthesis (154).

B.   *Aspergillus Enzymes*

In a symposium devoted to the *Genus Aspergillus,* Cohen reviews the proteases, and Barbesgaard describes industrial enzymes
(155).

C.   *Enzyme Production and Technology*

"Topics in Enzyme and Fermentation Biotechnology," Vol. 1,
edited by Wiseman, has chapters on fermentation technology related
to enzyme manufacture, Penicillin transforming enzymes, and glucose isomerase (156).

"Biotechnological Applications of Proteins and Enzymes,"
edited by Borak and Sharon, has several chapters on production
and application of enzymes (157).

"Industrial Enzymes," edited by Johnson, reviews enzyme technology in U.S. patents in the period 1970-76 (158).

REFERENCES

1. Aunstrup, K., *in* "Biotechnology and Fungal Differentiation" (J. Meyrath and J. D. Bu'Lock, eds.). Academic Press, New York (1977).
2. Vitkovic, L. and Sadoff, H. L., *J. Bact. 131*, 891 (1977).
3. Yoshida, K., Hidaka, H., Miyado, S., Shibata, U., Saito, K., and Yamada, Y., *Agr. Biol. Chem. 41*, 745 (1977).
4. Holmquist, B., *Biochemistry 16*, 4591 (1977).
5. Barach, J. T. and Adams, D. M., *Biochim. Biophys. Acta 485*, 417 (1977).
6. Sidler, W. and Zuber, H., *Eur. J. appl. Microbiol. 4*, 255 (1977).
7. Cheng, Y. E. and Aronson, A. I., *Arch. Microbiol. 115*, 61 (1977).
8. Lecadet, M. M., Lescourret, M. and Klier, A., *Eur. J. Bio-Chem. 79*, 329 (1977).
9. Setlow, P., *J. Biol. Chem. 251*, 7853 (1976).
10. Millet, J., *FEBS Letters 74*, 59 (1977).
11. Aiyappa, P. S., Traficante, L. J., and Lampen, J. O., *J. Bact. 129*, 191 (1977).
12. Aiyappa, P. S. and Lampen, J. O., *J. Biol. Chem. 252*, 1745 (1977).
13. Tsujita, Y. and Endo, A., *J. Bact. 130*, 48 (1977).
14. Tsujita, Y. and Endo, A., *J. Biochem. 81*, 1063 (1977).
15. Tsujita, Y. and Endo, A., *Biochem. Biophys. Res. Comm. 74*, 242 (1977).
16. Nakadai, T. and Nasuno, S., *Agr. Biol. Chem. 41*, 409 (1977).
17. Nakadai, T. and Nasuno, S., *J. Ferment. Technol. 55*, 273 (1977).
18. Nakadai, T. and Nasuno, S., *Agr. Biol. Chem. 41*, 1657 (1977).
19. Tanaka, N., Takeuchi, M., and Ichishima, E., *Biochim. Biophys. Acta 485*, 406 (1977).
20. Subramanian, E., Swan, I. D. A., Liu, M., Davies, D. R., Jenkins, J. A., Tickle, I. J., and Blundell, T. L., *Proc. Natl. Acad. Sci. USA 74*, 556 (1977).
21. Gripon, J-C., Rhee, S. H., and Hofmann, T., *Can. J. Biochem. 55*, 504 (1977).
22. James, M. N. G., Hsu, I-N., and Delbaere, T. J., *Nature 267*, 808 (1977).
23. Fruton, J. S., *Adv. Enzymol. 44*, 1 (1976).
24. Lenoir, L. and Auberger, B., *Le Lait 57*, 471 (1977).
25. Satoh, T., Beppu, T., and Arima, K., *Agr. Biol. Chem. 41*, 293 (1977).
26. Beuchat, L. R. and Basha, S. M. M., *Eur. J. Appl. Microbiol. 2*, 195 (1976).
27. Cohen, B. L. and Drucker, H., *Arch. Biochem. Biophys. 182*, 601 (1977).
28. Gripon, J-C., *Ann. Biol. anim. Bioch. Biophys. 17*, 283 (1977).

29. Abdelal, A. T. H., Kennedy, E. H., and Ahearn, D. G., *J. Bact. 130*, 1125 (1977).

30. Ogrydziak, D. M., Demain, A. L., and Tannenbaum, S. R., *Biochim. Biophys. Acta 497*, 525 (1977).

31. Sternberg, M., *Appl. Microbiology 20*, 135 (1976).

32. Pozsar-Hajnal, K., *Anal. Chem. 279*, 118 (1976).

33. Gripon, J-C., Desmazeaud, M. J., LeBars, D., and Bergerc, J-L., *J. Dairy Sc. 60*, 1532 (1977).

34. Rupnow, J. H., *Diss. Abstr. 37*, 3784 (1977).

35. Casey, J. P., *Die Stärke 29*, 196 (1977).

36. Seidman, M. *in* "Developments in Food Carbohydrate 1" (G. Birch and R. S. Shallonberger, eds.). Applied Science Publishers, London (1977).

37. Banks, W., *Carbohydrate Res. 57*, 301 (1977).

38. Fujimori, H., Ohnishi, M., Sakoda, M., Matsuno, R., and Hiromi, K., *J. Biochem. 82*, 417 (1977).

39. McWethy, S. J. and Hartman, P. A., *J. Bact. 129*, 1537 (1977).

40. Glymph, J. L. and Stutzenberger, F. J., *Appl. Env. Microbiol. 34*, 391 (1977).

41. Cho, Y. K. and Biley, J. E., *Enzyme Technology Digest 5*, 141 (1976).

42. Jolley, M. E. and Gray, C. J., *Carbohydrate Res. 49*, 361 (1976).

43. Moriyama, S., Matsuno, R., and Kamikuro, T., *Agr. Biol. Chem. 41*, 1985 (1976).

44. Watanabe, K., *J. Biochem. 80*, 379 (1976).

45. Pazur, J. H., Cepure, A., Okada, S., and Forsberg, L. S., *Carbohydrate Res. 58*, 193 (1977).

46. Smith, J. S. and Lineback, D. R., *Die Stärke 28*, 243 (1976).

47. Miah, M. N. N., Ueda, S., and Fukuoda, *Die Stärke 29*, 235 (1977).

48. Yamasaki, Y., Suzuki, Y., and Ozawa, J., *Agr. Biol. Chem. 41*, 755 (1977).

49. Iijuka, H. and Mineki, S., *J. Gen. Appl. Microbiol. 23*, 217 (1977).

50. Yuki, A., Watanabe, T., and Matsuda, K., *Die Stärke 29*, 265 (1977).

51. Mangallam, S., Subrahmangam, A., and Gobalkrishnan, K. S., *Current Science 46*, 16 (1977).

52. Urlaub, H. and Wöber, G., *Biochim. Biophys. Acta 522*, 161 (1978).

53. Suzuki, Y., Yuki, T., Kishigami, T., and Abe, S., *Biochim. Biophys. Acta 445*, 386 (1976).

54. Suzuki, Y., Tsuji, T., and Abe, S., *Appl. Env. Microbiol. 32*, 747 (1976).

55. Yamasaki, Y., Suzuki, Y., and Ozawa, J., *Agr. Biol. Chem. 41*, 1559 (1977).

56. Sorrentino, A. P., Zorzopulos, J., and Terenzi, H. F., *Arch. Biochem. Biophys. 180*, 232 (1977).

57. Napier, E. J., U.S. Patent 4,011,136 (1977).

58. Yamane, T. and Tsukano, M., *J. Ferment. Technol. 55*, 233 (1977).
59. Takasaki, Y. and Takahara, Y., U.S. Patent 3,992,261 (1976).
60. Takasaki, Y., *Agr. Biol. Chem. 40*, 1515 (1976).
61. Takasaki, Y., *Agr. Biol. Chem. 40*, 1523 (1976).
62. Horwarth, R. O., Lally, J. A., and Rotheim, P., U.S. Patent 4,011,139 (1977).
63. Brandt, C. J., Catley, B. J., and Awod, W. M., *J. Bact. 125*, 501 (1976).
64. Enevoldsen, B. S., Reimann, L., and Hansen, N. L., *FEBS Letters 79*, 121 (1977).
65. Harada, T., *Mem. Inst. Sci. Ind. Res. Osaka Univ. 34*, 49 (1977).
66. Inkerman, P. A. and Riddell, L., *Proc. Queensl. Soc. Sugar Cane Technol. 44*, 215 (1977).
67. Budtz Joergensen, E. and Kelstrup, J., *Acand. J. Dent. Res. 85*, 209 (1977).
68. Imai, K., Kobayashi, M., and Matsuda, K., *Agr. Biol. Chem. 41*, 1889 (1977).
69. Oi, S., Matsui, Y., Iizuka, M., and Yamamoto, T., *J. Ferment. Technol. 55*, 114 (1977).
70. Gorbacheva, I. V. and Rodionova, N. A., *Biochem. Biophys. Acta 484*, 79 (1977).
71. Baker, C. J., Whalen, C. H., and Bateman, D. F., *Phytopathology 67*, 1250 (1977).
72. Kanda, T., Wakabayashi, K., and Nishizawa, K., *J. Biochem. 79*, 989 (1976).
73. Sinner, M. and Dietrichs, H. H., *Holzforschung 30*, 50 (1976).
74. Matsuo, M., Yasui, T., and Kobayashi, T., *Agr. Biol. Chem. 41*, 1601 (1977).
75. Yamazaki, N., Sinner, M., and Dietrichs, H. H., *Holzforschung 30*, 101 (1976).
76. Zouchova, Z., Kocourek, J., and Musilek, V., *Folia Microbiol. 22*, 98 (1977).
77. Notario, V., Villa, T. G., and Villanueva, J. R., *Biochem. J. 159*, 555 (1976).
78. Nagasaki, S., Saito, K., and Yamamoto, S., *Agr. Biol. Chem. 41*, 493 (1977).
79. Lachance, M-A., Villa, T. G., and Phaff, H. J., *Can. J. Biochem. 55*, 1001 (1977).
80. Spano, L. A., Medeiros, J., and Mandels, M., *Resource Recovery and Conservation 1*, 279 (1976).
81. Ghose, T. K., *Adv. Biochem. Eng. 6*, 39 (1977).
82. Enari, T-M. and Markkanen, P., *Adv. Biochem. Eng. 5*, 3 (1977).
83. "Bioconversion of Cellulosic Substances into Energy, Chemicals and Microbial Protein" (T. K. Ghose, ed.). Proc. Symp. New Delhi, Febr. 1977. IIT New Delhi.
84. Reese, E. T., *Rec. Adv. Phytochem. 11*, 311 (1977).
85. Lee, S. E., Armiger, W. B., Watteeuw, C. M., and Humphrey, A. E., *Biotech. Bioeng. 20*, 141 (1978).

86. Simmons, E. G., Second Int. Mycological Congr., Tampa, FL, p. 618 (1977).

87. Montenecourt, B. S. and Eveleigh, D. E., *Appl. Env. Microbiol. 34*, 777 (1977).

88. Brown, D. E. and Zainudeen, M. A., *Biotech. Bioeng. 19*, 941 (1977).

89. Loewenbuerg, J. R. and Chapman, C. M., *Arch. Microbiol. 113*, 61 (1977).

90. Gum, E. K. and Brown, R. D., *Biochim. Biophys. Acta 446*, 371 (1976).

91. Nakayami, M., Tomita, Y., Suzuki, H., and Nisiwawa, K., *J. Biochem. 79*, 955 (1976).

92. Gong, C-S., Ladisch, M. R., and Tsao, G. T., *Biotech. Bioeng. 19*, 959 (1977).

93. Maguire, R. J., *Can. J. Biochem. 55*, 19 (1977).

94. Sternberg, D., Vijayakumar, P., and Reese, E. T., *Can. J. Microbiol. 23*, 139 (1977).

95. Wood, T. M. and McCrae, S. I., *Carbohydrate Res. 57*, 117 (1977).

96. Olutiola, P. O., *J. Gen. Microbiol. 102*, 27 (1977).

97. Olutiola, O. P., *Trans. Br. Mycol. Soc. 67*, 265 (1976).

98. Hurst, P. L., Nielsen, J., Sullivan, P. A., and Shepherd, M. G., *Biochem. J. 165*, 33 (1977).

99. Olutiola, P. O. and Cole, O. O., *Physiol. Plant. 39,* 243 (1977).

100. Olutiola, P. O. and Cole, O. O., *Physiol. Plant. 37,* 313 (1976).

101. Yamanaka, Y., *Diss. Abstr. 37*, 4581 (1977).

102. Olutiola, P. O., *Mycologia 68*, 1083 (1976).

103. Mooyong, M., Chahal, D. S., Swan, J. E., and Robinson, C. W., *Biotech. Bioeng. 19*, 527 (1977).

104. Forbes, R. S. and Dickinson, C. H., *Trans. Br. Mycol. Soc. 68*, 229 (1977).

105. Targonski, Z. and Szajer, C., *Acta Microbiol. Pol. 26*, 273 (1977).

106. Kanda, T., Wakabayashi, K., and Nisizawa, K., *J. Biochem. 79*, 977 (1976).

107. Borgio, P. and Sypherd, P. S., *J. Bact. 130*, 812 (1977).

108. Eberhart, B. M., Beck, R. S., and Goolsby, K. M., *J. Bact. 130*, 181 (1977).

109. Mizukoshi, S., Sugi, H., Mori, H., and Ichikushi, M., *J. Ferment. Technol. 55*, 548 (1977).

110. Olutiola, P. O., *Can. J. Microbiol. 22*, 1153 (1976).

111. Highley, T. L., *Material und Organismen 12*, 161 (1977).

112. Denison, D. A. and Koehn, R. D., *Mycologia 69*, 592 (1977).

113. Paice, M. G. and Jurasek, L., *Tappi for biol. wood chem.* 113 (1977).

114. Fanelli, C. and Cervone, F., *Trans. Br. Mycol. Soc. 68*, 291 (1977).

115. Lobanok, A. G., Zinchenko, O. N., Romanov, S. L., Smetanin, V. V., and Bogomazova, L. T., *Microbiologiya 45*, 620 (1976).

116. Stevens, B. J. H. and Payne, J., *J. Gen. Microbiol. 110*, 381 (1977).
117. Fujii, M. and Sakata, J., *Tappi for biol. wood chem.* 107 (1977).
118. Ohya, T., Yokoi, N., and Mase, T., U.S. Patent 3,983,002 (1976).
119. Beguin, P., Eisen, H., and Roupas, A., *J. Gen. Microbiol. 101*, 191 (1977).
120. Ng, T. K., Weimer, P. J., and Zeikus, J. G., *Arch. Microbiol. 114*, 1 (1977).
121. Tien Hung Chan, W. and Thayer, D. W., *Can. J. Microbiol. 23*, 1285 (1977).
122. Sinner, M., Parameswaran, N., Yamazaki, N., Liese, W., and Dietrichs, H. H., *Applied Polymer Symposium 28*, 993 (1976).
123. Holsinger, V. H., *Food Technology March*, 35 (1978).
124. Woychik, J. H. and Holsinger, V. H., *in* "Enzymes in Food and Beverage Processing" (R. L. Ory and A. J. St. Angelo, eds.), *ACS Symp. Ser. 47*, 67. ACS. Washington (1977).
125. San Jose, C., Asp, N-G., Burvall, A., and Dahlqvist, A., *J. Dairy Sci. 60*, 1539 (1977).
126. Hourigan, J. A., *Diss. Abstr. 37*, 6043 (1977).
127. Donelly, W. J., Fhaolain, I. N., and Patching, J. W., *Int. J. Biochem. 8*, 101 (1977).
128. Dürr, P. and Schobinger, U., *Alimenta 15*, 143 (1976).
129. Montedoro, G. and Bertuccioli, M., *Lebensm.-Wiss.u.-Technol. 9*, 225 (1976).
130. Cordonnier, R. and Marteau, G., *Bull. de L'O.I.V. 49*, 490 (1976).
131. Ferenczi, S. and Asvany, A., *Bull. de L'O.I.V. 5*, 43 (1977).
132. Cervone, F., Scala, A., Foresti, M., Cacace, M. G., and Noviello, C., *Biochem. Biophys. Acta 482*, 379 (1977).
133. Stewart, R. L., McCune, H. W., and Diehl, F. L., U.S. Patent 3,950,277 (1976).
134. Moskowitz, G. J., Shen, T., West, I. R., Cossaigne, R., and Feldman, L. I., *J. Dairy Science 60*, 1260 (1977).
135. Arnold, R. G., Shakani, K. M., and Dwivedi, B. K., *J. Dairy Sc. 58*, 1127 (1975).
136. Haas, G. J. and Lugay, J. C., U.S. Patent 3,968,255 (1976).
137. Okumura, S., Iwai, M., and Tsujusaka, Y., *Agr. Biol. Chem. 40*, 655 (1976).
138. Tsujisaka, Y., Okumura, S., and Iwai, M., *Biochim. Biophys. Acta 489*, 415 (1977).
139. Jensen, R. G. and Pitas, R. E., *Lipids 1* (1976) (R. Paoletti, G. Procellati, and G. Jacine, eds.). Raven Press, New York.
140. Nakamura, J., Maejima, K., and Tomoda, K., *J. Takeda Res. Lab. 35*, 1 (1976).
141. Sugiura, M., Oikawa, T., Hirano, K., and Inukai, T., *Biochem. Biophys. Acta 488*, 353 (1977).
142. Sugiura, M. and Oikawa, T., *Biochim. Biophys. Acta 489*, 262 (1977).

143. Isobe, M. and Sugiura, M., *Chem. Pharm. Bull. 25*, 1980 (1977).
144. Isobe, M. and Sugiura, M., *Chem. Pharm. Bull. 25*, 1987 (1977).
145. Watanabe, N., Ota, Y., Minoda, Y., and Yamada, K., *Agr. Biol. Chem. 41*, 1353 (1977).
146. Eriksson, K-E., Ander, P., Henningsson, B., Nilsson, T., and Goodell, B., U.S. Patent 3,962,033 (1976).
147. Ganga, P. S., Nandy, S. C., and Santappa, M., *Leather Science 24*, 8 (1977).
148. Parthasarathy, N. and Bose, S. M., *Acta Biochim. Pol. 23*,

149. Win, M. H., Disalvo, W. A., and Kenney, E. J., U.S. Patent 4,016,040 (1977).
150. Markussen, E. K. and Smith, A. W., German Patent Appl. 2730 481 (1977).
151. Coakley, W. T., Bater, A. J., and Lloyd, D., *Adv. Microbial Physiol. 16*,
152. Snoke, R. E. and Klein, G. W., U.S. Patent 4,055,469 (1977).
153. Juniper, C. P., How, M-J., Goodwin, B. F. J., and Kinshot, A. K., *J. Soc. Occup. Med. 27*, 3 (1977).
154. Priest, F. G., *Bact. Rev. 41*, 711 (1977).
155. "Genetics and Physiology of *Aspergillus*" (J. E. Smith and J. A. Pateman, eds.). Academic Press, New York (1977).
156. "Topics in Enzyme and Fermentation Biotechnology" (A. Wiseman, ed.), Vol. 1. Ellis Horwood, Chichester (1977).
157. "Biotechnological Applications of Proteins and Enzymes" (Z. Bohak and N. Sharon, eds.). Academic Press, New York (1977).
158. Johnson, J. C., "Industrial Enzymes Recent Advances." Noyes Data Corporation, Park Ridge, NJ (1977).

CHAPTER 7

AMINO ACIDS

Y. Hirose
K. Sano
H. Shibai

Central Research Laboratories
Ajinomoto Company, Inc.
Kawasaki, Japan

I.   INTRODUCTION

Many amino acids are currently produced in commercial quantities through fermentation processes. Some of these products are
eventually used as food and feed supplements, while others have a
therapeutic role in nutrition and medicine. The 1976 production
of amino acids in Japan was estimated at approximately 200,000
tons with a sales value of about $3000,000,000. In the same year,
production in other countries (the United States, France, Holland,
West Germany, Belgium, Italy, U.S.S.R., Korea, and Taiwan) totaled
about 100,000 tons. The Japanese amino acid production in 1976 is
listed in Table I, along with the routes for commercial production.
   Nearly all of the L-glutamic acid (manufactured as the monosodium salt) was used as a food seasoning, with minor amounts employed as raw material in a chemical process for the production of
a leather substitute. D,L-Methionine was the second most important of the amino acids produced and was used exclusively as a
nutritional supplement. The L-isomer produced by enzymatic resolution served as a therapeutic agent. The third most important
amino acid, L-lysine, produced as the monohydrochloride salt, was
used mainly as an animal feed additive with lesser amounts serving
medical purposes. Present in limited amounts in corn, rice, and
wheat, L-lysine has an important role in increasing the nutritional
value of these crops. L-Threonine and L-tryptophan are also nu-
tritionally important and may be produced in larger amounts when
production costs are reduced. Of the other amino acids listed in

TABLE I. Output of Amino Acids in Japan (1976)

Amino acid	Main route	Amount (tons/year)
L-Alanine	E, CE	10-50
DL-Alanine	C	150-200
L-Arginine	F	200-300
L-Aspartic acid	E	500-1,000
L-Aspargine	Ex	10-50
L-Citrulline	F	10-50
L-Cysteine	Ex	100-200
L-Cystine	Ex	100-200
L-DOPA	CE	80-200
Glycine	C	5,000-6,000
L-Glutamate (Na)	F	100,000
L-Histidine	F	100-200
L-Homoserine	F	10-50
L-Hydroxyproline	Ex	10-50
L-Glutamine	F	200-300
L-Isoleucine	F, Ex	10-50
L-Leucine	F, Ex	50-100
L-Lysine (HCl salt)	F	10,000
DL-Methionine	C	20,000
L-Methionine	CE	100-200
L-Ornithine	F	10-50
L-Phenylalanine	F, CE	50-100
L-Proline	F	10-50
L-Serine	I, CE	10-50
L-Threonine	F	50-100
L-Tryptophan	CE	20-50
DL-Tryptophan	C	20-40
L-Tyrosine	Ex	50-100
L-Valine	F	50-100

E, enzymatic synthesis; F, fermentative production; I,
microbial production from intermediate; C, chemical synthesis;
Ex, extraction from hydrolysate of protein; CE, chemical
synthesis and optical resolution.

Table I, L-alanine and glycine found use as flavor enhancers,
while L-cysteine was used as a quality-improving agent in bread
and as an antioxidant in fruit juices.

Almost all of the other amino acids mentioned in Table I were
produced for medicinal purposes. L-arginine, for example, alle-
viates hyperammonemia and liver disorders by stimulating arginase
activity in the liver. L-Cysteine treats bronchitis or nasal

catarrh and works with other amino acids in intravenous infusion
(especially while in post-operative surgery situations).   The
N-acyl derivatives of some amino acids aid in the preparation of
cosmetics, surface-active agents, fungicides, and pesticides.

The production of amino acids is now a large industry worldwide.   The field opened up with the discovery of monosodium L-
glutanate as the flavoring agent in konbu, a kelp-like seaweed
traditionally used as a seasoning in Japan (1).   In 1909, the
Ajinomoto Co. started the commercial production of monosodium L-
glutamate as a food seasoning from the acid-hydrolyzate of wheat
gluten or soybean protein.

The growth of the amino acid industry was accelerated by an
important development in the microbial production of L-glutamic
acid (2).   At present, most commercial amino acids result from the
microbial method.   Only L-cysteine and L-hydroxyproline are now
extracted from natural protein hydrolyzate, and two promising
microbial methods for L-cysteine production are now being
developed (3,4).   DL-Methionine, DL-alanine and glycine must still
depend on the chemical synthesis because of its strong economical
advantage.   When optical resolution is not necessary, the chemical
synthetic method of amino acids remains more economical.

In this review, we will describe the fermentation process for
amino acids, the characteristics of the microorganisms employed,
and the cultural conditions required.

For a more detailed background, there are excellent reviews of
the subject by Yamada, Kinoshita, Tsunoda, and Aida (5), Tsunoda
and Okumura (6), Kinoshita (7), Nakayama (8), and Yamada (9).

II.   DIRECT FERMENTATION METHOD

We can classify the production of amino acids by microorganisms
into three processes: (a) direct fermentation of amino acids from
carbon and nitrogen sources such as glucose and urea, (b) microbial
conversion of supplemented precursors to amino acids during cultivation, and (c) enzymatic conversion of economical substrates into
amino acids.

Direct fermentation may be divided into two subgroups according to the characteristics of the microorganisms employed: (a)
wild strains and (b) mutant strains, including both auxotrophic
and regulatory mutants.

We will describe representative cases in each group.

A.   Wild Strains

L-Glutamic acid is now produced exclusively by the fermentation of a wild strain of *Arthrobacter, Brevibacterium, Corynebacterium,* or *Microbacterium.*   Most of these L-glutamic acid-producing
bacteria are reported as gram positive, and nonmotile.   Most
importantly, they all required biotin for their growth.

Many investigations have clarified the role of biotin in the
L-glutamic acid production. The results are summarized as follows.
[1]   The greatest amount of L-glutamic acid accumulated in the
culture medium when the biotin concentration was suboptimal for
the maximum growth. More biotin supported abundant cell growth,
but seriously decreased the L-glutamic acid accumulation (10).
[2]   Even in the presence of excess biotin, the addition of
penicillin at the growth phase permitted the cells to accumulate
L-glutamic acid (11).
[3]   The addition of C_{16-18} saturated fatty acids or their
esters with hydrophilic polyalcohols also permitted the cells to
accumulate L-glutamic acid, even with excess biotin (12,13).
[4]   Oleic acid could replace biotin for their growth (14),
and, even with excess biotin, the oleic acid-requiring mutant
accumulated L-glutamic acid when cultured in an oleic acid-limited
medium (15).
[5]   The fact that cells grown with excess biotin could not
accumulate L-glutamic acid was due to the lack of permeability
rather than a lack of biosynthesizing activity (16). The L-
glutamic acid-producing cells, e.g. cells grown with limited biotin or treated with either penicillin or Tween 60, excreted intracellular L-glutamic acid when they were washed with a phosphate
buffer. Cells grown with excess biotin, however, did not. This
phenomenon was specific for L-glutamic acid and L-aspartic acid;
the other amino acids were washed from the cells even when grown
under biotin-rich conditions.
[6]   The critical biotin concentration for the accumulation of
L-glutamic acid was under 0.5 μg/g dry cells. With less biotin,
phospholipids in the cell membrane decreased remarkably. The same
evidence was reported in the case of L-glutamic acid accumulating,
oleic acid-requiring mutant and C_{16-18} saturated fatty acid-treated
cells. From these experiments, phospholipids such as cardiolipin,
phosphatidyl glycerol, and phosphatidyl inositol dimannoside appear
to be the key substances for the permeability of the cells to L-
glutamic acid (17).
[7]   The effect of penicillin on the permeability of the cells
to L-glutamic acid could not account for the decrease in the amount
of phospholipids. Under various concentrations of $NaNO_3$ in a medium for L-glutamic acid production under various osmotic pres-
sures, the amounts of L-glutamic acid accumulated by penicillin-
treated cells and polyoxyethylene monopalmitate-treated cells were
compared. L-glutamic acid accumulated by penicillin-treated cells
was inversely proportionate to the concentration of $NaNO_3$, while
the polyoxyethylene monopalmitate-treated cells remained unaffected
(18). In microscopic studies, cells excreting L-glutamic acid
which were treated with penicillin showed elongated or swollen
shapes suggesting imperfect cell wall synthesis. This evidence
leads to the conclusion that penicillin primarily attacks cell
wall synthesis, leaving cell membrane unprotected, and then proceeds to physically break down the permeability barrier.

Wild strains also accumulated L-valine, DL-alanine, D-alanine, L-alanine, L-glutamine, and N-acetyl-L-glutamine. *Paracolobacterium coliform* accumulated 15 g/l of L-valine from 100 g/l of glucose (19). Alanine was presumed to be initially synthesized in the cells as L-alanine and was later accumulated in the broth in racemic form after racemization by alanine racemase. It was produced by various strains, e.g. *Brevibacterium monoflagelum, Brevibacterium amylolyticum, Corynebacterium gelatinosum, Microbacterium album, Microbacterium ammoniaphilum,* and *Bacillus subtilis,* with yields of about 30-40% (5). In *Corynebacterium fascians,* D-alanine was accumulated in the medium (12 g/l) despite the existence of alanine racemase in the cells. The mechanism of D-alanine accumulation appears to be the result of a permeability barrier against L-alanine (20). On the other hand, L-alanine was accumulated by *Streptomyces aureofaciens* and *Streptomyces coelicolor* (16 g/l) (21). *Brevibacterium flavum* or *Corynebacterium glutamicum* produced L-Glutamine; the L-glutamic acid fermentation by the strains easily came to yield L-glutamine with a change in culture conditions. A high concentration of ammonium chloride, a weakly acidic pH, and the presence of zinc ions in the medium favored the L-glutamine production at the expense of L-glutamic acid accumulation (22). L-Glutamine was produced at the yield of 30% from some carbon sources (40 g/l). Recently, a potent L-glutamine producing mutant of *Brevibacterium flavum,* a sulfaguanidine-resistant strain, was bred. The yield was 39% and the amount was 39 g/l (23). N-acetyl-L-glutamic acid was a byproduct of the fermentation of L-glutamic acid or L-glutamine with sufficient aeration. The yield was 14% (5).

B. *Mutant Strains*

The small overproduction of amino acids by wild microorganisms in the culture media depends on a regulatory mechanism in the biosynthetic pathways, since almost all of them have no trouble producing the amino acids necessary for their own growth.

Two types of major regulation on amino acid biosynthesis are known: feedback inhibition and repression. Some other regulation mechanisms, attenuation (24) and catabolite repression (25), have been reported but clear evidence regarding amino acid fermentation is still lacking. The phenomenon of feedback inhibition was discovered in the L-tryptophan biosynthetic pathway in *Escherichia coli* (26). The molecular mechanism can be explained by allosteric protein theory (27), since the key enzyme of biosynthetic pathway, generally the first enzyme of the specific route, is an allosteric protein having a separate active site and regulatory site on its surface. The attachment of the inhibitor to the regulatory site makes some conformational change on the enzyme protein and affects the active site, causing a reversible inactivation of the enzyme. A decreased inhibitor concentration restores activity. This is the essence of the feedback inhibition mechanism.

Repression was first observed in the formation of aspartate-transcarbamylase (28). In this process, the end product controls the amount of enzymes in a biosynthetic pathway. The operon theory of Jacob and Monod (29) offers the following explanation of the repression mechanism. There are three types of genes: operator gene, structural gene, and regulator gene. If the active repressor attaches to the operator gene on the DNA, the transcription or transfer of the genetic code of the structural gene to the messenger RNA should be rejected. The active repressor is a complex of an apo-repressor, a protein coded in the regulatory gene, and a co-repressor, generally the end product of a biosynthetic pathway or its derivative. Thus, this regulation depends on both the concentration of end product as well as on the feedback inhibition mechanism. The existence of such regulation systems makes the wild microorganisms meager in amino acid production. For microorganisms to overproduce amino acids, then, these regulations must be subverted.

Auxotrophic mutants and regulatory mutants represent two means of artificially disorganizing such regulations. To produce some intermediate of amino acid biosynthesis, we can use the auxotroph whose pathway in the amino acid synthesis was blocked. The cultivation of this mutant with insufficient nutrient (end product) makes the cells free of feedback inhibition and/or repression, and the intermediate is thus overproduced. This approach is based on reports on auxotrophs of *Escherichia coli* (30,31). Its first application to amino acid overproduction was in L-ornithine, the fermentation of L-ornithine using citrulline auxotroph whose L-ornithine carbamyl-transferase had been genetically inactivated (32). When cultured with a low concentration of L-citrulline or L-arginine, the mutant accumulated much L-ornithine in the medium. In some special circumstances, the accumulated intermediate overflowed into the alternative biosynthetic pathway, with the auxotrophs overproducing some end products. The production of L-L-lysine by L-homoserine dehydrogenase blocked mutants of *Corynebacterium* (33) and *Brevibacterium* (34) has been achieved. In these bacteria, there was neither regulation on L-lysine specific biosynthetic pathway nor was there any lysine-degrading activity. In addition, neither mutant had a permeability barrier against L-lysine. In such a manner, auxotrophs can serve to obviate inhibition and/or repression, but almost all amino acids for protein synthesis cannot be overproduced by this method because they are themselves inhibitors and/or co-repressors. In cases where auxotrophs are not effective, we can use the second technique of artificial disorganization: regulatory mutants. The first evidence of disorganization was reported as analog resistant mutants (35). With its genetically inactivated regulatory site, the mutant may be desensitized from feedback inhibition and thus overproduce the end product. Derepressed mutants having genetically inactivated apo-repressor or operator functions can produce sizable quantities of end product. Regulatory mutants with genetically disordered regulation mechanisms presently produce many amino acids.

Most of the auxotrophs and regulatory mutants producing amino acids were derived from L-glutamic acid-producing bacteria, such as *Brevibacterium* or *Corynebacterium*, both because of the excellent assimilating activity of the carbon and nitrogen sources and because of the poor degrading activity of the amino acids produced.

1.   Auxotrophic Mutants.   L-Lysine production was the first case of the application of auxotrophs to the industrial production of amino acids.   The suboptimal concentration of the required nutrient for cell growth (either L-homoserine or L-methionine plus L-threonine) was necessary for the accumulation of L-lysine (Figure 1) (36).   The inhibitory effect of excess L-threonine on L-lysine production was the result of the feedback inhibition on aspartate kinase, a key enzyme for the synthesis of L-lysine, L-threonine, and L-methionine (Figure 2) (37).   The existence of 1 mM each of L-lysine and L-threonine inhibited aspartokinase activity at 94%; without L-threonine, it was 20% (37).   This is the main mechanism for the overproduction of L-lysine in the suboptimal condition of L-threonine (or L-homoserine) by homoserine auxotroph.   No other regulation on the L-lysine biosynthetic pathway of this strain has been observed (38).   In Table II are shown some auxotrophic strains feasible for commercial production.

Some amino acids are accumulated by a mutant having an auxotrophy apparently unrelated to the biosynthetic pathway of the accumulated amino acid, e.g. L-proline produced by isoleucine auxotroph.   In this case, the mechanism of overproduction is explained by the excess supply of ATP to the glutamate kinase, the key enzyme of L-proline biosynthesis.   The isoleucine auxotroph whose threonine dehydratase was inactive might have a high level of L-threonine which inhibited both aspartate kinase and homoserine kinase   resulting in the sparing of ATP (39).   Jensen referred to these regulatory interactions as "metabolic interlock" between small molecules and enzymes located in different, apparently remote, metabolic pathways (40).   The model for his paper was the activation of an enzyme of L-phenylalanine synthesis, prephenate dehydratase, by either L-leucine or L-methionine and the antagonistic effect of L-histidine on the inhibitory effect of 5-methyl-tryptophan.

2.   Regulatory Mutants.   A typical success in breeding of amino acid producers as regulatory mutants was the L-lysine producer of *Brevibacterium flavum* (41).   In *Brevibacterium flavum*, the L-lysine biosynthetic pathway was simply regulated at aspartate kinase by strong feedback inhibition depending on the concentration of both L-lysine and L-threonine (Figure 2).   Thus, if the regulatory site of aspartate kinase was inactivated, an overproduction of aspartate-β-phosphate could be expected.   Unlike L-lysine biosynthesis, L-threonine biosynthesis of this strain was known to have two other regulated reaction steps, homoserine

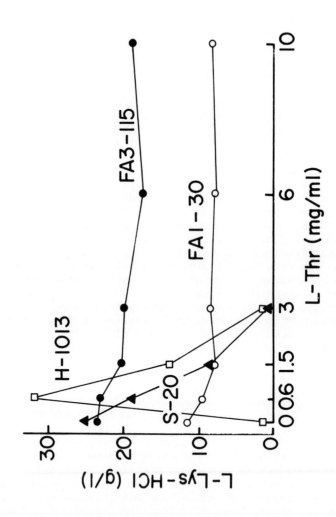

FIGURE 1. Effect of L-threonine on L-lysine production. The basal medium contained 100 g/L glucose and 2 g/L L-methionine. H-1013: homoserine auxotroph, S-20: threonine-, methionine-sensitive mutant, FA 1-30, FA 3-115: resistant mutants to 2-amino-ethyl-L-cysteine + L-threonine. All were derived from Brevibacterium flavum No. 2247.

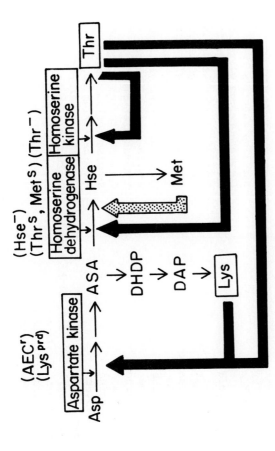

FIGURE 2. Regulation on lysine, threonine, and methionine biosynthesis in Brevibacterium flavum. → enzyme reaction, ➡ feedback inhibition, ⇨ repression.

TABLE II. Amino Acids Production by Auxotrophic Mutants

Amino acid	Requirement	Microorganism	Reference
L-Citrulline	arginine	Bacillus subtilis	(77)
		Corynebacterium glutamicum	(78)
L-Glutamic acid	oleic acid	Brevibacterium thiogenitalis	(15)
	glycerol	Corynebacterium alkanolyticum	(79)
L-Homoserine	threonine	Corynebacterium glutamicum	(80)
L-Leucine	phenylalanine	Corynebacterium glutamicum	(81)
	histidine		
L-Lysine	homoserine	Corynebacterium glutamicum	(33,82)
	threonine	Brevibacterium flavum	(36)
L-Ornithine	citrulline	Arthrobacter citreus	(32)
L-Phenylalanine	tyrosine	Corynebacterium glutamicum	(83)
L-Proline	isoleucine	Brevibacterium flavum	(84)
	histidine	Brevibacterium sp.	(85)
	serine	Kurthia catenoforma	(86)
L-Threonine	diaminopimelic acid, methionine	Escherichia coli	(87)
	methionine, valine	Escherichia coli	(88)
L-Tyrosine	phenylalanine, purine	Corynebacterium glutamicum	(89)
L-Valine	isoleucine or leucine	Corynebacterium glutamicum	(90)

dehydrogenase and homoserine kinase (38), so the overproduction of L-threonine could scarcely be expected by this aspartokinase mutant. In those circumstances, aspartate-β-phosphate or its derivative, L-lysine, for example, might be accumulated. In fact, L-lysine was exclusively accumulated in a biotin-rich medium.

The aspartate kinase desensitized mutant was expected to have the following specific characteristics:

(i) its growth might not be influenced by a lysine analog which inhibited the growth of wild strains by false-feedback inhibition on aspartate kinase;

(ii) it might accumulate a large amount of L-lysine in the minimal medium;

(iii) L-lysine producing activity of this mutant might not be restricted by exogenous L-threonine and L-lysine;

(iv) aspartate kinase activity of this mutant might not be inhibited by L-threonine and L-lysine.

Among these characteristics, (i) and (ii) were expected to be useful as screening markers of the mutant, and the breeding experiments depending on these expected characteristics were successfully performed. For characteristic (i), an analog of L-lysine, S-2-aminoethyl-L-cysteine (AEC), was employed and produced good results. This substance especially inhibited the growth of *Brevibacterium flavum* in the coexistence of L-threonine (Figure 3) (41), and this inhibition was eliminated by the supplement of a small amount of L-lysine. AEC might react as a false feedback inhibitor, so AEC-resistant mutants under the coexistence of threonine were isolated at the frequency of 5×10^{-2}, and 20% of them produced more than 4 g/L of L-lysine (as HCl salt). The wild parent strain produced 0.5 g/L. The highest amount of L-lysine produced in a commercial production medium with a carbon source of cane molasses was 33 g/L (27.5% yield from sugar), achieved by mutant FA 1-30. In a glucose medium, 32 g/L (32% yield) was the best accumulation by mutant FA 3-115 (41).

The mechanism of L-lysine overproduction by these mutants was investigated both *in vivo* and *in vitro*. At first, the inhibition of L-threonine on L-lysine production was studied by adding it to the culture medium. As shown in Figure 1, FA 3-115 was unaffected by an extremely high concentration of L-threonine (10 mg/ml) in contrast to the homoserine auxotroph, H-1013, whose L-lysine producing activity was completely inhibited by only 3 mg/ml of L-threonine. We may conclude that the mutation site of FA 3-115 was the regulatory site of aspartate kinase. The result of the *in vitro* study of aspartate kinase activities is shown in Figure 4 (42). In this experiment, a sonic extract of cells was precipitated with ammonium sulfate and used as an enzyme preparation. Aspartate kinase activities were estimated at various concentrations of L-lysine plus L-threonine. In the case of the wild type strain No. 2247, the half inactivation occurred at 0.3 mM of both L-lysine and L-threonine. In contrast, L-lysine producing mutants FA 1-30, FA 3-115, and X-15 had half inactivations at concentrations from 30-200 times higher. The mutant X-15 was derived from

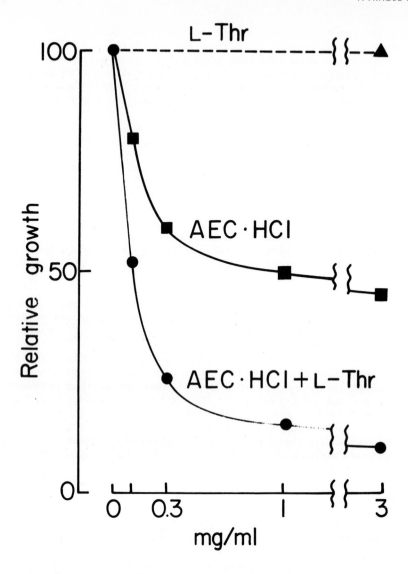

FIGURE 3. *Growth inhibition by 2-aminoethyl-L-cysteine (AEC) and L-threonine on Brevibacterium flavum.*

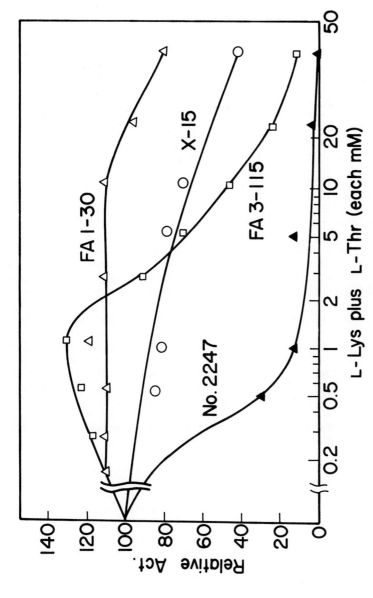

FIGURE 4. Effect of lysine and threonine on aspartate kinase activities. Sonic extract of the cells was precipitated with ammonium sulfate and used as enzyme source. No. 2247: wild type of Brevibacterium flavum. FA 1-30 and FA 3-115 were the mutants obtained as the resistant to AEC + L-threonine. X-15 was obtained as the resistant to AEC + L-threonine. X-15 was obtained as a lysine-excreting mutant on a minimal medium.

No. 2247 by the second breeding approach based on the supposed
characteristics of the regulatory mutant of aspartate kinase; this
mutant might produce much L-lysine in a minimal medium. The halo-
forming mutant colonies on lysine auxotroph on a minimal agar
plate were selected as L-lysine producers. About one-fifth of
these mutants had characteristics similar to those of AEC-resistant L-lysine producers (42). The rest were the threonine- or
methionine-sensitive mutants whose homoserine dehydrogenase was
about one-tenth that of the wild strain and the growth was consequently inhibited by the addition of threonine or methionine in a
minimal medium (42). A typical model of these sensitive mutants,
S-20, was used in the experiment shown in Figure 1. The improvement of L-lysine accumulation by the aspartate kinase desensitized
mutant was successful through the addition of resistance to α-
chloro-caprolactam and alanine auxotrophy. The maximal amount of
accumulation of L-lysine (HCl) was 46 g/L in a cane molasses
medium (43).

There was a third approach to obtain the regulatory mutant of
aspartate kinase. In *Pseudomonas putida* (44), the aspartate
kinase inactivated mutant was first obtained as diaminopimelic
acid, methionine, and threonine polyauxotroph, which was unsuc-
cessful in *Brevibacterium flavum*. Then, some revertants of this
polyauxotroph were derived, and their aspartate kinase was observed as desensitized enzymes. In the case of these *Pseudomonas*
revertants, however, L-lysine was scarcely accumulated at all because of high lysine-degradating enzyme activity (lysine oxyge-
nase).

Yeasts, such as *Candida periculosa* (45), *Saccharomyces lypo-
lytica* (46), and *Saccharomyces cerevisiae* (47) were very interesting items for L-lysine production studies. The synthetic pathway of L-lysine differs from that of bacteria, and a permeability
barrier exists against L-lysine which was not observed in bacteria. About 2 g/L of L-lysine was produced by the homocitrate syn-
thetase-desensitized mutant of *Candida periculosa*.

Many commercial investigations and applications of regulatory
mutants took place in terms of amino acid production. In addition
to L-lysine, such amino acids as L-threonine, L-isoleucine, L-
leucine, L-valine, L-arginine, L-histidine, L-phenylalanine, L-
tryptophan, and L-tyrosine were or can be produced commercially
by the regulatory mutants (Table III).

Those mutants escaped from repression and obtained as analog-
resistant are another type of regulatory mutant considered for
amino acid production. For example, L-tryptophan producers were
found in 5-fluoro-tryptophan-resistant mutants of *Bacillus subtilis* (48). One of them, FT-39, produced 2 g/L of L-tryptophan
from 100 l/L of glucose. Its anthranilate synthetase activity
was fully depressed: 300 times of that of the wild strain. The
five specific enzymes for L-tryptophan synthesis from chorismic
acid were known to be coordinately repressed in *Bacillus subtilis*.

Anthranilate synthetase was thus determined as the representative.
The addition of auxotrophy such as arginine, leucine, or purine to
FT-39 further improved this *Bacillus* system. As the result, 6 g/L
of L-tryptophan was produced.

The breeding of L-tryptophan producer was started earlier in
Brevibacterium than in *Bacillus subtilis*, but the 5-methyl-trypto-
phan-resistant mutants derived from the phenylalanine and tyrosine
polyauxotrophic mutant produced only 2 g/L of L-tryptophan at the
maximum (49). As the result of the subsequent studies on the
breeding of mutant as tryptophan analog-resistant, phenylalanine
analog-resistant and, phenylalanine-auxotrophic, 6.2 g/L of L-
tryptophan was produced. The overproduction mechanism of L-
tryptophan was explained as the escape from repression and feedback inhibition on anthranilate synthetase, 3-deoxy-D-arabino-
heptulosonate-7-phosphate synthetase, and the related enzymes
(50). L-Phenylalanine and L-tyrosine producers were also bred
with the same tactics. One of the m-fluoro-phenylalanine-resis-
tant mutants accumulated 2.2 g/L of L-phenylalanine with 1.9 g/L
of L-tyrosine and another 2.1 g/L of L-phenylalanine with negligible L-tyrosine (51).

III. PRECURSOR ADDITION METHOD

If some intermediate of the biosynthetic pathway of an objective amino acid is economically available, its addition into the
culture medium may be a useful technique for amino acid production. Since the regulation site of the biosynthetic pathway is
generally the first enzyme, the feeding of an intermediate into
the culture medium after the formation of biosynthetic enzymes may
result in a derepressed and desensitized condition of regulated
enzymes. L-Serine production from glycine is a case in point.
It was reported that 10 g/L of L-serine was produced from 20 g/L
of glycine by *Corynebacterium glycinophilum* (52). A single enzyme, serine-hydroxy-methyl-transferase, was reported to react on
the conversion of glycine to L-serine. Thus, it can be termed an
enzymatic method as described in the next section. In this case,
however, some cultivation was necessary for the supply of cofact-
or, tetrahydrofolic acid, whose reproduction depended on cell
metabolism. The participation of energy is a critical point in
discriminating between the precursor addition method and the
enzymatic method.

In Table IV, there is unique evidence that a regulatory mutant
of leucine biosynthesis of *Serratia marcescens* accumulated a particular amino acid, norvaline, at 7.4 g/L from 20 g/L of D- or L-
threonine added in the medium (53). Norvaline, thus produced, can
be converted to norleucine by a norleucine-resistant mutant, with
a yield of 4.7 g/L of norleucine from 10 g/L of norvaline (54).
Norvaline was a component of an antibiotic produced by *Bacillus
subtilis* (55).

TABLE III. Amino Acids Production by Regulatory Mutants

Amino acid	Selection	Microorganism	Reference
L-Arginine	canavanine^r	Escherichia coli	(91)
	arginine-hydroxamate^r	Bacillus subtilis	(92)
	D-serine^s, D-arginine^r, arginine-hydroxamate^r	Corynebacterium glutamicum	(93)
	2-thiazolealanine^r	Brevibacterium flavum	(94)
	substrate specificity	Serratia marcescens	(95)
L-Histidine	2-thiazolealanine^r, sulfaguanidine^r, α-amino-β-hydroxybutyric acid^r, ethionine^r, 2-aminobenzothiazole^r 1-, 2-, 4-triazolealanine^r, 6-mercaptoguanine^r, 8-azaguanine^r, 4-thiouracil^r, 6-mercaptopurine^r, 5-methyltryptophan^r	Brevibacterium flavum	(96)
	histidase$^-$, 1-, 2-, 4-triazole-alanine^r, 2-methylhistidine^r, 2-thiazolealanine^r	Corynebacterium glutamicum	(97)
	Revertant of histidine$^-$	Serratia malcescens	(98)
		Streptomyces	(99)
L-Isoleucine	α-amino-β-hydroxyvaleric acid^r, O-methyl-threonine^r	Brevibacterium flavum	(100)
	2-aminoethyl-L-cysteine^r	Brevibacterium flavum	(101)
	4-azaleucine^r	Bacillus subtilis	(102)
L-Leucine	2-thiazolealanine^r, methionine$^-$, isoleucine$^-$ α-aminobutyric acid^r, revertant of isoleucine$^-$	Brevibacterium lactofermentum	(103,104)
L-Lysine	2-aminoethyl-L-cysteine^r	Serratia marcescens	(98)
	α-chlorocaprolactam^r	Brevibacterium flavum	(41)
		Brevibacterium flavum	(43)

Amino acid	Selection	Microorganism	Reference
L-Phenylalanine	m-fluorophenylalanine^r, tyrosine$^-$, p-fluorophenylalanine^r, p-aminophenylalanine^r	Brevibacterium flavum	(105)
L-Proline	sulfaguanidine^r	Corynebacterium glutamicum	(106)
L-Serine	O-metyl-, serine^r, α-metyl-serine^r, iso-serine^r	Brevibacterium flavum	(107)
L-Threonine	α-amino-β-hydroxy-valeric acid^r, methionine$^-$	Corynebacterium glutamicum	(108)
L-Tryptophan	phenylalanine$^-$, 5-fluorotryptophan^r, 3-fluoro-tryptophan^r 5-metyl-tryptophan^r, tyrosine-hydroxamate^r, 6-fluoro-tryptophan^r, 4-methyl-tryptophan^r, p-ethylphenyl-alanine^r, p-amino-phenylalanine^r, tyrosine-hydroxamate^r, phenylalanine-hydroxamate^r	Brevibacterium flavum Brevibacterium flavum	(109,110) (111)
L-Tyrosine	m-fluoro-phenylalanine^r, 3-amino-tyrosine^r, p-amino-phenyl-alanine^r, p-ethyl-phenylalanine^r, tyrosine-hydroxamate^r,	Corynebacterium glutamicum Brevibacterium flavum	(112) (113)
L-Valine	phenylalanine$^-$ 2-thiazolealanine^r	Corynebacterium glutamicum Brevibacterium flavum	(114) (115)

TABLE IV. Amino Acids Production From Precursors

Amino acid	Precursor	Microorganism	Reference
L-DOPA	L-tyrosine	Pseudomonas melanogenum	(116)
L-Isoleucine	α-aminobutyric acid	Serratia marcescens	(117)
	α-aminobutyric acid	Bifidobacterium ruminale	(118)
	2-hydroxy-butyric acid,		
	α-bromobutyric acid	Bifidobacterium ruminale	(119)
L-Methionine	2-hydroxy-4-metyl-thiobutyric acid	Pseudomonas denitrificans	(120)
Norleucine	norvaline	Serratia marcescens	(54)
Norvaline	D-threonine, L-threonine	Serratia marcescens	(53)
L-Phenylalanine	2-hydroxy-3-phenyl-propionic acid	Pseudomonas denitrificans	(121)
L-Serine	glycine	Corynebacterium glycinophilum	(122)
	glycine	Pseudomonas sp.	(123)
L-Tryptophan	anthranilic acid	Hansenula anomala	(124)
	indole	Claviceps purpureus	(125)

IV. ENZYMATIC METHOD

Enzyme reaction is now used for the commercial production of
L-alanine and L-aspartic acid. In the case of L-alanine, the
decarboxylation of L-aspartic acid by L-aspartate-4-carboxy-lyase
is now commercialized (56). In spite of the existence of a power-
ful alanine producer, the direct fermentation process has not been
used because of the existence of alanine racemase which prevents
L-alanine accumulation. The optical resolution method and extraction from protein hydrolysate are at present more expensive.

The condensation of fumarate and ammonia by aspartase is the
commercial process for L-aspartic acid because of its economy and
simplicity (57). In addition, recent progress in the technology
of enzyme immobilization made this process even more convenient
(58).

An enzymatic production of L-cysteine from 2-amino-Δ^2-thiazo-
line-4-carboxylic acid (ATC), an intermediate in the chemical
synthesis of DL-cysteine, was recently reported (3). The microbial degrading enzyme of ATC was extensively investigated on both
stocked cultures and natural sources, and some strains belonging
to *Pseudomonas* were obtained as potent enzyme producers (3). They
accumulated about 6.1 g/L of L-cysteine plus L-cystine from 7.3
g/L of DL-ATC at the molar yield of about 100%. This suggests
that the substrate or intermediate might be racemized by a chemical or biochemical reaction during incubation; the maximum yield
was 31.4 g/L from 40 g/L of DL-ATC (59). Figure 5 shows the flow
of degradation of DL-ATC to L-cysteine proposed as a result of
enzymatic experiments (59). Three enzymes, ATC racemase, L-ATC
hydrolase, and S-carbamyl-L-cysteine (SCC) hydrolase, might be
included.

Similarly, the conversion of DL-ATC to L-cysteine was not a
single enzyme reaction, but it required no energy. Since it can
even be performed by sonic extract, it can be called an enzymatic
method. The merits of the enzymatic method for L-cysteine production, compared with the extraction method from the hydrolysate
of hair now in operation, are the possibility of less polution and
decreased cost resulting from mass production. There has been
other work on the enzymatic production of L-cysteine by the cysteine desulfhydrase of *Aerobactor aerogenes* from pyruvic acid,
ammonia, and Na_2S (as H_2S donor) (60). β-Chloro-L-alanine was
more suitable than pyruvic acid and ammonia, yet it was also more
expensive. Maximum L-cysteine accumulation was 48.5 g/L, and the
yield for β-chloro-L-alanine was 80.2% in the coexistence of 8%
acetone (61). The role of acetone was proposed to make a derivative of L-cysteine: 2,2-dimethyl-thiazoline-4-carboxylic acid.
The product inhibition of L-cysteine on cysteine desulfhydrase
could thus be avoided.

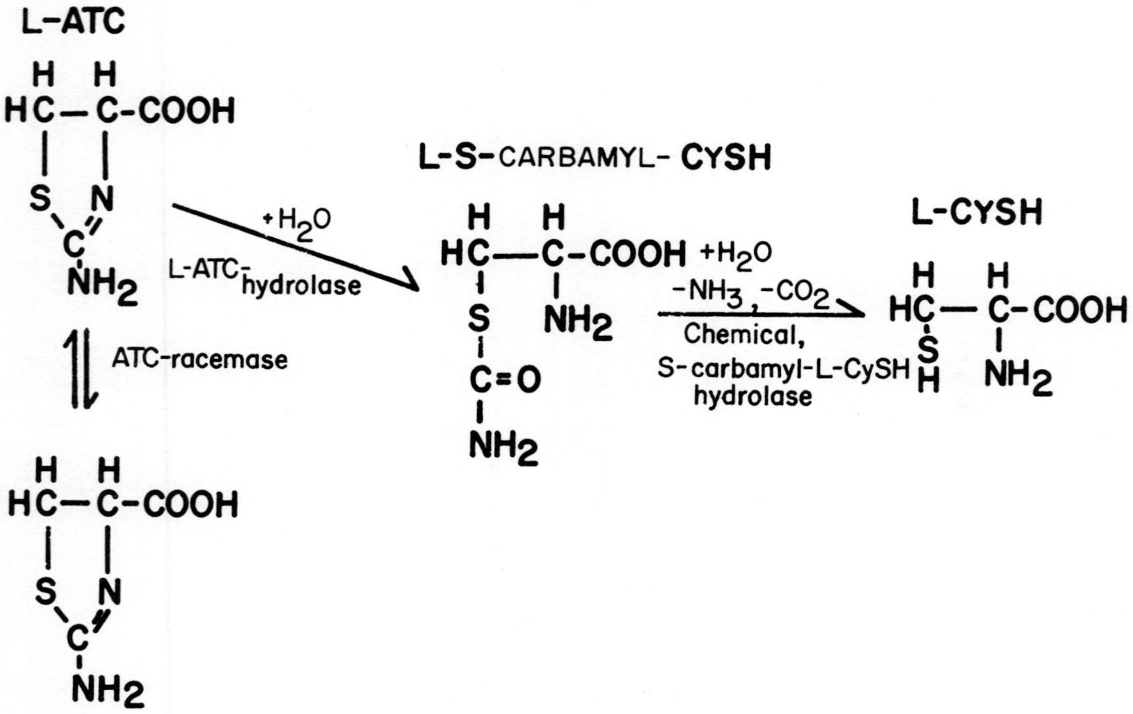

FIGURE 5. Enzymatic conversion of D–ATC to L–cysteine by Pseudomonas thiazolinophilum.

As described above, there are two types of enzyme reaction
used in the synthesis of amino acids: hydrolysis and synthesis.
Hydantoin and lactam ring compounds were asymmetrically reacted
by hydrolyzing enzymes and transformed to amino acids such as L-
glutamic acid, L-tryptophan, and L-lysine.   L-Glutamic acid was
produced from 10 g/L of DL-hydantoin-5-propionic acid at a yield
of 90% by the whole cells of *Bacillus brevis* (62).   In the case
of L-tryptophan from DL-5-indolyl-methyl-hydantoin, 7 g/L was
formed at the yield of 82% by *Flavobacterium aminogenes* (63).
Those hydantoins are rather easily racemized both enzymatically
or chemically in reaction conditions, since L-amino acids were
accumulated at a yield of more than 50%.   In contrast, the yield
of L-lysine produced from DL-α-amino-ε-caprolactam by yeast enzyme was less than 50% (64).   The racemization of the lactam by
the enzyme of *Achromobacter obae* was necessary for the complete
transformation of DL-α-amino-ε-caprolactam to L-lysine (65).

Another enzymatic method for amino acids production is the
application of a synthetic reaction such as aspartase and cysteine
desulfhydrase.   β-Tyrosinase and tryptophanase have a potency
that appears to have commercial application in the near future.
Both enzymes have been known as degradative enzymes, but the synthetic reaction was recently discovered to be active under organized conditions (66,67).   In the case of β-tyrosinase, 60 g/L of
L-tyrosine or L-DOPA was produced by *Erwinia herbicola* cells from
some economical substrates: phenol or pyrocatechol, pyruvate,
and ammonia (68).   One of the merits of these enzymatic methods
is the capability to produce unusual or unnatural amino acids such
as L-DOPA, which is difficult in direct fermentation.

V.   PROCESS CONTROL ON CULTIVATION OF MICROORGANISMS

To industrialize the amino acid production processes described
above, the large-scale submerged cultivation technique was necessary.   This technique was based on technology developed in the
industrialization of penicillin fermentation, and great advances
have been made during the growth of the amino acids industry.   To
describe the present state of process control in the fermentation
of amino acids, it may be convenient to classify the techniques:
(i) maintenance of pure culture condition, (ii) aeration and agitation, and (iii) control of pH and temperature.

A.   Maintenance of Pure Culture Condition

The prevention of contamination of the medium by microorganisms during cultivation is more difficult in commercial large tank
production than on a laboratory scale.

To protect against invasion of contaminants from the environment into the culture, air filtration and continuous heat sterilization of the medium are performed. In amino acid fermentation,
the raw materials are all easily soluble, so continuous heat sterilization is effective. There are three advantages to continuous
heating: (a) less energy used, (b) better quality control, and
(c) improved production (69).

To keep the air supply sterile, flasks with cotton plugs are
satisfactory. The characteristics of oxygen transfer of various
types of cotton plugs have been quantified in terms of the production of L-glutamic acid (70). In larger scale fermenters, air
sterilization is performed by filtration with a glass-wool filter.
Some theoretical concerns on the design and construction of air
filters has been reported (71).

B.   Aeration and Agitation Effectiveness

The biosynthesis of L-glutamic acid is an aerobic process.
The oxygen requirement for L-glutamic acid production from glucose
has been experimentally estimated as follows (72):

$$C_6H_{12}O_6 + 2.33\ O_2 \longrightarrow 0.82\ C_5H_9O_4N + 1.94\ CO_2$$

Oxygen may be considered as one of the raw materials consumed in
large amounts, so a quantitative discussion of oxygen transfer
during fermentation is indispensable for the economical construction and operation of commercial plants.

The following equations are the simplest expression of the
basis for discussing oxygen transfer during the fermentation:

$$r_{ab} = Kd(P_B - P_L) = KrM \qquad (P_L \geqslant P_{L\ crit})$$

$$< KrM \qquad (P_L < P_{L\ crit})$$

where r_{ab} is the rate of cell respiration (mole of O_2/ml.min); Kd,
oxygen absorption coefficient (mole/ml.min.atm); P_B, gas-phase
oxygen tension (atm); P_L, liquid-phase oxygen tension (atm); Kr,
cell's oxygen demand (mole/min/g of cell); M, cell density (g/ml);
$P_{L\ crit}$, critical level of liquid-phase oxygen for cell respiration (atm). The rate of cell respiration (r_{ab}) equals KrM at P_L
level above $P_{L\ crit}$; in other words, cell respiration is satisfied
when the oxygen supply is sufficient to maintain P_L above $P_{L\ crit}$.

Values of $P_{L\ crit}$ are usually less than 0.01 atm--too low to
be determined with conventional membrane-coated oxygen electrodes
whose ranges are above 0.008 atm. Since the determination of much
lower $P_{L\ crit}$ was indispensable in those studies, a new deductive
method was developed (Figure 6) (73). P_L and the redox potential
(E) of culture medium were measured simultaneously and plotted in

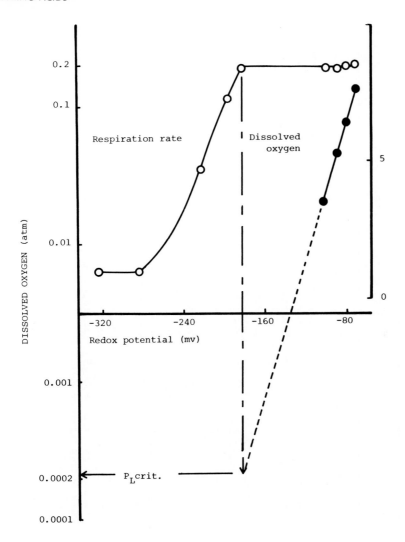

FIGURE 6. *Deduction of critical dissolved oxygen level
for cell's respiration in L-leucine fermentation.*

TABLE V. Amino Acids Production by Enzymatic Method

Amino acid	Reaction	Enzyme	Enzyme source	Reference
L-Amino acid	N-acyl-L-amino acid + H_2O → L-amino acid + acetic acid	aminoacylase	Aspergillus	(126,127)
L-Alanine	L-aspartic acid → L-alanine + CO_2	aspartate decarboxylase	Pseudomonas dacunhae	(128)
L-Aspartic acid	fumaric acid + NH_4^+ → L-aspartic acid	aspartase	Escherichia coli	(129)
L-Citrulline	L-arginine + H_2O → L-citrulline + NH_3	arginine deiminase	Escherichia coli	(130)
L-Cysteine	DL-2-amino-Δ^2-thiazoline-4-carboxylic acid + $2H_2O$ → L-cysteine + NH_3 + CO_2	ATC racemase, L-ATC hydrolase, S-carbamyl-L-cysteine hydrolase	Pseudomonas thiazolinophilum	(3)
	β-chloro-L-alanine + Na_2S (H_2S) → L-cysteine + $NaCl$ + $NaOH$	cysteine desulfhyrase	Aerobacter aerogenes	(4)
L-DOPA	pyrocatechol + pyruvate + NH_4^+ → L-DOPA	β-tyrosinase	Erwinia herbicola	(68)
L-Glutamic acid	DL-hydantoin-5-propionate + $2H_2O$ → L-glutamic acid + CO_2 + NH_3	L-glutamic acid-hydrolase	Bacillus brevis	(62)
5-Hydroxy-L-tryptophan	5-hydroxyindole + pyruvate + NH_4^+ → 5-hydroxy-L-tryptophan + H_2O	tryptophanase	Proteus rettgeri	(67)
L-Lysine	DL-α-amino-ϵ-caprolactam (ACL) + H_2O → L-lysine	ACL racemase, L-ACL hydrolase	Achromobacter obae, Cryptococcus laurentii	(65)

Amino acid	Reaction	Enzyme	Enzyme source	Reference
L-Phenylalanine	DL-phenylalanine-hydantoin + $2H_2O$ ⇌ L-phenylalanine + CO_2 + NH_3	L-phenylalanine-hydantoin hydrolase / N-carbamyl-L-phenylalanine hydrolase	Flavobacterium aminogenes	(131)
L-Tryptophan	DL-tryptophan-hydantoin + $2H_2O$ ⇌ L-tryptophan + CO_2 + NH_3	L-tryptophan-hydantoin hydrolase / N-carbamyl-L-tryptophan hydrolase	Flavobacterium aminogenes	(63)
	indole + pyruvate + NH_4^+ ⇌ L-tryptophan + H_2O	tryptophanase	Proteus rettgeri	(67)
	indole + L-serine ⇌ L-tryptophan + H_2O	tryptophan synthetase	Escherichia coli	(132)
	indole + L-serine ⇌ L-tryptophan + H_2O	tryptophanase	Proteus rettgeri	(133)
L-Tyrosine	phenol + pyruvate + NH_4^+ ⇌ L-tyrosine + H_2O	β-tyrosinase	Erwinia herbicola	(68)

Figure 6. There is a linear relationship between E and P_L in
logarithm. On the assumption that this linear relationship continues below 0.008 atm, the value of $P_{L\ crit}$ was deduced. In the
case of L-leucine fermentation, it was calculated at 0.0002 atm
(Figure 6). This new deductive method is useful for the precise
control of P_L under 0.008 and is included in the automatic control
system for amino acid fermentation (Figure 7).

Those studies discussing oxygen transfer in culture systems
quantitatively have corrected the conventional theory of the mechanism of lactic acid accumulation by L-glutamic acid producing
bacteria. Excess biotin did not create lactic acid accumulating
conditions; the oxygen deficiency caused the accumulation. In
fact, no lactic acid was accumulated in a biotin-excess medium
with a sufficient oxygen supply.

Although the production of amino acids depends on the oxygen
supply, its influence varied for each amino acid. The biosynthetic pathway of each acid may cause this. L-Glutamic acid, for
example, is biosynthesized by way of pyruvic acid, citric acid,
and α-ketoglutaric acid. In this process, 8 moles of $NADH_2$ and 3
moles of ATP are generated from NAD and ADP with the assimilation
of 1 mole of glucose. L-Lysine, on the other hand, is biosynthesized by way of pyruvic acid, citric acid, oxaloacetic acid, and
aspartic acid, forming 6 moles of $NADH_2$ and 2 moles of ATP from 1
mole of glucose. L-Leucine is synthesized from 1 mole of glucose
with the generation of 2 moles each of ATP and $NADH_2$. The amount
of $NADH_2$ formed in L-glutamic acid production exceeds that formed
in L-lysine production by 2 moles. This suggests that oxygen
shortage inhibits the production of L-glutamic acid more seriously. L-Leucine is formed not through the TCA cycle, but by way of
pyruvic acid. Therefore, maximum production occurs when the TCA
cycle is slightly inhibited by an oxygen shortage. However, a
more deficient oxygen condition might inhibit the reoxidization
of $NADH_2$, resulting in the accumulation of lactic acid in place
of L-leucine. The same may occur in L-glutamic acid and L-lysine
production (Figure 8).

C. *Automatic Control of Amino Acid Fermentation*

Figure 9 shows a typical design for a commercial fermenter for
amino acid production. Most of the microorganisms for amino acid
production are bacteria, and less power might be needed for agitation than for antibiotic fermentation, in which molds or actinomy-
cetes strains are used. But, because of the higher rate of sugar
consumption and respiration, the oxygen requirement is larger and
heat evolution per unit volume of culture media is more rapid.

One of the characteristics of amino acid fermentation is the
large quantity of nitrogen source required for the high ratio of
nitrogen contained in the amino acid molecule. The use of gaseous

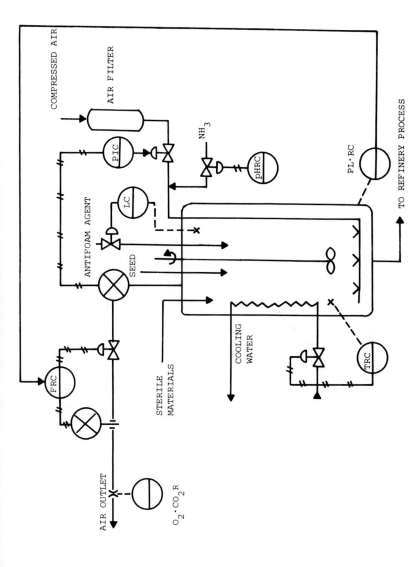

FIGURE 7. Design of automatically controlled fermentation process. FEC: flow recorder controller, LC: level controller, PIC: pressure indicator controller, pHRC: pH recorder controller, $P_L \cdot RC$: P_L and redox controller, $O_2 \cdot CO_2R$: O_2 CO_2 recorder.

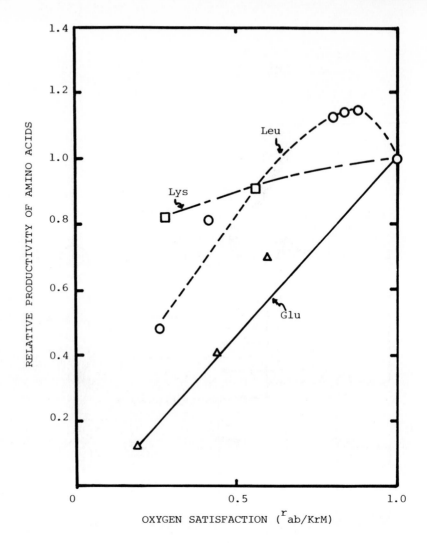

FIGURE 8. Relationship between relative productivity of amino
acids and degree of oxygen satisfaction.

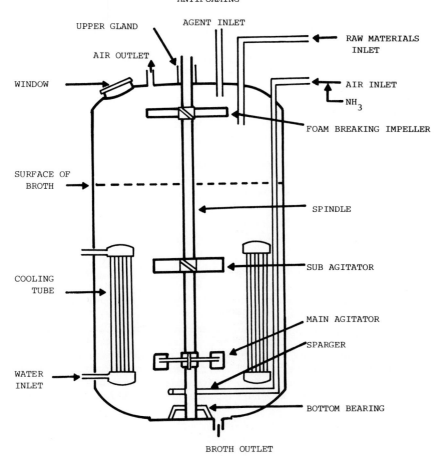

FIGURE 9. Design of submerged fermentor for amino acid fermentation processes.

ammonia was an important improvement in the process control of
fermentation, because it made the control of the pH more precise,
the equipment and the operation simpler than any others, and
avoided undesired dilution of the culture broth.

Two methods are used in conjunction to break the form: a
mechanical form-breaking impeller (Figure 9), and a chemical anti-
foam agent whose addition is automatically controlled by detection
of the foam with an electrode or watt meter to monitor the load
changes on the foam-breaking impeller.

Figure 7 shows a diagrammatic scheme of an automatically controlled fermentation process for amino acid production. The rate
of air flow, temperature, pH, and foaming are strictly controlled
by a computer system programmed to maintain maximum productivity.
Based on this scheme, commercial equipment was built for L-glutamic acid and has lowered labor costs greatly (74).

VI.   CONCLUSION

To respond to the growing need for food, feed, chemicals, and
pharmaceuticals, the amino acid industry is expanding rapidly.
To alleviate the food shortage resulting from the population ex-
plosion, the improvement of the protein efficiency of natural
food and feed by the supplement of amino acids may be one of the
most important contributions of the industry. DL-Methionine and
L-lysine already serve that purpose; L-tryptophan and L-threonine
are still too expensive. The industry must now improve the amino
acid-producing activities of microorganisms, introduce more economical raw materials, and further the economization of the production process.

REFERENCES

1.   Ikeda, K., *Journal of the Tokyo Chemical Society 30*, 820
     (1908).
2.   Kinoshita, S., Udaka, M., and Shimono, M., *J. Gen. Appl.
     Microbiol. 3*, 193 (1957).
3.   Sano, K., Yokozeki, K., Tamura, F., Yasuda, N., Noda, I., and
     Mitsugi, K., *Appl. Environ. Microbiol. 34*, 806 (1977).
4.   Ohgishi, H., Nishikawa, D., Kumagai, H., and Yamada, H.,
     Annual Meet. Agr. Chem. Soc. Japan, Abst., 90 (1977).
5.   Yamada, K., Kinoshita, S., Tsunoda, T., and Aida, K., "Micro-
     bial Production of Amino Acids." Kodansha, Tokyo, and
     Halsted Press, New York (1972).
6.   Tsunoda, T. and Okumura, S., *Proc. Internat. Symp. Convers.
     Manuf. Foodst. Microorganisms*, 229 (1972).

7. Kinoshita, S., *Rational Development of Amino Acid Fermentation Using Mutants: Microbiology-1976*, p. 526. American Society for Microbiology (1976).
8. Nakayama, K., *Process Biochemistry 12 (2)*, 4 (1976).
9. Yamada, K., *Biotechnol. Bioeng. 19*, 1563 (1977).
10. Tanaka, K., Iwasaki, T., and Kinoshita, S., *J. Agr. Chem. Soc. Japan 34*, 593 (1960).
11. Somerson, N. L. and Phillips, T., U.S. Patent 3,080,297 (1962).
12. Takinami, K., Okada, H., and Tsunoda, T., *Agr. Biol. Chem. 27*, 858 (1963); *28*, 114 (1964).
13. Takinami, K., Yoshii, H., Tsuri, H., and Okada, H., *Agr. Biol. Chem. 29*, 351 (1965).
14. Okumura, S., Tsugawa, R., Tsunoda, T., and Motozaki, S., *J. Agr. Chem. Soc. of Japan 36*, 204 (1962).
15. Kanzaki, T., Isobe, K., Okazaki, H., Mochizuki, K., and Fukuda, H., *Agr. Biol. Chem. 31*, 1416 (1967).
16. Shiio, I., Otsuka, S., and Katsuya, N., *J. Biochem. 53*, 333 (1963).
17. Takinami, K., Yamada, K., and Okada, H., *Agr. Biol. Chem. 30*, 674 (1966); *31*, 223 (1967).
18. Shibukawa, M., Kurima, M., Okabe, S., and Osawa, T., *Amino Acids and Nucleic Acids 17*, 61 (1968).
19. Udaka, S. and Kinoshita, S., *J. Gen. Appl. Microbiol. 5*, 159 (1960).
20. Yamada, S., Wada, M., Izuo, N., and Chibata, I., *Appl. Environ. Microbiol. 32*, 1 (1976).
21. Cerkes, L., Plachy, J., and Cerkesova, D., *Chem. Abst.* CA85-121812e (1976).
22. Nakanishi, T., Nakajima, J., and Kanda, K., *J. Ferment. Technol. 53*, 543 (1975).
23. Yoshinaga, F., Kikuchi, K., Tsuchida, T., and Okumura, S., Jpn. Patent Appl. Disclos. 51-44196 (1976).
24. Bertrand, K., Squires, C., and Yanofsky, C., *J. Mol. Biol. 103*, 319 (1976).
25. Hardmann, J. G., "Cyclic AMP," p. 433. Academic Press (1971).
26. Novic, A. and Szilard, L., "Dynamics of Growth Process," p. 21 (1954).
27. Monod, J., Changeux, J-P., and Jacob, F., *J. Mol. Biol. 6*, 306 (1963); Koshland, D. E. Jr., *Col. Spring Harbor Symp. Quant. Biol. 28*, 473 (1963).
28. Vogel, H. J., "Chemical Basis of Heredity," p. 276 (1957).
29. Jacob, F. and Monod, J., *J. Mol. Biol. 3*, 318 (1961).
30. Deway, D. L. and Work, E., *Nature 169*, 533 (1952).
31. Davis, B. D., *Nature 169*, 534 (1952).
32. Udaka, S. and Kinoshita, S., *J. Gen. Appl. Microbiol. 4*, 272 (1958).
33. Kinoshita, S., Kitada, S., and Nakayama, K., *J. Gen. Appl. Microbiol. 4*, 128 (1958).
34. Sano, K. and Shiio, I., *J. Gen. Appl. Microbiol. 13*, 349 (1967).

35. Adelberg, E. A., *J. Bacteriol.* 76, 326 (1958).
36. Sano, K. and Shiio, I., *J. Gen. Appl. Microbiol.* 13, 349 (1967).
37. Shiio, I. and Miyajima, R., *J. Biochem.* 65, 849 (1969).
38. Miyajima, R., Otsuka, S., and Shiio, I., *J. Biochem.* 63, 139 (1968).
39. Yoshinaga, H., *J. Gen. Appl. Microbiol.* 15, 387 (1969).
40. Jensen, R. A., *J. Biol. Chem.* 244, 2819 (1969).
41. Sano, K. and Shiio, I., *J. Gen. Appl. Microbiol.* 16, 373 (1970).
42. Sano, K. and Shiio, I., *J. Gen. Appl. Microbiol.* 17, 97 (1971).
43. Kubota, K., Tosaka, O., Yoshihara, H., and Hirose, H., Jpn. Patent Disclos. 51-19186 (1976).
44. Hermann, M., Thevenet, M. M., Coudert-Maratier, and Vandecasteale V-P., *Eur. J. Biochem.* 30, 100 (1972).
45. Soda, K., Tanaka, H., Takenouchi, E., and Nikolova, D., Abstract of papers, Fifth International Fermentation Symposium, Berlin, p. 496 (1976). Takenouchi, E., Nikolova, D., Awano, K., Soda, K., and Tanaka, H., *Agric. Biol. Chem.* 41, 615 (1977).
46. Gaillardin C-M., Sylvestre, G., and Heslot, H., *Arch. Microbiol.* 104, 89 (1975).
47. Haidaris, C. G. and Bhattacherjee, J. K., *J. Ferment. Technol.* 55, 189 (1977).
48. Shiio, I., Ishii, K., and Yokozeki, K., *Agr. Biol. Chem.* 37, 1991 (1973).
49. Shiio, I., Sato, H., and Nakagawa, M., *Agr. Biol. Chem.* 36, 2315 (1972).
50. Shiio, I., Sugimoto, S., and Nakagawa, M., *Agr. Biol. Chem.* 39, 627 (1975).
51. Sugimoto, S., Nakagawa, M., Tsuchida, T., and Shiio, I., *Agr. Biol. Chem.* 37, 2327 (1973).
52. Kubota, K., Kageyama, K., Shiro, T., and Okumura, S., *Amino Acids and Nucleic Acids* 23, 43 (1971).
53. Kisumi, M., Sugiura, M., Takagi, T., and Chibata, I., *J. Antibiot.* 30, 111 (1977).
54. Kisumi, M., Sugiura, M., and Chibata, I., *Appl. Environ. Microbiol.* 34, 135 (1977).
55. Nandi, P. and Sen, G. P., *Nature* 172, 871 (1953).
56. Chibata, I., Kamimoto, T., and Kato, J., *Appl. Microbiol.* 13, 638 (1965).
57. Kitahara, K., Fukui, S., and Misawa, M., *J. Gen. Appl. Microbiol.* 5, 74 (1959).
58. Chibata, I., Tosa, T., and Sato, T., *Methods in Enzymology* 44, 739 (1976).
59. Sano, K., Euchi, C., Yasuda, N., and Mitsugi, K., *Ann. Meet. Agr. Chem. Soc. Japan Abst.*, 431 (1977).
60. Kumagai, H., Choi, Y. J., Samejima, S., and Yamada, H., *Biochem. Biophys. Res. Commun.* 59, 789 (1974).

61. Ohgishi, H., Nishikawa, D., Kumagai, H., and Yamada, H.,
     Ann. Meet. Agr. Chem. Soc. Japan Abst., 90 (1977).
62. Tsugawa, R., Okumura, S., Ito, T., and Katsuya, *Agr. Biol.
     Chem. 30*, 27 (1966).
63. Sano, K., Yokozeki, K., Eguchi, Kagawa, T., Noda, I., and
     Mitsugi, K., *Agr. Biol. Chem. 41*, 819 (1977).
64. Fukumura, T., *Agr. Biol. Chem. 40*, 1695 (1976).
65. Fukumura, T., *Agr. Biol. Chem. 41*, 1509 (1977).
66. Yamada, H., Kumagai, H., Kashima, N., Torii, H., Enei, H.,
     and Okumura, S., *Biochem. Biophys. Res. Commun. 46*, 370
     (1972).
67. Nakazawa, H., Enei, H., Okumura, S., Yoshida, H., and Yamada,
     H., *FEBS Letters 25*, 43 (1972).
68. Enei, H., Nakazawa, H., Matsui, H., Okumura, S., and Yamada,
     H., *FEBS Letters 21*, 39 (1972).
69. Humphrey, A. E. and Deindoerfer, F. H., *Appl. Microbiol. 7*,
     256 (1959).
70. Hirose, Y., Sonoda, H., Kinoshita, K., and Okada, H., *Agr.
     Biol. Chem. 30*, 49 (1966).
71. Aiba, S., Humphrey, A. E., and Mills, N. F., "Biochemical
     Engineering," p. 270. New York-London (1973).
72. Okada, H. and Tsunoda, T., *Agr. Biol. Chem. 29*, 923 (1965).
73. Akashi, K., Ikeda, S., Shibai, H., Kobayashi, K., Hirose, Y.,
     Biotechnol. Bioeng. 20, 27 (1978).
74. Yamashita, S., Hoshi, H., and Inagaki, T., "Fermentation
     Advances" (D. Perlman, ed.), p. 444. Academic Press, New
     York-London (1969).
75. Hershfield, V., Boyer, H. W., Yanofsky, C., Lovett, M. A.,
     and Helinski, D. R., *Proc. Nat. Acad. Sci. USA 71*, 3455
     (1974).
76. Chakrabarty, A. M., *Proc. Nat. Acad. Sci. USA 70*, 1641
     (1973).
77. Shibuya, T., Ishida, M., Konishi, S., Okumura, S., and Shiro,
     T., *Amino Acids and Nucleic Acids 12*, 49 (1965).
78. Nakayama, K. and Hagino, H., *J. Agr. Chem. Soc. Japan 40*,
     377 (1966).
79. Kikuchi, M., Doi, M., Suzuki, M., and Naono, Y., *Agr. Biol.
     Chem. 36*, 1141 (1972).
80. Samejima, H., Nara, T., Fujita, T., and Kinoshita, S., *J.
     Agr. Chem. Soc. Japan 34*, 750 (1960).
81. Araki, K., Ueda, H., and Saigusa, S., *Agr. Biol. Chem. 38*,
     565 (1974).
82. Nakayama, K., Kitada, S., and Kinoshita, S., *J. Gen. Appl.
     Microbiol. 7*, 145 (1961).
83. Nakayama, K., Sato, Z., and Kinoshita, S., *J. Agr. Biol.
     Chem. Japan 35*, 142 (1961).
84. Yoshinaga, F., Konishi, S., Okumura, S., and Katsuya, N.,
     J. Gen. Appl. Microbiol. 12, 219 (1966).
85. Yamatodani, S., Suzuki, M., and Nakao, Y., *Amino Acids and
     Nucleic Acids 16*, 126 (1967).

188   *Y. HIROSE et al.*

86. Kato, J., Horie, H., Komatsubara, S., Kisumi, M., and Chibata,
    I., *Appl. Microbiol. 16*, 1200 (1968).
87. Huang, H. T., *Appl. Microbiol. 9*, 419 (1961).
88. Hirakawa, T., Tanaka, T., and Watanabe, K., *Amino Acids and
    Nucleic Acids 26*, 34 (1972).
89. Hagino, H., Yoshida, H., Kato, F., Arai, T., Katsumata, R.,
    and Nakayama, K., *Agr. Biol. Chem. 37*, 2001 (1973).
90. Nakayama, K., Kitada, S., Kinoshita, S., *J. Gen. Appl. Micro-
    biol. 7*, 52 (1961).
91. Maars, W. K., *Cold Spring Harbor Symp. Quant. Biol. 26*, 183
    (1961).
92. Kisumi, M., Kato, J., Sugiura, M., and Chibata, I., *Appl.
    Microbiol. 22*, 987 (1971).
93. Nakayama, K. and Yoshida, H., *Agr. Biol. Chem. 36*, 1675
    (1972).
94. Kubota, K., Onoda, T., Kamijo, H., Yoshinaga, F., and
    Okumura, S., *J. Gen. Appl. Microbiol. 19*, 39 (1973).
95. Kisumi, M., Takagi, T., and Chibata, I., *Amino Acids and
    Nucleic Acids 35*, 118 (1977).
96. Mihara, O., Kamijo, H., and Kubota, K., *Ann. Meet. Agr. Chem.
    Soc. Japan, Abst.* 112 (1973).
97. Araki, K., Shimojo, S., and Nakayama, K., *Agr. Biol. Chem.
    38*, 837 (1974).
98. Kisumi, M., Nakazawa, N., Takagi, T., and Chibata, I., *Ann.
    Meet. Agr. Chem. Soc. Japan Abst.* 30 (1975).
99. Sojak-Derkos, V. and Delic, V., *5th Int. Ferment. Symp. Abst.*
    143, Berlin (1976).
100. Shiio, I., Sasaki, A., Nakamori, S., and Sano, K., *Agr. Biol.
     Chem. 37*, 2053 (1973).
101. Ikeda, S., Fujita, I., and Hirose, Y., *Agr. Biol. Chem. 40*,
     517 (1976).
102. Ward, J. B. and Zahler, S. A., *J. Bacteriol. 116*, 727 (1973).
103. Tsuchida, T., Yoshinaga, F., Kubata, K., Momose, H., and
     Okumura, S., *Agr. Biol. Chem. 39*, 1149 (1975).
104. Momose, H. and Tsuchida, T., *1st Int. Cong. IAMS, Proc. I*,
     364, Tokyo (1975).
105. Sugimoto, S., Nakagawa, M., Tsuchida, T., and Shio, I., *Agr.
     Biol. Chem. 37*, 2327 (1973).
106. Hagino, H. and Nakayama, K., *Agr. Biol. Chem. 38*, 157 (1974).
107. Tsuchida, T., Kubota, K., Yoshinaga, F., and Hirose, Y., *23rd
     Symp. Amino Acids Nucleic Acids Abst.*, 4 (1974).
108. Yoshida, H. and Nakayama, K., *J. Agr. Chem. Soc. Japan 48*,
     201 (1974).
109. Shiio, I. and Nakamori, S., *Agr. Biol. Chem. 34*, 448 (1970).
110. Nakamori, S. and Shiio, I., *Agr. Biol. Chem. 36*, 1675 (1972).
111. Shiio, I., Sugimoto, S., and Nakagawa, M., *Agr. Biol. Chem.
     39*, 627 (1975).
112. Hagino, H. and Nakayama, K., *Agr. Biol. Chem. 39*, 343 (1975).
113. Sugimoto, S., Nakagawa, M., Tsuchida, T., and Shiio, I., *Agr.
     Biol. Chem. 37*, 2327 (1973).
114. Hagino, H. and Nakayama, K., *Agr. Biol. Chem. 37*, 2013 (1973).

115. Tsuchida, T., Yoshinaga, F., Kubota, K., and Momose, H., *Agr. Biol. Chem. 39*, 1319 (1975).
116. Tanaka, Y., Yoshida, H., and Nakayama, K., *Agr. Biol. Chem. 38*, 633 (1974).
117. Chibata, I., Kisumi, M., and Ashikaga, Y., *Amino Acids and Nucleic Acids 5*, 76 (1962).
118. Mattenzzi, D., Crociani, F., Emaldi, O., Selli, A., and Viviani, R., *Europ. J. Appl. Microbiol. 2*, 185 (1976).
119. Matsuchima, H., Murata, K., and Maze, Y., *J. Ferment. Technol. 53*, 443 (1975).
120. Wada, H., *J. Agr. Chem. Soc. Japan 48*, 303 (1974).
121. Wada, H., *J. Agr. Chem. Soc. Japan 48*, 351 (1974).
122. Kubota, K., Kageyama, K., Shiro, T., and Okumura, S., *J. Gen. Appl. Microbiol. 17*, 167 (1971).
123. Keune, H., Sahm, H., and Wagner, F., *Europ. J. Appl. Microbiol. 2*, 175 (1976).
124. Terui, G. and Enatsu, T., *J. Ferment. Technol. 40*, 120 (1962).
125. Malin, B. and Westhead, J., *J. Bioch. Microbiol. Eng. 1*, 49 (1961).
126. Tosa, T., *Biotech. Bioeng. 9*, 603 (1967).
127. Marconi, W., Bartoli, F., Cecere, F., Giovenco, S., Morisi, F., and Spotorno, G., *5th Int. Ferment. Symp. Abst.*, 296, Berlin (1976).
128. Chibata, I., Kakimoto, T., and Kato, J., *Appl. Microbiol. 13*, 638 (1965).
129. Kitahara, K., Fukui, S., and Misawa, M., *J. Gen. Appl. Microbiol. 5*, 74 (1959).
130. Yamamoto, K., Sato, T., Tosa, T., and Chibata, I., *Biotech. Bioeng. 16*, 1589 (1974).
131. Yokozeki, K., Sano, K., Eguchi, T., Yasuda, N., Noda, I., and Mitsugi, K., *Ann. Meet. Agr. Chem. Soc. Japan Abst.*, 238 (1976).
132. Marconi, W., Bartoli, F., Cecere, F., and Morisi, F., *Agr. Biol. Chem. 38*, 1343 (1974).
133. Fukui, S., Ikeda, S., Fujimura, M., Yamada, H., and Kumagai, H., *Europ. J. Appl. Microbiol. 1*, 25 (1975).

CHAPTER 8

YEASTS

H. J. Peppler

Whitefish Bay, Wisconsin

The yeast industry, a multiproduct business, has maintained effective programs of plant and process renovation, control systems improvement, production capacity expansion, and new product development for the food industry. In the United States, these major developments in the baker's yeast and food yeast operations contributed to an estimated overall annual unit growth rate of 2 to 4% in the market for yeast products. This report reviews some of these changes and trends in the yeast industry as gathered from trade information, patents, and other literature since early 1974.

I. YEAST PROPAGATION

The basic principles of commercial yeast processes and the use of yeast in the food and beverage industries were brought up to date in 1973 by Reed and Peppler (1). This practical monograph provides a broad introduction to the classification of yeasts, their biology and biochemistry, some of the laboratory procedures used, and the industrial application of yeasts in baking, brewing, wine making, distilled beverage production, food and feed yeast propagation and the manufacture of yeast-derived products, mainly extracts and enzymes. More detailed and comprehensive descriptions of the many aspects of yeast science and technology can be found in the three-volume edition of "The Yeasts" edited by Rose and Harrison (2).

Based on the incomplete survey reported by Perlman (3), which lacks data from the eastern nations of Europe, yeast is grown by more than 73 companies in at least 32 countries. Most of these operations produce only baker's yeast. In the United States alone, four major companies of baker's yeast operate 12 plants. These units supplied the baking industry with yeast products valued at about $120 million in 1976 (4). Food yeast and yeast-derived products were produced and marketed by eight companies-- three different baker's yeast growers, and 5 others. These are identified in Table I.

TABLE I. Principal U.S. Manufacturers of Yeasts and Yeast
          Products

	Baker's Yeast	Dried Yeast	Wine, Distillers, etc.	Extracts Lysates, etc.
Fleischmann Division Standard Brands, Inc. New York, New York	1[a]	1	1	1
Red Star Yeast Division Universal Foods Corp. Milwaukee, Wisconsin	1	1	1	1
Anheuser-Busch, Inc. St. Louis, Missouri	1	2		2
Federal Yeast Division Diamond-Shamrock Corp. Baltimore, Maryland	1			
Yeast Products, Inc. Clifton, New Jersey		1,2		2
Amber Laboratories Juneau, Wisconsin		2,4		2
Lake States Yeast Division St. Regis Paper Company Rhinelander, Wisconsin		3		
Boise-Cascade, Inc. Salem, Oregon		3		
Amoco Food Company Chicago, Illinois		5		
Stauffer Chemical Co. Westport, Connecticut		4		4
Kraft, Inc. Chicago, Illinois		4		

[a]Numbers identify carbon source on which yeast was grown:
1 = Molasses, 2 = Beer, 3 = Sulfite Liquor, 4 = Whey,
5 = Ethanol.

Commercial interest in microbial protein, popularly designated single-cell protein (SCP), in its biomass and extracted
forms, ran high until major economic, public health, and social
obstacles stalled production in existing plants in Italy and
Japan. The current problems and prospects of commercial-scale
plants for producing yeast as a protein source for livestock have
been reviewed in detail by Laskin (5), Litchfield (6,7), and
O'Sullivan (8). Meanwhile the Soviet Union, after opening its
huge Novo-Gorky petroprotein plant in 1974 (9,10), is advancing
plans toward an annual goal of one million metric tons of yeast
grown on purified liquid paraffins (11). With the quadrupling
of the price of world oil in 1973, alternate sources of fermentable carbonaceous materials for bioconversion to protein, especially by yeasts, are being evaluated at an accelerated pace.
Foremost in consideration are ethanol, methanol, cellulose,
starch, food processing byproducts, chemical plant effluents, and
other waste streams. Ratledge (12) discussed the variety and
potential of some of these alternate, low-cost, renewable substrates. An update of worldwide interest and current development
of microbial protein processes was presented at the recent Fifth
International Conference on Global Impacts of Applied Microbiology
(GIAM V) held in Bangkok, Thailand (13).

Substantial commercial production of yeast on alternate substrates is underway in three new operations: (a) ethanol is converted to food yeast (*Candida utilis*) in Minnesota (14), (b) whey
is fermented to food yeast (*Kluyveromyces fragilis*) in New York
and Wisconsin (15), and (c) the wastes from potato processing are
converted by a *Candida* species to a poultry feed supplement at
three locations in Maine (16,17). In Sweden, since 1973, a plant
is using the Symba Process (symbiotic culture of *Endomycopsis
fibuligera* and *Candida utilis*) to produce a feed supplement from
potato starch (18,19).

A. Baker's Yeast

The baker's yeast industry, generally regarded as being relatively mature, has grown slowly and steadily, following in part the
increase in population in some countries. Incomplete estimates
of world yeast production, shown in Table II, place the annual
baker's yeast volume at 187,700 tons (dry weight). In addition
to expanded capacity in existing plants, several new baker's
yeast factories have come on stream in the past five years: in
Denmark (1973), in Czechoslovakia (1974), in Zaire, and Bakers-
field, California (1975), in Brazil and Tabriz, Iran (1976).

Yamada (23) reported that eight baker's yeast factories in
Japan produced about 33,000 tons of yeast (dry weight) in 1975.

Growth of the baker's yeast market in the United States, as
revealed by baking industry statistics (4), is attributable mainly to the increase in population and the gain in per capita

TABLE II. Estimated Annual Yeast Production, 1977[a] (Dry Tons)

	Baker's Yeast	Dried Yeast[b]
Europe	74,000[c]	160,000[c]
North America	73,000	53,000
The Orient	15,000	25,000
United Kingdom	15,500	d
South America	7,500	2,000
Africa	2,700	2,500
Totals	187,700	242,500

[a]Based in part on surveys by Moo-Young (20), World Wide Survey
 of Fermentation Industries, 1967 (21), and private sources.
[b]Dried yeast includes food and fodder yeasts; data for petroleum-
 grown yeasts not available.
[c]Production figures for USSR not reported.
[d]None reported.

consumption of bread-type products. Projections for 1976, based
on comparable data for 1972, indicate that population gained
3.2%, per capita consumption rose 2.5%, and shipments of bread-
type products increased 5.5%.

In describing the main features of the new baker's yeast
plant in Denmark, Rosen (22) outlined processing procedures which
illustrate practices in modern yeast technology. Few factories
can match, however, the advanced electronic process control system installed and functioning in this plant. Another novel feature of the Danish plant is the pollution abatement system: process waste streams are concentrated by evaporation, yielding a
livestock feed known as condensed molasses solubles (CMS).

Many of the improvements, modifications and novel treatments
of yeast during propagation and processing have led to the grant-
ing of more than 180 patents in the United States since 1970.
The excellent detailed review of this comprehensive literature by
Johnson (24) in 1977 provides an invaluable reference and guide
to trends and potential developments in every segment of the
yeast field. The major areas of information covered, and the
frequency of patenting, are listed in Table III. About 75% of
the patents described deal with baker's yeast, food yeast and
yeast products for the food industry. Growing baker's yeast on
ethanol commercially appears to be a long-range prospect. Laboratory processes have been described by Ueda (25), Ridgway et al.
(26), Lindquist (27), Urakami (28), and Masuda et al. (29).

TABLE III. *Classification of Yeast-Related U.S. Patents (1970 to July 1977)[a]*

Category	Number issued
Yeast technology (apparatus, processing)	22
Growth on hydrocarbons	28
Growth on alcohols, acids, wastes	22
Production of chemicals	14
Use in baking and pasta products	24
Condiments and flavor enhancers	18
Reduced RNA	11
Yeast modification of food products	13
Isolated protein	5
Texturized yeast protein	7
Lysates and ruptured cells	7
Animal feed supplements	12
Total	183

[a]*As reviewed by Johnson (24).*

The need for faster leavening action in the commercial short-time, continuous dough systems has focused the search for yeast strains with high maltase activity. Lövgren and Hautera (30) have observed, however, that two different brands of baker's yeast which differ markedly in maltose fermenting ability have nearly the same leavening activity. They attribute this lack of correlation (i.e. high maltase action/high leavening) to a repression of the maltose uptake system which occurs in the presence of hexose in the dough. During the first two hours of dough fermentation, the concentration of maltose increases while the level of other sugars decreases. They concluded that a derepression of the maltose uptake system must occur when maltose utilization begins. Their studies with $U-^{14}C$ maltose showed that maltose is not a major source of CO_2 in the first hour of leavening action in the presence of glucose.

In contrast, Grzybowski and Majchrzak (31) observed an increase of 20 to 40% in the maltase activity of a baker's yeast treated with oxytetracycline (20 to 100 µg/ml aerated wort or yeast cream). The treated yeast reduced dough leavening time by about 13%, in comparison with untreated yeast.

An outstanding review of sugar transport and metabolism in yeast has been written by Barnett (32). It updates the field with 710 references through 1975.

B. Food Yeasts

In addition to the supply of yeast grown on molasses, four
new sources of food yeast have entered the market in the United
States since 1974:   (a) *Candida utilis* grown on synthetic ethanol
(14) and wood sugars in sulfite waste liquor (33); (b) *K. fragilis* from the fermentation of whey (15); and (c) a new facility,
adjacent to a new brewery, for recovering brewers yeast. These
plants are identified in Table I.

1. Ethanol-Grown Yeast. The first large-scale propagation
of yeast (*C. utilis*) on ethanol began in 1975 in Hutchinson,
Minnesota. About 7,000 tons of dried food yeast are produced
annually in an inorganic nutrient medium containing 100 to 500
ppm ethanol obtained from the hydration of ethylene (14). The
closed propagating system features two fermentors arranged in
parallel; it is operated continuously and with full automation.
As fermentor broth is withdrawn continuously, yeast is removed by
centrifuging, and the gas phase is returned to the bioreactors.
The yeast cream obtained is pasteurized before spray drying.
Certain modifications in substrate conposition and cream processing result in four products which differ in emulsion capacity,
waterbinding, flavor and nutritional value (14,34).

2. Whey-Grown Yeast. Whey is fermented with *K. fragilis* in
four commercial plants operated by three companies (Table I).
The process at Juneau, Wisconsin, the newest plant in the field,
is a semi-continuous, aerobic propagation in which the lactose
concentration is controlled automatically in the nonlimiting
range of 0.5 to 0.75%. This allows the formation of ethanol
which is recovered (15). For the production of food yeast, the
yeast cream obtained by centrifugation is spray dried. For feed
yeast, the whole fermentor broth is concentrated by evaporation
and then spray dried. Annual production is estimated at 5,000
dry tons.
At Stockton, Illinois, Swiss cheese is fermented in a modern
plant at the rate of 150,000 lbs/day (35). Ethanol is recovered
and shipped to Decatur where it is converted to vinegar.
Food yeast is the primary product from the whey conversion
operations in Visalia, California, and Endicott, New York.

3. Wood Sugar-Grown Yeast. When the Green Bay yeast plant
described by Kaiser and Jacobs (36) closed in 1967, only one
yeast plant utilizing spent sulfite liquor remained productive.
The Green Bay equipment was subsequently relocated, under new
ownership, to Salem, Oregon. Ammonia-base pulp mill waste liquor
is used in the new plant to produce about 5,000 tons annually of
dried *C. utilis*. Yeast harvested for food use is thrice-washed,
pasteurized and spray dried.

C. Feed Yeast

In view of Laskin's (5) comprehensive survey of commercial and pilot scale SCP processes and Litchfield's (6,7) review of comparative costs, only a footnote on treating wastes will be added here.

Three potato processors in Caribou, Maine, recover about six tons of feed supplement each day from 300,000 gal of high BOD (up to 14,000 ppm) waste water which is converted by a species of *Candida* (16,17). The compact aeration unit, designed and installed by Bio-Kinetics, Inc. (San Rafael, California) in 1976, reduces BOD by 80% in a five-hour cycle. A proliferation of these units is likely since an abundance of starchy foods and wastes is available for SCP production in almost every nation of the world. It is also to be noted that there is a preference for using yeasts in these processes: 42 of 54 plants surveyed by Moo-Young (20) in 1976 used processes based on yeast propagation.

Spencer-Martins and van Uden (46) tested 81 starch-assimilating yeasts for their ability to convert starch directly to microbial protein. Two species of *Lipomyces* converted 84 to 100% of the starch supplied. The most promising candidate for direct conversion of starch is *L. kononenkoae*.

Two other processes with commercial potential were reported in 1978: a) one removes lactic acid and reduces the nonprotein nitrogen of cheese whey with *Candida ingens*, a film-forming yeast (47); b) the other, in pilot stage, ferments acid-hydrolyzed straw in a semi-solid state (70% moisture) with *C. utilis* (48).

D. Process Control

Many process steps in yeast production can be regulated automatically, generally by sensors which signal the activation of pumps and pneumatic devices. During propagation, fermentor temperature, pH, foam suppressant demand, nutrient rates and aeration are under precise control in most plants. Molasses additions, generally at fixed and preset rates for a given propagation, may be controlled with greater precision by monitoring the ethanol concentration of the fermentor exit air (49). Wang *et al*. (50) combined an on-line computer with process sensors which determine cell concentration indirectly. Yeast growth rate and cell yield were regulated successfully. An alternate system for optimizing yeast production, described by Nyiri *et al*. (51), monitors the carbon:nitrogen input of the nutrient feed on the basis of the respiratory quotient ($RQ = \underline{d}\ CO_2/\underline{d}\ O_2$) which is calculated from the rates of carbon dioxide evolution and oxygen uptake of the culture, which is determined periodically. When RQ is approximately 1.0, maximal biomass develops.

The problems of process measurements in computer-coupled yeast-producing and related fermentation systems have been discussed by Swartz and Cooney (52) and Humphrey (60).

A most advanced electronic control system operating in the new Danish baker's yeast plant (22) automatically monitors start-up, propagation sequences and parameters, and harvesting.

II.   YEAST-DERIVED PRODUCTS

A.   Autolysed Yeast Extract

Autolysed yeast extracts (AYE) are food ingredients used as flavor and amino acid enhancement of foods (soups, sauces, gravies, cured meats, stews, snack foods, frozen pot pies, etc.). The extracts consist primarily of amino acids, peptides, poly-peptides and other soluble components of yeast cells resulting from hydrolytic activity of enzymes present in edible yeast. Autolysis of 100 lb yeast solids in cream at 40 to 50°C yields about 48 lb autolysed yeast extract (53). The insoluble residue, mainly cell wall material, is waste. The soluble portion is concentrated to a paste, powder or granules. In 1976 the domestic industry produced 4,000 tons of AYE, mainly from the autolysis of brewer's and baker's yeasts. Complete analyses of AYE were reported by the International Hydrolyzed Protein Council (53).

A related product, autolysed yeast, is a flake or powder form obtained by roller drum drying of the whole autolysate (cell fragments plus solubles). It contains only about 50% solubles.

B.   Isolated Cell Components

1. Ruptured Cells. Three new food ingredients with some unusual functional properties have been developed from mechanic-ally-ruptured baker's yeast: protein, glycan, and extract (38). In the process described by Newell et al. (54), chilled yeast cream (pH 4.5 to 6.5) is passed through a Manton-Gaulin homogen-izer (8,000 psig) three times, rupturing cell walls, releasing cell protein and solubles. Protein in the homogenate is extract-ed with mild alkali (pH 9.5, 45°C, 15 min) and centrifuged to remove yeast cell walls (yeast glycan). The alkaline extract is then acidified to pH 4.5, incubated one hour at 45°C, and centri-fuged to remove the insoluble yeast protein (55). The residual solubles are concentrated, cooked to improve flavor, and spray dried to yield yeast extract. The protein fraction contains less than 2% RNA (56), about 12% nitrogen, 12% carbohydrate, 11% lipid, and 2% ash (38). The yeast glycan fraction consists of 1.6% nitrogen, 88% carbohydrate, and less than 1% each of ash and

fat. Composition of the yeast extract is 7.7% nitrogen, 27% carbohydrate, 24% ash, and less than 1% fat; but it is high in
nucleic acids (10%).

A similar process for recovering protein from *C. tropicalis*
grown on n-paraffins was reported by Cunningham *et al.* (69).

2. RNA Reduction. Reduction of nucleic acid content of
yeast whole cells and isolated yeast protein can be achieved in
several ways: a) holding alkaline homogenates (pH 9.5) at 60°C
for 10 min (56,57); b) heat-shocking yeast cream at 68°C for 4 to
6 sec and incubating at 52.5°C for two hours, lowering the RNA
content of cells from 7% to 1 - 1.5%; c) activating endogenous
ribonuclease degradation of nucleic acids and leakage from the
cells. The latter two-step process (59) removed two-thirds of
the nucleic acid present in the yeast cells.

3. Microbial Protein. The status of microbial protein for
human consumption with respect to safety and nutrition was reviewed by Chen and Peppler (61). Various aspects of its use in
foods, either in the form of dead cells or isolated protein concentrates, were discussed: a) improvement of nutritional quality
and physical properties of whole cells; b) flavor and texture
improvements of protein concentrates; c) preparation of textur-
ized products; and d) functional properties of microbial protein
concentrates.

4. Extractable Components. Intracellular RNA of *C. utilis*
and other species of this genus, especially those sensitive to
potassium chloride, can be increased substantially (12 to 15%).
Highest yields (18%) were produced by a mutant of *C. lipolytica*
grown on n-paraffin, and *C. tropicalis* (16.9%) propagated on a
glycerol medium (62). RNA contents of 11 to 14.5% were found in
acetic acid-assimilating strains of *C. utilis* tested by Miyata
(63).

RNA can be extracted from yeast in alkaline solutions (pH 7.4
to 12.5) heated to 40°C. After stirring one hour, the suspension
is neutralized and centrifuged; RNA is precipitated at pH 2 (64).

A good portion of the 250 tons of nucleotide seasoning produced in Japan is processed from RNA extracted from *C. utilis*
grown on spent sulfite liquor (23). The residual cell solids of
the extraction process are used in animal feeds.

Glutathione may be extracted from brewer's yeast by treating
yeast cream (21% solids) with acetic acid, heating to 90°C, holding 5 min, and cooling rapidly (65). Glutathione is separated
from the extract as the copper salt.

With D-xylose as the sole carbon source for growth, *C. utilis*
was reported to produce xylitol in 10% yield (66). After immobilization in polyacrylamide gel, the same xylose-grown cells reduced xylose to xylitol with yields of 60 to 90%. The xylose-
grown cells also reduced D-ribose to ribitol.

Cells of *C. tropicalis* immobilized in polyacrylamide poly-styrene and aluminum alginate showed a greater rate (28%) of phenol oxidation than cell suspensions (67).

Astaxanthin, the principal carotenoid pigment in the red yeast *Phaffia rhodozyma*, induces pigmentation in rainbow trout (68). A diet with 15% red yeast pigmented trout in 43 days. When the diet was fed to lobsters, however, the yeast carotenoid was not readily accumulated.

REFERENCES

1. Reed, G. and Peppler, H. J., "Yeast Technology." AVI Publishing Co., Westport, CT (1973).
2. Rose, A. H. and Harrison, J. S., eds. "The Yeasts"; Vol. 1 "Biology of Yeasts" (1969); Vol. 2 "Physiology and Biochem-istry of Yeasts" (1970); Vol. 3 "Yeast Technology" (1970). Academic Press, London.
3. Perlman, D., *Chemtech. 7*, 434 (1977).
4. Bakery Trends, *Bakery Production and Marketing*, June (1977).
5. Laskin, A. I., *Ann. Rep. Ferment. Processes 1*, 151 (1977).
6. Litchfield, J. H., *Adv. Appl. Microbiol. 22*, 267 (1977).
7. Litchfield, J. H., *Food Technol. 31(5)*, 175 (1977).
8. O'Sullivan, D. A., *Chem. Eng. News 56(12)*, 12 (1978).
9. *Chem. Eng. News 52(33)*, 30 (1974).
10. *Food Eng.* p. 19, November (1974); p. 36, February (1976).
11. *Chemical Week 120(9)*, 20 (1977).
12. Ratledge, C., *Ann. Rep. Ferment. Processes 1*, 49 (1977).
13. Fifth International Conference on Global Impacts of Applied Microbiology (GIAM V). Bankok, Thailand, November (1977); Behrman, D., *ASM News 44*, 102 (1978).
14. *Food Processing 38(7)*, 90 (1977).
15. Bernstein, S. and Plantz, P. E., *Food Eng. 49(11)*, 74 (1977).
16. Dambois, I., Deeves, R., and Forwalter, J., *Food Processing 39(5)*, 156 (1978).
17. *Business Week*, March 14 (1977).
18. *Food Eng.*, p. 66 November (1976).
19. Jarl, K., *Food Technol. 23*, 1009 (1969).
20. Moo-Young, M., *Process Biochem. 11(10)*, 32 (1976).
21. World Wide Survey of Fermentation Industries, 1967. IUPAC Information Bull. No. 3, June (1971).
22. Rosen, K., *Process Biochem. 12(10)*, 10 (1977).
23. Yamada, K., "Japan's Most Advanced Industrial Fermentation Technology and Industry," The International Technical Infor-mation Institute, Tokyo (1977).
24. Johnson, J. B., "Yeasts for Food and Other Purposes." Noyes Data Corp., Park Ridge, New Jersey (1977).
25. Ueda, K., *Japan Kokai 76-35*, 471; *76-35*, 472 (1976).

26. Ridgway, J. A., Lappin, T. A., Benjamin, B. M., Corns, J. B., and Akin, C., U.S. Patent 3,865,691 (1975).
27. Lindquist, R. H., U.S. Patent 3,954,561 (1976).
28. Urakami, T., U.S. Patent 3,929,578 (1975).
29. Masuda, Y., Kato, K., Takayama, Y., Kida, K., and Nakanishi, M., U.S. Patent 3,868,305 (1975).
30. Lövgren, T. and Hautera, P., *European J. Appl. Microbiol. 4,* 37 (1977).
31. Grzybowski, R. and Majchrzak, R., *Acta Aliment. Pol. 3(1),* 49 (1977).
32. Barnett, J. A., *Adv. Carbohyd. Chem. Biochem. 32,* 125 (1976).
33. Anderson, R., Weisbaum, R. B., and Robe, K., *Food Processing,* p. 58, July (1974).
34. Andres, C., *Food Processing 38(11),* 87 (1977).
35. *Dairy & Ice Cream Field 159(11),* 48 (1976).
36. Kaiser, W. and Jacobs, W., *Food Processing 1,* 22 (1957).
37. *Wall St. Journal,* May 27 (1976); McCormick, R. D., *Food Product Dev. 7(6),* 17 (1973).
38. Seeley, R. D., *Food Product Dev. 9(7),* 46 (1975); *MBAA Tech. Quart. 14(1),* 35 (1977).
39. *Chem. Eng. News,* p. 15, Jan. 9 (1978); p. 11, Oct. 31 (1977).
40. Momose, H. and Gregory, K. F., *Appl. Environ. Microbiol. 35,* 641 (1978).
41. Tanner, R. D., Souki, N. T., and Russell, R. M., *Biotechnol. Bioeng. 19,* 27 (1977).
42. Okanishi, M. and Gregory, K. F., *Can. J. Microbiol. 16,* 1139 (1970).
43. Iguchi, T., Hayakawa, S., and Ohosawa, H., U.S. Patent 3,730,837 (1973).
44. Terui, S., British Patent 1,286,208 (1972).
45. Viikari, L. and Linko, M., *Process Biochem. 12(5),* 17 (1977).
46. Spencer-Martins, I. and van Uden, N., *European J. Appl. Microbiol. 35,* 29 (1977).
47. Ruiz, L. P., Gurnsey, J. C., and Short, J. L., *Appl. Environ. Microbiol. 35,* 771 (1978).
48. Grant, G. A., Han, Y. W., and Anderson, A. W., *Appl. Environ. Microbiol. 35,* 549 (1978).
49. Bach, H. P., Woeher, W., and Roehr, M., 5th Int. Ferm. Symp., Berlin (1976); *Biotechnol. Bioeng. 20, 799 (1978).*
50. Wang, H. Y., Cooney, C. L., and Wang, D. I. C., *Biotechnol. Bioeng. 19,* 69 (1977).
51. Nyiri, L. K., Toth, G. M., Parmenter, D. V., and Krishnaswami, C. S., U. S. Patent 4,064,015 (1977).
52. Swartz, J. R. and Cooney, C. L., *Process Biochem. 13(2),* 3 (1978).
53. International Hydrolyzed Protein Council, "Comments with Additional Data on SCOGS Tentative Evaluation of the Health Aspects of Protein Hydrolyzates as Food Ingredients--Report 37b." Washington, D. C., July 26 (1977).

54. Newell, J. A., Seeley, R. D., and Robbins, E. A., U.S.
     Patent 3,888,839 (1975).
55. Newell, J. A., Robbins, E. A., and Seeley, R. D., U.S.
     Patent 3,867,555 (1975).
56. Robbins, E. A., U.S. Patent 3,991,215 (1976).
57. Robbins, E. A. *et al.*, U.S. Patent 3,887,431 (1975).
58. Tannenbaum, S. R., Sinskey, A. J., and Maul, S. B., U.S.
     Patents 3,968,009 (1976); 3,720,585 (1973).
59. Chao, K. C., U.S. Patent 3,809,776 (1974).
60. Humphrey, A. E., *Process Biochem. 12(3)*, 19 (1977).
61. Chen. S. L. and Peppler, H. J., *Dev. Ind. Microbiol. 19*,
     79 (1978).
62. Akiyama, S., Doi, M., Arai, Y., Nakao, Y., and Fukuda, H.,
     U.S. Patent 3,909,352 (1975).
63. Miyata, S., Japan Kokai 76 54,975 (1976).
64. Kuninaka, A., Fujimoto, M., and Yoshino, H., Japan Kokai
     76 86,188 (1976).
65. Horie, Y., Katayama, H., Uchida, T., and Kuroiwa, Y.,
     Japan Kokai 76 76,483 (1976).
66. Okunev, O. N. *et al.*, *Prikl. Biokhim. Microbiol. 12(3)*, 356
     (1976); from *Chem. Abstr. 85*, 44859 (1977).
67. Hackel, U., Klein, J., Megnet, R., and Wagner, F., *European
     J. Appl. Microbiol. 1*, 291 (1975).
68. Johnson, E. A., Conklin, D. E., and Lewis, M. J., *J. Fish.
     Res. Board Canada 34 (12)*, 17 (1977).
69. Cunningham, S. D., Cater, C. M., Mattel, K. F., and
     Vanderzant, C., *J. Food Sci. 40*, 732 (1975).

CHAPTER 9

β-LACTAM ANTIBIOTICS

M. Gorman
F. M. Huber

The Lilly Research Laboratories
Eli Lilly and Company
Indianapolis, Indiana

I. INTRODUCTION

Research on β-lactam compounds in the year 1977 was characterized by the reporting of three developments which could have far-
reaching impact on the future of the use of this class of antibiotic in medicine (1-5). These are:

(1) The discovery of a new 7-acylamidocephem(1) in which the
acyl moiety contains an aminothiazole oxime function which exhibits 10-fold greater activity against strains of gram negative
bacteria belonging to both, classically, cephalosporin resistant
and sensitive genera than do older compounds.

(2) The advance in chemical synthetic procedures leading to
new β-lactams has yielded many highly altered cephems having carbon, oxygen, and nitrogen atoms at either the 1 or 2 positions.
These compounds are not only chemical laboratory curiosities but
they possess significant antibiotic activity on their own--often
surpassing the natural cephem analog (2,3).

(3) Additional information on thienamycin (4) and olivanic
acids (5) has shown these to be members of a large group of highly
active new antibacterials and β-lactamase inhibitors. Details
will be presented below on these discoveries.

II.   REVIEW LITERATURE

A number of review articles covering various aspects of β-
lactam research were published in 1977. The proceedings of a
meeting held at Cambridge, England in 1976 have been published
with the title: *Recent Advances in the Chemistry of β-Lactam
Antibiotics* (6). Several of these papers were referenced in last
year's review. Also dealing primarily with chemistry is Part II
of a review by E. I. Gunda and J. Cs. Jaszbereyi (2) covering many
of the chemical techniques used for total synthesis of novel β-
lactam compounds. In a book edited by D. Perlman (7)--"Structure
Activity Relationships (S.A.R.) Among the Semisynthetic Antibiotics"--there appears a series of articles pertaining to this
parameter of β-lactam research. Two of these chapters [one by
Price on penicillins (8) and one by Sassiver and Lewis on cephalosporins (9)] are reprinted from 1970 publications while the
other two [Price on penicillin (10) and Webber and Ott on cephalosporins (11)] complete the S.A.R. series from 1970 through the
beginning of 1977. The above book represents a novel idea in
editing and is a great help to those in antibiotic research. The
December 1977 supplement of the Japanese Journal of Antibiotics
is devoted to the proceedings of the 15th and 30th Anniversary
Symposium of the Institute of Microbial Chemistry and the Journal
of Antibiotics, held in Tokyo October 1977. It contains *inter
alia* β-lactam review chapters by E. P. Abraham consisting of a
survey of the research area (12), H. Aoki *et al.* on screening for
β-lactams (13), M. Hashimoto and T. Kamiya on chemical modification (14), T. Takahashi *et al.* on enzymatic acylation of cephalosporins and penicillins (15) and K. Kitano *et al.* on use of a
β-lactam super-sensitive *Pseudomonas* strain for screening (16).
Other reviews appearing this year include several on biosynthesis. One of these by D. J. Aberhart (17) concentrates primarily on the incorporation of labeled precursors aimed at establishing the reaction sequence from single amino acids to final
cephalosporin C and penicillin N while that by Vandamme (18) reviews what is known of enzymes involved in β-lactam antibiotic
synthesis. Y. Fujisawa (19) discusses in detail the steps from
deacetoxycephalosporin C to cephalosporin C. K. Kitano (20) discusses recent studies in establishing a system for detecting
trace amounts of new cephalosporins and the use of this method
for the improvement of production of β-lactam antibiotics.
A general background on cephalosporin antibiotic development
and related topics appeared by Wheeler (21) while Barza and Miao
(22) published a review of general biological properties of commercial cephalosporins. A review (23) of methods for introduction
of the 7α-methoxyl function into cephalosporins appeared.
Tipper and Strominger in 1965 (24) reported [reviewed histor-
ically this year (25)] the startingly simple explanation for the
mechanism of action of penicillin by inhibition of the steps of

peptidoglycan synthesis. This work proved to be the stimulus for
the synthesis of many novel new β-lactam derivatives as well as
prompting a great deal of research on the details of this mechanism. The current picture is much more complex since bacteria
have multiple penicillin sensitive enzymes. These are responsible
for the diverse morphological changes which take place when β-
lactam compounds interact with bacteria. A recent review by
Spratt (26) summarizes the current state of the mechanism of
action of penicillin. He describes in detail the newer methods
used to detect these multiple penicillin sensitive enzymes and
to analyze their functions in peptidoglycan synthesis.

Professor J. M. Ghuysen has reviewed his extensive contributions to the study of penicillin's interaction with a number of
dd-carboxypeptidases and transpeptidases in two reviews (27,28).
As commented upon by J. M. Frere (29), a point of major importance
introduced by the Belgium workers is that the enzyme-inhibitor
initial complex EI* is not stable. Degradation of the penicillin
occurs with concomitant reactivation of the enzyme. The cephalosporin complexes are more stable than the penicillin complex. Thus
the faster the decay of the EI* which leads to inactive antibiotic
fragments, the higher the concentration of antibiotic needed to
cause enzyme inhibition.

The action of β-lactam antibiotics may be described at the
molecular level as mentioned above or at the cellular level. Both
have been extensively studied. In the last year, G. N. Rolinson
and coworkers described in detail the differences between ampicillin and amoxycillin in terms of bactericidal effects, bacterio-
lytic effects and morphology of E. coli when cultured in the
presence of these compounds (30). They conclude that rate of
killing which is faster for amoxycillin might possibly have therapeutic significance for antibiotics of short half-life such as
β-lactam compounds.

III. PENICILLINS

Piperacillin (1), previously known as T1220, represents an
experimental penicillin with potent activity against Pseudomonas
and other gram negative bacteria.

This compound was prepared at Toyama Chemical Co. (31) and is
being developed by both Lederle Laboratories (32) and Toyama.
This acylureidopenicillin had an MIC of <2 for 70% of Pseudomonas
strains versus <64 for carbenicillin and it was also much more
active in vitro against Klebsiella which may indicate stability
to gram-negative penicillinase. In mouse infections of Pseudomonas, it was only slightly more active than carbenicillin (32).
In a second study (33), 91% of gram-negative isolates were susceptible to <8 mcg/ml of pipericillin as compared with only 66%
for carbenicillin.

1

Many compounds of this general structural type have been reported in previous years. This entry appears to be the most potent.
Whether it will represent a significant advance over carbenicillin
and ticarcillin remains to be seen. Other acylureidopenicillins
are described by Koenig *et al.* (34)

IV.   CEPHALOSPORINS

The first expanded spectrum cephalosporin to be widely studied
was cefamandole (*2*) (35,36). It is very potent against many gram-
negative bacteria including certain strains resistant to older
cephalosporins. It is quite resistant to many cephalosporinase
enzymes. More recently, several cephalosporins with similar properties were developed. Two of these, SCE 963 (37) (*3*) and cefuroxime (38) (*4*) have received extensive biological and chemical
evaluation.

2

3

4

5

This year three groups reported almost simultaneously on the combining of the aminothiazole present as part of SCE 963 with the *syn*-methyl oxime as present in cefuroxime to yield a new cephalosporin shown as *5*.

The first publication by the Roussel-Uclaf (1) group describes the synthesis of this 7-ACA derivative and points out that while the *anti*-isomer has weak activity, the *syn*-compound is 10-100 times as active (*in vitro*) against gram-negative bacteria as available reference cephalosporins. They follow this paper with a second report which designates the compound as HR 756 and mentions that it is active against *Pseudomonas* strains with a medium MIC of 61 µg/ml vs 342 µg/ml for carbenicillin (39). The new compound is active in treating mouse infections. The ED_{50} values in mice are better than cefazolin against all gram-negative and *Streptococcal* strains shown. The major weakness in the spectrum of this new antibiotic appears to be its activity against *Staphylococcus aureus* which is poor relative to cefazolin.

The information on HR 756 was extended in two papers presented by the Fujisawa group (40,41). They called HR 756 by the designation of FR 13301 (*5*) and showed that a second compound FR 13374 (*6*) has a similar activity pattern. The synthesis of the cephalosporin nucleus for *6* is described in Reference 14.

6

The activity of FR 13374 is similar to that of HR 756. The
similar activity of these different cephalosporins suggests the
importance of the side chain for the superior activity toward gram-
negative bacteria. Again FR 13374 was weaker than conventional
cephalosporins against *S. aureus*.

The third group to report on HR 756 was that from Takeda
Pharmaceutical Co. Their first paper (42) compares HR 756 with
the corresponding 3-carbamoyloxymethyl cephem (7) derivative and
the 3-tetrazoloylthiomethyl cephem (8). Again the unusual gram-
negative inhibition is a property of the *syn*-oxime isomer (shown).
The three compounds show only minor differences in *in vitro* activity. These new antibiotics must be strongly resistant to β-
lactamase activity. In their second paper (43) this group shows
that the corresponding free oximes (R = H, not CH_3) are also very
potent against gram-negative bacteria. All groups suggest that
further studies are in progress.

A detailed study of the effect of modification of the cephem
nucleus at C-3 on oral absorption of the resulting compounds was
reported in 1977 (44).

7: R = $OCONH_2$; R' = CH_3

8: R = [tetrazole structure]; R' = CH_3

9: R = $OCONH_2$; R' = H

10: R = [tetrazole structure]; R' = H

V. NUCLEAR MODIFIED CEPHALOSPORINS

As mentioned in this review last year, a synthesis of 1-carba
and 1-oxadethiocephalosporins were reported by Cama and Christensen (45,46) in 1974. Using either total synthesis similar to that
described in the above or starting with penicillin and converting
it to an azetidinone intermediate, a number of new β-lactam ring
systems or unusually substituted cephems were prepared. In general, results of only minimal antibacterial testing are given for
the new antibiotics, but compound 11 (47), the racemic-oxygen analog of cefamandole, is claimed to have activity equal to cefamandole. Starting from penicillin, the Shionogi group has also prepared novel 1-oxadethiocephalosporin analogs with carbenicillin-
like side chains (12) at the 7-position (48). The advantage of
penicillin as the starting material over a total synthesis is that
the final product is optically active.

Other nuclear analogs reported are represented by 13 (49,50)
with various R groups such as -OC$_2$H$_5$, H, CH$_3$, CH$_2$Ø and related
structures. Both the Bristol group (51) and the SKF workers (52)
report the 1-carba-2-thiacephem antibiotics (14).

Details of the chemistry of conversion of penicillins into new
β-lactam antibiotics are given in two papers from Beecham Laboratories that describe compounds of the type shown in 15 (53) and 16
(54). These cephalosporins are described as orally active and
their potency compares with cephalexin and cephaloglycin.

15: R = $-CH_2$⟨pyridyl⟩

16: R = $-CH_2$⟨phenyl⟩$-CO_2H$

Whether these complex chemical approaches will lead to economically viable antibiotics is still an unanswered question.

VI. NOCARDICIN

In the previous review we mentioned that nocardicin is a monocyclic β-lactam cell wall synthesis inhibitor that is of interest because of its antibacterial spectrum. The compound is active against *Pseudomonas* species and other gram-negative organisms (55). Its *in vitro* activity is weak and MIC values are strongly dependent on media constituents (56), except against specially selected strains "super-sensitive" to the nocardicins (13). Surprising was the observation that nocardicin A is much more active treating mouse infections, especially *Pseudomonas* strains, than antibiotics with superior MIC values (57). The pharmacokinetics in animals (58) also support the observation that nocardicin A may be of interest clinically.

Several new factors have been described from the nocardicin culture. The structures of these are shown as *17a-g* (59).

17f: HO—⟨ ⟩—C-CO— (with HON above, C double bonded to NON)

17g: HO—⟨ ⟩—CH-CO— (with NH$_2$ above)

As in the case of HR 756 (vida supra) the *syn*-oxime (*a*) is more active than the *anti*-compound (*b*) (13). It has been noted that nocardicin A decreases bacterial cell wall cross-linking (*trans*-peptidation) in a cell-free situation but has little effect on carboxypeptidase enzymes (13). A total synthesis of nocardicin has been reported (60).

VII.   CLAVULANIC ACID

Clavulanic acid is a β-lactamase inhibitor (61). It may be used together with penicillins or cephalosporins to protect them from destruction by these enzymes. The effect is to reduce their MIC and ED$_{50}$ values against various microorganisms. The structure (reviewed here last year) is shown as *18* (62).

18:   R = H

19:   R = COCH$_2$CH$_2$OH

A naturally occurring ester, *19*, has been reported (63). Two other derivatives isolated from the same organism, *Streptomyces clavuligerus*, are *20* and *21*. These structures are novel in that they possess no C-3 carboxyl group. They are reported to be active antifungal agents (64).

20:   R = COOH

21:   R = CH$_2$OH

VIII. THE THIENAMYCINS

The year 1977 has seen a proliferation in the number of new
natural compounds containing the 1-azabicyclo[3.3.0]hept-2-ene-
ring system. As predicted in the previous review (66), the β-lactam inhibitors from Beecham (MM 4550 and MM 13902) have now been
shown to be members of this series (67). The basic compound called
olivanic acid (22) has not been reported to be naturally occurring
as yet (67).

22: R = H, n = 0, R' = H

23: R = -SO$_3$H, n = 0,
      R' = -COCH$_3$

24: R = -SO$_3$H, n = 1,
      R' = -COCH$_3$

Compound 23 represents MM 13902 while MM 4550 is 24. The
stereochemistry of the olivanic acids has not been reported.
These same two compounds have been reported by workers in Japan
as MC 696-SY2-A and B (68). The structure of MC 696-SY2-A is also
represented by 23 and that of MC 696-SY2-B by 24. The producing
organism is *Streptomyces fulvoviridis* MC 696-SY2 for the latter
two materials and *Streptomyces olivaceus* for the former. While
the gross structures are identical, no direct chemical comparison
was made and no stereochemical indications were given in either
of these papers. Olivanic acid (22) has three asymetric centers
and thus each structure represents eight possible compounds.
Identity of these two series is far from certain in light of the
complexity of the epithienamycins described below.
The total synthesis of thienamycin has been accomplished by
the Merck group (69) and their paper was used as a vehicle to
first describe the stereochemistry of thienamycin (25).

25: R' = H

26: R' = COCH$_3$

The *trans*-stereochemistry of the β-lactam of thienamycin is
unique. All biologically active penicillins and cephalosporins
previously known have the *cis*-configuration at these two carbon
atoms. Perhaps this stereochemistry contributes to the β-lactamase stability of thienamycin.

N-Acetylthienamycin (*26*), first prepared chemically, has been reported to be naturally occurring, as 924A1 (70), produced by *Streptomyces cattleya* NRRL 8057. This culture also produces thienamycin.

Two additional isomeric N-acetyl thienamycins, represented by isomers of *26* are 890A1 and 890A3 (71). These compounds are produced by *Streptomycetes flavogriseus* (NRRL 8139, 8140). Removal of the N-acetyl function in these antibiotics may be accomplished enzymatically by treatment with *Protaminobacter ruber* and the isomeric thienamycins isolated (72).

At the 17th ICAAC Meeting two papers were presented on four compounds called N-acetyl *epi*thienamycins (73,74). From the evidence presented on structure and producing organism, it appears that 890A1 and 890A3 are N-acetyl *epi*thienamycin A and C and that N-acetyl *epi*thienamycin B and D are the corresponding N-acetyl olivanic acid isomers (*22*, R' = $COCH_3$). Further, compound C was shown to have the same configuration as N-acetyl thienamycin at C_5 and C_6 and differ only at C_8. Thus, N-acetyl-8-*epi*thienamycin is compound C. A and B have biological activity comparable to N-acetyl thienamycin while C and D possess relatively low antibacterial activity but better β-lactamase stability. Thus, the double bond (olivanic versus thienamycin side chain) has little effect on MIC level. Stereochemistry (*cis* or *trans* -H) at C_6 has little effect since thienamycin and compound B are both very active. C_8-Stereochemistry appears at this time from the limited data available to control the potency of this series. C_8-Stereochemistry has not been defined for any *epi*thienamycin other than C. All N-acetyl compounds in these series are devoid of activity against *Pseudomonas*. It seems that microorganisms capable of forming the thienamycin ring system are not very fastidious in producing substituents on that ring and thus the possibility of more thienamycin of olivanic acid related antibiotics being discovered is quite good.

Spratt has studied binding of thienamycin and clavulanic acid to penicillin binding proteins and shown that they bind most strongly to protein 2 and least to 3 (75). Thienamycin produced stable round *E. coli* cells at 0.1 μg/ml and, in contrast, clavulanic acid produced "lemon-shaped" cells at 30 μg/ml.

IX.   CULTURE STABILITY AND STRAIN IMPROVEMENT

A strain of *Penicillium chrysogenum* (B-991-41) that produces 10,370 units of penicillin per ml has recently been patented (76). This yield was obtained in a commercial medium containing lactose as a carbon source and phenylacetate as the precursor.

A mutant of *Cephalosporium acremonium* has been reported to synthesize 3.5 mg cephalosporin C per ml in a lactose-soybean meal medium (77). This mutant was resistant to cetyltrimethylammonium bromide.

In attempting to use genetic recombination in strain development, Aharonowitz and Demain (78) studied two different *Streptomycete* cultures. When crosses were undertaken with *S. lipmanii*
"prototroph-like" colonies resulted. Unfortunately, all such cultures segregated back to the parental type. Unlike the *S. lipmanii* system, crosses of *S. clavuligerus* gave much lower frequen-
cies of prototroph colonies. In two different crosses the recom-
binants did not segregate back. The authors concluded that *S.
lipmanii* was less suitable for genetic studies because it only
yielded heterokaryons.

X.   MICROBIOLOGICAL AND ENZYMATIC CONVERSIONS OF β-LACTAMS

The enzymatic alterations of penicillins and cephalosporins
have been recently reviewed by Moss (79). Since the last publication of this annal, several papers have been presented which
demonstrate microbiologic or enzymatic alterations of β-lactams.
With respect to the penicillins, ampicillin was reported to be
produced when a strain of azotobacter was incubated with 6-amino-
penicillanic acid and the methyl ester of D(-) phenylglycine (80).
In the reverse reaction, Lagerlof *et al.* (81) examined the production of 6-aminopenicillanic acid with immobilized *E. coli* acylase.
After testing numerous supporting materials, these authors found
that one preparation could be reused greater than 100 times.
In contrast to the penicillin acylase reports, no evidence
has yet been presented for an acylase to carry out a complimentary
reaction with cephalosporin C as a substrate. It has, however,
been reported that through a set of different reactions, the formation of 7-aminocephalosporanic acids from cephalosporins can be
achieved (82-84). In the latter system, the compounds are converted to the ketoadipyl and glutaryl derivatives and then hydrolyzed. The enzyme complex for this reaction is produced by a
fungus belonging to the genus *Gliocladium*. The transformation of
7-acylaminocephalosporins to 7-aminocephalosporins has been demonstrated when N-(N'-phenylthiocarbamyl)-cephalosporin C and 7-
benzyl-acetamido-desacetoxycephalosporanic acid (85,86). These
reactions were carried out by a culture of *Bacillus megaterium* and
an enzyme preparation from *E. coli*, respectively. The formation
of cephalosporins by N-acylation of their corresponding nucleus
has been well documented. Cephalexin was reported to be produced
from either the methyl ester of α-D-phenylglycine or 5-phenyl-
hydantoin and 7-aminodeacetoxycephalosporanic acid in the presence
of *Pichia hydantoinis* (87,88). Numerous bacteria have been found
to catalyze the N-acylation of 7-aminocephem compounds with α-amino
acid esters (15). Although the α-amino acid ester hydrolase would
not couple any of the N-substituted α-amino acid esters, it would
use a range of different esters of the same amino acid. The enzyme was immobilized on Curdlan 13140 and used for the continuous
synthesis of cephalexin.

XI. BIOSYNTHESIS

Investigators continue to probe the reasons underlying the
ability of methionine to stimulate cephalosporin C synthesis.
Kitano et al. (89) have examined the extent of this phenomenon in
fungi-producing cephalosporins. In this study the organisms were
classified into three categories with reference to their response
to methionine. These categories were: (a) stimulated, (b)
scarcely stimulated, and (c) not stimulated. Only approximately
20% of the strains tested were in category (a). No strains of
Paecilomyces were classified in that group. Although methionine
inhibited synthesis in group (c), cysteine stimulated antibiotic
formation. Komatsu and Kodaira (90) examined the metabolism of
sulfur in a C. acremonium mutant. This mutant was able to better
utilize sulfate for cephalosporin C synthesis than its parent.
These investigators found that the intracellular pool of cysteine
was increased by the addition of either methionine, norleucine,
or sulfate. Methionine and norleucine were found to stimulate
cysteine desulfhydrase. The mutant also had increased L-serine
sulfhydrylase activity. The latter seemed to account for its increased ability to utilize sulfate. Bost and Demain (91) have
reported the synthesis of radioactive penicillin N from L-$[^{14}C]$-
valine by a broken protoplast preparation of C. acremonium. The
preparation failed to synthesize any of the cephalosporins. In
another broken cell investigation, Brewer et al. (92) were able
to demonstrate the conversion of tritiated deacetoxycephalosporin
C to tritiated deacetylcephalosporin C. This reaction has also
been demonstrated by biological analysis by Fujisawa et al. (93).
The latter authors used a cell-free extract of C. acremonium and
assayed the products with P. aeruginosa P_sC^{ss}. The enzyme required
either NADH or NADPH and had a pH optima between 7 and 7.5. The
hydrocylase activity was not observed in mutants which only produced deacetoxycephalosporin C. At the same position on the 3-
hydroxymethylcephalosporins, Brewer et al. (94) have demonstrated
an O-carbamoyltransferase in Streptomyces clavuligerus. The enzyme required carbamoylphosphate as a substrate and the end products were detected by high-pressure liquid chromatography.

It is known that lysine inhibits penicillin synthesis and α-
aminoadipic acid reverses that inhibition. To better understand
this relationship, Friedrich and Demain (95) screened a number of
lysine analogs for the inhibition of growth and penicillin synthesis. The activity of many of these compounds was reversed by lysine. Sporulation was found to be more sensitive to most of the
lysine analogs than was growth and penicillin formation. In a
similar study, the same authors added different compounds in the
lysine biosynthetic pathway and observed that homocitrate reversed
the lysine inhibition. Thus homocitrate synthase was suggested as
the site which was affected by lysine in penicillin biosynthesis.

In order to further elucidate the penicillin biosynthetic pathway, several incorporation studies have been reported. Bycroft *et al.* (97) studied the incorporation of uniformly ^{14}C-labeled L-cysteine and L-valine into the benzylpenicillin synthesized by a high-producing strain of *P. chrysogenum*. They found that 25-40% of the label was incorporated into the penicillin molecule. Further examination with doubly labeled cysteine indicated that 40% of the ^{14}C and 34% of the tritium was present in the antibiotic. The role of amino acid racemases was discussed in relation to the results. Young *et al.* (98) have studied the stereospecific incorporation of cysteine into penicillin. They concluded that there is a net retention of the stereochemistry during the cyclization process involved in the formation of penicillin.

In studying the requirements for the optimal synthesis of nocardin A by *Nocardia uniformis*, Hosoda *et al.* (99) found that L-tyrosine, p-hydroxyphenylpyruvic acid, DL-p-hydroxymandelic acid and L-p-hydroxyphenylglycine all stimulated the synthesis of the antibiotic. Labeling studies indicated that tyrosine was incorporated into the two aromatic rings, serine into the β-lactam and homoserine into the 3-amino-3-carboxypropoxy moiety.

XII. CONCLUSION

The year 1977 has produced a wealth of new research on β-lactam antibiotics. We have tried not to cover those areas reviewed by others during this year but have instead listed major review articles. Three major areas of research, the development of HR 756, the appearance of many nuclear analogs of penicillin and cephalosporin, and the discovery of many new thienamycin related antibiotics have been discussed in depth. Significant advances in enzymological research and biosynthesis related to β-lactam antibiotics are covered.

REFERENCES

1. Bucourt, R., Heymes, R., Lutz, A., Penasse, L., and Perronet, J., *C. R. Acad. Sc. Paris Ser. D. 284*, 1847 (1977).
2. Gunda, E. T. and Jaszberenyi, J. Cs., *in* "Progress in Medicinal Chemistry 14" (G. P. Ellis and G. B. West, eds.), p. 181. North-Holland Publishing Co., Amsterdam, New York, Oxford (1977).
3. Hashimoto, M. and Kamiya, T., *Jap. J. Antibiot. 30*, Suppl., S-218 (1977).
4. Johnston, D. B. R., Schmitt, S. M., Bouffard, F. A., and Christensen, B. G., *J. Am. Chem. Soc. 100*, 313 (1978).

5. Brown, A. G., Corbett, D. F., Eglington, A. J., and Howarth, T. T., *J. Chem. Soc., Chem. Commun.* 523 (1977).
6. Elks, J., ed., "Recent Advances in the Chemistry of β-Lactam Antibiotics." The Chemical Society, Burlington House, London (1977).
7. Perlman, D., ed., "Structure-Activity Relationships Among the Semisynthetic Antibiotics." Academic Press, New York (1977).
8. Price, K. E., *in* "Structure-Activity Relationships Among the Semisynthetic Antibiotics" (D. Perlman, ed.), p. 1. Academic Press, New York (1977).
9. Sassiver, M. L. and Lewis, A., *in* "Structure-Activity Relationships Among the Semisynthetic Antibiotics" (D. Perlman, ed.), p. 87. Academic Press, New York (1977).
10. Price, K. E., *in* "Structure-Activity Relationships Among the Semisynthetic Antibiotics" (D. Perlman, ed.), p. 61. Academic Press, New York (1977).
11. Webber, J. A. and Ott, J. L., *in* "Structure-Activity Relationships Among the Semisynthetic Antibiotics" (D. Perlman, ed.), p. 161. Academic Press, New York (1977).
12. Abraham, E. P., *Jap. J. Antibiot. 30*, Suppl., S-1 (1977).
13. Aoki, H., Kunugita, K., Hosoda, J., and Imanaka, H., *Jap. J. Antibiot. 30*, Suppl., S-207 (1977).
14. Hashimoto, M. and Kamiya, T., *Jap. J. Antibiot. 30*, Suppl., S-218 (1977).
15. Takahashi, T., Kato, K., Yamazaki, Y., and Isono, M., *Jap. J. Antibiot. 30*, Suppl., S-230 (1977).
16. Kitano, K., Nara, K., and Nakao, Y., *Jap. J. Antibiot. 30*, Suppl., S-239 (1977).
17. Aberhart, D. J., *Tetrahedron 33*, 1545 (1977).
18. Vandamme, E. J., *in* "Advances in Applied Microbiology" (D. Perlman, ed.), p. 89. Academic Press, New York (1977).
19. Fujisawa, Y., *J. Takeda Res. Lab. 36*, 295 (1977).
20. Kitano, K., *J. Takeda Res. Lab. 36*, 105 (1977).
21. Wheeler, W. J., *Lloydia 40*, 519 (1977).
22. Barza, M. and Miao, P. V. W., *Am. J. Hosp. Pharm. 34*, 621 (1977).
23. Hiraoka, T., Sugimura, Y., Saito, T., and Kobayashi, T., *Heterocycles 8*, 719 (1977).
24. Tipper, D. J. and Strominger, J. L., *Proc. Nat. Acad. Sci. 54*, 1133 (1965).
25. Strominger, J. L., *Microbiology (Washington, D.C.)*, 177 (1977).
26. Spratt, B. G., *Sci. Prog. (Oxford) 65*, 101 (1978).
27. Ghuysen, J. M., "E. R. Squibb Lectures on Chemistry of Microbial Products. The Bacterial DD-Carboxypeptidase Enzyme System: A New Insight into the Mode of Action of Penicillin." Univ. Tokyo Press, Tokyo, Japan (1977).
28. Ghuysen, J. M., *J. Gen. Microbiol. 101*, 195 (1977).
29. Frere, J. M., *Biochem. Pharmacol. 26*, 2203 (1977).

30. Robinson, G. N., MacDonald, A. C., and Wilson, D. A., *J. Antimicrob. Chemother.* 3, 541 (1977).

31. Saikawa, I., Yasuda, T., Taki, H., Tai, M., Watanabe, Y., Sakai, H., Takano, S., Yoshida, C., and Kasuya, K., *Yakugaku Zasshi* 97, 987 (1977).

32. Kuck, N. A. and Redin, G. S., *Intersci. Conf. Antimicrob. Ag. Chemother.*, 17th New York, Paper No. 446 (abstr.) (1977).

33. Gerlach, E. H., Jones, R. N., Fuchs, P. C., Gavan, T. L., and Barry, A., *Intersci. Conf. Antimicrob. Ag. Chemother.*, 17th New York, Paper No. 451 (abstr.) (1977).

34. Konig, H. B., Metzger, K. G., Offe, H. A., and Schrock, W. A. *in* "Recent Advances in the Chemistry of β-Lactam Antibiotics" (J. Elks, ed.), p. 78. The Chemical Society, Burlington House, London (1977).

35. Kaiser, G. V., Gorman, M., and Webber, J. A., "Cefamandole - A Review of Chemistry and Microbiology." Paper presented at Symposium on Cefamandole, Boca Raton, Florida, March 17-19 (1977).

36. Levine, L. R. and McCain, E., *Intersci. Conf. Antimicrob. Ag. Chemother.*, 17th New York, Paper No. 342 (abstr.) (1977).

37. Numata, M., Minamida, I., Yamaoka, M., Shiraishi, M., Miyawaki, T., and Nishimura, T., *Intersci. Conf. Antimicrob. Ag. Chemother.*, 17th New York, Paper No. 44 (abstr.) (1977).

38. O'Callaghan, C. H. and Gregory, G. I., *Intersci. Conf. Antimicrob. Ag. Chemother.*, 17th New York, Paper No. 79 (abstr.) (1977).

39. Heymes, R., Lutz, A., and Schrinner, E., *Infection* 5, 259 (1977).

40. Mine, Y., Murakawa, T., Kamimura, T., Takaya, T., Nishida, M., Goto, S., and Kuwahara, S., *Intersci. Conf. Antimicrob. Ag. Chemother.*, 17th New York, Paper No. 147 (abstr.) (1977).

41. Murakawa, T., Okada, N., Sakamoto, H., Mine, Y., Nishida, M., Goto, S., and Kuwahara, S., *Intersci. Conf. Antimicrob. Ag. Chemother.*, 17th New York, Paper No. 148 (abstr.) (1977).

42. Ochiai, M., Aki, O., Morimoto, A., Okada, T., and Matsushita, Y., *Chem. Pharm. Bull.* 25, 3115 (1977).

43. Numata, M., Minamida, I., Tsushima, S., Nishimura, T., Yamaoka, M., and Matsumoto, N., *Chem. Pharm. Bull.* 25, 3117 (1977).

44. Scartazzini, R. and Bickel, H., *Heterocycles* 7, 1165 (1977).

45. Cama, L. D. and Christensen, B. G., *J. Am. Chem. Soc.* 96, 7582 (1977).

46. Guthikonda, R. N., Cama, L. D., and Christensen, B. G., *J. Am. Chem. Soc.* 96, 7584 (1977).

47. Firestone, R. A., Fahey, J. L., Maciejewicz, N. S., Patel, G. S., and Christensen, B. G., *J. Med. Chem.* 20, 551 (1977).

48. Narisada, M. and Nagata, W., Ger. Offen. 2,713,370 (1977).

49. Doyle, T. W., Belleau, B., Luh, B., Ferrari, C. F., and Cunningham, M. P., *Can. J. Chem.* 55, 468 (1977).

50. Doyle, T. W., Belleau, B., Luh, B., Conway, T. T., Menard, M., Douglas, J. L., Chu, D. T., Lim, G., Morris, L. R., et al., Can. J. Chem. 55, 484 (1977).
51. Doyle, T. W., Douglas, J. L., Belleau, B., Meunier, J., and Luh, B., Can. J. Chem. 55, 2873 (1977).
52. Bryan, D. B., Hall, R. F., Holden, K. G., Huffman, W. F., and Gleason, J. G., J. Am. Chem. Soc. 99, 2353 (1977).
53. Brain, E. G., Eglington, A. J., James, B. G., Nayler, J. H. C., Osborne, N. F., Pearson, M. J., Smale, T. C., Southgate, R., Tolliday, P., et al., J. Med. Chem. 20, 1086 (1977).
54. Brain, E. G., Eglington, A. J., Nayler, J. H. C., Osborne, N. F., Pearson, M. J., Smale, T. C., Southgate, R., Tolliday, P., Basker, M. J., and Sutherland, R., J. Med. Chem. 20, 1082 (1977).
55. Nishida, M., Mine, Y., Nonoyama, S., and Kojo, H., J. Antibiot. 30, 917 (1977).
56. Kojo, H., Mine, Y., and Nishida, M., J. Antibiot. 30, 926 (1977).
57. Mine, Y., Nonoyama, S., Kojo, H., Fukada, S., and Nishida, M., J. Antibiot. 30, 932 (1977).
58. Mine, Y., Nonoyama, S., Kojo, H., Fukada, S., and Nishida, J., J. Antibiot. 30, 938 (1977).
59. Hosoda, J., Konomi, T., Tani, N., Aoki, H., and Imanaka, H., Agr. Biol. Chem. 41, 2013 (1977).
60. Kamiya, T., in "Recent Advances in the Chemistry of β-Lactam Antibiotics" (J. Elks, ed.), p. 281. The Chemical Society, Burlington House, London (1977).
61. Neu, H. C. and Fu, K. P., Intersci. Conf. Antimicrob. Ag. Chemother., 17th New York, Paper No. 62 (abstr.) (1977).
62. Brown, A. G., Goodacre, J., Harbridge, J. B., Howarth, T. T., Ponsford, R. J., Stirling, I., and King, T. J., in "Recent Advances in the Chemistry of β-Lactam Antibiotics" (J. Elks, ed.), p. 295. The Chemical Society, Burlington House, London (1977).
63. Reading, C., Ger. Offen. 2,708,047 (1977).
64. Napier, E. J., Evans, R., Noble, D., Bushell, M. E., Webb, G., and Brown, D., Ger. Offen. 2,725,690 (1977).
65. Bentley, P. H., Gilpin, M. L., Hunt, E., Brooks, G., and Zomaya, I. I., American Chemical Society, Chicago, Paper No. 43 (abstr.), Sept. (1977).
66. Gorman, M. and Huber, F., Ann. Reps. Ferm. Proc. 1, 327 (1977).
67. Brown, A. G., Corbett, D. F., Eglington, A. J., and Howarth, T. T., J. Chem. Soc., Chem. Commun. 523 (1977).
68. Maeda, K., Takahashi, S., Sezaki, M., Iinuma, K., Naganawa, H., Kondo, S., Ohno, M., and Umezawa, H., J. Antibiot. 30, 770 (1977).
69. Johnston, D. B. R., Schmitt, S. M., Bouffard, F. A., and Christensen, B. G., J. Am. Chem. Soc. 100, 313 (1978).

70. Sawyer-Kahan, J., Kahan, F. M., Goegelman, R. T., Stapley, E. I., and Hernandez, S., Ger. Offen. 2,652,681 (1977).
71. Cassidy, P. M., Goegelman, R. T., Stapley, E. O., and Hernandez, S., Ger. Offen. 2,652,677 (1977).
72. Sawyer-Hakan, J. and Kahan, F. M., Ger. Offen. 2,652,678 (1977).
73. Stapley, E. O., Cassidy, P., Currie, S. A., Daoust, D., Goegelman, R., Hernandez, S., Jackson, M., Mata, J. M., Miller, A. K., Monaghan, R. L., Tunac, J. B., Zimmerman, S. B., and Hendlin, D., *Intersci. Conf. Antimicrob. Ag. Chemother.*, 17th New York, Paper No. 80 (abstr.) (1977).
74. Cassidy, P. J., Stapley, E. O., Goegelman, R., Miller, T. W., Arison, B., Albers-Schonberg, G., Zimmerman, S. B., and Birnbaum, J., *Intersci. Conf. Antimicrob. Ag. Chemother.*, 17th New York, Paper No. 81 (abstr.) (1977).
75. Spratt, B. G., Jobanputra, V., and Zimmerman, W., *Antimicrob. Ag. Chemother. 12*, 406 (1977).
76. Krasy Medic Prepara, U.S.S.R. 271-722 (1977).
77. Ebihara, Y., Umezu, Y., Imaizumi, A., Kamimoto, F., and Matsubara, S., Japan Kokai 77,105290 (1977).
78. Aharonowitz, Y. and Demain, A. L., *Europ. J. Appl. Microbiol. 4*, 125 (1977).
79. Moss, M. O., *Top. Enzyme Ferment. Biotechnol. 1*, 111 (1977).
80. Takeda, H., Matsumoto, I., Tomiyasu, M., Naito, M., Kawakami, T., and Matsuda, K., Japan Kokai 75,117990 (1975).
81. Lagerlof, E., Nathors-T-Westfelt, L., Ekstrom, B., and Sjoberg, B., *Methods Enzymol. 44*, 759 (1976).
82. Takeda, H., Matsumoto, I., and Matsuda, K., Japan Kokai 77,72886 (1977).
83. Takeda, H., Matsumoto, I., and Matsuda, K., Japan Kokai 77,38092 (1977).
84. Takeda, H., Matsumoto, I., and Matsuda, K., Japan Kokai 77,38092 (1977).
85. Nakagawa, N., Yamaguchi, T., and Watanabe, T., Japan Kokai 77,82791 (1977).
86. Savitskaya, E. M., Nys, P. S., Shchellenberg, N. N., Zinchenko, E. Ya., Ryabova, N. M., Levitov, M. M., Kol'tsova, E. V., Berezin, I. V., and Shvedas, V. K., U.S.S.R. 532-619 (1976).
87. Yoshida, N. and Ogino, S., Japan Kokai 77,31890 (1977).
88. Yoshida, N. and Ogino, S., Japan Kokai 77,31889 (1977).
89. Kitano, K., Kintaka, K., and Nakao, Y., *J. Ferment. Technol. 55*, 27 (1977).
90. Komatsu, K. and Kodaira, R., *J. Antibiot. 30*, 226 (1977).
91. Bost, P. E. and Demain, A. L., *Biochem. J. 162*, 681 (1977).
92. Brewer, S. J., Farthing, J. E., and Turner, M. K., *Biochem. Soc. trans. 5*, 1024 (1977).
93. Fujisawa, Y., Kikuchi, M., and Kanzaki, T., *J. Antibiot. 30*, 775 (1977).

94.   Brewer, S. J., Boyle, T. T., and Turner, M. K., *Biochem. Soc. trans 5*, 1026 (1977).
95.   Friedrich, C. G. and Demain, A. L., *Appl. Environ. Microbiol. 34*, 706 (1977).
96.   Friedrich. C. G. and Demain, A. L., *J. Antibiot. 30*, 760 (1977).
97.   Bycroft, B. W., Wels, C. M., Corbett, K., and Daloney, A. P., *in* "Recent Advances in the Chemistry of β-Lactam Antibiotics" (J. Elks, ed.), p. 12.   The Chemical Society, Burlington House, London (1977).
98.   Young, D. W., Morecombe, D. J., and Sen, P. J., *Eur. J. Biochem. 75*, 133 (1977).
99.   Hosoda, J., Tani, N., Konomi, T., Ohsawa, S., Aoki, H., and Imanaka, H., *Agric. Biol. Chem. 41*, 2007 (1977).

CHAPTER 10

AMINOGLYCOSIDE ANTIBIOTICS

Takashi Nara

Tokyo Research Laboratory
Kyowa Hakko Kogyo, Co., Ltd.
Tokyo, Japan

I. NEW AMINOGLYCOSIDES

New aminoglycosides of microbial origin, which have been reported during the last one or two years (from 1976 to 1978), are listed in Table I. The producing organisms and the antimicrobial activities are presented in the table, and the structures are shown in Figures 1 to 12.

All of the new antibiotics belonging to such groups as gentamicin, sisomicin, nebramycin and fortimicin are minor components present in the fermentation broths together with the major components. Whenever a new antibiotic is discovered from an organism, there is every possibility that the organism may elaborate at least several, sometimes 20, 30 or more minor components closely related to the major antibiotic. Particularly when the new major antibiotic is being worked out for further industrial development, chances of encountering minor components are greatly increased, because artificial mutation, works on cultural conditions and the availability of concentrated mother liquors resulting from tank fermentations will enable one to detect the minor antibiotics more readily which will *otherwise* remain to be undetected.

A great number of gentamicin and sisomicin minor components, which have been discovered by Schering scientists, are typical examples of the above explanation. One more minor component reported as gentamicin C_{2a}, as shown in Figure 1, is the 6'-C epimer of gentamicin C_2 and exhibits substantially the same antibacterial spectrum and potency *in vitro* as does gentamicin C_2 (1). This component was separated from other gentamicin components C_1, C_2, and C_{1a} by Craig countercurrent distribution (2).

223

TABLE I. New Aminoglycosides Discovered During the Last Year - 1977

Antibiotics	Producing organisms[a]	Activities[b]	Structure	References
Gentamicin group				
Gentamicin C2a	M. purpurea	G+, G-	Fig. 1	1,2
Compd. I-1(Aminoglycoside PC3)	M. purpurea mutant SC-1124	G+, G-, Myco.	Fig. 2	3,4
6'-Methylgentamicin A (Compd. II-2)	M. purpurea var. nigrescens	G+, G-, Myco.	Fig. 3	3
6'-Methylgentamicin A1 (Compd. III-1)	M. purpurea var. nigrescens	G+, G-, Myco.	Fig. 3	3
3"-N-Demethylgentamicin C2 (Compd. V-2)	M. purpurea var. nigrescens	G+, G-, Myco.	Fig. 3	3
4"-Demethylgentamicin C1 (Compd. VII-1)	M. purpurea var. nigrescens	G+, G-, Myco.	Fig. 3	3
4"-Demethylgentamicin C2 (Compd. VII-3)	M. purpurea var. nigrescens	G+, G-, Myco.	Fig. 3	3
4"-Demethylgentamicin C1a (Compd. VII-5)	M. purpurea var. nigrescens	G+, G-, Myco.	Fig. 3	3
Aminoglycoside PC2	M. purpurea mutant	Not reported	Fig. 4	4
Sisomicin group				
66-40C	M. inyoensis	Not reported	Fig. 5	5,6
Nebramycin group				
Oxyapramycin (Factor 7)	S. tenebrarius mutant	G+, G-	Fig. 6	7,8
Fortimicin group				
Fortimicin C	M. olivoasterospora	G+, G-	Fig. 7	9-11
Fortimicin D	M. olivoasterospora	G+, G-	Fig. 7	10,12
Fortimicin KE	M. olivoasterospora	G+, G-	Fig. 8	12
SF 1854	M. sp.	G+, G-	--c	13

Miscellaneous

LL-BM123α	Nocardia sp.	G+,	G-,	Myco.	Fig. 9	14,15
LL-BM123β_1	Nocardia sp.	G+,	G-,	Myco.	Fig. 10	14
LL-BM123β_2	Nocardia sp.	G+,	G-,	Myco.	--c	14
LL-BM123γ_1	Nocardia sp.	G+,	G-,	Myco.	Fig. 11	14
LL-BM123γ_2	Nocardia sp.	G+,	G-,	Myco.	Fig. 12	14

[a] M. = Micromonospora; S. = Streptomyces.
[b] G+ = Gram positive bacteria; G- = Gram negative bacteria; Myco. = Mycobacterium sp.
[c] Structure unknown.

225

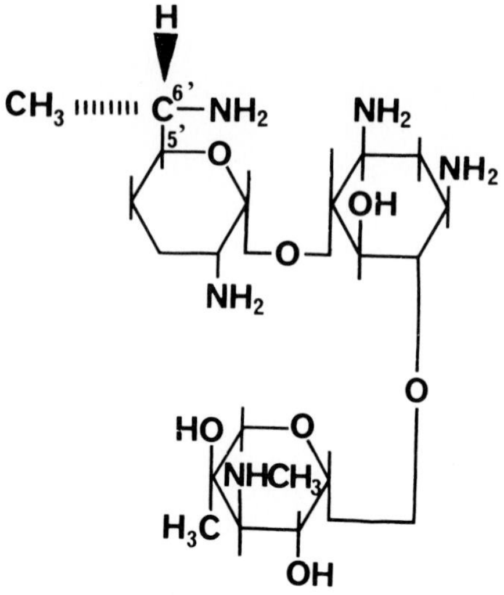

FIGURE 1.   Gentamicin C_{2a}

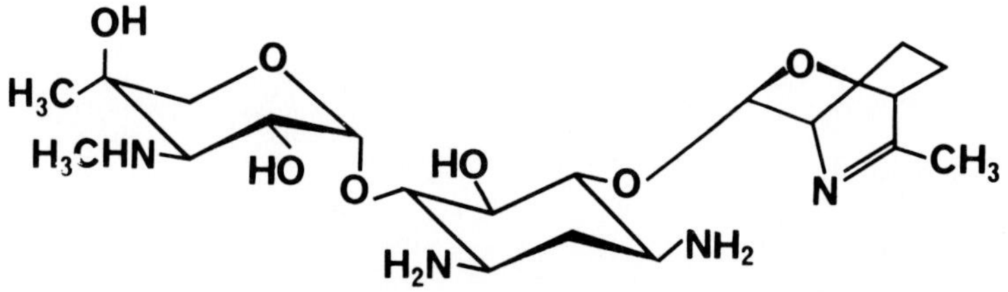

FIGURE 2.   Compound I-1 (Aminoglycoside PC3)

In addition to the Schering's works, seven new compounds of
gentamicin type (Compds. I-1, II-2, III-1, V-2, VII-1, VII-3, and
VII-5) have recently been reported by Hungarian investigators (3).
The structures are shown in Figures 2 and 3.   During the period
1972-1976 they isolated, from the culture broth of a new gentamy-
cin C-producing *Micromonospora purpurea* var. *nigrescens* (16), numerous metabolites including known gentamicin antibiotics and
other related metabolites together with several new substances.
The extensive chromatographic analysis of the crude gentamicin
obtained by ion-exchange process indicated the existence of about
50 basic, water-soluble components.   Seven new components of gentamicin type listed in Table I were thus discovered from these
investigations.   3"-N-Demethylgentamicin C_2 (Compd. V-2) was however already prepared from gentamicin C_2 chemically by Kyowa Hakko
chemists (17).   Compound I-1 (Figure 1), most unique structurally

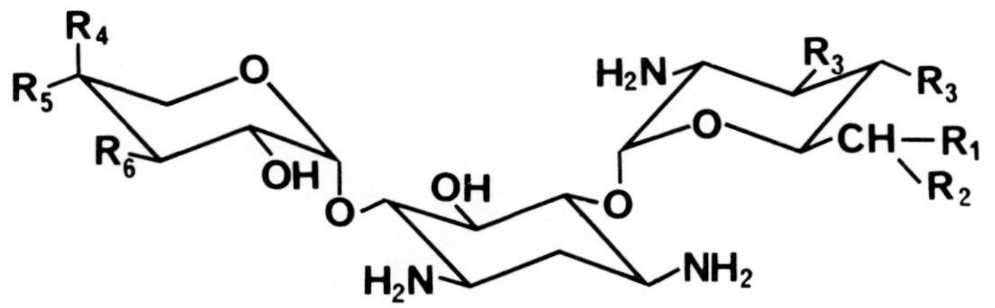

	Compd. No.	R_1	R_2	R_3	R_4	R_5	R_6
6' – Methylgentamicin A	II – 2	CH_3	OH	OH	H	OH	$NHCH_3$
6' – Methylgentamicin A_1	III – 1	CH_3	OH	OH	OH	H	$NHCH_3$
3'' – N – Demethylgentamicin C_2	V – 2	CH_3	NH_2	H	OH	CH_3	NH_2
4'' – Demethylgentamicin C_1	VII – 1	CH_3	$NHCH_3$	H	OH	H	$NHCH_3$
4'' – Demethylgentamicin C_2	VII – 3	CH_3	NH_2	H	OH	H	$NHCH_3$
4'' – Demethylgentamicin C_{1a}	VII – 5	H	NH_2	H	OH	H	$NHCH_3$

FIGURE 3. Compounds II-2, III-1, V-2, VII-1, VII-3, and VII-5.

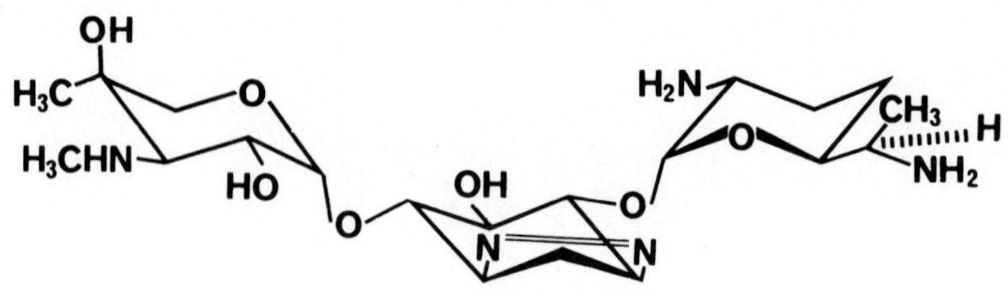

FIGURE 4.   Aminoglycoside PC2.

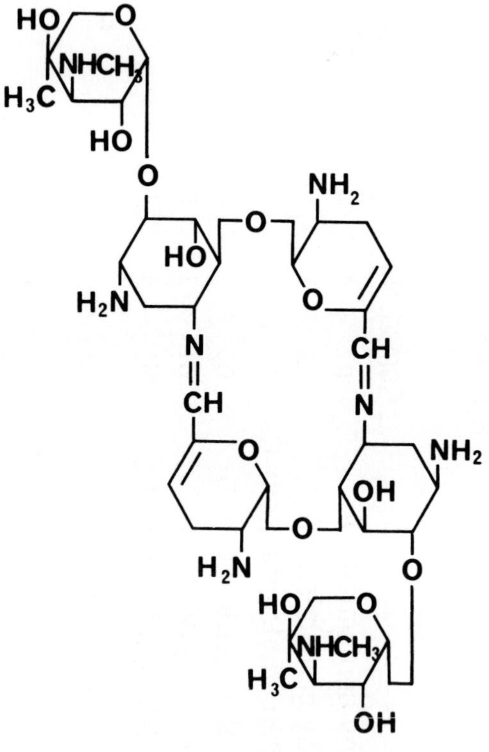

FIGURE 5.   66-40C.

among the 7 compounds, was isolated as aminoglycoside PC3, independently by Schering workers while working on biosynthesis from
gentamicin C_2 to gentamicin C_1 by a 2-deoxystreptamine negative
M. purpurea mutant (4).   Another aminoglycoside PC2 (Figure 4)
was also found during the investigation.

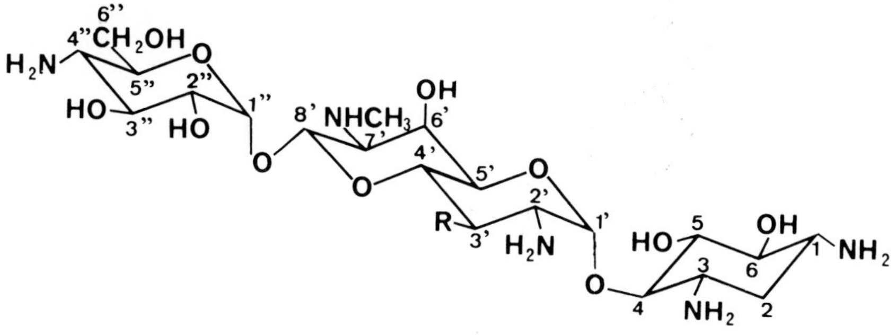

Apramycin (Factor 2)   R
Oxyapramycin (Factor 7)   ——
                                 H
                                 OH

FIGURE 6.   Oxyapramycin.

Aminoglycoside 66-40C (Figure 5) (5,6), having a novel dimeric
structure containing α,β-unsaturated imine groups was isolated
from the crude mixture of the minor components [66-40B (18,19),
66-40D (18,19) and garamine (20,21)] of the sisomicin fermentation. Though its activity was not reported, 66-40C can be used
as an intermediate in preparing sisomicin as well as 6'-N-alkyl-
sisomicins such as G-52 (22,23).

Oxyapramycin, previously designated nebramycin factor 7 (7),
was characterized as shown in Figure 6 (8). It is 3'-hydroxyapra-
mycin, a new analog of apramycin (factor 2) (24), and inhibits
the growth of microorganisms pathogenic to animal and plant life.
In particular, it exhibits a high degree of activity against
Gram-negative organisms, and is relatively nontoxic (7). Other
co-produced minors, factors 8, 9 and 10, in the nebramycin fermentation were also identified to known disaccharides, nebramine,
lividamine and neamine, respectively (8).

The existence of a number of minor components related to fortimicins A and B (25-28) has been suggested in the fortimicin
fermentation with M. olivoasterospora (26). Indeed, three new
fortimicins C (9-11), D (10,12), and KE (12) were isolated from
the beers and characterized by Kyowa Hakko scientists. As shown
in Figure 7, fortimicin C is 4-N-hydantoylfortimicin B and fortimicin D is 6'-C-demethylfortimicin A. Fortimicin KE, as shown in
Figure 8, is 6'-C-demethylfortimicin B. The purpurosamine portion of fortimicin D corresponds to that of gentamicin C_{1a}, that
is, purpurosamine C, while that of fortimicin A matches up with
that of gentamicin C_{2a}. Fortimicin KE is, in other words, 4-N-
desglycylfortimicin D. Both fortimicins C and D exhibit significant broad-spectrum activity against Gram-positive and negative

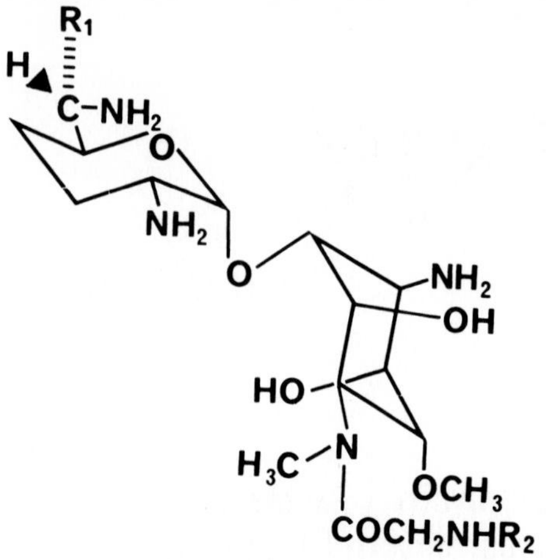

	R_1	R_2
Fortimicin A	CH₃	H
Fortimicin C	CH₃	CONH₂
Fortimicin D	H	H

FIGURE 7.   Fortimicins C and D.

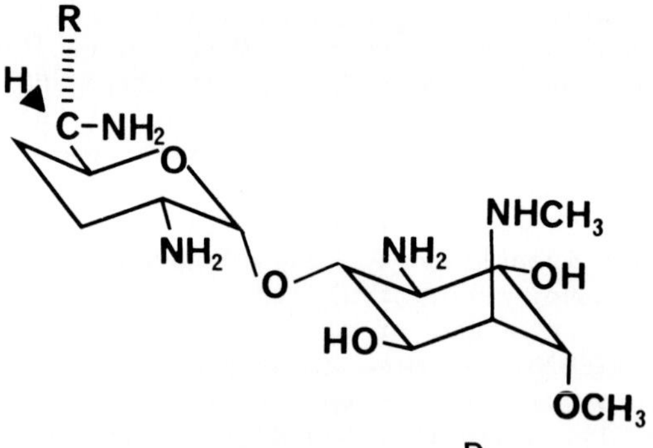

	R
Fortimicin B	CH₃
Fortimicin KE	H

FIGURE 8.   Fortimicin KE.

bacteria, particularly being active against all the resistant
cultures possessing such inactivation enzymes as AAC (6'), AAC
(2'), ANT (2"), APH (3')-I, APH (3')-II, and ANT (4'), except
AAC (3)-I.   This pattern of spectrum is quite similar to that
of fortimicin A, though the overall activity of fortimicins C
or D is slightly less than that of fortimicin A.   The finding
that fortimicin D (purpurosamine: gentamicin C_{1a} type) is
slightly less active than fortimicin A (gentamicin C_{2a} type),
is interesting in contrast with the gentamicin C_{1a} and C_{2a} relationship where gentamicin C_{1a} is significantly superior in activ-
ith to gentamicin C_{2a}.
   SF 1854 (13) obtained from *Micromonospora sp.* appears to belong to the fortimicin-group antibiotic.
   In addition to these minor components, a series of amino-
glycosides designated LL-BM 123 α, β_1, β_2, γ_1 and γ_2, was discovered by Lederle workers (14,15) whose structures (Figures 9,
10,11,12) are quite different from those of the minors, though

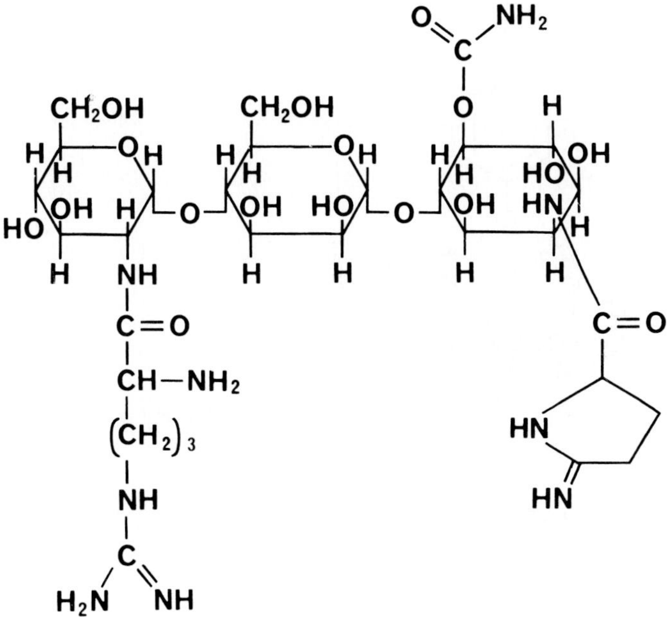

FIGURE 9.   LL-BM 123α.

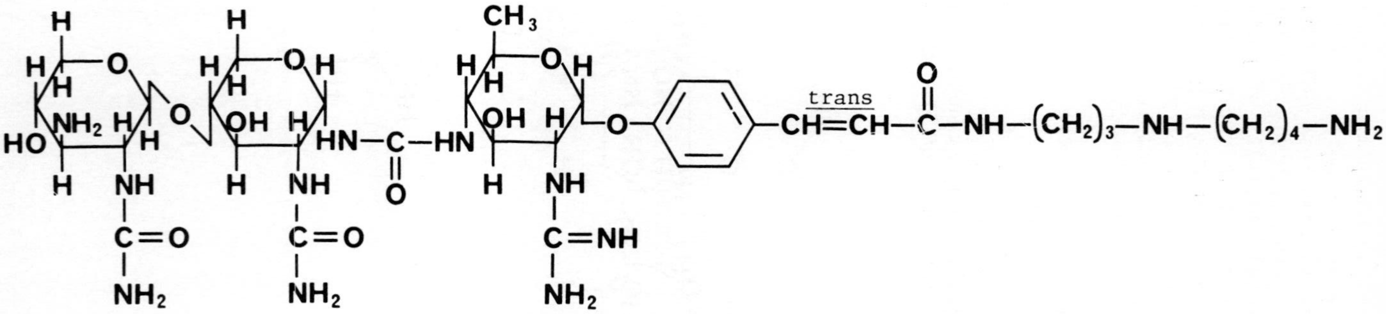

FIGURE 10. LL-BM 123β₁.

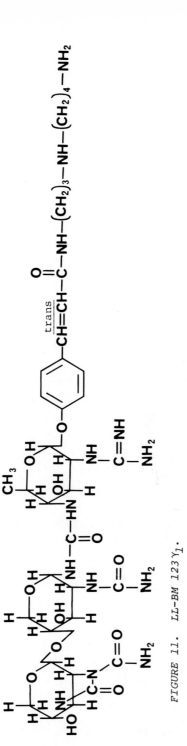

FIGURE 11. LL-BM 123 Y_1.

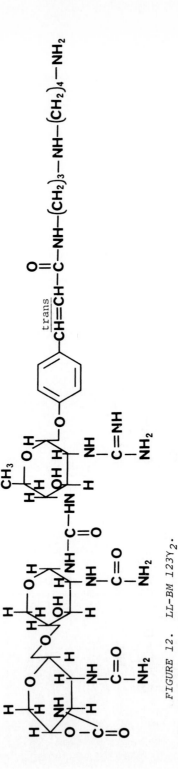

FIGURE 12. LL-BM 123Y₂.

the 4 components other than BM 123α do not belong to "amino-glycoside-aminocyclitol" antibiotics. All of the compounds are broadly active against Gram-positive and negative bacteria but generally less active than gentamicin. The order of activity of the antibiotics is BM 123$_{\gamma 1}$>$_{\gamma 2}$>β>α. It is of particular interest that BM 123$_{\gamma 1}$ has a significant activity against *Pseudo-monas aeruginosa*, almost comparable to that of gentamicin. LL-BM 123α was reported as remarkably nontoxic, but the toxicities of other four components have not yet been reported. As depicted in Figure 99, LL-BM 123α is a pseudotrisaccharide consisting of glucosamine, mannose and *myo*-inosamine-2, to which two strongly basic amino acids are attached. The other 4 components (LL-BM 123β_1, β_2, γ_1 and γ_2) are devoid of the *myo*-inosamine-2.

Some of the new aminoglycosides discovered during the period 1972-1976, which are listed in the author's last review (29), were more detailed in the subsequent year 1977.

Apramycin showed effect against enteric disease in cattle (30), and has been developed and practically used for therapeutic treatment of animals. Its structure was confirmed (24) by X-ray along with ^{13}CMR assignments (31).

Structure elucidation of LL-BM408 (LL-BM408α) was detailed in a recent paper (32). It was identified as ribosylparomamine and is much less active than its related antibiotics, ribostamycin and paromomycin.

Comparative studies on the accumulation in the kidney of sagamicin (33-36) and gentamicin components (C_1, C_{1a} and C_2) in-dicated that the accumulation is dependent on the chemical differ-ence in the substituents at 6'-C. The half life in the kidney of sagamicin was shortest, and it coincided with its lower nephro-toxicity. Furthermore, the bindings of aminoglycoside antibiotics including sagamicin with acidic mucopolysaccharide were worked out, which appear to be responsible for the affinity of the anti-biotics to organs. As a result, sagamicin combined more inten-sively than kanamycin or DKB (3',4'-dideoxykanamycin B), but less than gentamicin or neomycin. This order corresponds to their ex-tent of nephro- and oto-toxicity, suggesting that the polarity of aminoglycosides may partly at least contribute to their tissue affinity and tissue toxicity (37).

Sorbistins elaborated by *Pseudomonas sorbicinii*, which were first reported by Bristol-Banyu scientists (38-40), were subse-quently reported by Takeda (41), Lederle (42), and Merck (43) investigators. Sorbistins described by the latter two American companies are however biosynthesized by *Streptoverticillium* spe-cies, in contrast with *Pseudomonas* species reported by the former two Japanese groups.

The *in vitro* antibacterial activity of fortimicin A was com-pared with those of gentamicin, DKB, kanamycin and ribostamycin against 1091 bacterial clinical isolates (44). Fortimicin A was similar in activity to kanamycin and slightly less active than gentamicin and DKB, against aminoglycoside-susceptible strains, whereas it had relatively strong activity against *Serratia marcescens* and *Proteus inconstans* strains but weak activity against *P. aeruginosa* strains. Fortimicin A had appreciably greater activity against aminoglycoside-resistant Gram negative and positive bacteria, which can produce aminoglycoside inactivating enzymes except an aminoglycoside 3-N-acetyltransferase-I [AAC(3)-I].

X-Ray structure determination of crystalline fortimicin B molecule was carried out in order to confirm the structure proposed on chemical and spectroscopic grounds and to determine the absolute configuration uniquely (45). The molecule consists of purpurosamine and 1,4-diaminocyclitol which are bound together through the α-linkage. The absolute configuration of the entire molecule may be deduced by correlating the X-ray structure with the known absolute configuration of the 1,4-diaminocyclitol moiety. The numbering system and the stereoscopic view of the absolute configuration of the molecule are shown in Figure 13.

In parallel with the progress in the discoveries of the above new *microbial* products, a number of *semi-synthetic* aminoglycosides have been reported during the past year. Following the development and subsequent clinical use of DKB (46) and amikacin (1-N-L(-)-γ-amino-α-hydroxybutyryl kanamycin A) (47), netilmicin (Sch 20569) (48,49) has been undergoing clinical examination. As shown in Figure 14, netilmicin is a 1-N-ethyl sisomicin formed by reductive alkylation (48), and is more active than sisomicin against a series of clinical isolates and active against 97% of the sisomicin-resistant organisms (50). Compared to gentamicin, netilmicin is less nephrotoxic in rats (51), less toxic chronically in cats, but more toxic acutely in mice (49).

Other principal semi-synthetic aminoglycosides reported are: 5-*epi*-sisomicin (Sch 22591) (52,53), UK-18,892 (1-N-S-w-amino-2-hydroxybutyl kanamycin A) (54,55), 3'-deoxyseldomycin factor 5, 3'-*epi*-seldomycin factor 5 (56-58), 1-N-alkylseldomycin derivatives (59), 1-N-(*S*-4-amino-2-hydroxybutyryl)-gentamicin B (Sch 20287) and 1-N-(*S*-3-amino-2-hydroxypropionyl)-gentamicin B (Sch 21420)(60,61), 1-*epi*-amino, 1-desamino-1-hydroxy and 1-desamino-1-*epi*-hydroxy analogs of sisomicin, gentamicin C_1, C_{1a} and netilmicin (62), and 3"-demethyl derivatives of gentamicin C_1, C_{1a}, C_2 and sagamicin (17,63). The total synthesis of 3"-deoxydihydrostreptomycin was also reported (64).

II. MUTATIONAL BIOSYNTHESIS, MUTATION AND GENETIC ENGINEERING

Examples of mutational biosynthesis aimed to develop new semi-synthetic aminoglycosides, which were reported in the last year, are listed in Table II.

Mutational biosynthesis of 2-hydroxygentamicins and 5-deoxygentamicins by DOS⁻ mutants (VIb-3P, etc.) of *M. purpurea* was recently detailed (65,66), though listed in the author's last review (29). The C_1 and C_2 components of 2-hydroxygentamicin

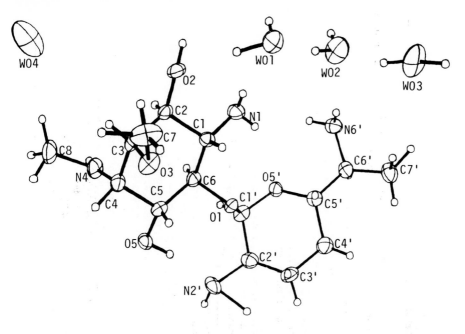

FIGURE 13.   The stereoscopic view of Fortimicin B structure.

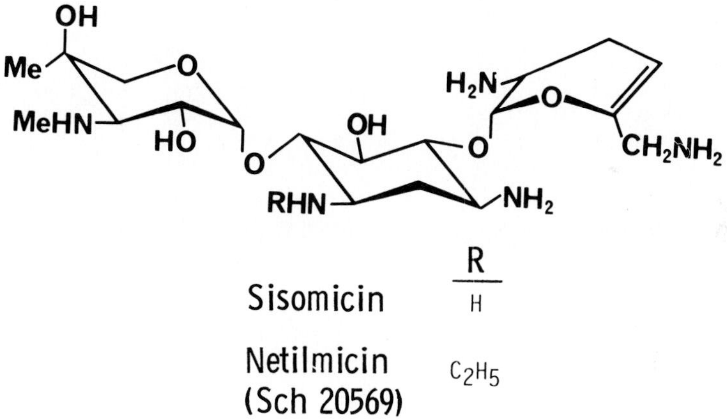

	R
Sisomicin	H
Netilmicin (Sch 20569)	C_2H_5

FIGURE 14.   Netilmicin.

TABLE II. Examples of Mutational Biosynthesis

Strains used[a]	Antibiotics produced by this strain	Type of[b] idiotroph	Inosamine derivatives added	New antibiotics formed	References
M. purpurea	Gentamicins	DOS⁻	Streptamine 2,4,6/3,5-Pentahydroxy-cyclohexanone Pentaacetate of 2,4,6/3,5-pentahydroxycyclohexanone Scyllo-inosamine-2	2-Hydroxygentamicin C_1 2-Hydroxygentamicin C_2	65,66
			2,5-Dideoxystreptamine 4,6-Hydrazino-1,3-cyclohexandiol 1,3-Di-N-benzylidine-2,5-dideoxystreptamine	5-Deoxygentamicin C_1 5-Deoxygentamicin C_2 5-Deoxygentamicin C_{1a}	
			2-epi-Streptamine	Epistreptamine analog of gentamicin?	
S.fradiae	Neomycin B Neomycin C	DOS⁻	2,6-Dideoxystreptamine	6-Deoxyneomycin B 6-Deoxyneomycin C	67
S.rimosus forma paromomycinus	Paromomycin I Paromomycin II	DOS⁻	2,6-Dideoxystreptamine	6-Deoxyparomomycin B 6-Deoxyparomomycin C	67
B. circulans	Butirosins	Neamine⁻ or DOS⁻	6'-N-Methylneamine 3',4'-Dideoxyneamine 3',4'-Dideoxy-6'-N-methylneamine 3',4'-Dideoxy-6'-C-methylneamine	6'-N-Methylbutirosins 3',4'-Dideoxybutirosins 3',4'-Dideoxy-6'-N-methylbutirosins 3',4'-Dideoxy-6'-C-methylbutirosins	68,69

[a] M = Micromonospora; S = Streptomyces; B = Bacillus.
[b] DOS = 2-Deoxystreptamine.

had broad-spectrum *in vitro* antibacterial activity similar to the gentamicin C_1 and C_2 components, but with greater activity against some gentamicin-resistant strains containing 2"-OH-nucleotidylating enzyme [ANT(2")]. It can be recalled that mutamicin 1 (2-hydroxysisomicin) became similarly active against gentamicin-resistant strains harboring ANT(2") (70). The LD_{50} (i.v.) in mice of the 2-hydroxygentamicin C complex indicated that it had approximately half the toxicity of the gentamicin C complex. A C_1, C_2, and C_{1a} mixture of 5-deoxygentamicins also had broad-spectrum activity, similar to the gentamicin complex. However, it exhibited improved activity against several gentamicin-acetylating strains of resistant bacteria such as those possessing AAC (3) and AAC (6').

The antibacterial spectra of 6-deoxyneomycins were very similar to those of neomycins, but 6-deoxyneomycin C was more potent against *E. coli*, *Proteus mirabilis*, *Staphylococcus aureus*, and *Salmonella typhimurium* than neomycin C whereas 6-deoxyneomycin B was less potent than neomycin B against these organisms. 6-Deoxyparomomycins I and II had only about 25% of the activity of the corresponding paromomycins (67).

Among 4 kinds of new butirosin analogs prepared by neamine- or DOS-requiring idiotrophs of *B. circulans*, 3',4'-dideoxy-6'-N-methylbutirosins A and B not only showed similar activities to butirosins against sensitive strains, but also were broadly active against butirosin-resistant bacteria possessing aminoglycoside inactivating enzymes, AAC (6')-I, AAC (6')-IV, APH (3')-II and AAC (2') (68,69).

The productivity of aminoglycosides bioconverted to new antibiotics by idiotrophs is often quite small (71), and the method has thus far suffered from the disadvantage that yields of new antibiotics have been too low for commercial exploitation (72).

Improvement of seldomycin factor 5 (SLD-5) (73-75) fermentation with *S. hofunensis* (MK 88) and its mutant 16G was attempted both by alteration of cultural conditions and by mutation (76). SLD-5 production by strain MK88 was dependent on the presence of Bacto-Peptone in the fermentation medium. Since an economical replacement for Bacto-Peptone is required for industrial fermentation, mutants were sought which would give good yields of SLD-5 with a less expensive nitrogen source. As shown in Table III, mutants 12-7 and E which are resistant to the threonine analog α-amino-β-hydroxyvaleric acid were found to give good yields of SLD-5 when Kyokuto-peptone was employed in the fermentation medium instead of Bacto-Peptone. Strains 12-7 and E also gave good yields with such inexpensive peptones as spray-dried lard water (SDLW) (Inland Molasses, Inc.) and liquid peptone Wp-100 (Inolex, Inc.).

Two actinophages active on MK88 were isolated from soil samples (76). Mutants resistant to one of the phages which is specific only for MK88 became asporogenous but did not show any appreciable change in SLD-5 production (Table III).

TABLE III.   Comparison of Seldomycin Factor 5 (SLD-5) Yields
by Mutants with Various Nitrogen Sources.

Strain	Marker	Maximal yields of SLD-5 (mcg base/ml)				
		Run 1		Run 2		
		Bacto-peptone	Kyokuto-peptone	Bacto-peptone	SDLW[a]	WP-100[a]
MK88		50	<50	<50		
U7-1	phage^{Rb}	90				
16G		200	50	459	160	149
12-7	αAHV^{Rb}	245	130	557	215	221
E	αAHV^R	420	420	480	541	488

[a]SDLW: spray-dried lard water; WP-100: liquid peptone.
[b]phage^R: resistance to phage 88-a; αAHV^R: resistance to
α-amino-β-hydroxyvaleric acid (76).

Plasmids have been implicated as determinants of several
phenotypic characters in *Streptomyces* species.   These include
fertility (77,78), melanin (79), aerial mycelium (80,81), antibiotic production (80,82-84) and antibiotic resistance (82,83).
The loss of one or more of these characters upon treatment of a
streptomycete with acridinium or phenanthridinium dyes has been
employed to indicate plasmid involvement in the expression of the
characters.   Acridines, for example, cause the loss of kasugamy-
cin and aureothricin production by *S. kasugaensis* (80).   Plasmid
involvement in the biosynthesis of the aminoglycoside antibiotics
has recently been suggested using similar techniques.
The treatment of a streptomycin-producing *S. bikiniensis* with
ethidium bromide or acriflavine resulted in the loss of the ability to produce streptomycin in 2-16% of the colonies isolated
from the treated spores (85).   The loss of streptomycin production was always accompanied by a decreased resistance to streptomycin.   None of the nonproducing isolates regained either the
ability to produce streptomycin or acquired resistance to that
antibiotic through repeated transfer of the cultures.   Treatment
with the dyes caused partial to total loss of the ability to produce aerial mycelium by *S. bikiniensis,* but the isolates regained
this ability upon repeated transfer to fresh medium.   The dyes
did not appear to effect pigment production by *S. bikiniensis.*
These studies and knowledge on the known action of these dyes
(86,87) suggest the possible involvement of plasmid (s) in the
production of streptomycin and in resistance to that antibiotic.
Investigations on aureothricin biosynthesis by *S. kasugaensis*
suggested that plasmid (s) may be involved in the biosynthetic
path from cystine to pyrrothine but not in the route from pyrrothine to aureothricin (88).   This observation indicates that plasmid (s) may be responsible for a biosynthetic path leading, from

TABLE IV.   Effect of DOS on KM Production by Acriflavine-
            Treated Isolates (89)

Additive	Concn. (μg/ml)	KM[a] production (μg/ml)		
		K-2j	311	811
None		17	0	0
DOS[b]	750	15	9	23
D-Glucosamine	750	20	0	0
myo-Inositol	750	15	0	0

[a]KM: Kanamycin A.
[b]DOS: Deoxystreptamine.

a primary metabolite, to the most characteristic "skeleton" for
the antibiotic, but not responsible for final paths leading to
the antibiotic itself and its related minor components, since
pyrrothine is the most characteristic and important "skeleton"
for aureothricin.   In other words, both biosynthesis from already
"preformed" basic structures to the antibiotic and interconver-
sions among its related minor components may not be under plasmid
control.

Another evidence that not final steps leading to an antibiotic and its related minor components but biosynthetic path-
ways(s) leading to a basic "skeleton" characteristic in the
secondary metabolites may be controlled by plasmid(s) has very
recently been obtained (89).   A kanamycin-producing strain, S.
kanamyceticus K-2j, was treated with acriflavine to eliminate
the kanamycin productivity.   As shown in Table IV, two isolates
(311 and 811) obtained by such treatment could biosynthesize
kanamycin only when deoxystreptamine (DOS) was fed to the cultures.   Thus, involvement of plasmid(s) in biosynthesis of DOS
moiety of kanamycins was suggested.

Genetic engineering using "plasmid" will, from now on, become
a useful tool to increase fermentation yields and to create new
antibiotics (90-92), since recent major technical advances in
molecular biology have made it possible to introduce foreign DNA
into E. coli using plasmids or phage derivatives as cloning
vehicles (93-95).

A very recent report by Davies et al. (96) will eventually
pave the way for the transfer of an antibiotic productivity from
one organism to another.   B. circulans NRRL B-3312, a nonpatho-
genic bacterium producing butirosin, contains an aminoglycoside
phosphotransferase that has a similar activity profile to the
neomycin phosphotransferases of clinically isolated antibiotic-
resistant bacteria.   Using colicinogenic factor El (Col El that
determines the colicin El production and resistance) derivative

as a vehicle, they have succeeded in the transfer of the gene-
determining neomycin phosphotransferase from *B. circulans* to *E.
coli*. Namely, purified DNA's from *B. circulans* and the plasmid
ColEl-Ap^R were digested with EcoRI endonuclease and the resulting
fragments covalently joined with polynucleotide ligase. The re-
combined DNA was used to transform *E. coli* and amplicillin-neomy-
cin resistant colonies were selected. Analysis of several clones
indicated that neomycin resistance in the *E. coli* transformants
was due to the presence of the *B. circulans* phosphotransferase
gene. This observation is consistent with the notion that anti-
biotic-modifying enzymes from antibiotic-producing organisms may
be the sources of antibiotic resistance in plasmid-containing
bacteria, as previously speculated by Benveniste and Davies (97).

A homology between aminoglycoside 3"-adenylyltransferase
[AAD(3")] and aminoglycoside 2"-nucleotidyltransferase [ANT(2")]
was suggested (98). This is unexpected, since these two enzymes
are apparently unrelated in view of the substrate profiles. Recombinant plasmids containing the ANT(2")-gene were constructed
and radioactively labeled complementary RNA's were prepared from
the recombinant plasmide and hybridized to a variety of plasmid
DNA's. The complementary RNA's hybridized with EcoRl fragments
of plasmids R5, R6 and R100 which contain the ADD(3")-gene. No
hybridization was found with DNA-fragments from plasmids coding
for other aminoglycoside-inactivating enzymes. Thus, although
the two enzymes have different substrate ranges, the existence
of homology between genes AAD(3") and ANT(2") suggests a common
evolutionary pathway. This is surprising in view of the fact
that no homology was detected between plasmids coded AAD(3") from
E. coli and *S. aureus*.

III. ANALYSIS, CULTURAL CONDITIONS AND GENERAL PHYSIOLOGY

More rapid, facile and precise qualitative and quantitative
methods to determine aminoglycoside antibiotics in the fermentation beers or crude materials are really needed both for new
antibiotic screening and for the routine monitoring of the industrial fermentation. Following the publication of a very useful book, "Chromatography of Antibiotics" by Wagman and Weinstein
(99), a few feasible analytical methods have been reported in
very recent years.

A method for quantitating the individual components of gentamicin during the progress of the gentamicin fermentation with
M. purpurea was developed by Schering scientists (100). The
fast, direct densitometric method of Wilson *et al.* (101), using
the ninhydrin chromogenic spray procedure after resolution by
thin-layer chromatography, is not sensitive enough to follow
directly the course of the fermentation. Since fluorescence is
10-100 times more sensitive than colorimetric procedures, fluorigenic labeling techniques were investigated. 4-Chloro-7-nitro-

benzo-2-oxa-1,3-diazole (NBD chloride), which reacts with primary and secondary amines while yielding a nonfluorescent hydrolysis product, was found to be the fluorigenic reagent of choice. Fluorimetric measurements were thus carried out *in situ* on the NBD chloride derivatives formed after thin-layer chromatography of the clarified fermentation broth. This procedure was 800 times as sensitive as its ninhydrin analog.

A similar fluorimetric method using NBD chloride was independently applied to the quantitative determination of fortimicins A and B in the fortimicin fermentation (102).

Gas-liquid chromatography of derivatized antibiotics has been reported (103,104). However, recent studies with high-pressure liquid chromatography (105,106) suggest that this technique is likely to become a preferred method for the identification of aminoglycosides and for the analysis of their mixtures.

For example, a fast, selective, and precise "high-performance" liquid chromatographic method for simultaneous, independent determination of kanamycin A and B was described by Bristol workers (105). Sample components were separated on a pellicular cation exchanger and monitored by fluorescence using post-column on-line derivatization. Less than 0.35 µg of kanamycin could be detected in as much as 7 µg kanamycin A injected. The detection limit for kanamycin A was less than 20 µg injected. Chromatographic analysis was less than 15 min per sample. The detection system has been further applied in their laboratories to the liquid chromatography of other primary amino-function-containing antibiotics such as ampicillin and amikacin.

A carbon thin-layer chromatographic method was devised by Kyowa Hakko scientists to effectively separate gentamicin, sisomicin, sagamicin and fortimicin groups of antibiotics (26). They modified the carbon thin-layer chromatography for the separation of aminoglycosides, which were initially developed by Brodasky (107) and Kondo *et al.* (108). Sisomicin, verdamicin and antibiotic G-52 were inseparable from gentamicin C_{1a}, C_2 and sagamicin, respectively, by paper chromatography using a solvent system consisting of lower layer of $CHCl_3$, CH_3OH and 17% NH_4OH (2:1:1, v/v). However, the carbon thin-layer chromatography clearly separated sisomicin from gentamicin C_{1a}. Good separation of verdamicin from gentamicin C_2 and of antibiotic G-52 from sagamicin could also be seen in this system. These data confirmed the usefulness of this carbon TLC as an effective analytical method to differentiate gentamicin components from their 4',5'-dehydro derivatives. Fortimicin A, though inseparable from gentamicin C_2 and verdamicin in the paper chromatographic system, was also distinct from these two antibiotics on this carbon TLC system.

Taxonomical studies on *M. olivoasterospora*, a fortimicin producer, were carried out in detail (109).

Recent discoveries of new aminoglycosides have arisen mainly from *Micromonospora* species belonging to Actinomycetales other than *Streptomycer sp.* (abbreviated as Rare Actinos).

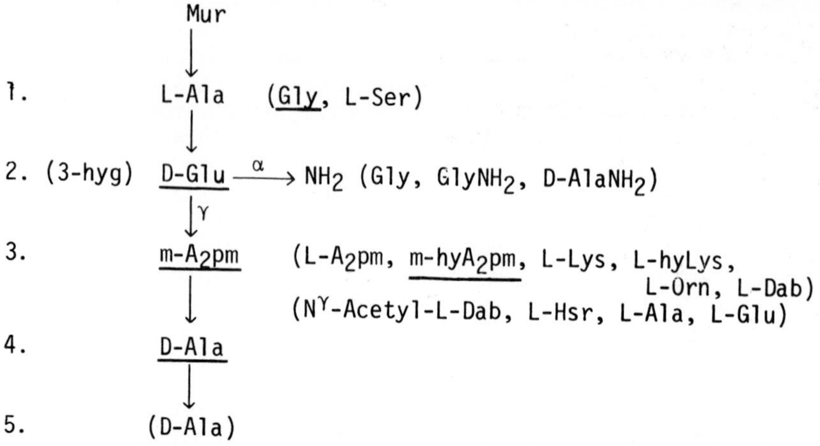
Mur
1. L-Ala (Gly, L-Ser)
2. (3-hyg) D-Glu α NH2 (Gly, GlyNH2, D-AlaNH2)
γ
3. m-A2pm (L-A2pm, m-hyA2pm, L-Lys, L-hyLys, L-Orn, L-Dab)
(Nγ-Acetyl-L-Dab, L-Hsr, L-Ala, L-Glu)
4. D-Ala
5. (D-Ala)

FIGURE 15. Variations of the peptide subunit in cell wall (114). Amino acids marked with underlines are the probable peptide subunit of Micromonospora sp. such as M. olivoastero-spora and M. sagamiensis.

Biochemical studies in the taxonomy of the Rare Actinos are indispensable not only for taxonomy itself but also for the recognition, during new antibiotic screening, of most of the genera belonging to Rare Actinos which usually lack distinctive morphological features (110). Useful biochemical markers are: 1) meso- or LL-diaminopimelic acid in the ce-l wall peptidoglycan, 2) sugar composition of polysaccharides, and 3) fatty acid spectrum of cell lipids (110,111). Such investigations were undertaken by Kyowa Hakko researchers with particular emphasis on fortimicins- and sagamicin-producing *Micromonospora* species (112,113).

One of the results they obtained is shown in Figure 15. This indicated variations of the peptide subunit in the cell wall of bacteria according to Schleifer and Kandler (114). The cell wall analysis of *M. olivoasterospora* (fortimicins producer) and *M. sagamiensis* (sagamicin producer) indicated that the cell wall consists of, from the muramic acid side, glycine, D-glutamic acid, meso- (and 3-hydroxy-meso-) diaminopimelic acid, and D-alanine in this order. It is interesting to find that, in the *Micromonospora* species, glycine is attached directly to muramic acid while L-alanine is attached to muramic acid in *Streptomyces* species. Further elucidation of the peptide sequence in the cell wall will hopefully clarify whether the sequence is a key specific for the genera belonging to Rare Actinos.

Not only the cell wall constituents but also the phospholipids, fatty acids, pigments and antibiotic sensitivities of these *Micromonospora* species were analyzed by the same workers

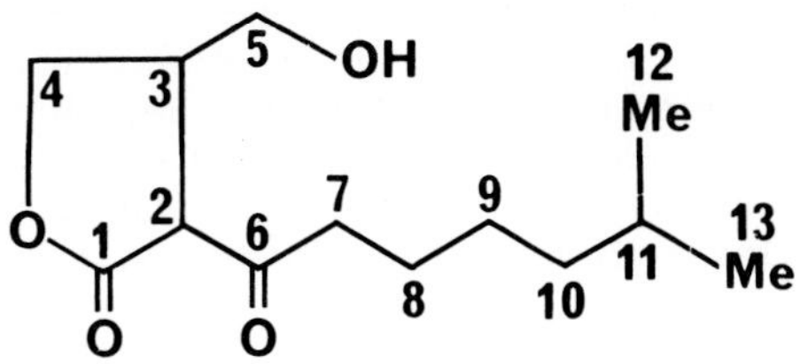

FIGURE 16. *A-Factor.*

(112). For example, the phospholipids of *M. olivoasterospora*
(fortimicin producer) consists of phosphatidylethanolamine (1.00),
phosphatidylinositol mannosides (0.74), phosphatidylinositol
(0.52), bisphosphatidylglycerol (0.21) and phosphatidylglycerol
(trace). The number in the parenthesis shows the quantitative
ratios analyzed as phosphorus.

Selective methods for isolation of Rare Actinos from natural
sources and the characteristics of Rare Actinos were reported
briefly (113) based on a number of previous reports.

While working on sagamicin and fortimicin fermentations with
Micromonospora species, three kinds (φMm-1, φMm-2 and φMm-3) of
Micromonospora phages were isolated from the surrounding soils
(113,115). Phage φMm-1 attacks all the *Micromonospora*, one *Actinoplanes* and a few *Streptomyces* species tested, φMm-2 attacks
only all of the *Micromonospora* species tested and φMm-3 is active
only against several species of *Micromonospora*. Therefore, φMm-2
phage may be used for identification of *Micromonospora* species.
Two types of phages infecting *M. purpurea* ATCC 15835 were isolated separately by Kikuchi and Perlman (116). Phage φUW21 is a
monovalent phage attacking only *M. purpurea* ATCC 15835 and Phage
φUW51 is a polyvalent attacking many strains of *Micromonospora*,
one strain of *S. griseus* and also *Nocardia mediterranei* ATCC
13685.

Streptoalloteichus hindustanus, a new genus belonging to Rare
Actinos, was reported (117,118) to coproduce nebramycin factors
II, IV, and V' together with major products, tallysomycins A and
B belonging to the bleomycin-phleomycin group.

It was observed by the author's group (113) that a major component of antibiotic 460 previously reported as a new antibiotic
complex (119) is identical with neomycin B.

An A-factor capable of stimulating streptomycin formation by
Actinomyces streptomycini was reported which could be isolated
from certain *Actinomyces* strains (120). The A-factor was purified 2×10^5-fold from the culture broth. One mg of the purest
preparations induces the formation of 5×10^4 mg streptomycin in
the A-factor-defective mutant 1439. Its chemical structure was
recently defined as 2S-isocapryloyl-3R-oxymethyl-γ-butyrolactone
(121), as shown in Figure 16. This factor thus shows no structural relation to any part of streptomycin molecule.

A significant barbital effect on streptomycin biosynthesis in
S. griseus, which had been reported by Ferguson *et al.* (122) in
1957, was reconfirmed on the complex medium, whereas no effect
could be demonstrated on the near defined medium (123). Examina-
tions of the broths showed that the mycelium of the actinomycete
only in the complex medium containing barbital was not disrupted
and partially lyzed. In agreement with this, the barbital containing broth was thick and foaming. Barbital may exhibit a
positive and economical feasible effect on the streptomycin fermentation, but the effect is presumably strain dependent.

Development of chemically defined media often leads to the
discovery of key factors both for the growth of an antibiotic-
producing organism and for the antibiotic biosynthesis. Such
attempts were made to find any key factor(s) involved in seldomycin and fortimicin fermentations.

Development of a chemically defined medium for seldomycin
factor 5 production by *S. hofunensis* showed that vitamin B_{12}
stimulated SLD-5 synthesis appreciably (76).

A chemically defined medium was also devised in order to
study the requirements for fortimicin A production by *M. olivoasterospora* KY 11515 (102). Soluble starch was the best carbon
source, and NH_4Cl and NH_4NO_3 were suitable nitrogen sources both
for growth and fortimicin production. L-Arginine, L-asparagine,
L-aspartic acid and L-glutamic acid were somewhat stimulatory for
growth and antibiotic formation. L-Serine stimulated only antibiotic production. The most important finding was that vitamin
B_{12}, cobalt and nickel exhibited marked stimulatory effects on
fortimicin A production (102). Cobalt is presumably involved in
formation of vitamin B_{12} by *M. olivoasterospora,* as reported in
other species of the genus *Micromonospora* (124). Therefore a
part of the cobalt effects can be ascribed to that of vitamin
B_{12}. The effect of cobalt on antibiotic production was, however,
greater than that of vitamin B_{12} in this study.

Regarding these cobalt effects, Tilley *et al.* reported the
involvement of cobalt in two C-methylation steps leading to gentamicin C components and sagamicin in the gentamicin fermentation
(125). Hence cobalt levels in media affect the gentamicin production markedly. The author's group also observed similar cobalt effects on the sagamicin fermentation with *M. sagamiensis*
(126). Involvement of cobalt in the C-methylation is of utmost
interest in conjunction with the one of the features characteristic in the *Micromonospora* antibiotics that is the occurrence
of $-N \cdot CH_3$, $-O \cdot CH_3$ and $-S \cdot CH_3$ as can be seen in the structures of
the sisomicin-gentamicin-sagamicin group antibiotics, fortimicins,
and 3-thiomethylrifamycin S and SV (127).

IV.   BIOSYNTHETIC PATHWAYS AND METABOLIC REGULATION

According to Rinehart and Stroshane (128), possible biosynthetic routes from D-glucose to deoxystreptamine (DOS) are shown
in Figure 17.   It might be expected that DOS would be biosynthe-

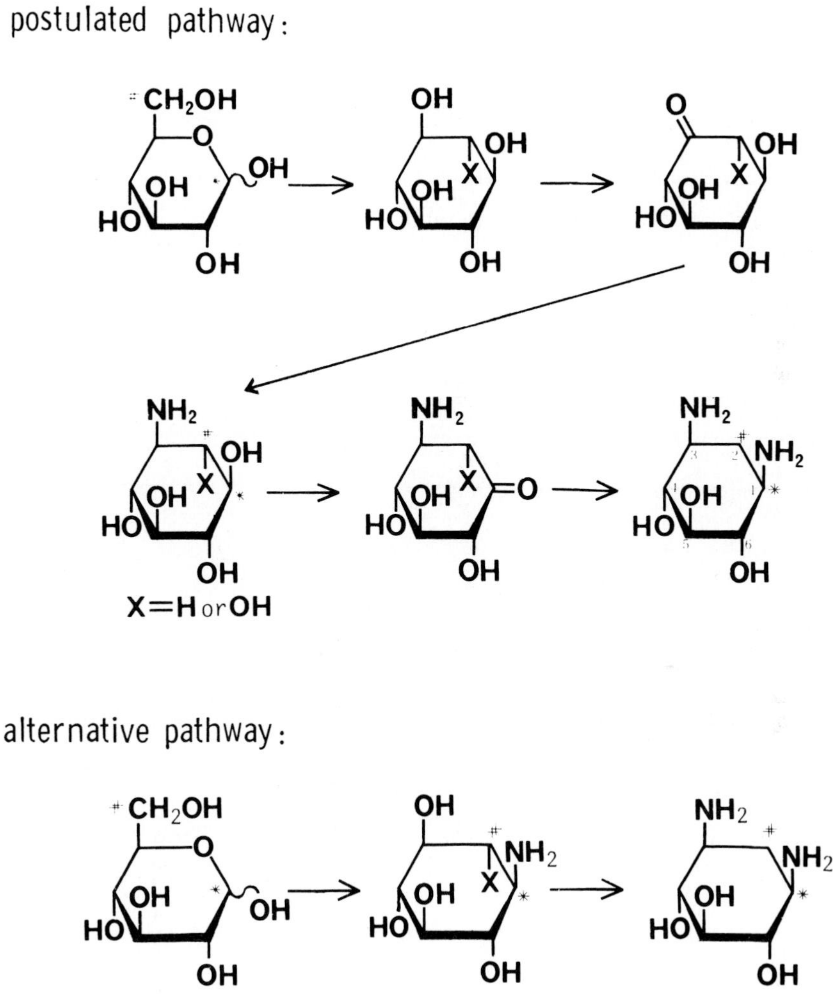

postulated pathway:

X=H or OH

alternative pathway:

FIGURE 17.   Possible pathways from glucose to deoxystreptamine (128).

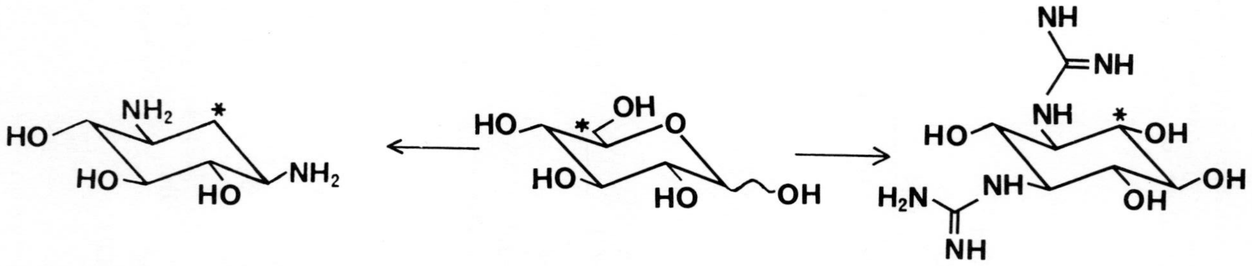

2-Deoxystreptamine

Streptidine

FIGURE 18. Pathways from glucose to streptidine and 2-deoxystreptamine.

sized from glucose in a similar manner to streptidine (in streptomycin) and actinamine (in spectinomycin). However, it does not
seem to be the case since, for instance, myo-inostitol, an intermediate in streptidine biosynthesis, is not incorporated into the
DOS-containing neomycin (128). Furthermore, as depicted in
Figure 18, labeling experiments have shown that the positioning
of the nitrogen functions with respect to the glucose precursor
is different for streptidine and DOS (129,130).

As already described in II. MUTATIONAL BIOSYNTHESIS, MUTA-
TION AND GENETIC ENGINEERING, a DOS-requiring idiotroph (VIb-3P)
of $M.$ $purpurea$ was able to biosynthesize 2-hydroxygentamicin,
when streptamine or 2,4,6/3,5-pentahydroxycyclohexanone (inosose:
X = OH in Figure 17) was added to the fermentation (66). As
shown in Figure 17, Rinehart and Stroshane (128) have suggested
a deoxyinosose (X-H in Figure 17) as an intermediate in the biosynthetic pathway to DOS in the DOS aminoglycoside antibiotics.
In light of the above result with inosose in the idiotroph fermentation, it became apparent that $M.$ $purpurea$ VIb-3P may be a
mutant blocked somewhere before the suggested deoxyinosose intermediate in the pathway to DOS. Incidentally, in the isosose-fed
fermentation, streptamine could be isolated from the broth, indicating that the inosose was converted to streptamine by $M.$ pur-
$purea$ VIb-3P (66).

There have appeared two papers which can reconfirm two final
6'-N-methylation steps leading to gentamicin C_1 and sagamicin
(gentamicin C_{2b}). The two processes were previously postulated
by Testa and Tilley (131). Firstly the biosynthetic relationship
between gentamicin C_2 and C_1 was elucidated by Schering people
(4). (Methyl-^{13}C, ^{14}C)-Gentamicin C_1 was prepared by incubating
a DOS negative $M.$ $purpurea$ mutant with (methyl-^{14}C)-gentamicin
C_2 and (methyl-^{13}C)-L-methionine. The cmr spectrum of the gentamicin C_1 isolated from the (methyl-^{13}C)-methionine fed fermentation showed that carbon enrichment occurred only for the 6'-N-
methyl group. The ratio of the specific ^{14}C-radioactivity of the
gentamicin C_1 isolated to that of the gentamicin C_2 reisolated
from the fermentation was 1:1.15. The data show that gentamicin
C_2 is a biosynthetic precursor of gentamicin C_1.

Incidentally, they detected two new aminoglycosides designated as PC2 (Figure 4) and PC3 (Figure 2; identical to compd.
I-1) as shown in Table I of I. NEW AMINOGLYCOSIDES.

Secondly, biotransformation of gentamicin C_{1a} to sagamicin
was studied by Kyowa Hakko group (132). The conversion of gentamicin C_{1a} into sagamicin with resting cells of $M.$ $sagamiensis$
and (methyl-^{14}C)-L-methionine or (methyl-^{14}C)-S-adenosyl-L-
methionine was confirmed definitely. The radioactivity incorporated into sagamicin was 16.7% and 4.1% with methionine and
S-adenosylmethionine, respectively. The lower efficiency of incorporation observed with the latter compound might be attributed
to the instability of the compound in the medium and/or poor
transportation through the cell membrane.

Gentamicin C_{2b} (sagamicin) was also found to be biotrans-
formed from sisomicin by *M. rhodorangea* capable of producing
antibiotic G-418 (6'-C-methylgentamicin X_2) (133). An attempt
to transform sisomicin to 6'-N-methylsisomicin (antibiotic G-52)
using this strain led unexpectedly to the formation of gentamicin
C_{2b} rather than G-52. The mechanisms involved in the biotransformation are 6'-N-methylation and (4'-5')-reduction. The (4'-
5')-reduction reaction could not be monitored, which should have
been one of the two enzymatic reactions involved in the biotransformation of sisomicin to gentamicin C_{2b}. On the other hand, the
progression of the methylation was followed by chasing the $^{14}CH_3$
label from the L-[methyl-^{14}C] methionine. At present, it is not
known whether the gentamicin C_{2b} is formed via (i) the 6'-N-
methylation followed by the (4'-5')-reduction of sisomicin, (ii)
the reduction followed by the methylation, or (iii) simultaneous
reactions of the two.

In connection with the above finding on sisomicin transformation, it is of utmost interest to observe the existence of
sisomicin as a minor component in the gentamicin fermentation
with *M. purpurea* var. *nigrescens* (3). This suggests that a
(4'-5')-unsaturation reaction involved in the bioconversion of
antibiotic JI-20A into sisomicin (134) may occur not only in the
producers of sisomicin-type antibiotics but in those of gentami-
cin-sagamicin-type.

D-Glucose-u-^{14}C was applied to a paromomycin fermentation
with *S. albus* var. *metamycinus*. The distribution of radioactivity in paromomycin I showed that there is no fragmentation
of the glucose chain during the biosynthesis of glucosamine,
ribose and paromose I (135).

Pearce *et al.* demonstrated that a paromomycin-producing
organism *S. rimosus* forma *paromomycinus* can incorporate neamine
into neomycin, suggesting that the probable first step in the
subunit assembly of neomycin is the formation of neamine (136).

Mutation works on an antibiotic producer often lead to the
discovery of an unexpected metabolite related to the antibiotic,
which are known to be produced by an organism quite differnet
from the producer. For example, a mutant of a neomycin-producing
S. fradiae was found which synthesizes ribostamycin instead of
neomycin (137). New colonies producing neomycin again were obtained after a reverse mutation. The finding that this mutant
probably blocked in one of the last steps of neomycin biosynthesis accumulates ribostamycin indicates ribostamycin might be an
intermediate in the biosynthesis of neomycin. It was also noted
that the ribostamycin production is much higher in the conditions
of neomycin production than in those of ribostamycin (respectively 1.8 and 0.5 mg/ml), while *S. ribosidificus* (a ribostamycin
producer) produces under the same conditions 0.05 and 0.75 mg/ml,
respectively.

The two findings, 1) that ribostamycin is an intermediate between neamine and neomycin (137) and 2) ribosylparomamine occurs in a paromomycin-producer (32), suggest that ribosylparomamine may be an intermediate between paromamine and paromomycin.

Putting together both postulated pathways from the above results on neomycin (136,137) and a probable pathway for butirosins biosynthesis, which was proposed from works on mutational biosynthesis by *B. circulans* mutants (69), a biosynthetic pathway for ribostamycin, ribosylparomamine (30), neomycin, paromomycin, butirosins and the derivatives may be postulated as shown in Figure 19.

Since aminoglycoside-modifying enzymes originally found in clinical resistant organisms may exist in aminoglycoside-producing organisms, more emphasis should be placed to these enzymes in terms of the aminoglycoside biosynthesis and its metabolic regulation. The following three items will be described below: 1) new aminoglycoside-modifying enzymes discovered in the last year, 2) new inactivation mechanisms for new aminoglycosides, and 3) new inactivation of aminoglycosides by the producing organisms.

Three new enzymes to be added to those listed in Mitsuhashi's proposal (138) for the nomenclature of aminoglycoside-modifying enzymes are: aminoglycoside 3'-phosphotransferase type IV [APH (3')-IV], aminoglycoside 2"-phosphotransferase [APH (2")] and aminoglycoside 4'-nucleotidyltransferase [ANT (4')]. All the enzymes were found in clinical isolateds of Gram positive *Staphylococcus* species.

The first enzyme APH (3')-IV found in clinical isolates of *S. aureus* is plasmid-mediated and can phosphorylate amikacin (139). This phosphotransferase is distinct from those previously described since it catalyzes the modification of 3'-hydroxyl group of amikacin. Surprisingly, those strains possessing the enzyme remain susceptible to amikacin. This may be ascribed partly to the fact that the modification of amikacin occurs at a slower rate than that of kanamycin. A similar phenomenon has also been observed with several *E. coli* strains, carrying an enzyme APH (3')-II, that are resistant to neomycin and kanamycin but susceptible to the related aminoglycoside seldomycin factor 5 (73-75); the enzyme extracted from these strains is capable of phosphorylating seldomycin but at a slower rate than neomycin and kanamycin (139). A 3'-phosphotransferase from *S. aureus* and *S. epidermidis*, which appears to be similar to the enzyme APH (3')-IV, has recently been described (140).

The second new enzyme APH (2") originated from *S. aureus* of clinical source can phosphorylate gentamicin and netilmicin most readily, and kanamycin, tobramycin and amikacin less readily (141,142). The structure of the product of inactivation of gentamicin C_1 was determined to be gentamicin C_1-2"-phosphate. One of the reasons for the recent emergence of gentamicin-resistant *S. aureus* is thus probably the occurrence of this enzyme in the clinical isolates.

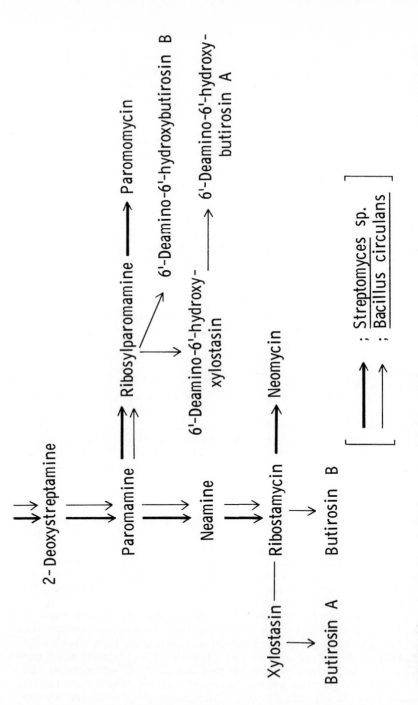

FIGURE 19. Postulated pathway for biosynthesis of ribosylparomamine, paromomycin, ribostamycin, neomycin, butirosins and related compounds.

The third enzyme is aminoglycoside-4'-nucleotidyltransferase ANT (4') obtained from *S. aureus* (143) and *S. epidermidis* (144). This enzyme is also plasmid-mediated and can adenylylate 4'-hydroxyl group of kanamycins, tobramycin, lividomycin, neomycins, butirosins, ribostamycin and amikacin.   This ANT (4') may be important as one of resistant mechanisms in *S. aureus* for amikacin. A similar enzyme was also obtained from *Bacillus brevis*, a non-clinical isolate, whose crude extract converted, for example, xylostasin into 4'-adenylylxylostasin in the presence of ATP and divalent metal ions (Mg^{++}, Mn^{++} or Co^{++}) (145).

New inactivation mechanisms for new aminoglycosides such as fortimicin A, seldomycin factor 5 and apramycin have been elucidated recently.

It was previously observed that two new different aminoglycoside antibiotics fortimicin A (25) and seldomycin factor 5 (74) did not inhibit *E. coli* KY8348, which is resistant to gentamicin C and sisomicin due to the aminoglycoside 3-N-acetyltransferase I [AAC (3)-I] of the organism.   This requires that there is a cross resistance between gentamicin C and fortimicin A or seldomycin factor 5 in *E. coli* KY8348, although these three antibiotics are structurally quite different from each other.   Subsequent studies were made to isolate and determine structurally the inactivated fortimicin A and seldomycin factor 5 resulting from enzymatic reaction with the *E. coli* enzyme.   It was then concluded that fortimicin A and seldomycin factor 5 were inactivated by the aminoglycoside-3-N-acetyltransferase I [AAC (3)-I] of *E. coli* KY8348, resulting in the formation of 1-N-acetylfortimicin A and 3-N-acetylseldomycin factor 5, respectively (146).   An enzyme extract obtained from a clinical isolate *P. aeruginosa* GN3054, which is resistant to fortimicin A, was also found to acetylate 1-N-amino group of the fortamine by the same enzyme [AAC (3)-I] (44).   Fortimicin A is thus active against all the resistant cultures possessing AAC (6'), AAC (2'), ANT (2"), APH (3')-I, II, and ANT (4') except this enzyme AAC (3)-I.

Apramycin (nebramycin factor 2) has likewise been known to be active against all the resistant cultures having a variety of known aminoglycoside-inactivating enzymes.   However, recent studies with *Salmonella, Klebsiella* and *Escherichia* species isolated from apramycin-treated swines indicated that these organisms are resistant to apramycin and the mechanism of resistance is 3-N-acetylation of the deoxystreptamine (see Figure 6) by an enzyme AAC (3) occurring in the organisms (147).   It is thus interesting to see that gentamicin (sisomicin and sagamicin), fortimicin A, seldomycin factor 5 and apramycin, all of which differ structurally greatly from each other, are in common susceptible to the enzyme AAC (3).

Two structural comparisons can be made of seldomycin factor 5 with gentamicins X and A or with 66-40B and 66-40D (18,19) in terms of suitable substrates for AAC (3)-I.

Firstly, gentamicin X is susceptible to this enzyme, but gentamicin A is not inactivated by this enzyme (148). A structural difference of gentamicin X from gentamicin A is the presence of 4"-methyl in the garosamine moiety of gentamicin X and its absence in gentamicin A, and 4"-OH of gentamicin X (axial) is an epimer of that of gentamicin A (equatorial) (74).

Secondly, antibiotic 66-40B, which has the *ribo* configuration at C-4" and is thus more like the kanamycins than the gentamicin C type, is inactivated by AAC (3)-I. However, antibiotic 66-40D, even though it possesses the C-4" *arabino* configuration analogous to that of garosamine, resists inactivation by AAC (3)-I (149).

These two considerations suggest that suitable substrates for AAC (3)-I must have a substitute such as a methyl group on the aminohexose that is linked at the 6-position of DOS. When speculated in an analogous way, it may be 4"-O-methyl group in the xylopyranose moiety of seldomycin factor 5 that determines the susceptibility of seldomycin factor 5 to AAC (3)-I.

A few reports have appeared, in the last year, on inactivated aminoglycosides modified by the producing organisms.

Butirosin-3'-phosphotransferase, which can form 3'-phosphobutirosin A from butirosin A, ATP and Mg^{++} with a cell-free extract of the butirosin-producing *B. vitellinus*, was purified 1000 fold from the cells of the organism (150). Aminoglycoside substrates for this purified enzyme were butirosin A, xylostasin, ribostamycin, kanamycin B, neomycin and paromomycin. Similarly, a cell-free preparation of aminoglycoside 3'-phosphotransferase was obtained from a butirosin-producing *B. circulans* (151). This enzyme phosphorylated butirosin A, ribostamycin, kanamycins A and B, but not lividomycin A, and this substrate requirement was the same as that of APH (3')-II type found in resistant bacteria. This enzyme was, however, different from the APH (3')-II in its behavior during affinity chromatography using kanamycin A-Sepharose 4B (152) since it did not bind to the affinity column.

The phosphatase-less mutants of a butirosin-producing *B. vitellinus* were found to accumulate 6'-N-pyrophosphoamide butirosin A. Further mutation of one of the phosphatase-less mutants led to the accumulation of 6'-O-pyrophospho-6'-deamino-6'-hydroxy butirosin A instead of the 6'-N-pyrophosphoamide butirosin A (153).

An unknown lividomycin-like substance accumulated prior to formation of lividomycin during the lividomycin fermentation with *S. lividus* (154). This accumulation was enhanced by the increase of phosphate concentrations in the fermentation medium while lividomycin production and alkaline phosphatase levels in the broth were lowered. This unknown substance was subsequently identified as lividomycin-6'-phosphate, thus suggesting probable involvement of phosphorylation and dephosphorylation reactions in the biosynthesis of lividomycin.

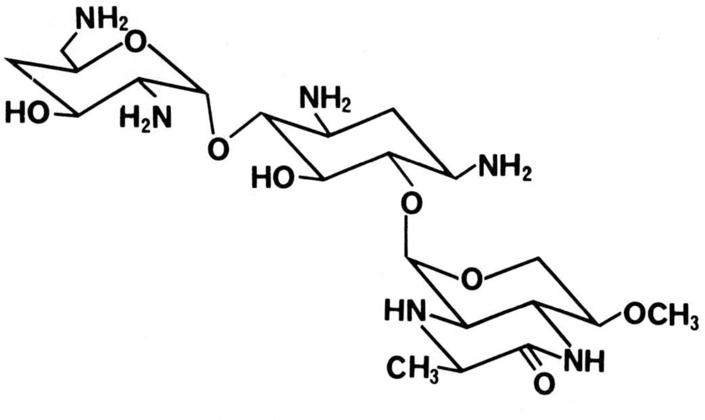

FIGURE 20.   Inactivation product of seldomycin factor 5.

Simple methods for the selective dehydroxylation of aminoglycosides (for example, kanamycin B, neamine, xylostasin, ribostamycin, paromomycin I, etc.) by a combination of enzymatic and
chemical reactions were reported by Takeda group (155):   the
former is phosphorylation of aminoglycosides by using enzymes
APH (3') from resistant strains while the latter involves transformation of phosphates into 3'-deoxyaminoglycosides by treatment
with silylating agents and subsequent hydrogenation.   Although
highly speculative, it is likely that, if the latter *chemical*
reaction would occur enzymatically, the biosynthesis of 3'-deoxy-
aminoglycosides from the corresponding aminoglycosides could
follow the two-step pathway via the 3'-phosphate forms, since
the occurrence of some 3'-phosphoaminoglycosides and phosphotransferases APH (3') in the producing organisms has been well
known.

A number of workers (156-161) have reported that streptomycin-
producing strains of *S. griseus* and *S. bikiniensis* can phosphorylate streptomycin.   However, an actinophage-resistant streptomycin
producing survivor obtained from the nonstreptomycin-producing *S.
griseus* NRRLB-2926 does not have the streptomycin-phosphorylating
system (162).   Such a culture may be the exception to the observation of Dowding and Davies (161) that most aminoglycoside-producing streptomycetes have abilities for inactivating the antibiotic.

Seldomycin factor 5 yields have been noticed to drop rather
rapidly at a later stage of the seldomycin fermentation with *S.
hofunensis,* suggesting the aminoglycoside inactivation by an enzymatic system occurring in the producing organism itself (73,76).
Subsequent enzymatic studies revealed that seldomycin factor 5
was inactivated completely by a cell-free extract of *S. hofunensis* in the presence of glucose and ATP at pH 6.6 (163).   This enzyme system was very specific only for seldomycin factor 2 and

factor 5, but none or little of the other aminoglycosides such as neomycin B, kanamycin A, butirosin A, gentamicin C_{1a}, sagamicin and fortimicin A was substrate for the system. One of 3 sugars (galactose, D-ribose, and N-acetylglucosamine) and one of 3 nucleotides (UTP, GTP and GMP) can be used as two cofactors instead of glucose and ATP, respectively. Several inactivation products resulting from the *in vitro* reaction were also detected in the *in vivo* fermentation. A typical fermentation time course showed that the inactivation activity emerged from the beginning of growth, increased as the growth progressed and reached a maximum almost at the same time when the antibiotic titers reached a maximum. One of the major inactivation products was isolated from the reaction mixture and its structure was determined as shown in Figure 20. This inactivation reaction taking place both *in vitro* and *in vivo* appears to be a rather complicated, new type of mechanism that differs greatly from known aminoglycoside inactivations such as acetylation, phosphorylation and nucleotidylation.

As described in III. ANALYSIS, CULTURAL CONDITIONS, AND GENERAL PHYSIOLOGY, A-factor (Figure 16) was found to stimulate streptomycin production by a mutant 1439 of *Actinomyces streptomycini* (120). In this mutant, the transamidinase catalyzing the formation of streptidine, the core of the streptomycin molecule, by transfer of guanidine groups from arginine to streptamine, is measurable only after addition of the A-factor. Thus, differential gene expression is evidently involved in its regulatory effect.

As shown in Figure 21, aminoglycosides such as streptomycin and kanamycin appear to be shunt products diverging from a pathway leading to the cell wall (29,113,164). Indeed, addition of cell wall inhibitors to medium has been reported to increase production of aminoglycoside antibiotics.

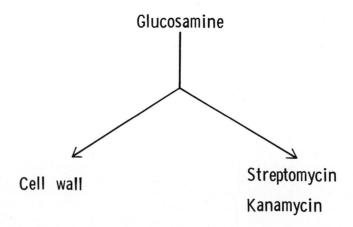

FIGURE 21. *Biosynthesis of Aminoglycosides.*

For example, bacitracin and D-cycloserine exhibited a simula-
tory effect on kanamycin formation by *S. kanamyceticus* with slight
inhibition of cellular growth. This stimulation might be due to
accumulation of cell wall intermediates--aminosugar and sugar--
which are shunted to the pathway of kanamycin synthesis (165).
Penicillin G, in subinhibitory concentrations (1 to 5 µg/ml), was
added to cultures of *S. griseus* in different stages of its life
cycle. The inhibitor decreased streptomycin production, when
young cells were treated; however, there was an increase in streptomycin formation when penicillin was added to older cultures.
Thus, it may be possible that the biosynthesis of streptomycin
has some correlation with a certain type of cell wall (e.g.,
cross wall), the biosynthesis of which is inhibited by penicillin,
whereby streptomycin is increased (166). A question arises here
as to whether in other aminocyclitol antibiotics (neomycin, kanamycin, paromomycin, gentamicin, etc.) in which the structure of
the DOS component is very similar to that of streptidine, DOS may
also be an ingredient in the cell wall of the producer strains,
as streptidine is in *S. griseus* (167). This speculation has been
supported by a recent finding that cell wall inhibitors such as
bacitracin can certainly stimulate production of sagamicin (gentamicin C_{2b}) by *M. sagamiensis* when added to a certain stage of
fermentation, resulting in simultaneous repression of glucosamine
incorporation into the cell wall (164). Further investigation
was made to see a relationship between streptomycin and cell wall
synthesis by *S. griseus* by Nomi and coworkers (168). Sites of
inhibition of cell wall synthesis by addition of enduracidin or
bacitracin were sought for in the organism. More accumulation of
glucosamine-6-phosphate and N-acetylglucosamine-1-phosphate was
observed by the treatment. Studies on the time course of streptomycin fermentation in the absence of cell wall inhibitor showed
that the progress of streptomycin synthesis matched up well with
the decrease of cell wall synthesis and with the more accumulation of glucosamine-6-phosphate and N-acetylglucosamine-1- phos
phate.
    Several carbon sources cause catabolite repression of N-
acetylkanamycin amidohydrolase in *S. kanamyceticus*. This enzyme,
presumably the last enzyme in kanamycin biosynthesis, is repressed by glucose, fructose, lactose, mannose and maltose, with
lactose and fructose causing the most severe effect. cAMP was
reported to relieve glucose repression (169). It is hoped that
this isolated finding of an effect of cAMP on actinomycete metabolism is confirmed in the near future (170).

V.   REVIEW ARTICLES AND BOOKS

    Structure-activity relationships in aminoglycoside antibiotics
were reviewed by Price, Godfrey, and Kawaguchi (148) and Kawaguchi
(1971). Two general reviews on the chemistry, fermentation and

biological aspects of aminoglycoside-aminocyclitol antibiotics were written by Daniels (72) and Cox, Richardson and Ross (172). Some mention was made by Nara, Kawamoto, Okachi and Oka (113) of general physiology, biosynthesis, and metabolic regulation in the aminoglycoside fermentations. A part of metabolic regulation and genetic aspects on aminoglycoside biosynthesis was written by Nakayama (164) and Hopwood (173). An annual review on aminocyclitol and other antibiotics was written by Hoeksema and Davenport in "Annual Reports in Medicinal Chemistry," Vol. 12 (174).

REFERENCES

1. Daniels, P. J. L. and Marquez, J. A., U.S. Patent 3,984,395, October 5, 1976.
2. Bryne, K. M., Kershner, A. S., Maehr, H., Marquez, J. A., and Schaffner, C. P., *J. Chromatogr. 131,* 191 (1977).
3. Bérdy, J., Pauncz, J. K., Vajna, Z. M., Horváth, G., Gyimesi, J., and Koczka, I., *J. Antibiotics 30,* 945 (1977).
4. Daniels, P. J. L., Weinstein, J., Condon, R. G., and Lee, B. K., Abstracts, 17th Interscience Conference on Antimicrobial Agents and Chemotherapy (17th ICAAC), No. 156. New York, NY, October 12-14, 1977.
5. Mallams, A. K., Tkach, R. W., and Davies, D. H., U.S. Patent 4,009,328, February 22, 1977.
6. Davies, D. H., Mallams, A. K., McGlotten, J., Morton, J. B., and Tkach, R. W., *J. Chem. Soc. (Perkin I)* 1407 (1977).
7. Stark, W. M., U.S. Patent 3,853,709, December 10, 1974.
8. Dorman, D. E., Paschal, J. W., and Merkel, K. E., *J. Amer. Chem. Soc. 98,* 6885 (1976).
9. Nara, T., Okachi, R., Yamamoto, M., Mori, Y., Sato, M., Sugimoto, M., and Shimizu, Y., Japan Kōkai Patent S52-83, 513, July 12, 1977.
10. Sugimoto, M., Ishii, S., Iida, T., Sato, M., Okachi, R., Shirahata, K., Mori, Y., Matsubara, I., and Nara, T., Abstracts, Annual Meeting of the Agricultural Chemical Society of Japan, Nagoya, No. 2P-24, April 1-4, 1978.
11. Sato, M., Iida, T., Mori, Y., Matsubara, I., and Nara, T., Abstracts, the 98th Annual Meeting of the Pharmaceutical Society of Japan, Okayama, No. 5K 2-3, April 3-5, 1978.
12. Iida, T., Shirahata, K., Matsubara, I., Sugimoto, M., Ishii, S., Okachi, R., and Nara, T., Japan Kōkai Patent S53-56,640, May 23 (1978) and Japan Kōkai Patent Appl. No. S52-2338, January 14 (1977).
13. Shomura, T., Ohba, K., Watanabe, H., Omoto, J., Tsuruoka, T., Kojima, M., Inoue, S., and Niida, T., Japan Kōkai Patent S52-15,896, February 5, 1977.
14. Martin, J. H., Tresner, H. D., and Porter, J. N., U.S. Patent 4,007,167, February 8, 1977.

15. Ellestad, G. A., Martin, J. H., Morton, G. O., Sassiver, M. L., and Lancaster, J. E., *J. Antibiotics 30,* 678 (1977).
16. Gadó, I., Bérdy, J., Koczka, I., Horváth, I., Járay, M., and Zlatos, G., Hungarian Patent 168,778, December 30, 1973.
17. Tomioka, S., Fukuhara, T., and Mori, Y., Japan Kōkai Patent S51-86,444, July 29, 1976.
18. Davies, D. H., Greeves, D., Mallams, A. K., Morton, J. B., and Tkach, R. W., *J. Chem. Soc. (Perkin I),* 814 (1975).
19. Lee, B. K., Condon, R. G., Wagman, G. H., and Weinstein, M. J., *J. Antibiotics 29,* 677 (1976).
20. Kugelman, M., Mallams, A. K., and Vernay, H. F., *J. Antibiotics 26,* 394 (1973).
21. Reimann, H., Cooper, D. J., Mallams, A. K., Jaret, R. S., Yehaskel, A., Kugelman, M., Vernay, H. F., and Schumacher, D., *D. Org. Chem. 39,* 1451 (1974).
22. Marquez, J. A., Wagman, G. H., Testa, R. T., Waitz, J. A., and Weinstein, M. J., *J. Antibiotics 29,* 483 (1976).
23. Daniels, P. J. L., Jaret, R. S., Nagabhushan, T. L., and Turner, W. N., *J. Antibiotics 29,* 488 (1976).
24. O'Connor, S., Lam, L. K. T., Jones, N. D., and Chane, M. O., *J. Org. Chem. 41,* 2087 (1976).
25. Nara, T., Yamamoto, M., Kawamoto, I., Takayama, K., Okachi, R., Takasawa, S., Sato, T., and Sato, S., *J. Antibiotics 30,* 533 (1977).
26. Okachi, R., Takasawa, S., Sato, T., Sato, S., Yamamoto, M., Kawamoto, I., and Nara, T., *J. Antibiotics 30,* 541 (1977).
27. Egan, R. S., Stanaszek, R. S., Cirovic, M., Mueller, S. L., Tadanier, J., Martin, J. R., Collum, P., Goldstein, A. W., DeVault, R. L., Sinclair, A. C., Fager, E. E., and Mitscher, L. A., *J. Antibiotics 30,* 552 (1977).
28. Cirolami, R. L. and Stamm, J. M., *J. Antibiotics 30,* 564 (1977).
29. Nara, T., "Aminoglycoside Antibitics" *in* "Annual Reports on Fermentation Processes" (D. Perlman, ed.), Vol. I, pp. 299-326. Academic Press, Inc., New York (1977).
30. Pankhurst, J. W., *Vet. Record 99,* 107 (1976).
31. Wenkert, E. and Hagaman, W. E., *J. Org. Chem. 41,* 701 (1976).
32. Kirby, J. P., Borders, D. R., and Van Lear, G. E., *J. Antibiotics 30,* 175 (1977).
33. Nara, T., Kawamoto, I., Okachi, R., Takasawa, S., Yamamoto, M., Sato, S., Sato, T., and Morikawa, A., *J. Antibiotics 28,* 21 (1975).
34. Okachi, R., Kawamoto, I., Takasawa, S., Yamamoto, M., Sato, S., Sato, T., and Nara, T., *J. Antibiotics 27,* 793 (1974).
35. Egan, R. S., DeVault, R. L., Mueller, S. L., Levenberg, M. L., Sinclair, A. C., and Stanaszek, R. S., *J. Antibiotics 28,* 29 (1975).
36. Daniels, P. J. L., Luce, C., Nagabhushan, T. L., Jaret, R. S., Schumacher, D., Reimann, H., and Ilavsky, J., *J. Antibiotics 28,* 35 (1975).

37. Tanaka, M., Deguchi, T., Ishii, A., Nakamura, N., Sato, K., Shimizu, M., and Hara, T., Abstracts, 10th International Congress of Chemotherapy, No. 385, Zurich, Switzerland, September 18-23, 1977.
38. Tsukiura, H., Hanada, M., Saito, K., Fujisawa, K., Miyaki, T., Koshiyama, H., and Kawaguchi, H., J. Antibiotics 29, 1137 (1976).
39. Tomita, K., Hoshino, Y., Uenoyama, Y., Fujisawa, K., Tsukiura, H., and Kawaguchi, H., J. Antibiotics 29, 1147 (1976).
40. Konishi, M., Kamata, S., Tsuno, T., Numata, K., Tsukiura, H., Naito, T., and Kawaguchi, H., J. Antibiotics 29, 1152 (1976).
41. Nara, K., Sumino, Y., Asai, M., and Akiyama, S., Japan Kōkai Patent S51-123,886, October 28, 1976.
42. Kirby, J. P., VanLear, G. E., Morton, G. O., Gore, W. E., Curran, W. V., and Borders, D. B., J. Antibiotics 30, 344 (1977).
43. Kahan, F. M., Putter, I., and Hernandez, S., Japan Kōkai Patent S52-128,313, October 27, 1977.
44. Ōhashi, H., Kawabe, H., Sato, K., and Kurashige, S., Abstracts, 2nd Tokyo Symposium of Microbial Drug Resistance, No. IIIA-3. Tokyo, October 26-28, 1977.
45. Hirayama, N., Shirahata, K., Ōhashi, Y., Sasada, Y., and Martin, J. R., Acta Crystallographica B34, in press (1978).
46. Umezawa, H., Umezawa, S., Tsuchiya, T., and Okazaki, Y., J. Antibiotics 24, 485 (1971).
47. Kawaguchi, H., Naito, T., Nakagawa, S., and Fujisawa, K., J. Antibiotics 25, 695 (1972).
48. Wright, J. J., J. Chem. Soc. Chem. Comm. 206 (1976).
49. Miller, G. H., Arcieri, G., Weinstein, M. J., and Waitz, J. A., Antimicrob. Ag. Chemotherap. 10, 827 (1976).
50. Flournoy, D. J., Antimicrob. Ag. Chemotherap. 10, 864 (1976).
51. Luft, F. C., Yum, M. N., and Kleit, S. A., Antimicrob. Ag. Chemotherap. 10, 845 (1976).
52. Miller, G. H., Moss, E., Chiu, P. J. S., and Waitz, J. A., 16th Interscience Conference on Antimicrobial Agents and Chemotherapy (16th ICAAC), No. 59. Chicago, IL, October 27-29, 1976.
53. Fu, K. P. and Neu, H. C., 17th ICAAC, No. 250 (1977).
54. Richardson, K., Jevons, S., and Moore, J. W., 17th ICAAC, No. 149 (1977).
55. Jevons, S., Andrews, R. J., Brammer, K. W., Cheeseman, H. E., and Richardson, K., 17th ICAAC, No. 150 (1977).
56. Carney, R. E. and McAlpine, J. B., 17th ICAAC, No. 155 (1977).
57. Matsushima, H. and Mori, Y., J. Antibiotics 30, 390 (1977).
58. Matsushima, H., Kitaura, K., and Mori, Y., Bull. Chem. Soc. Japan 50, 3039 (1977).

59. Wright, J. J., Daniels, P. J. L., Mallams, A. K., and Naga-bhushan, T. L., U.S. Patent 4,002,608, January 11, 1977.

60. Nagabhushan, T. L., Cooper, A. B., Tsai, H., and Daniels, P. J. L., 17th ICAAC, No. 249 (1977).

61. Fu, K. P. and Neu, H. C., 17th ICAAC, No. 250 (1977).

62. Mallams, A. K., Davies, D. H., Boxler, D. L., Vernay, H. F., and Reichert, P., 17th ICAAC, No. 251 (1977).

63. Tomioka, S. and Mori, Y., Abstracts, Annual Meeting of the Agricultural Chemical Society of Japan, Nagoya, No. 20-24, April 1-4, 1978.

64. Sano, H., Tsuchiya, T., Kobayashi, S., Hamada, M., Umezawa, S., and Umezawa, H., *J. Antibiotics 29*, 978 (1976).

65. Rosi, D., Goss, W. A., and Daum, S. J., *J. Antibiotics 30*, 88 (1977).

66. Daum, S. J., Rosi, D., and Goss, W. A., *J. Antibiotics 30*, 98 (1977).

67. Cleophax, J., Gero, S. D., Leboul, J., Akhtar, M., Barnett, J. E. G., and Pearce, C. J., *J. Amer. Chem. Soc. 98*, 7110 (1976).

68. Ito, Y., Takeda, K., and Yamaguchi, T., Japan Kōkai Patent S52-97,938, August 17, 1977.

69. Takeda, K., Kinumaki, A., Furumai, T., Yamaguchi, T., Ohshima, S., and Ito, Y., *J. Antibiotics 31*, 247 (1978).

70. Testa, R. T., Wagman, G. H., Daniels, P. J. L., and Wein-stein, M. J., *J. Antibiotics 27*, 917 (1974).

71. Shier, W. T., Ogawa, S., Hichens, M., and Rinehart, K. L., *J. Antibiotics 26*, 551 (1973).

72. Daniels, P. J. L., "Aminoglycoside - Aminocyclitol and Related Antibiotics" in "Kirk/Othmer - Encyclopedia of Chemical Technology," Vol. II. John Wiley and Sons, Inc., New York (1978).

73. Nara, T., Yamamoto, M., Takasawa, S., Sato, S., Sato, T., Kawamoto, I., Okachi, R., Takahashi, I., and Morikawa, A., *J. Antibiotics 30*, 17 (1977).

74. Sato, S., Takasawa, S., Sato, T., Yamamoto, M., Okachi, R., Kawamoto, I., Iida, T., Morikawa, A., and Nara, T., *J. Antibiotics 30*, 25 (1977).

75. McAlpine, J. B., Sinclair, A. C., Egan, R. S., DeVault, R. L., Stanaszek, R. S., Cirovic, M., Mueller, S. L., Goodley, P. C., Mauritz, R. J., and Wideburg, N. E., *J. Antibiotics 30*, 39 (1977).

76. Shimizu, M., Takahashi, I., and Nara, T., *Agr. Biol. Chem. 42*, 653 (1978).

77. Vivian, A. and Hopwood, D. A., *J. Gen. Microbiol. 64*, 101 (1970).

78. Vivian, A., *J. Gen. Microbiol. 69*, 353 (1971).

79. Gregory, K. F. and Huang, J. C. C., *J. Bacteriol. 87*, 1287 (1964).

80. kanishi, M., Ohta, T., and Umezawa, H., *J. Antibiotics 23*, 45 (1970).

81. McCann, P. A., Redshaw, P. A., and Pogell, B. M., *Federation Proc. 35,* 1585 (1976).

82. Kirby, R., Wright, L. F., and Hopwood, D. A., *Nature 254,* 265 (1975).

83. Akagawa, H., Okanishi, M., and Umezawa, H., *J. Gen. Microbiol. 90,* 336 (1975).

84. Wright, L. F. and Hopwood, D. A., *J. Gen. Microbiol. 95,* 96 (1976).

85. Shaw, P. D. and Piwowarski, J., *J. Antibiotics 30,* 404 (1977).

86. Waring, M., *in* "Antibiotics. III. Mechanism of Action of Antimicrobial and Antitumor Agents" (J. W. Corcoran and F. E. Hahn, eds.), pp. 141-165. Springer-Verlag, Heidelberg (1975).

87. Wolfe, A. D., *in* "Antibiotics. III. Mechanism of Action of Antimicrobial and Antitumor Agents" (J. W. Corcoran and F. E. Hahn, eds.), pp. 203-233. Springer-Verlag, Heidelberg (1975).

88. Okanishi, M., Koshichi, K., Ichihara, K., and Umezawa, H., Abstracts, Annual Meeting of the Agricultural Chemical Society of Japan, Tokyo, No. 1B-2, April 1-4, 1977.

89. Hotta, K., Okami, Y., and Umezawa, H., *J. Antibiotics 30,* 1146 (1977).

90. Umezawa, H., *Kagaku* (in Japanese) *46,* 130 (1976).

91. Okanishi, M., *Hakko to Kogyō* (in Japanese) *34,* 435 (1976).

92. Okanishi, M., *Amino Acid-Nucleic Acid 35,* 15 (1977).

93. Helinski, D. R., *Ann. Rev. Microb. 27,* 437 (1973).

94. Chakrabarty, A. M., *Ann. Rev. Genet. 10,* 7 (1976).

95. Cohen, S. N., Chang, A. C. Y., Boyer, H. W., and Helling, R. B., *Proc. Natl. Acad. Sci., USA 70,* 3240 (1973).

96. Courvalin, P., Weisblum, B., and Davies, J., *Proc. Natl. Acad. Sci. USA 74,* 999 (1977).

97. Benveniste, R. and Davies, J., *Proc. Natl. Acad. Sci. USA 70,* 2276 (1973).

98. Yagisawa, M., Courvalin, P. M., DeWilde, M., and Davies, J., 17th ICAAC, No. 22 (1977).

99. Wagman, G. H. and Weinstein, M. J., "Chromatography of Antibiotics." Elsevier Scientific Publishing Company, Amsterdam-London-New York (1973).

100. Kabasakalian, P., Kalliney, S., and Magatti, A. W., *Anal. Chem. 49,* 953 (1977).

101. Wilson, W. L., Richard, G., and Hughes, D. W., *J. Pharm. Sci. 62,* 282 (1973).

102. Yamamoto, M., Okachi, R., Kawamoto, I., and Nara, T., *J. Antibiotics 30,* 1064 (1977).

103. Tsuji, K. and Robertson, J. H., *Anal. Chem. 42,* 1661 (1970).

104. Omoto, S., Inouye, S., and Niida, T., *J. Antibiotics 24,* 430 (1971).

105. Mays, D. L., Van Apeldoorn, R. J., and Lauback, R. G., *J. Chromatogr. 120,* 93 (1976).

106. Peng, G. W., Gadalla, M. A. F., Peng, A., Smith, V., and Chiou, W. L., *Clin. Chem. 23*, 1838 (1977).

107. Brodasky, T. F., *Anal. Chem. 35*, 343 (1963).

108. Kondo, S., Sezaki, M., and Shimura, M., *J. Antibiotics Ser. B. (in Japanese) 17*, 1 (1964).

109. Kawamoto, I., Yamamoto, M., and Nara, T., Abstracts, Annual Meeting of the Agricultural Chemical Society of Japan, Tokyo, No. 2D-26, April 1-4, 1977.

110. Kroppenstedt, R. M. and Kutzner, H. J., *Experientia 32*, 318 (1976).

111. Buchanan, R. E. and Gibbons, N. E., "Bergey's Manual of Determinative Bacteriology," 8th Ed., p. 658. The Williams and Wilkins Company, Baltimore, 1974.

112. Kawamoto, I., Oka, T., and Nara, T., Abstracts, The Annual Meeting of the Actinomycetologist, Tokyo, No. 4, May 20, 1977.

113. Nara, T., Kawamoto, I., Okachi, R., and Oka, T., *Japanese J. Antibiotics 30 (Supplement)*, 174 (1977).

114. Schleifer, K. H. and Kandler, O., *Bacteriol. Rev. 36*, 407 (1972).

115. Katsumata, R., Adachi, S., and Takayama, K., Abstracts, Annual Meeting of the Agricultural Chemical Society of Japan, Tokyo, No. 2B-4, April 104, 1977.

116. Kikuchi, M. and Perlman, D., *J. Antibiotics 30*, 423 (1977).

117. Kawaguchi, H., Tomita, K., Tsukiura, H., and Konishi, M., Japan Kōkai Patent S52-31,001, March 9, 1977.

118. Kawaguchi, H., Tsukiura, H., Tomita, K., Konishi, M., Saito, K., Kobaru, S., Numata, K., Fujisawa, K., Miyaki, T., Hatori, M., and Koshiyama, H., *J. Antibiotics 30*, 779 (1977).

119. Weinstein, M. J., Luedemann, G. M., Wagman, G. H., and Marquez, J. A., U.S. Patent 3,454,696, July 8, 1969.

120. Luckner, M. and Nover, L., "23. Secondary Metabolism and Cell Differentiation" *in* "Molecular Biology, Biochemistry and Biophysics" (M. Luckner, L. Nover and H. Böhm, eds.), pp. 22-24. Spring-Verlag, Berlin, Heidelberg, New York (1977).

121. Kleiner, E. M., Pliner, S. A., Soifer, V. S., Onoprienko, V. V., Balashova, T. A., Rozynov, B. V., and Khokhlov, A. S., *Bioorganitcheskaja Chimia 2*, 1142 (1976).

122. Ferguson, J. H., Huang, H. T., and Davisson, J. W., *Appl. Microbiol. 5*, 339 (1957).

123. Heding, H. and Gurtu, A. K., *J. Antibiotics 30*, 879 (1977).

124. Wagman, G. H., Gannon, R. D., and Weinstein, M. J., *Appl. Microbiol. 17*, 648 (1969).

125. Tilley, B. C., Testa, R. T., and Doman, E., The 31st Meeting of the Society for Industrial Microbiology, Kingston, RI, No. 26, August 17-22, 1975.

126. Kawamoto, I., Okachi, R., and Nara, T., *J. Antibiotics*, in press (1978).

127. Celmer, W. D., Cullen, W. P., English, A. R., Jefferson, M. T., Oscarson, J. R., Boutein, J. B., and Sciavolino, F. C., 15th Interscience Conference on Antimicrobial Agents and Chemotherapy, No. 260. Washington, D.C., September 24-26, 1975.

128. Rinehart, K. L. and Stroshane, R. M., *J. Antibiotics 29,* 319 (1976).

129. Rinehart, K. L., Malik, J. M., Nystrom, R. S., Stroshane, R. M., Truit, S. T., Taniguchi, M., Rolls, J. P., Haak, W. J., and Ruff, B. A., *J. Amer. Chem. Soc. 96,* 2263 (1974).

130. Munro, M. H. G., Taniguchi, M., Rinehart, K. L., Gottlieb, D., Stoudt, T. H., and Rogers, T. O., *J. Amer. Chem. Soc. 97,* 4782 (1975).

131. Testa, R. T. and Tilley, B. C., *J. Antibiotics 29,* 140 (1976).

132. Deguchi, T., Okumura, S., Ishii, A., and Tanaka, M., *J. Antibiotics 30,* 933 (1977).

133. Lee, B. K., Bailey, J. V., Condon, R. G., Marquez, J. A., Wagman, G. H., and Weinstein, M. J., *Antimicrob. Ag. Chemotherap. 12,* 335 (1977).

134. Testa, R. T. and Tilley, B. C., *J. Antibiotics 28,* 573 (1975).

135. Köster, H., Liebermann, B., and Reuter, G., *Z. Allgem. Mikrobiol. 17,* 433 (1977).

136. Pearce, C. J., Barnett, J. E. G., Anthony, C., and Akhtar, M., *Biochem. J. 159,* 601 (1976).

137. Baud, H., Betencourt, A., Peyre, M., and Penasse, L., *J. Antibiotics 30,* 720 (1977).

138. Mitsuhashi, S., "Drug-Inactivating Enzymes and Antibiotic Resistance" (S. Mitsuhashi, L. Rosival and V. Krcmery, eds.), p. 115. Spring-Verlag, Berlin (1975).

139. Courvalin, P. and Davies, J., *Antimicrob. Ag. Chemotherap. 11,* 619 (1977).

140. Kayser, F. H., 16th ICAAC, No. 204, 1976.

141. LeGoffic, F., Martel, A., Moreau, N., Capmau, M. L., Soussy, C. J., and Duval, J., *Antimicrob. Ag. Chemotherap. 12,* 26 (1977).

142. Nagabhushan, T. L., Cooper, A. C., Daniels, P. J. L., Davies, J., and Hoffman, B., 17th ICAAC, No. 21, 1977.

143. LeGoffic, F., Martel, A., Capmau, M. L., Baca, B., Goebel, P., Chardon, H., Soussy, C. J., Duval, J., and Bouanchaud, D. H., *Antimicrob. Ag. Chemotherap. 10,* 258 (1976).

144. Santanam, P. and Kayser, F. H., *J. Infect. Dis. 134,* S33 (1976).

145. Shirafuji, H., Kida, M., and Yoneda, M., Abstracts, Annual Meeting of the Agricultural Chemical Society of Japan, Kyoto, No. 2I-21, April 1-4, 1976.

146. Sato, S., Iida, T., Okachi, R., Shirahata, K., and Nara, T., *J. Antibiotics 30,* 1025 (1977).

147. Davies, J. and O'Connor, S., *Antimicrob. Ag. Chemotherap. 13,* in press (1978).

148. Price, K. E., Godfrey, J. C., and Kawaguchi, H., *Adv. Appl. Microbiol. 18*, 191 (1974).

149. Price, K. E., Godfrey, J. C., and Kawaguchi, H., "Effect of Structural Modifications on the Biological Properties of Aminoglycoside Antibiotics Containing 2-Deoxystreptamine" *in* "Structure-Activity Relationships Among the Semisynthetic Antibiotics" (D. Perlman, ed.), pp. 239-395. Academic Press, Inc., New York (1977).

150. Nakahama, K., Shirafuji, H., Nogami, A., Kida, M., and Yoneda, M., Abstracts, Annual Meeting of the Agricultural Chemical Society of Japan, Yokohama, No. 1L-19, April 1-4, 1977.

151. Matsuhashi, Y., Sawa, T., Kondo, S., and Takeuchi, T., *J. Antibiotics 30*, 435 (1977).

152. Matsuhashi, Y., Yagisawa, M., Kondo, S., Takeuchi, T., and Umezawa, H., *J. Antibiotics 28*, 442 (1975).

153. Shirafuji, H., Nakahama, I., Nogami, A., Kida, M., and Yoneda, M., Abstracts, Annual Meeting of the Agricultural Chemical Society of Japan, Yokohama, No. 1L-20, April 1-4, 1977.

154. Kimizuka, F., Naito, N., Kumagaya, K., Obayashi, A., and Tanabe, O., Abstracts, Annual Meeting of the Agricultural Chemical Society of Japan, Yokohama, No. 1L-21, April 1-4, 1977.

155. Okutani, T., Asako, T., Yoshioka, K., Hiraga, K., and Kida, M., *J. Amer. Chem. Soc. 99*, 1278 (1977).

156. Miller, M. S. and Walker, J. B., *J. Bacteriol. 99*, 401 (1969).

157. Walker, J. B. and Skorvaga, M., *J. Biol. Chem. 248*, 2435 (1973).

158. Nimi, O., Ito, G., Sueda, S., and Nomi, R., *Agr. Biol. Chem. 35*, 848 (1971).

159. Nimi, O., Ito, G., Ohata, Y., Funayama, S., and Nomi, R., *Agr. Biol. Chem. 35*, 856 (1971).

160. Benveniste, R. and Davies, J., *Proc. Natl. Acad. Sci. U.S. 70*, 2276 (1973).

161. Dowding, J. and Davies, J., "Mechanisms and Originins of Plasmid-Determined Antibiotic Resistance" *in* "Microbiology-1974" (D. Schlessinger, ed.), p. 179. American Society for Microbiology, Washington, D.C. (1975).

162. Ogawa, Y. and Perlman, D., *J. Antibiotics 29*, 1112 (1976).

163. Sato, S., Shimizu, M., Iida, T., and Nara, T., Abstracts, Annual Meeting of the Agricultural Chemical Society of Japan, Nagoya, No. 2P-18, April 1-4, 1978.

164. Nakayama, K., *Amino Acid-Nucleic Acid 36*, 1 (1977).

165. Basak, K. and Majumdar, S. K., *Folia Microbiol. 21*, 43 (1976).

166. Barabás, G. and Szabó, G., *Antimicrob. Ag. Chemother. 11*, 392 (1977).

167. Szabó, G., Barabás, G., Vályi-Nagy, T., and Magyar, Z.,
      Acta Microbiol. Acad. Sci. Hung. 12, 109 (1965).
168. Ikeda, A., Koseki, A., Yoshimura, Y., Nimi, O., and Nomi,
      R., Abstracts, Meeting of the Fermentation Technology
      Society of Japan, Osaka, No. 306, November 10-12, 1977.
169. Satoh, A., Ogawa, H., and Satomura, Y., *Agr. Biol. Chem.
      40*, 191 (1976).
170. Drew, S. W. and Demain, A. L., *Ann. Rev. Microbiol. 31*,
      343 (1977).
171. Kawaguchi, H., *Japanese J. Antibiotics 30 (Supplement)*,
      190 (1977).
172. Cox, D. A., Richardson, K., and Ross, B. C., "The Amino-
      glycosides" *in* "Topics in Antibiotic Chemistry" (P. G.
      Sammes, ed.), Vol. 1, pp. 1-90. Ells Horwood, Ltd. (1977).
173. Hopwood, D. A. and Merrick, M. J., *Bacteriol. Rev. 41*, 595
      (1977).
174. Hoeksema, H. and Davenport, L. C., *Ann. Rep. Med. Chem. 12*,
      110 (1977).

CHAPTER 11

MICROBIAL TRANSFORMATIONS OF ANTIBIOTICS

M. Shibata
M. Uyeda

Faculty of Pharmaceutical Sciences
Kumamoto University
Kumamoto, Japan

In the last several years, enzymatic reactions have been
elucidated through which some antibiotics are inactivated by
antibiotic-resistant strains. By the use of these reactions with
mild but inherent specificities, preparations of new derivatives
of antibiotics with superior activities have been attempted.
Microbial transformations of antibiotics have been detailed (1-3)
and, in addition, a number of papers on this subject have been
published. Novel antibiotics also have been prepared by "directed biosynthesis" and "mutational biosynthesis." In most of the
cases, modified antibiotics showed lower activities but some of
them exhibited improved characteristics (lower toxicities or the
higher antibiotic activities) than the normal products. These
techniques appear to become important methods for antibiotic-
transformation. In this review, we have included pertinent information on this subject.

I. INDIRECT TRANSFORMATIONS

A. Modification by Directed Biosynthesis

A few attempts for the formation of a modified antibiotic have
been made by the addition of inhibitors or precursors to a fermentation medium (4-6). The addition of several methylation inhibitors to the fermentation medium of Streptomyces aureofaciens
(7) or S. griseus (8) effected the production of 7-chloro-6-
demethyltetracycline or N-demethyl-streptomycin, in addition to

267

the normal products. Sulfonamide and sulfanilamide inhibited N-methylation, rather selectively, resulting in the production of N-demethyllincomycin by *S. lincolnensis* (9). The addition of 5-fluorouracil to *S. cacaoi* resulted in the formation of 5-fluoro-polyoxins L and M with the broad antibacterial spectrum (10).

The addition of 4-aminosalicylic acid to the culture medium of *S. caelestis* resulted in the production of desalicetin 2'-(4-aminosalicylate) with a spectrum similar to that of celesticetin (11).

In the bleomycin fermentation, the addition of 1,2-diamino-ethane, dimethylamine, morpholine, guanine, N-(3-aminopropyl)-1,3-diaminopropane, N-methyl-N-(3-aminopropyl)-1,3-diaminopropane, N'-n-butyl-N-(3-aminopropyl)-1,3-diaminopropane and N'-(1-phenyl-ethyl)-N-(3-aminopropyl)-1,3-diaminopropane effected the produc-tion of new bleomycins which contained the corresponding amine. In most cases these new bleomycins showed higher antibiotic activity than that of bleomycin A_2 (12).

In the presence of *cis*-4-methylproline, *S. parvullus* produced two additional actinomycins, designated K_{1c} and K_{2c} in which the proline sites were replaced by *cis*-4-methylproline. Analogously, actinomycins K_{1t} and K_{2t} were produced in the presence of *trans*-4-methylproline (13).

B. *Modification by Blocked Mutants*

Modified antibiotic may be expected to be formed by mutants, blocked in intermediate steps of antibiotic synthesis. Mutant 22227a of *S. caelestis* (14) produced 7-0-demethylcelesticetin different from the normal product, celesticetin. Mutant 22218a of the same streptomycete (15) produced N-demethylcelesticetin and N-demethyl-7-0-demethylcelesticetin (Figure 1).

In the studies of platenomycin cosynthesis (16), four basic glycosides [3-0-propionyl-5-mycaminosyl-platenolides I and II, 9-dehydro demycarosyl platenomycin and demycarosyl platenomycin (17)] and two neutral macrocylic lactones [platenolides I and II (18)] were isolated from the fermentation broth of the blocked mutants of *S. platensis* subsp. *malvinus*. All these intermediates were transformed into platenomycin by the growing culture or washed mycelium of other mutants of the same organism. Among these compounds, 9-dehydrodemycarosyl platenomycin and demycarosyl platenomycin were weakly active against Gram-positive bacteria and *Klebsiella pneumoniae* (19).

A mutant of neomycin-producing *S. fradiae* produced ribostamy-cin. Colonies were obtained by reverse mutation which resulted in the formation of neomycin. From these results, ribostamycin was implicated as an intermediate in the biosynthesis of neomycin (20).

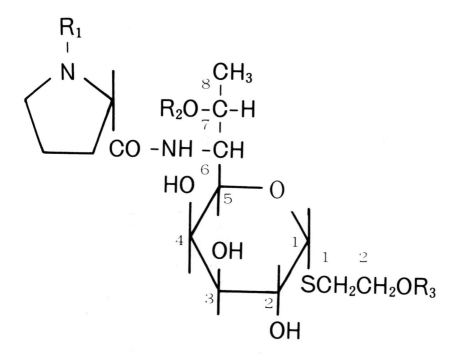

FIGURE 1.   Structures of celesticetins.

	R_1	R_2	R_3
Celesticetin	CH_3	CH_3	salicylate
7-O-Demethylcelesticetin	CH_3	H	salicylate
N-Demethylcelesticetin	H	CH_3	salicylate
N-Demethyl-7-O-demethylcelesticetin	H	H	salicylate
Desalicetin 2'-(4-amino-salicylate)	CH_3	CH_3	4-aminosalicylate

The impact of cephalosporin antibiotics on medicine stimulated the search for new cephem compounds by various mutants of cephalosporin C-producing *Cephalosporium acremonium*. As a result, the productions of N-acetyl deacetoxycephalosporin C (21), deacetoxycephalosporin C (22,23), deacetylcephalosporin C (24), 7-(D-5-amino-5-carboxyvaleramido)-3 (1,1-dimethyl-2-amino-2-carboxyethyl-thiomethyl)-3-cephem-4-carboxylic acid (25), D-5-amino-5-carboxyvaleramido-(5-formyl-4-carboxy-2H,3H,6H-tetrahydro-1,3-thiazinyl) glycine (26) and 7-(5-amino-5-carboxypentamido)-3-methylthiomethyl-3-cephem-4-carboxylic acid (27) were demonstrated by the various mutants of the same organism.

A number of lysine-requiring auxotrophs of *Acremonium chrysogenum* were investigated for incorporation of side-chain precursors and for accumulation of β-lactam compounds. One of the auxotrophs, *A. chrysogenum* ATCC 20389, was found to use *L*-S-carboxymethylcysteine as a side-chain precursor for the synthesis

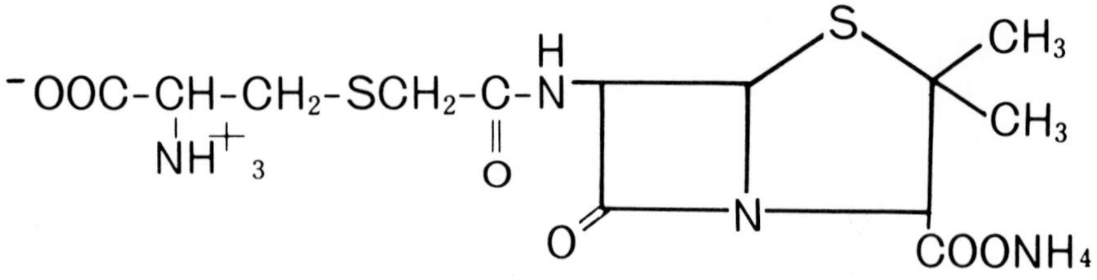

FIGURE 2.   Structure of RIT 2214.

of a new penicillin, RIT-2214. RIT-2214 was identified as 6-(D)-
{[(2-amino-2-carboxy)-ethylthio]-acetamido}-penicillanic acid by
spectral analysis, bioactivity, elucidation of side-chain structure and semisynthesis. It exhibited a broad antibiotic spectrum
with an *in vitro* potency slightly less than that of ampicillin,
and showed no activity against penicillin-resistant organisms,
but afforded better protection than ampicillin against most of
the infections tested (28).

C.   *Modification by Mutational Biosynthesis (Mutasynthesis)*

A novel method for preparing semisynthetic aminoglycoside
antibiotics was developed in 1969 by using mutants of *S. fradiae*
incapable of producing the 2-deoxystreptamine portion of neomycin.
When 2-deoxystreptamine was added to the fermentation, the antibiotic was formed. Similarly, streptamine and 2-epistreptamine
were incorporated into new antibiotics, hybrimycins A_1, A_2, B_1
and B_2 by the 2-deoxystreptamine-negative mutants of the same
organism (29,30).
Since then, numerous modified aminoglycoside antibiotics have
been prepared by this technique. These antibiotics include hybrimycins C_1 and C_2 (2-hydroxyparomomycins I and II) (30,31),
1-N-methyl-, 2-hydroxy-, 2-epihydroxy-, and 3',4'-dideoxyribo-
stamycins (32), 6'-deamino-6'-hydroxy-1-N-methyl- and 6'-deamino-
6'-hydroxy-2-epihydroxy-kanamycins (32), mutamicins I and II (2-
hydroxysisomicin and 5-deoxysisomicin) (33), 2-hydroxybutirosin,
and 5-deoxybutirosamine (34,35), 3'-chloro-3'-deoxy-, and 3'-
deoxybutirosins A (36), streptomutin A (37), 2-hydroxygentamicin
(38,39) and 5-deoxygentamicin (38-40). Some derivatives such as
5-deoxysisomicin and 2-hydroxygentamicin C, exhibit higher activity especially against antibiotic-resistant strains and less toxicity than the parent sisomicin and gentamicin.

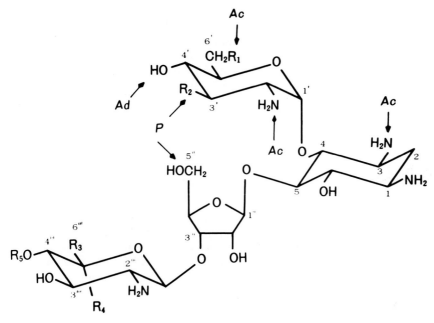

FIGURE 3.   Structures of neomycins.

	R_1	R_2	R_3	R_4	R_5
Neomycin B	NH_2	OH	H	CH_2NH_2	H
Neomycin C	NH_2	OH	CH_2NH_2	H	H
Paromomycin	OH	OH	$\begin{cases} H \\ CH_2NH_2 \end{cases}$	$\begin{cases} CH_2NH_2 \\ H \end{cases}$	H
Lividomycin A	OH	H	H	CH_2NH_2	$mannose$
Lividomycin B	OH	H	H	CH_2NH_2	H

The terms "mutational biosynthesis" (37) and "mutasynthesis" (37) were proposed for the production of new metabolites by mutants blocked in the biosynthetic pathway to the secondary metabolite. The term "idiotroph" was proposed to identify such mutants (37).

Mutational biosynthesis was reviewed in Vol. 1 of this series (41). Additional literature includes the bioconversion of paromamine, neamine, gentamicins A_2, A and X_2 and antibiotic JI-20A (6'-amino-gentamicin X_2) into sisomicin by a deoxystreptamine-negative mutant of *M. injoensis*. Based upon the specificity of

the structural configuration of these compounds which were converted to sisomicin and those which were not, a pathway for the
biosynthesis of sisomicin was proposed (42).

In a similar way, a paromamine-negative mutant of *M. purpurea*
blocked in the production of gentamicin converted gentamicins C_2
or C_{1a} into gentamicins C_1 or C_{2b}, respectively. Both of these
conversions require an N-methylation step at the 6'-position.
Antibiotic JI-20A was transformed to gentamicin C_{1a} and C_{2b},
while antibiotic JI-20B (6'-C-methyl JI-20A) was transformed to
gentamicins C_2 and C_1. Gentamicins A and X_2 were also transformed into gentamicin complex by the mutant. The products of
these transformations reveal that the mutant is able to carry out
the enzymatic steps leading to gentamicin C complex and include
C-methylation, epimerization, dehydroxylation, and N-methylation
(43).

The technique of mutational biosynthesis employed not only
deoxystreptamine-negative mutants, but also a neamine-(2-deoxy-
streptamine-contining pseudodisaccharide) negative mutant. 3'-
Deoxyneamine and 3'-deoxyxylostasin or 3'-chloro-3'-deoxyneamine
and 3'-chloro-3'-deoxyxylostasin were transformed into 3'-deoxy-
butirosin A or 3'-chloro-3'-deoxybutirosin A by a neamine-negative
mutant of *B. vitellinus* (36).

II.   DIRECT TRANSFORMATION

A.   *Acylation*

   1.   Chloramphenicol. Besides the acylations of chloramphenicol by *E. coli, S. aureus, S. epidermidis* and *S. coelicolor*, etc.,
chloramphenicol was acylated by the spores, washed mycelium or
whole cultures of *S. griseus* (44) and by a mutant of *Myxococcus
xanthus* (45).

   In the case of *M. xanthus*, 1-acetyl and 3-acetyl esters of
chloramphenicol were identified as inactivation products and the
same derivatives as well as 3-propionyl, 3-*iso*butyryl, and 3-
*iso*valeryl esters of chloramphenicol were formed by *S. griseus*.
In the comparative studies of plasmid elimination with acriflavin
and ethidium bromide, the tyrosinase-determining gene was located
on a plasmid while the location of the gene for the chloramphenicol acetyltransferase (CAT) in *S. griseus* has not yet been
assigned (46).

   Several biochemical similarities between the staphylococcal
and R factor-mediated types of CAT are known (47,48), although
they differ in primary sequence. In order to elucidate minor
distinctions among staphylococcal CATs, four of these enzymes
were further investigated (47). Each was purified and was shown
to exist as a tetrameric protein with a native molecular weight
of 80,000 and an identical subunit size of 20,000. Each exhibited
identical catalytic and immunological properties and was capable

of undergoing reversible denaturation in 6M guanidine hydrochloride. Hybrids were formed between pairs of each of the purified enzymes. However, they possessed variable sensitivity to heat denaturation and mercuric ion inhibition. These properties cannot as yet be correlated with specific structural features.

The distribution of CAT in various species of microorganisms including the chloramphenicol- and corynecin-producer was examined. None of the cell-free extracts of chloramphenicol- or corynecin-producing strains possessed CAT activity and a possible relationship between the origin of the enzymes involved in the biosynthesis of antibiotics and of the enzymes involved in the resistance mechanism was discussed (49).

2. *Aminoglycosides.* In addition to the acetylation of kanamycin by the kanamycin acetyltransferase [AAC(6') -I] from *E. coli* K 12 (R5) (50), the 6'-N-acetylation of 3',4'-dideoxykanamycin B (DKB) (51) was demonstrated by a similar enzyme from *Ps. aeruginosa* GN315. Subsequently, other aminoglycoside antibiotics such as ribostamycin (52), 4'-deoxykanamycin (53), amikacin (53, 55), butirosins A and B (53), tobramycin (53), neomycin (54), gentamicins C_{1a} and C_2 (53,54), sisomicin (56,57) and related antibiotics (53,54) were also found to be inactivated through 6'-N-acetylation by similar aminoglycoside 6'-N-acetyltransferases ([AAC(6')-I], kanamycin acetyltransferase) from *Ps. aeruginosa* and *E. coli.*

In subsequent studies on the structural requirements of substrate antibiotics for the action of the *Ps. aeruginosa* enzyme, it was indicated that concurrent 6'-N-alkylation and 1-N-acylation may yield active derivatives resistant to this enzyme (53). Tobramycin was also acetylated by aminoglycoside 6'-N-acetyltransferase I-like enzymes of *Klebsiella pneumoniae* and *Enterobacter cloaceae* (58).

The acetylation of kanamycin, amikacin and tobramycin was demonstrated by another 6'-N-acetylating enzyme from *Moraxella glueidii*. From the difference of substrate specificity, the name aminoglycoside 6'-N-acetyltransferase II [AAC(6')-II] was proposed (59).

A new R factor-mediated aminoglycoside acetyltransferase was isolated from *Ps. aeruginosa* GN4925. Kanamycin, DKB and 6'-methyl DKB were acetylated at the 6'-N position by this enzyme except amikacin, kanamycin C and gentamicin C_1 and the name aminoglycoside 6'-N-acetyltransferase 3 was proposed (60) (tentatively referred to as [AAC(6')-III] hereafter).

Other aminoglycoside 6'-N-acetyltransferases were identified in *Ps. aeruginosa* 3796 and in the kanamycin producing *S. kanamyceticus*. These enzymes were compared to other aminoglycoside 6'-N-acetyltransferases from various sources. They had somewhat similar substrate range but differed in their ability to modify tobramycin, neomycin B, butirosin and amikacin. The *Ps. aeruginosa* 3796 acetyltransferase was thought to be very similar to aminoglycoside 6'-N-acetyltransferase III [AAC(6')-III] (61).

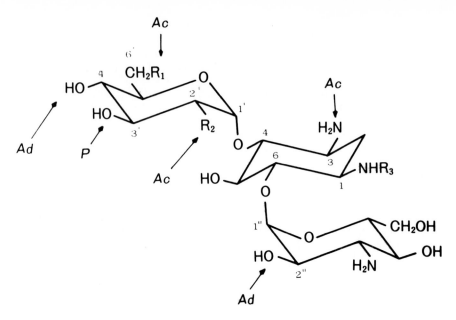

FIGURE 4. Structures of kanamycins. DKB is 3',4'-dideoxy-kanamycin B and tobramycin is 3'-deoxykanamycin B. Symbols are as follows and so forth; Ac: Acetylation; P: Phosphorylation; Ad: Adenylylation; AHBA: 4-Amino-2-hydroxybutyrate.

	R_1	R_2	R_3
Kanamycin A	NH_2	*OH*	*H*
Kanamycin B	NH_2	NH_2	*H*
Kanamycin C	*OH*	NH_2	*H*
Amikacin	NH_2	*OH*	*AHBA*

The acetylation of gentamicin C components was demonstrated with the enzyme preparation from *Ps. aeruginosa* 99 (62). Genta-mycin and sisomicin were acetylated by a similar enzyme from *Ps. aeruginosa* 130 (gentamicin acetyltransferase, aminoglycoside 3-acetyltransferase, [AAC(3)-I]) and the inactivated compound was identified as 3-N-acetylgentamicin C_{1a} (63). A similar amino-glycoside 3-acetyltransferase I was also identified in *E. coli* carrying R factor (*E. coli* K12 C600 R135) (64). Recently 3-N-acetylribostamycin was found to be produced enzymatically from ribostamycin by *S. ribosidificus* (65).

Another 3-N enzymatic acetylation of gentamicin, tobramycin and kanamycin by *E. coli* 176 was reported. From the difference in the isoelectric points, this enzyme appears to be an isoenzyme of [AAC(3)-I] and the name, aminoglycoside 3-N-acetyltransferase

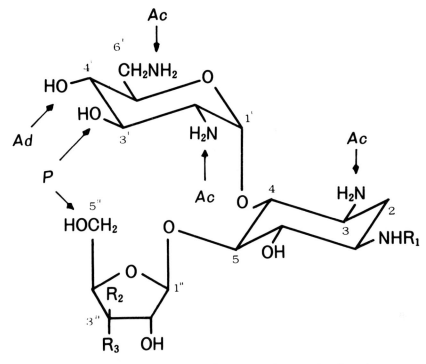

FIGURE 5.   *Structures of ribostamycin and butirosins.*

	R_1	R_2	R_3
Ribostamycin	H	H	OH
Butirosin A	AHBA	OH	H
Butirosin B	AHBA	H	OH

II [AAC(3)-II] was proposed (66). A new aminoglycoside 3-N-
acetyltransferase (gentamicin acetyltransferase III, [AAC(3)-III])
was also identified in *Ps. aeruginosa* PST, which possesses a wider
substrate range than any such enzyme so far discovered in resistant bacteria (67). In general, neomycin B and paromomycin are
not acetylated by [AAC(3)-I] and [AAC(3)-II] while they and gentamicin C_1 as well as kanamycins A and B were acetylated by
[AAC(3)-III]. The only agents which do not serve as substrates
for this enzyme were butirosin and amikacin, the 1-N-hydroxy-
aminobutyric acid derivatives.

     Other new gentamicin acetyltransferases which are character-
ized by the 2'-N-acetylation of aminoglycoside antibiotics were
found in the extracts of *S. spectabilis* (spectinomycin producer)
(68) and *Providencia sp.* 164 (69). The 2'-amino group of a number of aminoglycoside antibiotics (gentamicin, tobramycin, buti-

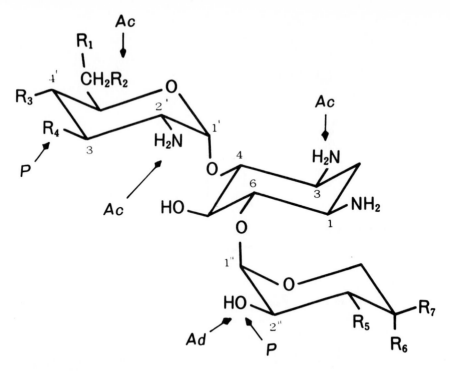

FIGURE 6.   Structures of gentamicins.   Sisomicin is 4,5-
dehydrogentamicin C_{1a}.

	R_1	R_2	R_3	R_4	R_5	R_6	R_7
Gentamicin A	H	OH	OH	OH	$NHCH_3$	H	OH
Gentamicin A_2	H	OH	OH	OH	OH	OH	H
Gentamicin X_2	H	OH	OH	OH	$NHCH_3$	OH	CH_3
Gentamicin C_{1a}	H	NH_2	H	H	$NHCH_3$	OH	CH_3
Gentamicin C_2	CH_3	NH_2	H	H	$NHCH_3$	OH	CH_3
Gentamicin C_1	CH_3	$NHCH_3$	H	H	$NHCH_3$	OH	CH_3

rosin, sisomicin, kanamycins A and B) was acetylated by gentamicin
acetyltransferase II ([AAC(2')]).   A *Providencia* strain was found
to produce an enzyme quite similar to   AAC(2') .

     Recently, gentamicin acetyltransferase I [AAC(3)-I] of *E.
coli* C600 JR88 was purified to homogeneity.   The purified enzyme
was found to be a tetrameric protein of 63,000 molecular weight
containing no tryptophan and to have a V_{max} value of 3.4 $\pm$ 0.2
µ mol/min/mg at pH 8 and a Km value of 0.3 $\pm$ 0.08 µM for gentamicin C_{1a} (71).   Very little enzymological information is available for these enzymes.

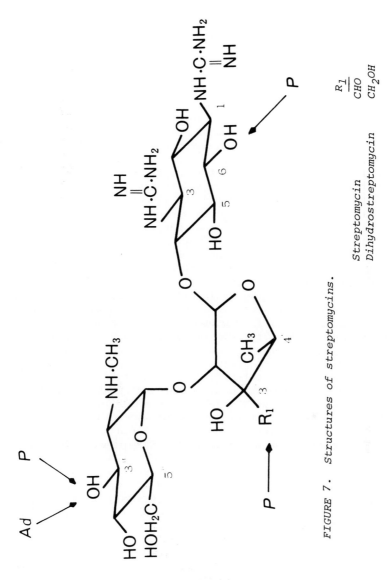

FIGURE 7. Structures of streptomycins.

3. *Others*. The M component of verginiamycin was found to be
modified by whole cells or cell-free enzyme preparations of an *S.
aureus* strin (71). This reaction proceeds by enzymatic acetylation
of the secondary alcoholic function of the molecule, followed by
a rapid chemical degradation of the O-acetylated product (72).
As in the case of chloramphenicol acetyltransferase (73), a
higher level of acetylating activity was found in cells grown in
the presence of the M factor, and both enzymes had several properties in common. However, the new enzyme differed in substrate
specificity.

Microbial transformation of daunorubicin has recently received
attention as a technique for preparing modified daunorubicins for
antitumor testing. Daunorubicin transformation products include
daunorubicinol (74), 7-deoxydaunomycinone and 7-deoxydaunorubici-
nol aglycone, etc. (75-77). In addition, daunorubicin was transformed into N-acetyldaunorubicin by *B. cereus* var. *mycoides*.
Daunorubicinol was also converted to N-acetyldaunorubicinol (78).

Leucomycin A_1 was converted to leucomycin A_3 (the 3-0-acetyl
derivative of leucomycin A_1) by washed mycelia of *S. kitasatoen-
sis* 66-14-3 (79). The effect of butyrate was not observed in the
resting cell system. The production of leucomycins A_1 and A_3 was
affected by butyrate and glucose in growing but not in washed
cells. Glucose was an inducer of this enzyme system and butyrate
tended to inhibit it (79,80).

4"-Depropionyl maridomycin III was reacylated in the presence
of acetyl CoA to maridomycin V (4"-acetyl maridomycin III) by the
cell-free extract of *S. hygroscopicus*, No. B-5050, the maridomycin producer (81). The same reacylation was also demonstrated by
other strain, *Streptomyces sp.* K-342 than the maridomycin-produc-
ing strain (82).

Lankacidin C was esterified to lankacidin C-8-butyrate in the
presence of methylbutyrate by culture broth and by cell-free extract of *B. megaterium* IFO 12108. In a similar way, 8-isobutyryl,
8-valeryl, and 8-isovaleryl esters of lankacidin C were produced.
Lankacidin C-8,14-dibutyrate was hydrolyzed to lankacidin C-14-
butyrate by the same organism (83). Some lankacidin C monoesters
(8- or 14-ester) were found to be superior to lankacidin C in
antimicrobial activity, protecting effects and toxicity; lankacidin C-14-butyrate showed preferable properties in protecting
and antitumor effects by oral administration in mice (84).

The existence of deacetylcephalosporin C acetyltransferase
was demonstrated in the cell-free extracts of the cephalosporin
C-producing *C. acremonium* (85). The pH 7.0-7.5 was optimal for
its activity and the enzyme required Mg^{++} as a cofactor (85). A
similar enzyme was purified 104-fold and deacetylcephalosporin C
and acetyl CoA were reaction substrates (87).

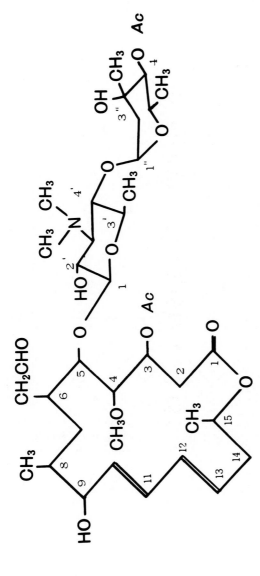

FIGURE 8. Structures of leucomycins. Ac: acyl group.

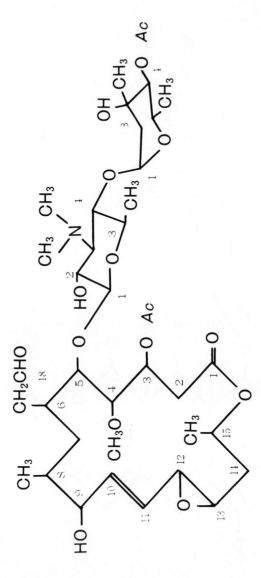

FIGURE 9. Structures of maridomycins. Ac: acyl group.

B. *Deacylation*

1. *Macrolide*. Among T-2636 antibiotics, N-containing lipo-
philic antibiotics of lankacidin group, T-2636A (88) and D (both
containing C-14 acetyl group) were deacylated to give T-2636C and
F (89), respectively, by partially purified enzyme (88) from *S.
rochei var. volubilis* strain No. T-2636. T-2636C (deacetylated
product of A) showed about 20 times higher activity against *S.
lutea* than T-2636A and T-2636F about 10 times higher potency than
T-2636D.

Reports and a review (90) have been published on microbial
and chemical transformation of 16-membered macrolide antibiotics.
The acyl group in the 4"-position of mycarose has been reported
to play an important role in their antimicrobial property (91).
Microbial deacylation of 4"-acyl group was reported in many
macrolide antibiotics such as leucomycin [by *Diaporth sp.* (92),
Mucor sp. (93) and bacteria (94)], maridomycin and 9-propionyl-
maridomycin [by *Streptomyces sp.* (95,96) and bacteria including
B. megaterium IFO 91277 (94)], josamycin [by bacteria (94)],
niddamycin [by *Streptomyces, Cunninghamella* and *Penicillium sp.*
(93)], antibiotic SF-837 [by *Mucor, Streptomyces, Trichosporon
sp.* (97)] and 9-acyl-SF-837 [by *Mucor* and *Aspergillus sp.*, etc.
(98)]. Although the removal of the acyl group has resulted in
the lowering of the antibacterial activity, the deacylated products will be useful substrate for improved antibiotics by the
introduction of new acyl groups.

2. *Others*. Antitumor antibiotics of the olivomycin (NSC-A-
649) and chromomycin (NSC-135052) classes were transformed into
deacylated analogs by *Whetzelinia sclerotiorum* (99).

3-Acetyldeoxynivalenol was deacylated to give deoxynivalenol,
a trichothecene mycotoxin by *Fusarium nivale, F. roseum* and *F.
solani*; 7,15-diacetyl-deoxynivalenol obtained by acetylation of
deoxynivalenol by *F. solani*, was deacylated to give 7-acetyldeoxy-
nivalenol (100). The ester at C-7 was not hydrolyzed. Regio-
selectivity in the microbial modification of trichothecene has
been demonstrated (101).

The final steps in the biosynthesis of cephalosporin C proceed *via* deacetoxycephalosporin C and deacetylcephalosporin C.
Cephalosporin C-negative mutants were found to accumulate deacetylcephalosporin C exclusively (24). The accumulation by mutant
No. 81 (102) was carried out by extracellular cephalosporin C
acetylhydrolase which had not yet been demonstrated in *C. acremonium*. Independently, the same enzyme was demonstrated in *C. acremonium*, C-462 (103) grown under conditions where the enzyme synthesis is regulated by the nature of the carbon source (104).

C.   Phosphorylation

1.   *Aminoglycoside*. Kanamycin (see Figure 3) is known to be
phosphorylated at the 3'-hydroxyl group by kanamycin phosphotransferase I (neomycin phosphotransferase I, aminoglycoside 3'-phos-
photransferase I, [APH(3')-I]) in the presence of ATP and Mg^{++}
(105). This enzyme was purified 1170 fold by gel filtration and
DEAE-Sephadex A-25 column chromatography, is very sensitive to
ultraviolet light and has been stabilized in the presence of
-S-S- reductants (106). Lividomycin was phosphorylated also at
the 5"-hydroxyl group by enzymes from *Ps. aeruginosa* TI-13 (107,
108), *E. coli* Kl2 ML1410 R81 (109) and *S. aureus* (110). In subsequent studies, it was shown that [APH(3')-I] from *E. coli* Kl2
J5 Rll-2, phosphorylated the 3'-hydroxyl group of kanamycin and
the 5"-hydroxyl group of lividomycin A and that the enzyme caused
cross resistance between them (110).

The 3'-hydroxyl group of kanamycin, neomycin and butirosin
(see Figures 3 and 5) was phosphorylated by new enzymes, kanamycin phosphotransferase II (neomycin phosphotransferase II, aminoglycoside 3'-phosphotransferase II, [APH(3')-II]) from *E. coli*
JR66/W677 (112) and *Ps. aeruginosa* Ps 49 (113). Similar enzymes
were identified in *Providencia stuartii* (114) and *Bacillus circulans* (115). The 3'-hydroxyl group of kanamycin, neomycin, paromomycin and ribostamycin, and the 5"-hydroxyl group of lividomycin (see Figure 3) and 3',4'-dideoxyribostamycin (but not butirosin) were phosphorylated by [APH(3')-I], while the former four
antibiotics and butirosin (except lividomycin and 3',4'-dideoxy-
ribostamycin) were phosphorylated by [APH(3')-II] (112,113,115).

3'-Phosphotransferases I in *Ps. aeruginosa* and R factor-
carrying *E. coli* were different from each other in chromatographic behavior, molecular weight, pH optimum and K_i value, while
[APH(3')-II] showed the same characteristics (115). On the other
hand, the *B. circulans* enzyme and [APH(3')-II] showed the same
substrate requirements but differed from the latter in immunological behavior (116).

Aminoglycoside 3'-phosphotransferase II from *E. coli* JR66/
W677 was purified by buffer extraction, dialysis, kanamycin-
Sepharose 4B affinity chromatography, Diaflo ultrafiltration and
column chromatography. The enzyme was purified 56.5 fold with a
7.6% yield and was homogenous by electrophoresis and Sephadex
G-100 gel filtration. The amino acid composition was determined
and a molecular weight of 25,000 was estimated by sodium dodecyl-
sulfate-urea-polyacrylamide gel electrophoresis (117).

In addition to the inactivation of antibiotics such as kanamycin, neomycin, paromomycin and ribostamycin by [APH(3')-I] and
[APH(3')-II], both the 3'-hydroxyl group of butirosin and the
5"-hydroxyl group of lividomycin A were phosphorylated by a new
enzyme isolated from *Ps. aeruginosa* 21-75. This enzyme was purified by affinity chromatography using dibekacin-Sepharose 4B or

lividomycin A-Sepharose 4B followed by DEAE-Sephadex A-50 chromatography. It was characterized by kinetic studies and named
aminoglycoside 3'-phosphotransferase III ([APH(3')-III]) (118).

In addition to the usual substrate antibiotics for [APH(3')],
the 3'-phosphorylation of amikacin was demonstrated in clinical
isolates of *S. aureus*. This new [APH(3')] was different from
3'-phosphotransferase and other phosphotransferases in the substrate range and immunological behavior (119).

The selective phosphorylation of 5"-hydroxyl group of ribostamycin and 2"-O-phosphorylation of gentamicins (sisomicin) were
carried out by a new enzyme from *Ps. aeruginosa* GN573 (120) and
S. aureus R. Palm. The latter enzyme (aminoglycoside 2"-phos-
photransferase, [APH(2")]) was found to have a high specificity
toward gentamicins and showed 5.8 and 28,000 for the isoelectric
point and the molecular weight, respectively (121). The inactivation of antibiotics was detailed (122,123).

Immobilization of aminoglycoside phosphotransferases from
resistant bacteria were reported. Continuous phosphorylation of
kanamycin B and dihydrostreptomycin was carried out efficiently
on a column of immobilized phosphotransferases. Immobilized
streptomycin phosphotransferase was found to be more resistant
to heating than the soluble preparation and remained active upon
repeated use (124). Novel and efficient methods for the preparation of 3'-deoxyaminoglycoside were indicated. 3'-Deoxykanamycin
B, 3'-deoxyxylostasin and 3'-deoxyribostamycin were prepared by a
combination of enzymatic phosphorylation and subsequent chemical
reactions (125).

    2. *Streptomycin.* Streptomycin 6-phosphotransferase of *S.
griseus* was studied by Nomi *et al.* (126,127) and Walker *et al.*
(128-132). The enzyme was purified 200 fold by DEAE-Sephadex
A-25 and Sephadex G-100 column chromatography, and required ATP
and 10^{-2}M Mg^{++}. The enzyme was most stable at pH 8.0 and lost
the activity after 15 min at 40°C (131). The corresponding positions of dihydrostreptomycin, streptidine and 2-deoxystreptidine
were also phosphorylated by the enzyme (132).

Streptomycin 3"-phosphate and dihydrostreptomycin 3"-phosphate
were formed by other streptomycin-phosphorylating enzymes (streptomycin 3"-phosphotransferases) isolated from E. coli JR35 (133),
S. griseus, S. bikiniensis (132,134) and *Ps. aeruginosa* TI-13
(135-137). Dihydrostreptomycin 3'α-6-diphosphate was also formed
from ATP and dihydrostreptomycin 6-phosphate with fresh nondialyzed sonicates of mature mycelia of *S. bikiniensis* ATCC 11062
(132,134). New isolates of streptomycin-resistant *E. coli* were
found to inactivate streptomycin in large amounts. The inactivation product was isolated and treatment with alkaline phosphatase
resulted in the liberation of inorganic phosphate and a strepto-
mycin-like compound without any antibiotic activity. From the

difference of sensitivity to butyl-streptomycylamine, the enzyme
system of these strains was presumed to be different from strep-
tomycin-phosphotransferase and streptomycin-adenyltransferase
(138).

   3. *Clindamycin*. Clindamycin was converted into inactive
clindamycin 3-phosphate by *S. coelicolor* (139). An *in vivo* study
in rats revealed lower blood levels of the 3-phosphate ester when
compared with its injectable from (the 2-phosphate ester), but
both esters were metabolized in a manner similar to that of
clindamycin (140).

D. *Nucleotidylation*

   Besides the adenylylation of streptomycin (141) and spectinomycin (142) by *E. coli* and the nucleotidylation of clindamycin by
S. coelicolor (143,144), adenylylation of aminoglycoside antibiotics was further investigated. Gentamicin C components and
kanamycin were adenylylated by the enzyme preparation from *E.
coli* K12 JR66/W677 (gentamicin-kanamycin nucleotidyltransferase,
[AAD(2")]) (145). Similar adenylylation was demonstrated in *K.
pneumoniae* 3020, 3694, *E. coli* ML1410 R^+100 and *E. coli* K12-
carrying R factor from *K. pneumoniae* (146,147).
   One of the inactivated compounds of dideoxykanamycin (DKB)
was determined to be 3',4'-DKB 2"-adenylate (148). As DKB and
gentamicin are inactivated by the enzyme of *E. coli* K12 JR66/W677,
the inactivated gentamicins C_1, C_{1a} and C_2 were postulated to be
their respective 2"-adenylates (149). 3',4'-Dideoxykanamycin B
was by the same enzyme solution transformed to DKB 2"-guanylate
or DKB 2"-inosinate in the presence of GTP or ITP, respectively
(150).
   The sonic extract of *Ps. aeruginosa* POW also inactivated
gentamicin, tobramycin, sisomicin, and kanamycins A and B in the
presence of ATP. This extract was similar to the R factor-
mediated gentamicin adenylyltransferase ([AAD(2")]) from *Entero-
bacteriaceae* (151) which was isolated from R^+ *E. coli* W677/HJR66
and partially purified. Gentamicin, kanamycin, tobramycin and
their isomers served as substrates while gentamicin C_2 had the
lowest Km and the highest V_{max} values (152).
   In addition, a clinical isolate of *S. aureus* was found to
inactivate a variety of aminoglycoside antibiotics with the exception of the gentamicin components. The enzyme preparation
from this strain modified the 4'-hydroxyl function of these antibiotics by adenylylation (tobramycin adenylyltransferase,
[ANT(4')-I], [AAD(4')]) (153).
   New isolates of *S. aureus* inactivated streptomycin and spectinomycin by adenylylation, although the adenylylated positions
of either drug have not yet been established. The adenylylated

streptomycin was shown to be different from 3"-adenylyl-strepto-
mycin, indicating the possibility of existence of an enzyme that
differs from streptomycin 3"-adenylyltransferase of *E. coli* (154).

E. Hydrolysis

1. *β-Lactam*. The amide bond in β-lactam ring of penicillin
or cephalosporin is hydrolyzed by β-lactamases. This hydrolysis
is very important in medicine, because the existence of β-lactamase is a major mechanism of bacterial resistance to β-lactam
antibiotics (155).

β-Lactamases are produced by a wide variety of microorganisms.
Depending on the difference of the origin, some of them hydrolyze
cephalosporins much more rapidly than penicillins while the reverse is true for other enzymes. Most of the semisynthetic penicillins and cephalosporins have been found to be susceptible to
at least one β-lactamase (156). The properties (substrate profile, molecular weight, amino acid sequence and electrical charge)
of different β-lactamases were recently described (157).

β-Lactamases from Gram-negative bacteria were divided into
five main classes containing 15 different types of the enzyme
(158). In addition to the known β-lactamases, novel R factor-
mediated β-lactamases in *Bordetella bronchiseptica* (159), *Klebsiella aerogenes* (160) and *Ps. aeruginosa* HL (161) and a new
species-specific β-lactamase of *Enterobacter aerogenes* (162) were
demonstrated.

2. *Peptide*. Enzymatic conversion of penicillin to 6-amino-
penicillanic acid (6-APA) is prominent in the preparation of
chemotherapeutical important semisynthetic penicillins (163).
Numerous studies on penicillin acylase, an enzyme which catalyzes this conversion, have been made.

Its occurrence is widespread in bacteria, fungi, actinomy-
cetes and yeasts, and two types (bacterial and fungal) were found
which differed in the hydrolyzing activity of benzylpenicillin
and phenoxymethylpenicillin (165,166). In addition to this conversion, the enzyme also facilitates the reaction in the opposite
direction and this brings about the synthesis of penicillin from
6-APA and a suitable side-chain (167). The synthetic reaction
proceeds more readily at slightly acid pH values, whereas the
hydrolysis is usually faster at slightly alkaline pH values
(166-168).

Penicillins such as benzyl-, *n*-heptyl-, *DL*-α-hydroxybenzyl-,
p-hydroxybenzyl-, 3,4-dihydroxybenzyl-, α-aminobenzyl-, phenoxy-
methyl-, and α-carboxybenzylpenicillins, etc. were synthesized by
the reverse reaction (167-172). Similar enzymes were recently
demonstrated also in *Ps. melanogenum* (173) and *Brevibacterium
cerinum* (174). Various properties of bacterial and fungal penicillin acylases were described (166).

On the other hand, extensive searches failed to locate the corresponding enzyme capable of producing 7-aminocephalosporanic acid (7-ACA) from cephalosporin C. However, other N-acylcephalosporins such as 7-phenoxyacylcephalosporin and cephalothin were successfully cleaved enzymatically to 7-ACA. At present, 7-ACA, the starting material for the preparation of semisynthetic cephalosporins, is obtained by an efficient chemical hydrolysis of cephalosporin C (171,175-177).

Enzymatic synthesis of cephalosporins such as cephalexin and its analogs was carried out first (corresponding organic acid esters and 7-aminocephem compounds) by an acylase from *Pseudomonadaceae*. The enzyme was named α-amino acid ester hydrolase (178,179). It was purified from *Xanthomonas citri*, was most active at pH 5.5-6.5 and 35-40°C, and showed 3.5mM of Km value for cephalexin deacylation (180). Similarly, cephalexin and other cephalosporins were synthesized with the entrapped *E. coli* penicillin acylase (181) and with the *Kluyvera citrophila* acylase (182,183). The purified *Kluyvera* acylase showed 63,000 and 8.12 for the molecular weight and isoelectric point, respectively, and gave 1.4mM of Km value for cephalexin hydrolysis (184).

A new isolate, a Gram-negative, nonmotile bacterium (NRRL B-3652), was found to hydrolyze the amide bond of novobiocin. The two reaction products were isolated and identified as 3-[3-methylbuten-2-yl]-4-hydroxybenzoic acid and novenamine (3-amino-4-hydroxy-7-noviosyl-8-methylcoumarin) (185). An enzymatic hydrolysis of bleomycin B_2 to bleomycinic acid and agmatine by a *Fusarium* acylagmatine amidohydrolase was also demonstrated (186). These degradation products (novenamine and bleomycinic acid) are expected to be convenient substrates for the preparation of novel semisynthetic antibiotics.

3.   *Lactone*.   Mikamycin B was found to be inactivated by washed cells or cell-free preparations of *S. mitakaensis*. An enzyme hydrolyzing its lactone linkage was named mikamycin B lactonase and the reaction product was identified as mikamycin B acid (187). The enzyme was purified 1400 fold by ammonium sulfate fractionation, column chromatography and obtained as a single protein preparation. The molecular weight, optimum pH and temperature were 29,000, pH 7.0 and 27°C, respectively. The Km value for mikamycin B was found to be 1.43×10^{-5}M (188).

4.   *Glycoside*.   As indicated by the degradation of validamycin A by *Ps. denitrificans* (189), validamycins are susceptible to microbial attack. In subsequent studies, validamycin A (VA-A $\overset{\beta}{\leftarrow}$ Glu) and D(VA-A $\overset{\alpha}{\leftarrow}$ Glu) were shown to be hydrolyzed to D-glucose and validoxylamine A(VA-A) by *Erwinia aroideae* IFO 3830, *Corynebacterium aquaticum* IFO 12154, *Oospora destructor* IFO 8556, *Candida intermedia* and others. The conversion of validamycin C (Glu $\overset{\beta}{\leftrightarrow}$ VA-A $\overset{\beta}{\leftarrow}$ Glu), E(VA-A $\overset{\beta}{\leftarrow}$ Glu $\overset{\alpha}{\leftrightarrow}$ Glu) and F (Glu $\overset{\alpha}{\leftrightarrow}$ VA-A $\overset{}{\leftarrow}$ Glu) into validamycin A by selective hydrolysis of an

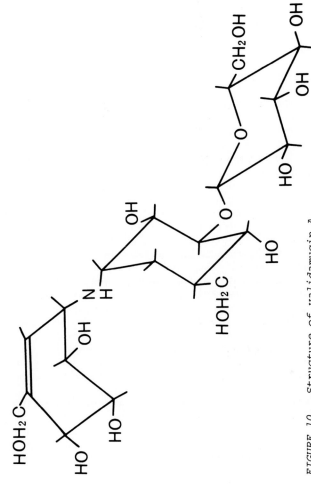

FIGURE 10. Structure of validamycin A.

α-glucosidic linkage was also demonstrated by *Endomycopsis fibuliger* IFO 0109, *Endomyces decipiens* IFO 0102 and *Candida intermedia* (190). The significance of this selective hydrolysis is important because validamycins C, E and F are considerably less active than validamycin A.

　　5. *Others*. Enzymatic conversion of toyocamycin to sangivamycin by *Streptomyces rimosus* was also demonstrated. The enzyme, toyocamycin nitrile hydrolase was isolated and partially purified from the soluble fraction of the organism (191).

F. Oxidation and Reduction

　　Dihydroabikoviromycin was dehydrogenated to abikoviromycin by *S. olivaceus* SF 973. The purified enzyme catalyzing this reaction was most active at around pH 7 and 40 - 45°C. Its molecular weight was about 36,000 (192). 11-Demethyltomamycin was also enzymatically converted to oxotomaymycin by an intracellular constitutive enzyme of *S. achromogenes* (193).

　　After the conversion of tylosin to relomycin has been reported (194), the reduction of aldehydic group was demonstrated also in other 16-membered macrolides. Maridomycin (MDM) III, 9-propionyl MDM III and josamycin were transformed to 18-dihydro MDM III, 18-dihydro-9-propionyl MDM III and 18-dihydrojosamycin, respectively, by the action of *Nocardia mexicana* IFO-3927 (195). 4"-Depropionyl MDM III (196) formed by deacylation from parent MDM III was also transformed to 18-dihydro-4"-depropionyl MDM III by the action of *S. lavendulae* strain No. K-122. In these cases, reduction of the aldehyde group resulted in a marked decrease of the *in vitro* antimicrobial activity.

　　As previously demonstrated for mammalian metabolism (197,198), daunomycin, an anthracycline antibiotic possessing antitumor activity, was transformed to 7-deoxydaunomycinone (76) by the crude enzyme preparation of *S. steffisburgensis*, probably *via* an NADH-dependent reductive glycosidic cleavage.

　　Furthermore, 7-deoxydaunomycinone was transformed to 7-deoxydaunomycinol aglycone (C-13 dehydro derivative) by an NADPH-linked keto reductase (76). Direct reductive cleavage was then applied to the anthracycline antibiotics such as steffimycin B, nogalamycin, cinerubin A and daunomycin and was carried out by whole cells and cell-free extract of *Aeromonas hydrophila*, *Citrobacter freundii* and *E. coli* (77). Some degree of anaerobicity was required for the cleavage by all three organisms.

　　Ketonec carbonyl reduction of steffimycinone to steffimycinol ($\geq$C=O → $\geq$C-OH) was also carried out by *S. nogalater* UC^R-2783 and *S. peuceticus var. caesius* IMRU-3920/UC^R-5633 (199). These organisms and a cell-free extract of the former catalyze the reduction of C-10 carbonyl with NADPH as a cofactor.

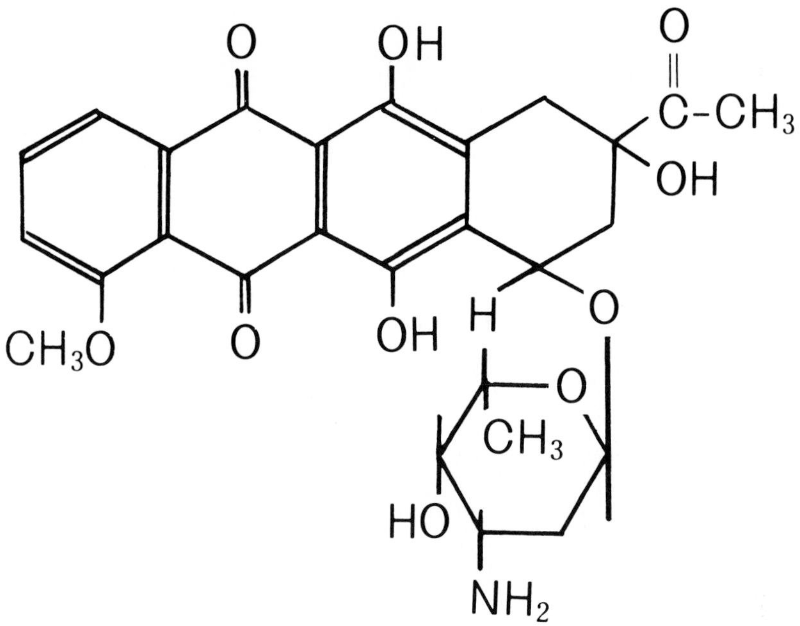

FIGURE 11. Structure of daunomycin.

Related to this reaction, daunomycinone was transformed to dihydrodaunomycinone by the mutant strain, S. aureofaciens B-96 which normally produces the glycoside aureovocin (200).   The reduction of daunorubicin to daunorubicinol was first reported using S. lavendulae ATCC 8644, S. roseochromogenus ATCC 13400, Corynebacterium simplex ATCC 6946, and Bacterium cyclooxydans ATCC 12673 (201).   Daunorubicinol can also be prepared by direct fermentation.

Other workers (74) reported that reduction of the side chain carbonyl of daunorubicin and N-acetyldaunorubicin by Corynebacterium equi FCRC 151 under aerobic conditions, resulted in daunorubicinol and N-acetyldaunorubicinol, respectively.

G. Methylation (Carboxymethylation, Hydroxymethylation and
    Transmethylation)

In addition to N-acetylation, N- and O-phosphorylation and O-adenylylation, N-carboxymethylation of aminoglycoside antibiotics was also observed (202,203). A new inactive product of ribostamycin (SF-733), 3-N-carboxymethyl ribostamycin, was obtained from the beer of S. ribosidificus 25-83 which has been grown in a medium containing D-xylose. In this case, the pentose

metabolism of the strain is thought to play a role in the biosynthesis of carboxymethyl group, as previously indicated by O-
carboxymethylation of rifamycin B from rifamycin SV (204).

Hydroxymethylation of antibiotics was also observed (205).
N-Demethylclindamycin (>N-H), the biotransformation product of
clindamycin, was converted to N-demethyl-N-hydroxymethylclinda-
mycin (>N-CH$_2$OH) by *S. lincolnensis*.

As an example of transmethylation, erythromycin C (containing
L-mycarose moiety) was transformed into erythromycin A (containing
L-cladinose moiety) by a partially purified particulate enzyme of
S. erythreus (erythromycin C:S-adenosyl-*L*-methionine transmethyl-
ase) (206). Erythromycin D (207), which is a key intermediate in
the erythromycin biosynthesis, was also transmethylated by the
same enzyme preparation to form erythromycin B.

H. Amination and Deamination

The interconversion between formycin and formycin B has been
shown (208,209) and the formycin B-aminating enzyme of *Streptomyces sp.* MA406-A-1 was purified 7.7-fold. It catalyzes the
following reaction:

formycin B + aspartate → formycin + fumarate

From this and other findings, it was suggested that under certain
conditions formycin B would be converted to formycin by a novel
enzyme(s) rather than by the action of the enzyme system including adenylosuccinate synthetase and adenylosuccinate lyase (210).

Ketomycin (3-cyclohexeneglyoxylic acid) was converted to 3-
cyclohexeneglycine by *B. subtilis* (211). A relationship between
the mechanism of resistance to ketomycin and the reduced capacity
of this conversion by a ketomycin-resistant mutant of *E. coli* K12
was discussed (212).

An enzyme catalyzing the deamination of the cytosine moiety
of blasticidin S was extracted from a strain of *Aspergillus
terreus*. The purified blasticidin S deaminase showed a high
specificity toward blasticidin S derivatives and was found to
have 30,000 molecular weight and 4.35 isoelectric point (213).

I. Hydroxylation

In addition to the conversion of (+) 5'-hydroxygriseofulvin
(equatorial) by *S. cinereocrocatus* NRRL 3443 (214), griseofulvin
was transformed to (+) 5'-hydroxygriseofulvin (axial) and 6'-
hydroxymethylgriseofulvin by the action of *Cephalosporium curtipes*
(215).

Narbomycin (216), 14-membered macrolide antibiotic, was hydroxylated at the C-12 position to form picromycin (C-12 hydroxylnarbomycin) by washed cells of *S. zaomyceticus* MCRL-0405, a picromycin producer.

Maridomycin I (MDM I) and josamycin (JM) were hydroxylated at β-position of 4"-isovaleryl group to 3'''-hydroxymaridomycin I (HMDM I) and 3'''-hydroxyjosamycin (HJM), respectively, by *S. olivaceus* 219 (217). Antimicrobial activities of these hydroxylated products (HMDM I and HJM) were 20-50% lower than their respective substrates. Protective effect of HJM against *S. aureus* by oral administration, however, was similar to that of JM. HJM and HMDM I were resistant to rat liver homogenate and bacterial esterase, which hydrolyzed JM and MDM I to 4"-deisovaleryljosamycin and 4"-deisovalerylmaridomycin I, respectively.

J. *Transglycosylation and Glycosidation*

In search for aminoglycoside derivatives with resistance to the enzyme inactivation and with improved oral absorption properties, neamine (neomycin A, a degradation product of neomycins B and C) was subjected to Pan's transglycosidation reaction (219) in the presence of maltose (glycosyl donor) and Clarase^R. The resulting 5-glucosylneamine is more active than neamine against the organisms tested, although it did not inhibit *E. coli* resistant to neomycin B which inactivates neomycin B and kanamycin by acylation (218). In contrast, glycosylated kanamycin A obtained by the same procedure resulted in decreased antibiotic potency *in vitro* and *in vivo* (220).

Synthesis of new validamycin derivatives (190) was attempted by microbial transglycosidation from validoxylamine A, a common moiety of validomycins, which are antibiotics used in agriculture. Besides the conversion of validoxylamine A to validamycin D (maltose as an α-glucosyl donor) or A (cellobiose as a β-glucosyl donor) (190) by various strains of bacteria or *Rhodotorula sp.*, β-D-galactosyl-validoxylamine A was obtained from validoxylamine A in the presence of lactose (as a β-galactosyl donor) by the action of *Rhodotorula glutinis* IFO 1382. This compound had a decreased potency but showed promise in the semisynthesis of new validamycins.

Maezawa *et al.* (216) succeeded in the bioconversion of biologically inactive narbonolide and picronolide into active narbomycin and picromycin, respectively, by glycosidation of the aglycone by means of washed cells of *S. narbonensis* ISP 5016. Rosamicin consists of an aglycone identical to that of cirramycin A$_1$ and desosamine which is usually found in 12- or 14-membered macrolide antibiotics (221). It was postulated that a new antibiotic might be obtained by combining a sugar normally present in 16-membered macrolide antibiotics with the aglycone of 14-membered macrolides. Accordingly, glycosidation of narbonolide (222) with mycaminose was attempted by feeding narbonolide to the fermentation of platenomycin-producing *S. platensis* subsp. *malvinus* MCRL-0388 and its blocked mutant. As a result, two new compounds, 5-0-mycaminosyl narbonolide and 9-dihydro-5-0-mycaminosyl narbonolide, were formed.

A new antibiotic, 3-0-oleandosyl-5-0-desosaminylerythronolide A oxime (223), was produced from erythronolide A oxime by the oleandomycin-producing culture, *S. antibioticus* ATCC 11891. This compound was found to be less active, but more stable to acid, than erythromycin A oxime and erythromycin A.

K.   *Other Transformations*

Erythromycin A was degraded to erythronolide, erythralosamine and two unknown products by the growing, broken or lyophilized cells of *Pseudomonas sp.* 56. The enzyme system was found to be constitutive, localized in the cell membrane fraction and specific to erythromycin A (224).

Transformation of the quinone ring of rifamycin S into γ-pyrone ring of rifamycin G was demonstrated by washed cells of *Nocardia mediterranea*. This inactive compound was also produced together with the rifamycin complex in normal *N. mediterranea* fermentation (225).

In addition to the polymyxin-hydrolyzing enzyme produced by a pseudomonad, an extracellular neutral protease was obtained from *B. polymyxa*. The enzyme was purified 50-fold and decomposed polymyxin E but was ineffective to polymyxin D (226).

Antimycin A was transformed into a more polar product by vegetative growth or spores of *Aspergillus ochraceus* (AYF-219). The structure of transformation product was not identified but a mixture of two acids formed by the cleavage of the dilactone in the molecule was indicated (227).

Enzymatic conversion of sterigmatocystine into aflatoxin B_1 by cell-free extracts of *Aspergillus parasiticus* was also demonstrated. The conversion was proposed to occur by an oxidative cleavage of the ring (228).

Isomerization of the nucleoside antibiotic showdomycin to isoshowdomycin was carried out by growing and resting cells of *Streptomyces sp.* No. 383 (229). Isomerization of novobiocin to its inactive form was also reported using an extracellular enzyme of *Actinomyces (streptomyces) spheroides*, strain 35 (230).

In addition to microbial epoxidations of steroids, an efficient epoxidation of *cis*-propenylphosphonic acid to (-)-*cis*-1,2-epoxipropylphosphonic acid (fosfomycin) was carried out by *Penicillium spinulosum* (231).

The reversible conversions (O=C⟨ ⇌ HO-CH) between carbomycin A and maridomycin II, and between carbomycin B and leucomycin A_3 at C-9 position were demonstrated by the washed cells of *S. hygroscopicus* B-5050. Moreover, the conversions (-CH=CH- → -CH-CH-)

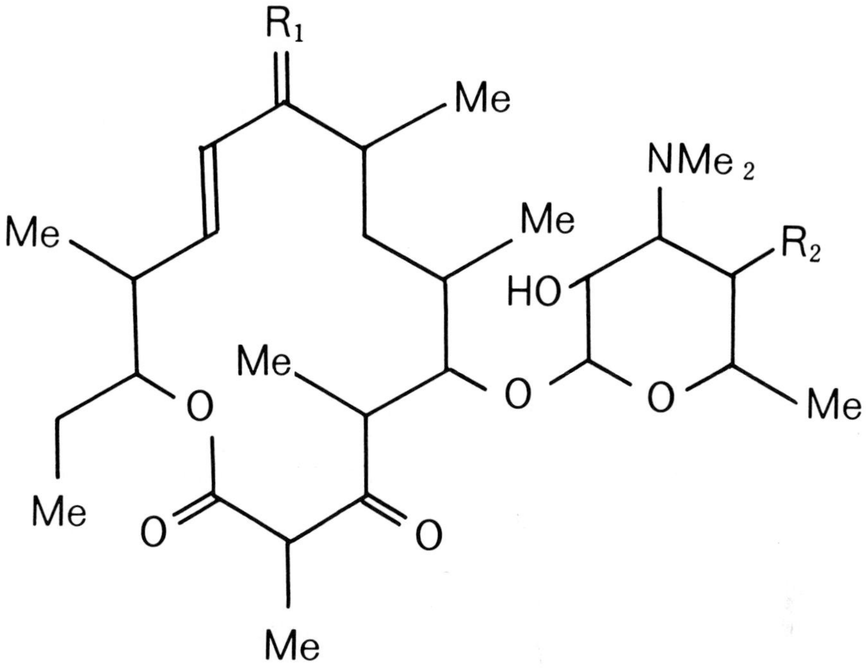

FIGURE 12.   *Structures of narbomycins.*

	R_1	R_2
5-0-Mycaminosyl narbonolide	*O*	*OH*
9-Dihydro-5-0-mycaminosyl narbonolide	*OH,H*	*OH*
Narbomycin	*O*	*H*

of leucomycin A_3 to carbomycin A by the intact cells of the mutant strain were also observed. These results indicated interconversion among leucomycin A_3, carbomycin A, carbomycin B and maridomycin II (232).

In addition to the conversion of 4"-depropionylmaridomycin (MDM) III, 18-dihydro MDM III and 18-dihydro-4"-depropionyl MDM III, as described above (95,96), *Streptomyces sp.* No. K-245 transformed MDM III into four derivatives (A_1, A_2, A_3 and A_4). A_1, the main product, was found to have a C 18 aldehyde group and C 4"-propionyl group but possessed no antibiotic activity. The relationship between the derivatives of the A group and those of MDM III was also discussed (233).

REFERENCES

1. Sebek, O. K. and Perlman, D., *Adv. Appl. Microbiol. 14*, 123
    (1971).
2. Sebek, O. K., *Lloydia 37*, 115 (1975).
3. Kieslich, K., "Microbial Transformations." Georg Thieme
    Publishers, Stuttgart (1976).
4. Goodman, J. J. and Matrishin, M., *J. Bacteriol. 82*, 615
    (1961).
5. Goodman, J. J. and Miller, P. A., *Biotech. Bioeng. 4*, 391
    (1962).
6. Niedleman, S. L., Bienstock, E. and Bennet, R. C., *Biochim.
    Biophys. Acta 71*, 199 (1963).
7. Perlman, D., Heuser, L. J., Semar, J. B., Frazier, W. R. and
    Boska, J. A., *J. Am. Chem. Soc. 83*, 4481 (1961).
8. Neidleman, S. L., Albu, E. and Bienstock, E., *Biotech. Bio-
    eng. 5*, 87 (1963).
9. Argoudelis, A. D., Johnson, L. E. and Pyke, T. R., *J. Anti-
    biot. 26*, 429 (1973).
10. Isono, K., Crain, P. F., Odiorne, T. J., McCloskey, J. A.
    and Suhadolnik, R. J., *J. Am. Chem. Soc. 95*, 5788 (1973).
11. Argoudelis, A. D., Coats, J. H. and Johnson, L. E., *J. Anti-
    biot. 27*, 738 (1974).
12. Fujii, A., Takita, T., Shimada, N. and Umezawa, H., *J. Anti-
    biot. 27*, 73 (1974).
13. Katz, E., Williams, W. K., Mason, K. T. and Mauger, A. B.,
    Antimicrob. Ag. Chemoth. 11, 1056 (1977).
14. Argoudelis, A. D., Coats, J. H., Lemaux, P. G. and Sebek,
    O. K., *J. Antibiot. 25*, 445 (1972).
15. Argoudelis, A. D., Coats, J. H., Lemaux, P. G. and Sebek,
    O. K., *J. Antibiot. 26*, 7 (1973).
16. Furumai, T. and Suzuki, M., *J. Antibiot. 28*, 770 (1975).
17. Furumai, T. and Suzuki, M., *J. Antibiot. 28*, 775 (1975).
18. Furumai, T. and Suzuki, M., *J. Antibiot. 28*, 783 (1975).
19. Furumai, T., Takeda, K. and Suzuki, M., *J. Antibiot. 28*,
    789 (1975).
20. Baud, H., Betencourt, A., Peyre, M. and Penasse, L., *J.
    Antibiot. 30*, 720 (1977).
21. Traxler, P., Treichler, H. J. and Nüesch, J., *J. Antiobiot.
    28*, 605 (1975).
22. Queener, S. W., Capone, J. J., Radue, A. B. and Nagarajan,
    R., *Antimicrob. Ag. Chemoth. 6*, 334 (1974).
23. Fujisawa, Y., Kitano, K. and Kanzaki, T., *Agric. Biol. Chem.
    39*, 2049 (1975).
24. Fujisawa, Y., Shirafuji, H., Kida, M., Nara, K., Yoneda, M.
    and Kanzaki, T., *Agric. Biol. Chem. 39*, 1295 (1975).
25. Kitano, K., Kintaka, K., Suzuki, S., Katamoto, K., Nara, K.
    and Nakao, Y., Abst. Ann. Meet., Soc. Ferment. Technol.,
    Japan, p. 244 (1975).

26. Fujisawa, Y. and Kanzaki, T., *J. Antibiot. 28*, 372 (1975).
27. Kanzaki, T., Fukita, T., Shirafuji, H. and Fujisawa, Y., *J. Antibiot. 27*, 361 (1974).
28. Troonen, H., Roelants, P. and Boon, B., *J. Antibiot. 29*, 1258 (1976).
29. Shier, W. T., Rinehart, Jr., K. L. and Gottlieb, D., *Proc. Nat. Acad. Sci. U.S. 63*, 198 (1969).
30. Shier, W. T., Rinehart, Jr., K. L. and Gottlieb, D., U.S. Patent 3,669,838, June 13 [*C. A. 77*, 150,584 (1972)].
31. Shier, W. T., Schaefer, P. C., Gottlieb, D. and Rinehart, Jr., K. L., *Biochemistry 13*, 5073 (1974).
32. Kojima, M. and Satoh, A., *J. Antibiot. 26*, 784 (1973).
33. Testa, R. T., Wagman, G. H., Daniels, P. J. L. and Weinstein, M. J., *J. Antibiot. 27*, 917 (1974).
34. Claridge, C. A., Bush, J. A., Defuria, M. D. and Price, K. E., *Devel. Indust. Microbiol. 15*, 101 (1974).
35. Taylor, H. D. and Schmitz, H., *J. Antibiot. 29*, 532 (1976).
36. Nogami, I., Arai, Y., Kida, M. and Hiraga, K., Japan Kokai Patent S51-1694, January 8 (1976).
37. Nagaoka, K. and Demain, A. L., *J. Antibiot. 28*, 627 (1975).
38. Rosi, D., Goss, W. A. and Daum, S. J., *J. Antibiot. 30*, 88 (1977).
39. Daum, S. T., Rosi, D. and Goss, W. A., *J. Antibiot. 30*, 98 (1977).
40. Daum, S. T., Rosi, D. and Goss, W. A., *J. Am. Chem. Soc. 99*, 283 (1977).
41. Nara, T., "Annual Reports on Fermentation Processes" (D. Perlman, ed.), Vol. 1, pp. 311-314. Academic Press, New York (1977).
42. Testa, R. T. and Tilley, B. C., *J. Antibiot. 28*, 573 (1975).
43. Testa, R. T. and Tilley, B. C., *J. Antibiot. 29*, 140 (1976).
44. El-Kersh, T. A. and Plourde, J. R., *J. Antibiot. 29*, 292 (1976).
45. Burchard, R. P. and Parish, J. H., *Antimicrob. Ag. Chemoth. 7*, 233 (1975).
46. El-Kersh, T. A. and Plourde, J. R., *J. Antibiot. 29*, 1189 (1976).
47. Sands, L. C. and Shaw, W. V., *Antimicrob. Ag. Chemoth. 3*, 299 (1973).
48. Shaw, W. V., "Methods in Enzymology" XLIII (D. Perlman, ed.), p. 752. Academic Press, New York (1975).
49. Nakano, H., Matsuhashi, Y., Takeuchi, T. and Umezawa, H., *J. Antibiot. 30*, 76 (1977).
50. Umezawa, H., Okanishi, M., Utahara, R., Maeda, K. and Kondo, S., *J. Antibiot. 20*, 136 (1967).
51. Yagisawa, M., Naganawa, H., Kondo, S., Takeuchi, T. and Umezawa, H., *J. Antibiot. 25*, 495 (1972).
52. Yamamoto, H., Yagisawa, M., Naganawa, H., Kondo, S., Takeuchi, T. and Umezawa, H., *J. Antibiot. 25*, 747 (1972).

53. Yagisawa, M., Kondo, S., Takeuchi, T. and Umezawa, H.,
     J. Antibiot. 28, 486 (1975).
54. Benveniste, R. and Davies, J., *Biochemistry 10*, 1787 (1971).
55. Kawabe, H., Naito, T. and Mitsuhashi, S., *Antimicrob. Ag.
     Chemoth. 7*, 50 (1974).
56. O'Hara, K., Kono, M. and Mitsuhashi, S., *J. Antibiot. 27*,
     349 (1974).
57. O'Hara, K., Kono, M. and Mitsuhashi, S., *Antimicrob. Ag.
     Chemoth. 5*, 558 (1974).
58. Minshew, B. H., Holmes, R. K., Sanford, J. P. and Baxter,
     C. R., *Antimicrob. Ag. Chemoth. 6*, 492 (1974).
59. LeGoffic, F. and Martel, A., *Biochimie 56*, 893 (1974).
60. Kawabe, H., Kondo, S., Umezawa, H. and Mitsuhashi, S.,
     Antimicrob. Ag. Chemoth. 7, 494 (1975).
61. Haas, M., Biddlecome, S., Davies, J., Luce, C. E. and
     Daniels, P. J. L., *Antimicrob. Ag. Chemoth. 9*, 945 (1976).
62. Mitsuhashi, S., Kobayashi, F. and Yamaguchi, M., *J. Anti-
     biot. 24*, 400 (1971).
63. Brzezinska, M., Benveniste, R., Davies, J., Daniels, P. J. L.
     and Weinstein, J., *Biochemistry 11*, 761 (1972).
64. Umezawa, H., Yagisawa, M., Matsuhashi, Y., Naganawa, H.,
     Yamamoto, H., Kondo, S. and Chabbert, Y. A., *J. Antibiot.
     26*, 612 (1973).
65. Kojima, M., Ezaki, N., Amano, S., Inouye, S. and Niida, T.,
     J. Antibiot. 28, 42 (1975).
66. LeGoffic, F., Martel, A. and Witchitz, J., *Antimicrob. Ag.
     Chemoth. 6*, 680 (1974).
67. Biddlecome, S., Haas, M., Davies, J., Miller, G. H., Rane,
     D. F. and Daniels, P. J. L., *Antimicrob. Ag. Chemoth. 9*,
     951 (1976).
68. Benveniste, R. and Davies, J., *Proc. Nat. Acad. Sci. U.S. 70*,
     2276 (1973).
69. Chevereau, M., Daniels, P. J. L., Davies, J. and LeGoffic,
     F., *Biochemistry 13*, 598 (1974).
70. Yamaguchi, M., Mitsuhashi, S., Kobayashi, F. and Zenda, H.,
     J. Antibiot. 27, 507 (1974).
71. Williams, J. W. and Northrop, D. B., *Biochemistry 15*, 125
     (1976).
72. DeMeester, C. and Rondelet, J., *J. Antibiot. 29*, 1297 (1976).
73. Suzuki, Y., Okamoto, S. and Kono, M., *J. Bacteriol. 92*, 798
     (1966).
74. Aszalos, A. A., Bachur, N. R., Hamilton, B. K., Langlykke,
     A. F., Roller, P. P., Sheikh, M. Y., Sutphin, M. S., Thomas,
     M. C., Wareheim, D. A. and Wright, L. H., *J. Antibiot. 30*,
     50 (1977).
75. Wiley, P. F. and Marshall, V. P., *J. Antibiot. 28*, 838
     (1975).
76. Marshall, V. P., Reisender, E. A., Reineke, L. M., Johnson,
     L. H. and Wiley, P. F., *Biochemistry 15*, 4139 (1976).

77. Marshall, V. P., Reisender, E. A., and Wiley, P. F., *J. Antibiot. 29*, 966 (1976).
78. Hamilton, B. K., Sutphin, M. S., Thomas, M. C., Wareheim, D. E., and Aszalos, A. A., *J. Antibiot. 30*, 425 (1977).
79. Ōmura, K., Miyazawa, J., Takeshima, H., Kitao, C., Atsumi, K. and Aizawa, M., *J. Antibiot. 29*, 1131 (1976).
80. Ōmura, K., Miyazawa, J., Takeshima, H., Kitao, C. and Aizawa, M., *J. Antibiot. 30*, 193 (1977).
81. Uchida, M., Suzuki, M., Miyagawa, K., Sugita, N., Sawada, H. and Higashide, E., Abst. Ann. Meet. Agric. Chem. Soc., p. 86. Japan (1975).
82. Uyeda, M., Mori, S., Morita, M., Ogata, T., Mori, M. and Shibata, M., *J. Antibiot. 30*, 1130 (1977).
83. Nakahama, K., Harada, S. and Igarasi, S., *J. Antibiot. 28*, 390 (1975).
84. Harada, S., Yamazaki, T., Hatano, K., Tsuchiya, K. and Kishi, T., *J. Antibiot. 26*, 647 (1973).
85. Fujisawa, Y., Shirafuji, H., Kida, M., Nara, K., Yoneda, M. and Kanzaki, T., *Nature, New Biol. 246*, 154 (1973).
86. Fujisawa, Y. and Kanzaki, T., *Agric. Biol. Chem. 39*, 2043 (1975).
87. Liersh, M., Nüesch, J. and Treichler, H. J., Abst. Int. Symp. Gent. Ind. Microorg., 2nd., p. 48 (1974).
88. Higashide, E., Fugono, T., Hatano, K. and Shibata, M., *J. Antibiot. 24*, 1 (1971).
89. Fugono, T., Harada, S., Higashide, E. and Kishi, T., *J. Antibiot. 24*, 23 (1971).
90. Ōmura, S. and Nakagawa, A., *J. Antibiot. 28*, 401 (1975).
91. Ōmura, S., Katagiri, M., Umezawa, I., Komiyama, K., Maekawa, T., Sekikawa, K., Matsumae, A. and Hata, T., *J. Antibiot. 21*, 532 (1968).
92. Abe, J., Watanabe, T., Take, T., Sato, S., Yamaguchi, T., Asano, K., Hata, T. and Ōmura, S., Japan Kōkai Patent S48-4555 (1973).
93. Theriault, R. J., U.S. Patent 3,784,447 (1974), [*C. A. 80*, 81043 (1974)].
94. Nakahama, K., Izawa, M., Muroi, M., Kishi, T., Uchida, M. and Igarasi, S., *J. Antibiot. 27*, 425 (1974).
95. Nakahama, K., Kishi, T. and Igarasi, S., *J. Antibiot. 27*, 487 (1974).
96. Shibata, M., Uyeda, M. and Mori, S., *J. Antibiot. 28*, 434 (1975).
97. Takashi, S., Inoue, S., Ezaki, N., Tsuruoka, T., Amano, T., Watanabe, H. and Niida, T., Japan Kōkai Patent S48-29148 (1973), [*C. A. 80*, 144395 (1974)].
98. Niida, T., Inoue, S., Shomura, T., Omoto, S., Watanabe, H., Nomiya, B. and Koeda, T., Japan Kōkai Patent S48-72389 [*C. A. 80*, 35826 (1974)].
99. Schmitz, H. and Claridge, C. A., *J. Antibiot. 30*, 635 (1977).

100. Yoshizawa, T. and Morooka, N., *Appl. Microbiol. 29*, 54 (1975).

101. Yoshizawa, T. and Morooka, N., *Appl. Microbiol. 30*, 38 (1975).

102. Fujisawa, Y., Shirafuji, H. and Kanzaki, T., *Agric. Biol. Chem. 39*, 1303 (1975).

103. Nüesch, J., Hinnen, A., Liersch, M. and Treichler, H. J., "Genetics of Industrial Microorganisms" (K. D. MacDonald, ed.), p. 451. Academic Press, Inc., London (1976).

104. Hinnen, A. and Nüesch, J., *Antimicrob. Ag. Chemoth. 9*, 824 (1976).

105. Umezawa, H., Okanishi, M., Kondo, S., Hamano, K., Utahara, R., Maeda, K. and Mitsuhashi, S., *Science 157*, 1559 (1967).

106. Sakagami, Y., Takaishi, N. and Hachimori, A., *J. Antibiot. 27*, 248 (1974).

107. Kobayashi, F., Yamaguchi, M. and Mitsuhashi, S., *Antimicrob. Ag. Chemoth. 1*, 17 (1972).

108. Kondo, S., Yamamoto, H., Naganawa, H., Umezawa, H. and Mitsuhashi, S., *J. Antibiot. 25*, 483 (1972).

109. Yamaguchi, M., Koshi, T., Kobayashi, F. and Mitsuhashi, S., *Antimicrob. Ag. Chemoth. 2*, 142 (1972).

110. Kobayashi, F., Koshi, T., Eda, J., Yoshimura, Y. and Mitsuhashi, S., *Antimicrob. Ag. Chemoth. 4*, 1 (1973).

111. Umezawa, H., Yamamoto, H., Yagisawa, M., Kondo, S. and Takeuchi, T., *J. Antibiot. 26*, 407 (1973).

112. Yagisawa, M., Yamamoto, H., Naganawa, H., Kondo, S., Takeuchi, T. and Umezawa, H., *J. Antibiot. 25*, 748 (1972).

113. Brzezinska, M. and Davies, J., *Antimicrob. Ag. Chemoth. 3*, 266 (1973).

114. Marengo, P. B., Chenoweth, M. E., Overturf, G. D. and Wilkins, J., *Antimicrob. Ag. Chemoth. 6*, 821 (1974).

115. Matsuhashi, Y., Yagisawa, M., Kondo, S., Takeuchi, T. and Umezawa, H., *J. Antibiot. 28*, 442 (1975).

116. Matsuhashi, Y., Sawa, T., Kondo, S. and Takeuchi, T., *J. Antibiot. 30*, 435 (1977).

117. Matsuhashi, Y., Sawa, T., Takeuchi, T. and Umezawa, H., *J. Antibiot. 29*, 204 (1976).

118. Umezawa, Y., Yagisawa, M., Sawa, T., Takeuchi, T., Umezawa, H., Matsumoto, H. and Tazaki, T., *J. Antibiot. 28*, 845 (1975).

119. Courvalin, P. and Davies, J., *Antimicrob. Ag. Chemoth. 11*, 619 (1977).

120. Kida, M., Igarashi, S., Okutani, T., Asako, T., Hirago, K. and Mitsuhashi, S., *Antimicrob. Ag. Chemoth. 5*, 92 (1974).

121. LeGoffic, F., Martel, A., Moreau, N., Capmau, M. L., Soussy, C. J. and Duval, J., *Antimicrob. Ag. Chemoth. 12*, 26 (1977).

122. Umezawa, H., *Adv. Carbohyd. Chem. Biochem. 30*, 183 (1974).

123. Haas, M. J. and Dowding, J. E., "Methods in Enzymology" (J. H. Hash, ed.), Vol. XLIII, pp. 611-627. Academic Press, New York (1975).

124. Umezawa, H., Matsuhashi, Y., Yagisawa, M., Yamamoto, H., Kondo, S. and Takeuchi, T., *J. Antibiot. 27*, 358 (1974).

125. Okutani, T., Asako, T., Yoshioka, K., Hiraga, K. and Kida, M., *J. Am. Chem. Soc. 99*, 1278 (1977).

126. Nomi, R., Nimi, O. and Kado, T., *Agric. Biol. Chem. 32*, 1256 (1968).

127. Nomi, R., Nimi, O. and Kado, T., *Agric. Biol. Chem. 33*, 1454 (1969).

128. Miller, A. L. and Walker, J. B., *J. Bacteriol. 99*, 401 (1969).

129. Miller, A. L. and Walker, J. B., *J. Bacteriol. 104*, 8 (1970).

130. Nimi, O., Ito, G., Sueda, S. and Nomi, R., *Agric. Biol. Chem. 35*, 848 (1971).

131. Nimi, O., Ito, G., Ohata, Y., Funayama, S. and Nomi, R., *Agric. Biol. Chem. 35*, 856 (1971).

132. Walker, J. B. and Skorvaga, M., *J. Biol. Chem. 248*, 2435 (1973).

133. Ozanne, B., Benveniste, R., Tipper, D. and Davies, J., *J. Bacteriol. 100*, 1144 (1969).

134. Walker, M. S. and Walker, J. B., *J. Biol. Chem. 245*, 6683 (1970).

135. Kobayashi, F., Yamaguchi, M. and Mitsuhashi, S., *Jap. J. Microbiol. 15*, 381 (1971).

136. Kobayashi, F., Yamaguchi, M., Sato, J. and Mitsuhashi, S., *Jap. J. Microbiol. 16*, 15 (1972).

137. Kawase, H., Kobayashi, F., Yamaguchi, M., Utahara, R. and Mitsuhashi, S., *J. Antibiot. 24*, 651 (1971).

138. Diedrichsen, A., Bang, J. and Heding, H., *J. Antibiot. 30*, 83 (1977).

139. Coats, J. H. and Argoudelis, A. D., *J. Bacteriol. 108*, 459 (1971).

140. Brodasky, T. F. and Lewis, C., *J. Antibiot. 25*, 230 (1972).

141. Umezawa, H., Takasawa, S., Okanishi, H. and Utahara, R., *J. Antibiot. 21*, 81 (1968).

142. Benveniste, R., Yamada, T. and Davies, J., *Infec. Immunity 1*, 109 (1970).

143. Argoudelis, A. D. and Coats, J. H., *J. Am. Chem. Soc. 93*, 534 (1971).

144. Argoudelis, A. D., Coats, J. H. and Mizsak, S. A., *J. Antibiot. 30*, 474 (1977).

145. Benveniste, R. and Davies, J., *FEBS Letters 14*, 293 (1971) [*C.A. 75*, 60114y (1971)].

146. Kobayashi, F., Yamaguchi, M., Eda, J., Higashi, F. and Mitsuhashi, S., *J. Antibiot. 24*, 719 (1971).

147. LeGoffic, F. and Chevereau, M., *CR Hebd Seances Acad. Sci., Ser. C. Sci. Chim. 274*, 535 (1972) [*B.A. 54*, 1083 (1972)].

148. Yagisawa, M., Naganawa, H., Kondo, S., Hamada, M.,
      Takeuchi, T. and Umezawa, H., *J. Antibiot. 24*, 911 (1971).
149. Umezawa, H., *Adv. Carbonyd. Chem. Biochem. 30*, 207 (1974).
150. Yagisawa, M., Naganawa, H., Kondo, S., Takeuchi, T. and
      Umezawa, H., *J. Antibiot. 25*, 492 (1972).
151. Kabins, S., Nathan, C. and Cohen, S., *Antimicrob. Ag.
      Chemoth. 5*, 565 (1974).
152. Smith, A. L. and Smith, D. H., *J. Infec. Diseases 129*,
      391 (1974).
153. LeGoffic, F., Martel, A., Capmau, M. L., Baca, B., Goebel,
      P., Chardon, H., Soussy, C. J., Duval, J. and Bouanchaud,
      D. H., *Antimicrob. Ag. Chemoth. 10*, 258 (1976).
154. Kawabe, H., Inoue, M. and Mitsuhashi, S., *Antimicrob. Ag.
      Chemoth. 5*, 553 (1974).
155. Abraham, E. P., "Biosynthesis and Enzymatic Hydrolysis of
      Penicillins and Cephalosporins," pp. 42-45. University of
      Tokyo Press, Tokyo (1974).
156. Ross, G. W. and O'Callaghan, C. H., "Methods in Enzymology"
      (J. H. Hash, ed.), Vol. XLIII, p. 70. Academic Press, New
      York (1975).
157. Thatcher, D. and Richmond, M. H., "Methods in Enzymology"
      (J. H. Hash, ed.), Vol. XLIII, pp. 640-687. Academic Press,
      New York (1975).
158. Richmond, M. H. and Sykes, R. B., *Adv. Microb. Physiol. 9*,
      31 (1973).
159. Yaginuma, S., Terakado, N. and Mitsuhashi, S., *Antimicrob.
      Ag. Chemoth. 8*, 238 (1975).
160. Petrocheilou, V., Sykes, R. B. and Richmond, M. H.,
      Antimicrob. Ag. Chemoth. 12, 126 (1977).
161. Labia, R., Guione, M., Masson, J., Philippon, A. and
      Barthelemy, M., *Antimicrob. Ag. Chemoth. 11*, 785 (1977).
162. Letarte, R., Devaud-Felix, M., Pechere, J. and Allard-
      Leprohon, D., *Antimicrob. Ag. Chemoth. 12*, 201 (1977).
163. Price, K. E., "Structure-Activity Relationships Among the
      Semisynthetic Antibiotics" (D. Perlman, ed.), p. 7.
      Academic Press, New York (1977).
164. Cole, M., *Process Biochem. 2* , 35 (1967) [*C. A. 67*, 31525n
      (1967)].
165. Claridge, C. A., Luttinger, J. R. and Lein, J., *Proc. Soc.
      Exp. Biol. Med. 113*, 1008 (1963).
166. Cole, M., Savidge, T. and Vanderhaeghe, H., "Methods in
      Enzymology" (J. H. Hash, ed.), Vol. XLIII, p. 699. Academic
      Press, New York (1975).
167. Rolinson, G. N., Batchelor, F. R., Butterworth, D., Comeron-
      Wood, J., Cole, M., Eustace, G. C., Hart, M. V., Richards,
      M. and Chain, E. B., *Nature 187*, 236 (1960).
168. Kaufmann, W. and Bauer, K., *Naturwiss. 47*, 474 (1960).
169. Claridge, C. A., Gourevitch, A. and Lein, J., *Nature 187*,
      237 (1960).
170. Cole, M., *Biochem. J. 115*, 747 (1969).

171. Nara, T., Okachi, R. and Misawa, M., *J. Antibiot.* 24, 321 (1971).
172. Nara, T., Misawa, M., Okachi, R. and Yamamoto, M., *Agric. Biol. Chem.* 35, 1676 (1971).
173. Okachi, R. and Nara, T., *Agric. Biol. Chem.* 37, 2797 (1973).
174. Nara, T., Misawa, M. and Okaji, M., Japan Kōkai Patent, S51-07757 (1976).
175. Huang, H. T., Seto, T. A. and Shull, G. M., *Appl. Microbiol.* 11, 1 (1963).
176. Sassiver, M. L. and Lewis, A., "Structure-Activity Relationships Among the Semisynthetic Antibiotics" (D. Perlman, ed.), p. 89. Academic Press, New York (1977).
177. Morin, R. B., Jackson, B. G., Flynn, E. H. and Roeske, R. W., *J. Am. Chem. Soc.* 84, 3400 (1962).
178. Takashashi, T., Yamazaki, Y., Kato, K. and Isono, M., *J. Am. Chem. Soc.* 94, 4035 (1972).
179. Takahashi, K., Yamazaki, Y., Kato, K., Takahashi, T. and Kawahara, K., Abst. Ann. Meet. Japan Agric. Chem. Soc., p. 287 (1973).
180. Takahashi, K., Yamazaki, Y. and Kato, K., Abst. Ann. Meet. Japan Agric. Chem. Soc., p. 287 (1973).
181. Marconi, W., Bartoli, F., Cecere, F., Galli, G. and Morisi, F., *Agric. Biol. Chem.* 39, 277 (1975).
182. Shimizu, M., Masuike, T., Fujita, H., Kimura, K., Okachi, R. and Nara, T., *Agric. Biol. Chem.* 39, 1225 (1975).
183. Shimizu, M., Masuike, T., Fujita, H., Iida, T., Kimura, K. and Nara, T., *Agric. Biol. Chem.* 39, 1745 (1975).
184. Shimizu, M., Okachi, R., Kimura, K. and Nara, T., *Agric. Biol. Chem.* 39, 1655 (1975).
185. Sebek, O. L. and Hoeksema, H., *J. Antibiot.* 25, 434 (1972).
186. Umezawa, H., Takahashi, Y., Fuji, A., Saino, T., Shirai, T. and Takita, T., *J. Antibiot.* 26, 117 (1973).
187. Kim, C. H., Otake, N. and Yonehara, H., *J. Antibiot.* 27, 903 (1974).
188. Kim, C. H., Endo, T. and Yonehara, H., *Agric. Biol. Chem.* 40, 1559 (1976).
189. Kameda, Y. and Horii, S., *J.C.S. Chem. Comm.* 1972, 446 (1972).
190. Kameda, Y., Horii, S. and Yamano, T., *J. Antibiot.* 28, 299 (1975).
191. Takayoshi, U. and Suhadolnik, R. J., *Arch. Biochem. Biophys.* 162, 614 (1974).
192. Tsuruoka, T., Shomura, T., Ogawa, Y., Egami, N., Watanabe, H., Amano, S., Inouye, S. and Niida, T., *J. Antibiot.* 26, 168 (1973).
193. Hurley, L. H., Gairola, C. and Das, N. V., *Biochemistry 15*, 3760 (1976).
194. Feldman, L. I., Dill, I. K., Holmlund, C. E., Whaley, H. A., Patterson, E. L. and Bohonos, N., *Antimicrob. Ag. Chemoth. 1963*, 54 (1964).

195. Nakahama, K. and Igarasi, S., *J. Antibiot.* 27, 605 (1974).
196. Shibata, M., Uyeda, M. and Mori, S., *J. Antibiot.* 28, 434 (1975).
197. Bachur, N. R. and Gee, M., *Fed. Proc.* 31, 835 (1972).
198. Asbell, M., Schwartzbach, E., Bullock, F. J. and Yesair, D. W., *J. Pharmacol. Exp. Ther.* 182, 163 (1972).
199. Wiley, P. F., Koert, J. M., Elrod, D. W., Reisender, E. A. and Marshall, V. P., *J. Antibiot.* 30, 649 (1977).
200. Karnetová, J., Matĕjů, J., Sedmera, P., Vokoun, J. and Vanĕk, Z., *J. Antibiot.* 2ᴤ, 1199 (1976).
201. Florent, J., Lunel, J. and Renaut, J., Neue Vorfahren zur Herstellung des Antibiotikums 20789 R. P., German Patent 2,456,139, May 28 (1975).
202. Kojima, M., Inouye, S. and Niida, T., *J. Antibiot.* 26, 246 (1973).
203. Kojima, M., Inouye, S. and Niida, T., *J. Antibiot.* 28, 48 (1975).
204. Lancini, G. C., Gallo, G. G., Sartori, G. and Sensi, P., *J. Antibiot.* 22, 369 (1969).
205. Argoudelis, A. D., Coats, J. H. and Magerlein, B. J., *J. Antibiot.* 25, 191 (1972).
206. Corcoran, J. W., "Methods in Enzymology" (J. H. Hash, ed.), Vol. XLIII, p. 487. Academic Press, New York (1975).
207. Majer, J., Martin, J. R., Egan, R. S. and Corcoran, J. W., *J. Am. Chem. Soc.* 99, 1620 (1977).
208. Umezawa, H., Sawa, T., Fukagawa, Y., Koyama, G., Murase, M., Hamada, M. and Takeuchi, T., *J. Antibiot.* 18, 178 (1965).
209. Sawa, T., Fukagawa, Y., Homma, Y., Wakashiro, T., Takeuchi, T. and Hori, M., *J. Antibiot.* 21, 334 (1968).
210. Ochi, K., Yashima, S. and Eguchi, Y., *J. Antibiot.* 28, 965 (1975).
211. Keller-Schielein, W., Poralla, K. and Zähner, H., *Arch. Mikrobiol.* 67, 339 (1969).
212. Jackson, J. H. and Umberger, H. E., *Antimicrob. Ag. Chem.* 3, 510 (1973).
213. Yamaguchi, I., Shibata, H., Seto, H. and Misato, T., *J. Antibiot.* 28, 6 (1975).
214. Andres, W. W., McGahren, W. J. and Kunstann, M. P., *Tetrahedron Letters 1969-43*, 3777 (1969).
215. Bod, P., Szarka, E., Gyimesi, J. and Horváth, G., *J. Antibiot.* 26, 101 (1973).
216. Maezawa, I., Hori, T., Kinumaki, A. and Suzuki, M., *J. Antibiot.* 26, 771 (1973).
217. Nakahama, K., Kishi, T. and Igarasi, S., *J. Antibiot.* 27, 433 (1974).
218. Endō, T. and Perlman, D., *J. Antibiot.* 25, 681 (1972).
219. Pan, S. C., Nicholson, L. W. and Kolochov, P., *Arch. Biochem. Biophys.* 42, 406 (1953).
220. Endō, T. and Perlman, D., *J. Antibiot.* 25, 751 (1972).

221. Reimann, H. and Jaret, R. S., *J. Chem. Soc., Chem. Comm.*
      1972, 1270 (1972).
222. Maezawa, I., Kinumaki, A. and Suzuki, M., *J. Antibiot. 29,*
      1203 (1976).
223. LeMahieu, R. A., Ax, H. A., Blount, J. F., Carson, M.,
      Despreau, C. W., Pruess, D. L., Scannell, J. P., Weiss, F.
      and Kierstead, R. W., *J. Antibiot. 29,* 729 (1976).
224. Flickinger, M. C. and Perlman, D., *J. Antibiot. 28,* 307
      (1975).
225. Lancini, G. and Sartori, G., *J. Antibiot. 29,* 466 (1976).
226. Woyczikowska, B., Pass, L., Girdwoyn, M. and Raczynska-
      Boyanowska, K., *Acta Biochim. Pol. 20,* 285 (1973) [*B. A. 57,*
      25322 (1974)].
227. Singh, K. and Rakhit, S., *J. Antibiot. 24,* 704 (1971).
228. Singh, R. and Hsieh, D. P. H., *Appl. Environmental Microbiol.*
      31, 743 (1976).
229. Ozaki, M., Kariya, T., Kato, H. and Kimura, T., *Agric. Biol.*
      Chem. 36, 451 (1972).
230. Batyrova, A. Sh. and Egorov, N. S., *Antibiotiki 19,* 1089
      (1974).
231. White, R. F., Birnbaum, J., Meyer, R. T., Ten Broeke, J.,
      Chemerda, J. M. and Demain, A. L., *Appl. Microbiol. 22,* 55
      (1971).
232. Suzuki, M., Takamaki, T., Miyagawa, K., Ono, H., Higashide,
      E. and Uchida, M., *Agric. Biol. Chem. 41,* 419 (1977).
233. Shibata, M., Uyeda, M. and Mori, S., *J. Antibiot. 29,* 824
      (1976).

CHAPTER 12

CYTOTOXIC AND ANTITUMOR COMPOUNDS
FROM FERMENTATIONS

A. Aszalos

Frederick Cancer Research Center
National Cancer Institute
Frederick, Maryland

J. Berdy

Research Institute for Pharmaceutical Chemistry
Budapest, Hungary

I. INTRODUCTION

The success of antitumor antibiotics like Adriamycin, Daunorubicin, Bleomycin, and Actinomycin D in cancer chemotherapy have
led many research groups around the world to search for still more
novel antibiotics.
    Due to these efforts, the National Cnacer Institute, along
with other groups, is now studying an impressive list (1,2) of
recently discovered antitumor antibiotics. Discovered through
current screening methods, most of these antibiotics are cell
toxic agents or active compounds in animal model systems (3,4)
and are essentially inhibitors of both normal and malignant cell
growth. This inhibition of cell growth generally manifests itself
on the molecular level by (a) covalent binding followed by DNA
scission [Bleomycin (5) and Neocarzinostatin (6)], (b) by covalent
binding to DNA [Mitomycin C (7)] or (c) by noncovalent binding to
DNA [Adriamycin (8)]. Host toxicity is thus a nearly inevitable
component of present tumor chemotherapy. To modify this pattern,
various *in vitro* prescreen methods are now under consideration,
such as erythrocyte differentiation (9), the agglutination test
(10), the Ames test (11),   genetically manipulated or very

sensitive microorganisms (12,13), and assorted enzyme inhibition
tests (14).   It should be mentioned that polysaccharide and protein type antitumor materials have different modes of action different from those previously described, yet, with the exception
of macromomycin, no such compound has yet established itself in
the clinic.   For *in vitro* screening, the models used most frequently are the L1210 and P388 lymphoid leukemias in mice.   The
minimum activity criteria is set at 50% prolongation of survival
(T/C x 100 $\geq$ 150).   The shortcomings of these screening systems
are well known, resulting from the schedule dependency of different drugs and from the differences between murine cancers with
high growth factors and slow-growing solid tumors.   Researchers
are now attempting to select reproducibly transplantable cancers
that show a pattern of drug response which parallels the pattern
of human cancer drug responsiveness (15).   Preclinical studies
continue with drug-sensitive and drug-resistant human cancers
which can be grown as solid tumors in T-cell deficient or immuno-
suppressed mice (16).

The detection of natural substances like antitumor antibiotics,
which would utilize metabolic differences between normal and malignant cells, has recently drawn interest.   Unfortunately, our present knowledge of metabolic differences is such that, other than
enhanced protein, DNA and RNA build-up, and carbohydrate utilization, we can find only occasional qualitative differences between
a malignant cell and its normal counterpart (17).   These occasional differences appear in absolute requirements for amino acids
such as asparginase (18) and cysteine (19).   Cancer chemotherapy
based on synthetic amino acid analogs and amino acid cleaving enzymes (20) aims at utilizing these differences.   Recently enzymes,
like glyoxalase and adenosin, which may plan an important role in
the metabolism of cancerous cells, have been successfully used in
finding antibiotic inhibitors of tumor growth (21).

Efforts to use antibiotics to take advantage of the differences
between normal and malignant cell membranes have also met with
success.   Bestatin (22) proved an inhibitor of aminopeptidases,
which may well have to do with the differences between normal and
malignant cell walls.   Other enzymes, like esterazes, alkaline
phosphatase, and sialidase, were also used as prescreen systems.
These enzymes appear to be connected to surface differences between normal and transformed cells.

Reviews dealing with all aspects of antitumor antibiotics have
recently been published.   One of the most comprehensive works,
edited by Sartorelli and Johns, deals in detail with modes of
action, antitumor spectra, toxicity, and other relevant characteristics of antitumor compounds (23).   J. Fuska has published a comprehensive listing of antitumor antibiotics known in 1974 (25).
Symposia on aspects of pharmacodynamics, toxicology, and prescree-
methods of anticancer antibiotics have also been held (24).

Advanced research has continued unabated in the last few years: I. H. Goldberg, *et al.* has detailed the interaction of antineoplastic antibiotics with nucleic acids (26) and summarized screening models, modes of action, therapeutic usefulness, toxic effects, and the pharmacology of antitumor antibiotics (27); H. J. Issag, *et al.* designed a thin-layer chromatographic classification of the most important antitumor antibiotics for the quick identification of "unknown" antibiotics in crude preparations (28); and the infrared spectra were shown useful in the rapid identification of known antibiotics (29).

The last fifteen years' activities of one of the largest antibiotic research groups in the world, the Institue of Microbial Chemistry led by Dr. H. Umezawa, have also been recently summarized (30).

One of the most comprehensive collections of antibiotics obtained by fermentation lists about 4,500 compounds (31). This compilation, together with a collection of compounds originating from plants or animals, was recently computerized for quick identification purposes (32). This listing mentions about 800 antibiotics active in some tumor model system. This chapter deals with the 160 of these compounds discovered since 1974. Recent developments concerning some previously discovered antibiotics will also be mentioned.

II.   SACCHARIDE COMPOUNDS

This class comprises those compounds containing mainly saccharides. Such compounds on the cell surface of *Bacillus Calmette-Guerin (BCG)*, it is believed, are responsible for its usefulness in clinical trials. *BCG* is believed to act through nonspecific host-immune stimulation (33), and the rest of the compounds in this class may have a similar mode of action. Whether lipids attached to the saccharide backbone play a significant part in the immune stimulation remains unclear (34). In the case of *BCG*, however, it has been found that both the lipid and the polysaccharide fractions are necessary to cause the regression of established tumors (35).

The investigation of components of *Mycobacterium butyricum* yielded similar results (36). If pure polysaccharides are water-soluble but not   hydrolyzed by host enzymes, they usually exhibit antitumor activity regardless of their sugar composition and physical structure. Cellulose, for example, is inactive, while O-methyl-cellulose shows considerable activity. High molecular weight compounds show more activity than those with a low molecular weight (37).

The mode of action of these polysaccharides is connected with host-immune stimulation. Previous studies in this field have been summarized by Whistler, Bushway, and Singh (38).

Researchers have compared the effects of bacterial lipopolysaccharides on different cell lines, and the immunological mechanism of tumor cell growth inhibition has also been theorized (39).
Studies have considered the induction of interferon by some of
these polysaccharides as one possible mode of action (40,41).
Research workers have also examined the mechanism of neutralization of charges on cell surfaces by charged polysaccharides like
DEAE-dextran (42) and gum tragacanth (43).

Because of the interesting modes of action of polysaccharide-
type antitumor compounds and their relatively minor cytotoxic
effects (44), the search for new ones has continued. A good number have been discovered since 1974.

Lipopolysaccharide isolated from *Proteus vulgaris* caused complete regression of subcutaneously inoculated Ehrlich carcinoma
in mice in 30% of cases tested. It was concluded that a humoral
factor other than antibody was responsible (45). A polysaccharide
of high molecular weight which inhibited sarcoma 180 in mice was
likewise isolated from *Suillus* fungi (46). *Streptomyces tumor-
coagulans* (47) has produced a compound yielding similar results.

The lipopolysaccharide fraction of *Proteus mirabilis* has also
caused the regression of Ehrlich carcinoma (48). A modification
of this lipopolysaccharide resulted in a nontoxic, nonpyrogenic,
but effective antitumor complex containing glucosamine, fatty
acids, and 2-keto-deoxy-octanioc acid residues (49). Scleroglucan
has been isolated from *Sclerotium glucanium* (50) and has proven to
be homogeneous and to possess a main chain of (1→3)-β-D-gluco-
pyranosyl units with every third unit carrying a (1→6)-β-D-gluco-
pyranosyl group. With this material, complete regression was observed in sarcoma-bearing mice in seven out of ten cases.

The antitumor lipopolysaccharides, serratigan and serratiman-
nan, isolated from *Serratia marcescens*, were shown to have α-(→3)
galactan and α-(1→2) plus α-(1→3) mannan residues, respectively
(51,52). *Streptomyces flavochromogenes* produced a glycoprotein
containing 90% sugar and 10% protein, which inhibited the growth
of both sarcoma 180 and Ehrlich ascites tumors (53). Another glycoprotein with antitumor properties was isolated from *Phellinus
linteus* (54), while *Streptomyces myxogenes* produced an olygo-
saccharide, SF-1130 (55).

PS-K, the protein-bound polysaccharide, isolated from *Coriolus
versicolor*, showed marked activity against sarcoma 180 in mice
(56). Aqueous extractions of the fungus *Boletus* (57) and the
mushroom *Hygrocybe* (58) both yielded polysaccharide-type antitumor
agents. A new type of antitumor glycopeptide with N-aminoacylated
glucosamine structures was also found to be active against sarcoma
180 and L-1210 tumors in mice (59). In addition, a possible polysaccharide-type material was obtained from the culture filtrate of
Streptomyces hachijoensis (60).

An extract of *Salmonella enteritidis* was shown to increase the
activity of macrophages *in vitro* and *in vivo* (61). Zymosan extracted from yeast cells extended the life of rats bearing benzo-

pyrine-induced tumors (62). Two polysaccharide-type antitumor
compounds were isolated from a marine bacterium (63) and from
Streptomyces mashuensis (64) fermentations.

The chemical structure of galactomannan from the cell wall of
Aspergillus niger was also recently reported (65).

Another polysaccharide was isolated from a *Cyclomyces* species
and shown to have tumor inhibitory properties in mice (66). Structural studies on the β-D-glucan antitumor material isolated from
Coriolus versicolor were conducted (67,68). The total synthesis
of minosaminomycin, a sugar-containing antibiotic, was achieved
(69).

III.   ANTHRACYCLINES

The success of adriamycin in the clinical treatment of certain
solid tumors has led both to the isolation of a variety of related
antibiotics and to the synthesis of many structural analogs and
derivatives. Table I lists the names of nautrally-occurring
anthracyclines with the corresponding microorganisms to date, and
Table II shows the structures of natural anthracycline antibiotics
developed since 1974.

Researchers have published many detailed discussions of adriamycin therapy (70); adriamycin itself has been the subject of many
chemical studies since 1974. Many O-acyl derivatives have been
made and shown to have activities equivalent to that of the parent
compound (71). N-acyl derivatives, particularly the N-octanoyl
and N-dodecanoyl derivatives, have shown T/C values > 300 in the
P388 model (72). The N-trifluoro-acetyl-adriamycin 14-valerate,
(AD-32) (73), showed superior activity to that of its parent compound in model systems. The mode of action of this compound was
investigated and shown, unlike adriamycin, not to be based on DNA
intercalation (74,75). Modes of action other than DNA intercalation have also been suggested for adriamycin and daunorubicin
(76,77). Many attempts have been made to eliminate the cardiac
toxicity side effect of these compounds through chemical modification (78,79). Most of the isolated and chemically modified daunorubicin and adriamycin compounds and their biological activities
have also recently been described (80).

Other newly discovered anthracyclines include baumycin A_1, A_2,
B_1, and B_2. They are 4'-substituted glycosides with different
stereochemistry in the substituents (86). Baumycin C_1 and C_2
were shown to be N-formyl daunorubicin and N-formyl daunorubicinol, respectively. Of this series of compounds, Baumycin A_1 and
A_2 strongly inhibit the growth of cultured L-1210 cells (87).
Carminomycin (88) was shown to be desmethyl daunorubicin, and
its absolute stereochemistry was established (89,90).

The use of the daunorubicin DNA complex in chemotherapy has
been studied in relation to that of the parent compound (81,82).
Pharmacodynamic studies were conducted with daunorubicin and

TABLE I. Sources of Anthracycline Antitumor Antibiotics

Anthracycline	Producing Organism
Aclacinomycin	S. galilaeus
Aklavin	S. species A 1165
Aranciamycin	S. echinatus Tu 303
Baumycin	S. coeruleorubidus
Beromycin	S. griseoruber var. beromycini
Carminomycin	A. carminata
Ciclamycin	S. capoamus (4670 1A 37)
Ciclacidin	S. capoamus (4670 1A 37)
Cinerubin	S. cinereoruber var. fructofermentans
Cirolemycin	S. bellus var. cirolerosus
Cytotetrin	S. griseoflavus
Daunorubicin	S. coeruleorubidus (8899-31723)
	S. bifurcus 23219
	S. griseus var. rubidofaciens (32041)
	S. peucetius
Doxorubicin	S. peucetius var. caesius or carneus
Dannosaminyl-Daunorubicin	S. peuceticus var. carneus
Ericamycin	Streptomyces SE 548
Figaroic acid	Streptosporangium C31-751
Galirubin	S. galilaeus JA 3043
Isorhodomycin	S. purpurascens
Lateriomycin	S. griseoruber 71070
Leukaemomycin	S. griseus
Marcellomycin	Actinosporangium sp. C36, 145
Marimycin	S. mariensis
Miniatomycin	Streptomyces 4362
Mitochromin	S. viridochromogenes
Musettamycin	Actinosporangium sp. C-36, 145

Mycetin	*S. janthinus 117-S. violans 167*
	A. violatus-A. violarus
Nocardorubin	*Nocardia narashinoensis 76*
Nogalamycin	*S. nogalater*
Pillaromycin	*S. flavovirens 65786*
Pyrromycin	*Streptomyces DOA 1205*
Quinocycline	*S. aureofaciens*
Retamycin	*S. olindensis*
Requinomycin	*S. filamentosus*
Reticulomycin	*S. rubrireticuli*
Rhodorubin	*S. galilaeus*
Rhodomycetin	*S. griseus*
Rhodomycin	*S. purpurascens*
Rubomycin	*S. coeruleorubidus*
Rutilantin	*Streptomyces A-220*
Ryemycin	*S. ryensis*
Steffimycin	*S. steffisburgensis*
Tauromycetin	*S. tauricus nov. sp.*
Trypanomycin	*S. diastochromogenes*
Vaccinocidin	*Actinomyces 3933/13*
Violacin	*Actinomyces 2732/3*
	Macrospora violaceus
Violamycin	*S. violaceus*
Violarin	*S. violaceus and S. coelicolor*
A 1683	*Streptomyces 1683*
A 195	*S. spadicis*
B 5794	*Streptomyces 5794*
FA 313	*S. chromovarious*
LL-AH-272	*S. platensis*
S 583 A-R	*S. purpurascens*
M-770	*S. violascens var. rubescens*
135/I	*S. jantinus 135/I*
719	*S. violaceus 719*
5888	*S. galilaeus*

adriamycin (83), and it was shown that daunoribicinol forms intracellularly from daunorubicin and that this enzymatic reduction occurs much less frequently with adriamycin (84).

Two new types of anthracyclines, aclacinomycin A and B (N-dimethyl-daunosamine trisaccharide derivatives) have shown T/C values of 300 in the L-1210 leukemia system and have inhibited the trowth of L-1210 cells *in vitro* (85).

Compared to daunorubicin and adriamycin, it appears that carminomycin is less cardiotoxic and better adsorbed from the gastrointestinal tract (91). The adsorption differences were attributed to variances in the partition coefficients of these compounds (92).

Figaroic acid (93) was described as a new anthracycline complex produced by *Streptosporangium* C-31751. It appears in the inactive precursor form, which is activated by HCl hydrolysis, presumably by hydrolyzing off materials from the precursor.

Leukaemomycin (94) was isolated from the culture filtrate of *Streptomyces griseus*. It is composed of four known anthracyclines: rubomycin B (leukaemomycin B_1), daunorubicin (leukaemomycin C), dihydrodaunorubicin (leukaemomycin D), and daunosaminyldaunorubicin (leukaemomycin B_2).

The structures of the compounds marcellomycin, musettamycin, and pyrromycin, which belong to the "Bohemic acid" complex, were established (95). These compounds exhibit a moderate tumor inhibitory effect in the L-1210 leukemia system (96).

Microbiological side-chain reduction of daunorubicin was demonstrated to yield daunorubicinol with the same stereochemistry as that produced in mammalian tissues (97) by the same biotransformation reaction.

N-acetylation of both daunorubicin and daunorubicinol was shown to occur by microbiological culture (98). Other biotransformations of anthracyclines yielded steffimycinol (99) and different 7-deoxyaglycones (100).

The rhodirubins, a group of six compounds, have been shown to have ε-pyrromycinone as their chromophore, like members of the Bohemic acid group. Yet their oligosaccharide moieties are different. The full structures of both rhodorubin A and B were established (101). Steffimycin and steffimycin B were produced by a culture of *S. elgreteus*, but only steffimycin B has shown inhibitory effect to L-1210 mouse leukemia cells *in vitro* (102). Violamycin A and B were compared to daunorubicin and were found to have less mitotic activity (103). Structurally, violamycin A was demonstrated to be a series of aglycones, ε-isorhodomycinone, β-rhodomycinone, and α_2-rhodomycinone, each coupled to rhodosamine. Violamycin B is a complex containing di- and trisaccharides of ε-isorhodomycinone, β-rhodomycinone, and α_2-rhodomycinone (104).

The reported antibiotic FA-313 is believed to be an anthracycline based on gross characteristics (105). Nineteen anthracyclic compounds were produced by *S. galilaeus* MA 144-M1 (106), and some members of this group have been shown to have the same alycon as components of the Bohemic acid group and the rhodorubins, while others have the same aglycon as the aclacinomycins. One of the most interesting members of this group is MA 144-El, an aglycone dimer covalently linked at the 7 position. New components of the fermentation of *S. galilaeus* were isolated, from which component Ul showed the same *in vivo* activity as aclacinomycin A (106a).

The stereochemical requirement of the substituent at the C-9 position of the anthracycline structure was recently determined by pharmacological measurements and by the intercalating ability of different stereoisomers with DNA (107). Aklavin, which was discovered earlier, was shown to be identical with l-deoxypyrromycin (108).

IV. QUINONE TYPE COMPOUNDS

Several new quinone type antitumor compounds have been detected in the past four years. One of these, napthyridinomycin, produced by *Streptomyces lusitanus*, was shown to interact with DNA by the formation of a covalent binding, similar to mitomycin C (109). Asteriquinone, 2,5-bis[N-(1",1"-dimethyl-2"-propenyl)-indol-3'yl]-3,6-dihydroxy-1,4-benzoquinone, was isolated from the fermentation micelium of *Aspergillus terreus* and found to suppress implanted Ehrlich carcinoma without notable toxicity to the host (110).

Sterigmatocystins were isolated from a fermentation of an *Aspergillus* species. Of six of these compounds, four (I-IV) have been shown to prolong the survival of mice bearing L-1210 and P388 (111).

An orange-red basic antibiotic named antibiotic 54 isolated from the fermentation broth of *Streptomyces nitrosporeus* (112) and found to inhibit the growth of sarcoma 180 in mice. A series of antitumor compounds designated M92-BA4, -BA5, -BN1, -BN2, -BN3, and -VA2 were isolated from the fermentation of *Micromonaspora verruculosa* (113). Cytrimycin, produced by *Streptomyces katsunumaensis*, was shown to be a close structure analog of chromomycin A_2 and active against L-1210 and L-5178 cells (114). The fermentation of *Actinomyces olivovariabilis* produced Variacyclomycin A and B, the latter proving active against HeLa cells (115).

A weekly active antitumor compound, medermycin, was isolated from a *Streptomyces* recognized as an analog of antibiotic 289 and luteomycin (116). SS-228Y, a perhydroxyquinone-type antibiotic active against the Ehrlich ascites tumor, was produced from a marine microorganism of the *Chainia* (117) species and its structure established (118).

Two griseorhodins, FCRC-57G and FCRC-57-U, were isolated, their activity against KB cells established as 24 µg/ml (ED_{50}), and their structures determined (119).

Several chemical and biochemical studies were conducted with previously discovered quinone-type antibiotics. Damavaricin C derivatives were made through the oxidative hydrolysis of strep-tovaricin C and subsequent etherification. These new derivatives inhibit the focus formation of animal cells by RNA tumor virus *in vitro*, an activity which could not be detected with any strepto-varicins (120). Mitomycin A and C were totally synthesized (121); the structures of kidamycin (122), pluramycin and neopluramycin (122a) were chemically elucidated; the alkylation of biological macromolecules by mitomycin antibiotics was studied (123); and, through studying the biosynthesis of streptovaricin precursors, prostreptovaricins were discovered (124).

V. ACTINOMYCINS

Since actinomycin D has proven its value in clinical use against child leukemia, investigations into new actinomycins and modifications of existing ones have continued.

Among new actinomycins, a complex designated 70,501, was iso-lated from the fermentation of *Micromonospora floridensis*. Through high-voltage electrophoresis followed by chromatography in a second dimension, some of these compounds were shown to contain amino acids hitherto undetected in actinomycins (125). Yet another ac-tinomycin-type compound, 472A, was recently reported (126). When azetidin-2-carboxylic acid was fed to actinomycin D fermentation, one or both prolines were replaced by this compound, and two new actinomycins, azetomycin I and azetomycin II (dependent on the number of replaced prolines), were isolated (129). Both new acti-nomycins were found to be as biologically active as actinomycin D.

Three new actinomycins were synthesized when DL-pipecolic acid was fed in the culture medium of *Streptomyces antibioticus*. Acti-nomycin Pip 2 contains two residues of pipecolic acid, while acti-nomycin Pip 1α and 1β each contain one residue of pipecolic acid along with prolin or 4-oxopipecolic acid, respectively, at the amino-acid site of the actinomycin molecule (128). Additional studies revealed that L-pipecolic acid, but not D-pipecolic acid, gets incorporated into the newly formed actinomyces (129). In similar studies, when cis and trans-4-methyl proline were fed to the fermentation of *Streptomyces parvullus*, four new antibiotics, K_{1c}, K_{2c}, K_{1t}, and K_{2t}, were produced. It was shown that 4-methyl-proline replaces one (K_{1c} and K_{1t}) proline or two (K_{2c} and K_{2t}) prolines in these new actinomyces (130). These antibiotics are less active against microorganisms and less potent inhibitors of nucleic acid synthesis than their parent compound.

The previously discovered actinomycin D_0 was studied in com-parison with actinomycin D_1 for its interaction ability with DNA and its antimicrobial activity. Actinomycin D_0 proved 100-fold less active in each area than actinomycin D (131).

Two biosynthetic actinomycins, actinoleucin Au_6I and actinoleucin Au_6II, were isolated. A leucin-containing peptide is
attached to the quinoid part in the former, and to the benzoid
nucleus in the latter (132).

Among semisynthetic actinomycins, 7-nitro and 7-amino actinomycin D matched the parent compound in the inhibition of several
experimental tumors (133). It was also shown that by the replacement of the 2-amino group by hydrogen or a 3-hydroxy propylamino
group the 2-amino group is important but not necessary for the
activity of the actinomycin molecule (134).

Other studies demonstrated the importance of the lacton group
in the actinomycin molecule. If converted to a lactam group, the
resulting molecule is considerably less active in murine tumor
systems than the original compound (135). Structures of large
numbers of actinomycins were related to their antitumor activity
(136). A two-dimensional characterization of amino acids in actinomycin hydrolysates was also described (137). By this technique,
a new member of the actinomycin Z family, X-4357g, was proven to
contain β,γ dihydroxyaminobutyric acid.

VI. AMINO ACIDS AND PEPTIDES

Some of these compounds are specific enzyme inhibitors and
were discovered by screening with purified enzyme systems. It
was demonstrated, for example, that aminopeptidases appear on the
cell surface and hydrolyze substrates in the medium (138,139). It
was postulated that these aminopeptidases might inhibit the hydrolysis of proteins which are involved in cell-cell recognition processes and that they might regulate tumor growth. This enzyme inhibition might also increase or decrease the activity of cells involved in immunity because these inhibitors bind to the enzymes on
the cell surface (140).

Common screening methods like the *in vivo* P388 system or the
in vitro KB cell-line system also revealed peptide-type antibiotics in the fermentation broth. In fact, the aminopeptidase inhibitor bestatin (22) was discovered as a result of this screening
method.

By screening against aminopeptidase B of actinomycin culture
filtrates,   bestatin was revealed. It also inhibits leucine
aminopeptidase, but fails to inhibit trypsin, chymotrypsin, elas-
tase, papain, or pepsin. Its toxicity is very low, even with
doses of 300 mg/kg (i.v.) in mice, and it was found to increase
the number of antibodies forming cells in dd/y mice (141).

Bestatin augments the immune resistance and suppresses the
growth of tumors caused by a second infusion of Ehrlich carcinoma
cells. It also acts synergistically with bleomycin in the treatment of different model cancers (141). The structure of bestatin
is [(2S,3R)-3-amino-2-hydroxy-4-phenylbutanoyl] - L-leucine,
(142), and the structure of the novel amino acid component in

bestatin was found by x-ray crystallography to be (2S,3R)-3-amino-2-hydroxy-4-phenylbutanioc acid (143). After bestatin was synthesized (144), researchers conducted structural activity relations with synthetic analogs (145).

The microbial metabolite KF-77-AG-6 was discovered by screening with an *in vitro* enzyme system. This compound is a part of the previously discovered antipain molecule, and its structure is [(S)-1-carboxy-2-phenylethyl] carbamoyl-L-arginine (146).

The antimetabolite U-43,757, which has significant activity against L-1210 lymphocytic leukemia, was isolated from culture filtrate of *Streptomyces sviceus* (147). Its structure is (αS,4S,5R)-α-amino-3-chloro-4-hydroxy-4,5-dihydroisoxazolacetic acid. This compound along with its closely related analog, U-42, 126, was found to inhibit L-aspargine synthesis *in vitro* as well as *in vivo*. This inhibitory effect appears linked to its mode of action (148).

Feldamycin was isolated from the culture filtrate of *Streptomyces ficellus* (149). It has low inhibitory activity against L-1210 mouse leucemia cells, and its structure was shown to contain N-methylhistidine and a new amino acid designated feldamycin acid (150). Another cell toxic agent, chlamidocin, was isolated from culture filtrate of *Diheterospora chlamydosporia* and its structure elucidated (151). Cyclosporin A and C were also detected as antifungal agents (152), but were shown to have immunosuppressive properties (154).

An alazopeptin related antibiotic, OS-3256B, was isolated from culture filtrate of *Streptomyces candidus*. The administration of the antibiotic to L-1210 tumor-bearing CDF_1 mice resulted in a considerable extension of life span (155).

An interesting Vitamin B_{12} antimetabolite, N^5-hydroxy-L-arginine, was found to be produced by *Bacillus cereus* 439. This compound acted synergistically with L-lysine against KB cells (156).

The crystal structure of piperazinedione, antibiotic 593A, was also determined (157). It had been shown previously that leupeptin inhibits skin carcinogenesis (158), but recent studies suggest that it promotes bladder carcinogenesis if administered during the cancer promotion step rather than the cancer initiation step (159). In sum, these experiments reveal that different scheduling of leupeptin administration in nitrosamine-induced carcinogenesis may shed light on the different phases of carcinogenesis.

VII.   BLEOMYCIN-TYPE COMPOUNDS

While searching for a phleomycin-type antibiotic without renal toxicity, Dr. Umezawa discovered bleomycin in 1966 (160). Since that time, the therapeutic effects of bleomycin on squamous cell carcinoma, lymphoma, and some testicular tumors have been confirmed in clinics, and many review articles have appeared on this

compound (161,162). Bleomycins obtained from fermentation broths
are A-1, demethyl A-2, A-2'a, A-2'b, A-2'c, A-5, A-6, B-1, B-2,
B-4, and B-6. It had previously been demonstrated that bleomycin
caused scission of DNA, and recent tests show that the terminal
amino group is not essential for this action (162). Yet this
scission of DNA requires the amino group of the α-aminocarboxamide
group (164). It was established that bleomycin-resistant cells
contain a bleomycin-inactivating enzyme, bleomycin hydrolase (165)
which is inactivated by bestatin (22), so that the action of bleomycin can be enhanced by simultaneous use of the two antibiotics
in resistant cells. The pharmacological action of bleomycin revealed that bleomycin exists in a Cu^{++} complex in the tissues and
that this complex breaks before bleomycin enters the cell nucleus
and exerts its effect on DNA (166).

Many biochemical papers have been published on bleomycin, on
the biological behavior of the cobalt complex (167), on interaction with DNA in cell-free and intact cell systems (168), on the
biosynthesis of new bleomycins (169), and on the mode of action
(170-172). Chemical studies on various components of bleomycin
have also been reported (173-176).

Two bleomycin related antibiotics, tallysomycin A and B, were
isolated from an unusual streptomyces strain. These antibiotics
showed broad antibacterial and antifungal activities *in vivo* and
have induced phage in lysogenic bacteria (177). When their structures were elucidated (178),   it was found that the major difference between tallysomycins and bleomycins is that the former
contains additional sugar moiety and possesses different side
chains. Platomycin A and B were shown to be related to bleomycins,
but, based on chromatographic mobilities, they are different from
any previously described antibiotic of this type. The biological
activity spectra of these two antibiotics are like those of the
bleomycins in their activity against gram-positive and negative
bacteria and against different model tumors (179).

Victomycin (XK-49-1-B-2) was isolated from the fermentation
broth of *Streptosporangium riolaceochromogenes* MK49. On the basis
of ultraviolet spectrum and chromatographic behavior, it proved
different from other bleomycin-type compounds. It is active
against gram-positive and negative bacteria, sarcoma 180, and
Ehrlich ascites carcinoma (180).

A bleomycin-type antibiotic, SF-1771, was isolated from the
growth medium of *Streptomyces toyocaensis* (181). The antibiotic
was shown active against experimental tumors and a variety of bacteria. Another bleomycin-type compound, with the same general
biological characteristics, SS-10-B, was isolated from the fermentation of *Streptomyces olivogriseus* (182).

Previous names of Tallysomycin A and B were BU2231A and BU2231B
respectively (183).

The action of bleomycin on superhelical DNA was studied by S.
L. Ross and R. E. Moses (184).

VIII.   ANTIBIOTICS OF PROTEINOUS NATURE

Proteinous microbial products which have molecular weights over 1,500 and which inhibit tumor growth in experimental animals are rarer than those with lower molecular weights. However, because of the mode of action of these high molecular weight compounds, there is great interest in their isolation and biological activity. Many of these antibiotics were reported earlier: actinogan, enomycin, flamulin, iomycin A, marinamycin, melanomycin, neocarzinostatin, peptimycin, A-216, A-280, and raromycin.

Macromomycin, also discovered earlier, has been the subject of many studies. It was purified to homogeneity and found to inhibit L1210 leukemia, P388 leukemia, B16 melanoma, and Lewis lung carcinoma (185).

Macromycin's mode of action is connected to the inhibition of DNA synthesis and to the enhancement of the immunogenicity of tumors (187,188). It has also been suggested recently that macromomycin may bind selectively to the surface of tumor cells and thereby exert its selective cytostatic effect (189).

Another protein antibiotic discovered recently, macracidmycin, which inhibits Ehrlich ascites carcinoma, has a therapeutic index over 30, a molecular weight of 35-38,000, and a weak acidic character (190).

A protein which inhibits the growth of sarcoma 180 was named sporamycin (191). Actinocarcin, a new basic polypeptide, inhibits the growth of Ehrlich carcinoma but shows no antimicrobial activity (192). Similarly, renastacarcin (antibiotic 9091-GSC-8) demonstrates no microbiological activity but inhibits Ehrlich and sarcoma 180 tumors in mice (193). Three antitumor glycopeptides with molecular weights of 1,000, 2,000, and 10,000 were isolated from the culture broth of *Lactobacillus bulgaricus* (194). A polypeptide antibiotic with a molecular weight of 5,500 and both a chromophore and phosphoric acids, but which is quite different from roseolic acid, was shown to have moderate antitumor activity in the P388 leukemia system (195).

A polypeptide called gamba, isolated from a *Pseudomonas* strain, has shown moderate antitumor activity (196), while another polypeptide, VI-7501, was isolated from a *Streptomyces* strain and shows antitumor activity against ascites sarcoma (197).

The possible use of Concanavalin A in cancer chemotherapy was discussed (198), while the previously discovered compound enomycin was shown to inhibit protein synthesis in a reticulocyte lysate system (198). The structures of actinoxanthin (200) and neocarzinostatin (201) and a revised structure for Echinomycin (Quinomycin A) were reported (202,203).

The effects of the modification of the side-chain amino and carboxyl groups on the chemical and biological properties of neocarzinostatin were studied. It was shown that the amino groups (alanine-1 and lysine-20) are not essential to the antitumor

activity of this protein with 109 amino acids (204). In studying
the action mechanism of the antitumor protein cesalin, it was established that the antibiotic inhibits Na^+ and K^+-ATP-ase in KB
cells, but not in rat brain and kidney cells or human erythrocytes
(205).

IX. CYCLIC COMPOUNDS

A variety of heterocyclic and alicyclic compounds with antitumor activity have recently been detected. Among the heterocyclic compounds, neothramycin A and B are 1,4-benzodiazepin-type
compounds isolated from the culture filtrate of *Streptomyces* MC
916-C4. These compounds have shown marked therapeutic effect on
L-1210 mouse leukemia and Yoshida rat sarcoma (206).

An indicator-type compound, XK-46, was isolated from the fermentation of thermophilic *Streptomyces sp.* MK-46 (207). The compound inhibits the activity of tyrosinase hydrolase and is also
active against Ehrlich and sarcoma 180 tumors. Baciphelacin
was isolated from the culture filtrate of *Bacillus thiaminolyticus*
IFO 3967/B-1-7 and proven active against P388 lymphatic leukemia,
producing a 50% increase in the survival time of tumor-bearing
mice (208).

The antibiotic ladacamycin (5-azacytidin) was isolated from
fermentation broth of *Streptoverticilium ladakanus* and proven active against T-4 lymphoma in mice (209).

Polyoxins, produced by *Streptomyces cocaoi*, are nucleoside
antibiotics. The bioxynthesis of these compounds was studied in
detail by K. I. Sono and R. J. Suhadolnick (210). Vermiculine, a
previously discovered compound, was recently demonstrated to be
active against Ehrlich carcinoma, sarcoma 37, and lymphoadenoma
L-5178 (211). An antitumor substance, PSX-1, was isolated from a
fermentation broth of *Penicillium stipitatum Thom* that also produced duclauxin and several tropolones (212). Chlorocarcin A was
found to be coproduced with chlorocarcin B and C and mimosamycin
by *Streptomyces levendulae*. The compound contains chlorine and
has exhibited marked activity against murine tumors and Ehrlich
carcinoma (213).

Two polyether-type antibiotics, laidlomycin (214) and antibiotic A-130 (215), have shown toxicity against mammalian cells.

Compounds that inhibit the enzyme sialidase and which may play
a role in cell-cell recognition were isolated from a *Streptomyces*
fermentation. These compounds, siastatin A and B, exhibited different activities against sialidases isolated from different sources (216).

Researchers also clarified the structure of the antitumor
antibiotic sybiromycin (217).

The X-ray crystal structure of p-bromophenacyl septamycin, a
polyether antibiotic, was determined (5) (218), as was the crystal
structure of streptonigrin (219).

9-Methylstreptimidone, a new glutarimide-type compound, was obtained from a *Streptomyces* culture filtrate (200) and proven to inhibit the growth of HeLa, L, and rabbit kidney cells as well as inhibiting placque formation by different viruses. A new amino-nucleoside, 9-(2'-amino-2'-deoxypentofuranosyl)-guanine was produced by an *Aerobacter sp.* (221), with activity against HeLa cells *in vitro* and sarcoma 180 tumors *in vivo*. A compound, vertisporin, which exhibits cytotoxicity against HeLa cells, was isolated from the fermentation. Fermentation of the fungus *Verticimonosporium diffractum* produced vertisporin, which exhibits cytotoxicity against HeLa cells.

An interesting compound called quadrone was isolated from the fermentation broth of *Aspergillus terreus* (223). Its structure was determined by X-ray crystallography, and the compound has proven active against human epidermoid carcinoma of the nasopharynx *in vitro* and P388 lymphocytic leukemia in mice.

Among homocyclic compounds, two interesting p-terphenyls, compounds A and E, were isolated from *Aspergillus candidus* fermentation with compound A showing an inhibition to the growth of HeLa cells (224). The same fermentation produced compound B, or Xanthoascin, which inhibits the growth of HeLa cells, but causes cardiotoxicity in experimental animals (225). The antibiotic terphenyllin was discovered simultaneously with the above compound (226), and is identical in structure to compound A.

The antitumor antibiotic, calvatic acid, was discovered simultaneously by two groups. It was isolated from fermentation broth of *Calvatia craniformis* (227) and *Calvatia lilacina* (228) and was found to be active against L-1210 leukemia and Yoshida sarcoma.

Lambdamycin (229), an antibiotic identical with chartreusin, was isolated from fermentation of *Streptomyces glaucoachromogenes*. It is an indicator-type compound with digitalose and fucose sugar components and inhibits the growth of L-1210 cells while showing some activity against gram-positive bacteria.

Some time ago, Szent-Györgyi suggested (230) that the methyl-glyoxal level of cells was involved in the regulation of cell proliferation; cells that contain high levels of enzymes which convert methylglyoxal tend to become cancerous. The inhibition of the gloxalase enzymes was thought to be a good screening method for finding natural anticancer agents. In a program to isolate such agents, Dr. Umezawa's group has isolated MS-3, a glyoxalase inhibitor (231,232). The component was shown to inhibit the growth of Yoshida rat sarcoma cells *in vitro*. Another glyoxyalase inhibitor produced by *Streptomyces griseosporeus* was shown to inhibit HeLa cells *in vitro* and both Ehrlich carcinoma and L-1210 leukemia *in vivo* (233). This compound differs from MS-3 in that it inhibits the glyoxalase enzymes both of liver and yeast. It was also shown to react with glutathione, a cofactor of the glyoxalase enzyme.

Active against several mammalian cells *in vitro*, PR toxin was isolated from the fermentation of *Penicillium rogueforti* (234). Researchers determined its structure and the structure of the previously discovered antitumor gancidin W (234a).

X. CYTOCHALASINS

Cytochalasins proved to be very useful as *in vitro* biological investigative tools. They also have some selective toxicity to transformed cells. Several new compounds of this class have been discovered recently, and their primary site of action appears to be on the cell surface.

Chaetoglobosins A-F are cytotoxic metabolites of *Chaetomium globosum* (235), and the structures of C, D, E, and F have recently been elucidated (236). From the same fermentation, chaetoglobosins G and J were also isolated, and their structure and stereochemistry soon established (237).

Cytochalasin G, a new member of this class, was isolated from the fermentation of an unidentified *Nigrosabulum* (238), and its structure elucidated by X-ray crystallography.   A fungus, *Phomopsis paspali*, was isolated from the grain of *Paspalum scrobiculatum*, and cultivated to yield a toxic substance, paspaline A, from the fermentation medium (239). It possesses a structure which related it to cytochalasin D. From the fermentation of *P. Paspelli*, two novel-type cytochalasins, kodo-cytochalasin-1 and kodo-cytochalasin-2,   have been isolated (240).

XI. ANTITUMOR ANTIBIOTICS YET UNRELATED TO THE ABOVE CATEGORIES

This section covers those antibiotics which are chemically uncharacterized and those which do not belong to any of the above categories. To the latter group belong the ansamitocins.   The isolation of these compounds from the fermentation broth of a *Nocardia* species (241) raised considerable interest. Maytansine, which is in the advanced stages of clinical testing, was previously obtained in minute quantities from wood. The availability of these maytansine-like compounds through fermentation makes this important drug type more accessible. This finding also suggests the possibility that other compounds presently isolated from wood may also be obtainable by microbial fermentation.

A complex mixture of amino acids, carbohydrates, aminosugars, and lipids was obtained from the mycelium of *Mycobacterium smegmatis* by water-hexene extraction. The complex had antitumor and antiviral effects without the complications which arise from using whole cells for these chemotherapeutic purposes (242). Another cell extract from *Penicillium stipitatum* yielded a fraction which

contains mainly free fatty acids. This fraction was shown to inhibit the growth of Ehrlich ascites cells (243), the same cells
which were shown to be inhibited by strobilurin A and B (244).
The antibiotic lacon-V was produced by a *Lactococcus* and was shown
to be active against mammalian cells (245). From a *Pseudomonas*
species, another mammalian cell active antibiotic, Y-9569, was
produced (246).

The compound P11-55 was isolated from the marine microorganism
species *Vibrio* and found to have both anticancer and antiulcer
activity (247). A *Pseudomonas* species produced the substance
PS46-B1 which has anticancer activity *in vivo* (248). Anticancer
materials were found to be produced by the microorganisms *Inonotus
cuticularis* (249), *Pleurotus ostreatus* (250), and *Lactiporus sul-
phureus* (251). The antibiotic U-43120 produced by *Streptomyces
paulus* was shown to be active against P338 leukemia in mice (252).

Nocamycin was isolated from the fermentation of *Nocardiopsis
syringae* (253), while two antibiotics were isolated from the fermentation of a *Mycoplasma* species. One of them, factor II, exhibits a strong cytotoxicity against KB cells (254).

REFERENCES

1. Wood, H. B. Jr., Report of the Division of Cancer Treatment,
    NCI, Vol. 2, p. 346. U.S. Dept. of Health, Education and
    Welfare, Public Health Service, NIH. Bethesda, MD (1974).
2. Apple, M. A., New Anticancer Drug Design: Past and Future
    Strategies, *in* Cancer, a Comprehensive Treatise, Chemotherapy,
    (F. F. Becker, ed.), Vol. 5, p. 614. Plenum, NY (1977).
3. Goldin, A., Carter, S., and Mantel, *in* "Antineoplastic and
    Immunosuppressive Agents" (A. C. Sartorelli and D. G. Johns,
    eds.), p. 12. Springer, New York, NY (1974).
4. Venditti, J., *in* "Pharmacological Bases of Cancer Chemother-
    apy," p. 243. Williams and Wilkins, Baltimore, MD (1975).
5. Haidle, C. W., *Mol. Pharmacol. 7*, 645 (1971).
6. Beerman, T. and Goldberg, I. H., *Biochem. Biophys. Res.
    Commun. 59*, 1254 (1974).
7. Gale, E. F., Cundliffe, E., Reynolds, P. E., Richmond, M. H.,
    and Waring, M. J., "The Molecular Basis of Antibiotic Action,"
    p. 246. John Wiley, New York, NY (1972).
8. DiMarco, A., Arcamone, F., and Zunino, F., *in* "Antibiotics,
    Mechanisms of Action of Antimicrobial and Antitumor Agents"
    (J. W. Corcoran and F. E. Hahn, eds.), p. 101. Springer,
    Berlin (1974).
9. Ebert, P. S., Wars, I., and Buell, D. N., *Cancer Research
    36*, 1809 (1976).
10. Hwang, K. M., and Sartorelli, A. C., *Biochem. Pharmacol. 24*,
    1149 (1975).

11. Benedict, W. F., Baker, M. S., Haroun, L., Choi, E., and Ames, B. N., *Cancer Res. 37*, 2209 (1977).
12. Hanka, L. J., *Cancer Treatment Reports 61*, 591 (1977).
13. Bradner, W. T., *in* "Fundamentals in Cancer Chemotherapy, Antibiotics and Chemotherapy" (F. M. Schabel, ed.), Vol. 23, p. 4. S. Karger AG, Basel (1978).
14. Sandberg, A. A., Kirani, R. Y., Yamanada, H., Varkarakis, M. J., and Murphy, G. P., *Cancer Chem. Rep. Part 1 59*, 175 (1975).
15. Muggia, F. M., Bono, V. H., Jr., and Devita, V. T., *in* "Fundamentals in Cancer Chemotherapy, Antibiotics, and Chemotherapy" (F. M. Schabel, ed.), Vol. 23, p. 42. S. Karger A. G., Basel (1978).
16. Giovanella, B. C., *Proc. Amer. Assoc. Cancer Res. 17*, 124 (1976).
17. Potter, V., Walker, P., and Goodman, J., *Gann Monogra. 13*, 121 (1972).
18. Newman, R. E. and McCoy, T. A., *Science 124*, 126 (1956).
19. Ohnuma, T., Waligunda, J., and Holland, J. F., *Cancer Res. 31*, 1640 (1971).
20. Ren, J. R. and Handschumacher, R. E., *in* "Cancer, A Comprehensive Treatise, Chemotherapy" (F. F. Becker, ed.), Vol. 5, p. 957. Plenum, New York, NY (1977).
21. Umezawa, H., "Enzyme Inhibitors of Microbial Origin." University of Tokyo Press, Tokyo (1972).
22. Umezawa, H., Aoyagi, T., Suda, H., Hamada, M., and Takeuchi, T., *J. Antibiot. 29*, 97 (1976).
23. "Antineoplastic and Immunosuppressive Agents" (A. C. Sartorelli and D. G. Johns, eds.), Part II. Springer, New York, NY (1975).
24. Fuska, J., *Adv. Appl. Microbiol. 18*, 259 (1976).
25. 10th International Congress of Chemotherapy, Zurich, Sept. 18-22 (1977).
26. Goldberg, I. H., Beerman, T. A., and Poor, R., *in* "Cancer, A Comprehensive Treatise, Chemotherapy" (F. F. Becker, ed.), Vol. 5, p. 427. Plenum, New York, NY (1977).
27. Goldberg, I. H., Beerman, T. A., and Poor, R., *in* "Cancer, A Comperhensive Treatise, Chemotherapy" (F. F. Becker, ed.), Vol. 5, p. 599. Plenum, New York, NY (1977).
28. Issaq, H. J., Barr, E. W., Wei, T., Meyers, C., and Aszalos, *J. Chromatog. 133*, 291 (1977).
29. Strauss, D. G., *J. Antibiot. 27*, 805 (1974).
30. Institute of Microbial Chemistry 1962-1977 (H. Umezawa, ed.). Center for Academic Publications, Tokyo, Japan (1977).
31. Berdy, J., *Adv. Appl. Microbiol. 18*, 309 (1974).
32. Bostian, M., McNitt, K., Aszalos, A., and Berdy, J., *J. Antibiot. 30*, 633 (1977).
33. Smith, R. D., *The Sciences 1976*, 21.
34. Mihich, E., Westphal, O., Luderitz, O., and Neter, E., *Proc. Soc. Exp. Biol. Med. 107*, 916 (1961).

35. Azuma, I., Ribi, E. E., Meyer, T. J., and Zbar, B., *J. Natl. Cancer Inst. 52*, 95 (1974).

36. Esber, H. J., Hagopian, M., and Bogden, A. E., *J. Natl. Cancer Inst. 53*, 209 (1974).

37. Oka, S., Kumano, N., Sato, K., Tamari, T., Matsuda, K., Hirai, H., Oguma, T., Ogawa, K., Kiyooka, S., and Miyao, K., *Proc. 6th Intern. Congr. Chemother. 1*, 122 (1969).

38. Whistler, R. L., Bushway, A. A., and Singh, P. P., *Adv. Carbohydrate Chem. 37*, 266 (1976).

39. Ralph, P. and Nakoinz, I., *Nature 249*, 49 (1974).

40. Lackovic, V., Borechy, L., Sihl, D., Masler, L., and Bauer, S., *Proc. Soc. Exp. Biol. Med. 134*, 874 (1970).

41. Ho, M., *Science 146*, 1472 (1967).

42. Larsen, B. and Olsen, K., *Eur. J. Cancer 4*, 157 (1968).

43. Roe, E. M. F., Smyth, H., and Flahavin, E., *Cancer Res. 32*, 2067 (1972).

44. Holland, J. F., Roboz, J., Weld, N., and Bekesi, G. B., *Proc. Am. Assoc. Cancer Res. 15*, 466 (1974).

45. Yamazaki, M., Ohkuma, S., and Mizumo, D., *Gann. 65*, 337 (1974).

46. Ohtsuka, J., Ueno, S., Yoshikumi, C., Hirose, F., Ohmura, F., Fugii, T., Ohhara, M., Wada, T., and Takahashi, E., Japan Patent 76 00173 (1976).

47. Ikegawa, T. and Sawa, Y., Japan Patent 75 160493 (1975).

48. Arai, M., Nakahara, M., Hamano, K., and Okazahi, H., *Agr. Biol. Chem. 39*, 1813 (1975).

49. Nakahara, M., Kitahara, N., Hamato, K., Arai, M., and Okazahi, H., *Agr. Biol. Chem. 39*, 1821 (1975).

50. Singh, P. P., Whistler, R. L., Tokuzu, R., and Nakahara, W. K., *Carbohydr. Res. 37*, 245 (1974).

51. Ikekawa, T. and Ikeda, Y., *Chem. Pharm. Bull. 23*, 163 (1975).

52. Ikekawa, T. and Ikeda, Y., *Chem. Pharm. Bull. 22*, 78 (1974).

53. Shirakawa, S., Ikekawa, T., and Oishi, K., Japan Patent 75 77595 (1975).

54. Sugiura, M., Kunihisa, M., and Nishigaki, Y., Japan Patent 73 40997 (1973).

55. Omoto, S., Shomura, T., Kondo, Y., Inouye, S., and Niida, T., *Meija Seika Kenhyu Nempo 14*, 10 (1975).

56. Ohno, R., Imai, K., Yokomahu, S., and Yamada, K., *Gann 65*, 679 (1975).

57. Ohtsuka, S., Veno, S., Yoshikumi, C., Hirose, F., Ohmura, Y., Fujii, T., Ohhara, M., Wada, T., and Takahashi, E., Japan Patent 76 06725 (1976).

58. Ohtsuka, S., Veno, S., Yoshikumi, C., Hirose, F., Ohmura, Y., Fujii, T., Ohhara, M., Wada, T., and Takahashi, E., Japan Patent 75 07129 (1975).

59. DeBarbieri, A., DiVittorio, P., Perrone, F., Mougeri, M., Agosteo, A. P., Zappa, M., and Temelcon, O., 10th Intern. Congr. Chemother., Abst. 521. Zurich (1977).

60. Soeda, M., German Patent 2,615,099 (1976).

61. Juy, D., Bona, C., and Chidid, L., *C. R. Acad. Sci. 278*, 2859 (1974).

62. Matthies, E., Pfordte, K., and Ponsold, W., *Arch. Geschwulst-forsch. 41*, 110 (1973).

63. Hamuro, J., Fukuhara, K., and Hirose, Y., Japan Patent 77 47993 (1977).

64. Bardalaye, P. C. and Nordin, J. H., *J. Biol. Chem. 252*, 2584 (1977).

65. Okutani, K., *Nippon Suisan Gakkeishi 43*, 323 (1977).

66. Ohtsuka, S., Veno, S., Yoshikumi, C., Hirose, F., Ohmura, Y., Wada, T., Fujii, T., and Takahashi, E., U.S. Patent 4,051,314 (1977).

67. Hirase, S., Nahai, S., Akatsu, T., Kobayashi, A., Oohara, M., Matsunagas, K., Fujii, M., Kodaira, S., and Fujii, T., *Yakugaku Zasshi 96*, 413 (1976).

68. Inoue, Y. and Chujo, R., *Carbohydr. Res. 56*, 351 (1977).

69. Iinuma, K., Kondo, S., Maeda, K., and Umezawa, H., *Bull. Chem. Soc. Japan 50*, 1850 (1977).

70. Carter, S. K., *J. Nat. Cancer Inst. 55*, 1265 (1975).

71. Prasad, K. N., Gilmer, K., Sahu, S. K., and Becker, G., *Cancer Res. 35*, 77 (1975).

72. Aszalos, A., Sutphin, M., Wright, L. H., Hoyer, B. H., Dour-os, and Langlykke, A. F., 10th I.U.P.A.C. Symposium, Abstr. C19. Dunedin, New Zealand, August 23-27 (1976).

73. Israel, M., Modest, E. J., and Frei, E., *Cancer Res. 35*, 1365 (1975).

74. Krishan, A., Israel, M., Modest, E. J., and Frei, E., *Cancer Res. 36*, 2114 (1976).

75. Facchinetti, T., Mantovani, A., Cantoni, R., Cantoni, K., Pantarotto, C., and Salmona, M., *Biochem. Pharmacol. 26*, 1953 (1977).

76. Gozalvez, M., Blanco, M., Hunter, J., Miko, M., and Chance, B., *Europ. J. Cancer 10*, 567 (1976).

77. Murphee, S. A., Cunningham, L. S., Hwang, K. N., and Sarto-relli, *Biochem. Pharmacol. 25*, 1227 (1976).

78. Plowman, J. K., Kelley, S. P., and Fine, P. L., *Proc. Am. Assoc. Cancer Res. 15*, 373 (1974).

79. Duarte-Karim, M., Ruysschaert, J. M., and Hildebrand, J., *Biochem. Biophys. Res. Comm. 71*, 658 (1976).

80. Arcamone, F., *Lloydia 40*, 45 (1977).

81. Ohnuma, T., Holland, J. F., and Chen, J. H., *Cancer Res. 35*, 1761 (1975).

82. Atassi, G., Duarte-Karim, M., and Tagnon, H. J., *Europ. J. Cancer 11*, 309 (1975).

83. Takanashi, S. and Bachur, N. R., *J. Pharmacol. Exp. Ther. 195, 4 (1975)*.

84. Bachur, N. R., *Biochem. Pharmacol. Supplement 2*, 207 (1974).

85. Oki, T., Matsuzawa, Y., Yoshimoto, A., Numata, K., Kitamura, I., Hori, S., Tahamatsu, A., Umezawa, H., Ishizuka, M., Naga-nawa, H., Suda, H., Hamada, M., and Takeuchi, T., *J. Anti-biot. 28*, 830 (1975).

86. Takahashi, Y., Naganawa, H., Takeuchi, T., Umezawa, H., Komi-
     yama, T., Ohi, T., and Inui, T., *J. Antibiot. 30*, 622 (1977).
87. Komiyama, T. M., Matsuzawa, Y., Ohi, T., Inui, T., Takahashi,
     Y., Naganawa, H., Takeuchi, T., and Umezawa, H., *J. Antibiot.
     30*, 619 (1977).
88. Brazhnikova, M. G., Zbarsky, V. B., Potapova, N. P., Sheinher,
     Y. N., Vlasova, T. F., and Bozynov, B. N., *Antibiotiki 18*,
     1059 (1973).
89. Pettit, G. R., Einck, J. J., Herald, C. L., Ode, R. H., Von
     Dreele, R. B., Brown, P., Brazhikova, M. G., and Gause, G.
     F., *J. Am. Chem. Soc. 97*, 7387 (1975).
90. Wani, M. C., Taylor, H. L., Wall, M. E., McPhail, A. T., and
     Onan, K. D., *J. Am. Chem. Soc. 97*, 5954 (1975).
91. Brazhnikova, M. B., Zbarsky, V. B., Ponomarenko, V. I., and
     Potapova, N. P.,
92. Formelli, F., DiMarco, A., Casazza, A. M., Pratesi, G.,
     Supino, R., and Mariani, A., 10th Int. Congress of Chemo-
     therapy, Abstr. 493. Zurich (1977).
93. Bradner, W. T., Bush, J. A., and Nettleton, D. E., German
     Patent 2,628,487 (1977).
94. Strauss, D. and Fleck, W., *Z. Allg. Microbiol. 15*, 615 (1975).
95. Nettleton, D. E., Bradner, W. T., Bush, J. A., Coon, A. B.,
     Moseley, J. E., Myllymaki, R. W., O'Herron, F. A., Schrieber,
     R. A., and Vulcano, A. L., *J. Antibiot. 30*, 525 (1977).
96. Bradner, W. T. and Misiek, M., *J. Antibiot. 30*, 519 (1977).
97. Aszalos, A. A., Bachur, N. R., Hamilton, B. K., Langlykke,
     A. F., Roller, P. P., Sheikh, M. Y., Sutphin, M. S., Thomas,
     M. C., Wareheim, D. A., and Wright, L. H., *J. Antibiot. 30*,
     50 (1977).
98. Hamilton, B. K., Sutphin, M. S., Thomas, M. C., Wareheim, D.
     A., and Aszalos, A. J., *J. Antibiot. 30*, 425 (1977).
99. Wiley, P. F., Koert, J. M., Elrod, D. W., Reisender, E. A.,
     and Marshall, V. P., *J. Antibiot. 30*, 649 (1977).
100. Marshall, V. P., Reisender, E. A., Reineke, L. M., Johnson,
     J. H., and Wiley, R. P., *Biochemistry 15*, 3664 (1976).
101. Kitamura, I., Shibanoto, N., Oki, T., Inui, T., Naganawa, H.,
     Ishizuka, M., Masuda, T., Takeuchi, T., and Umezawa, H., *J.
     Antibiot. 30*, 616 (1977).
102. Brodsky, T. F. and Reusser, F., *J. Antibiot. 27*, 809 (1974).
103. Seeber, C. and Fleck, W., *Z. Allg. Microbiol. 14*, 503 (1974).
104. Fleck, W., Strauss, D., Koch, W., and Prauser, P., *Z. Allg.
     Microbiol. 14*, 551 (1974).
105. Ichihashi, M., Mori, H., Yamada, T., Sugi, H., Fujikawa, N.,
     Japan Patent 77 12992 (1977).
106. Ohi, T., Shibamoto, N., Matsuzawa, Y., Ogaswara, T., Yoshi-
     moto, A., Kitamura, I., Inui, T., Naganawa, H., Takeuchi, T.,
     and Umezawa, H., *J. Antibiot. 30*, 683 (1977); Hori, S.,
     Shirai, M., Hirano, S., Oki, T., Inui, T., Tsukagoshi, S.,
     Ishizuka, M., Takeuchi, T., and Umezawa, H., *Gann 68*, 685
     (1977).

107. Penco, S., Angellucci, F., Viverani, A., Arlandini, E., and Arcamone, F., *J. Antibiot. 30*, 764 (1977).
108. Kumar, V., Remers, W. A., and Grulich, R., *J. Antibiot. 30*, 881 (1977).
109. Kluepfel, D., Baker, H. A., Piattoni, G., Sehgal, S. N., Sidorowicz, A., Singh, K., and Vezina, C., *J. Antibiot. 28*, 497 (1975).
110. Yamamoto, Y., Kiriyama, N., Shimizu, S., and Koshimura, S., *Gann Monogr. 67*, 623 (1976).
111. Bradner, W. T., Bush, J. A., Myllimaki, R. W., Nettleton, D. E., and O'Herron, F. A., *Antimicrob. Agents Chemother. 8*, 1596 (1975).
112. Kikuchi, M., Yamamoto, S., and Tanaka, N., Japan Patent 73 10293 (1973).
113. Okuda, A. and Awadaguchi, S., Japan Patent 76 33195 (1976).
114. Horikoshi, S. and Takahashi, T., Japan Patent 76 13593 (1975).
115. Gromova, M. V., Lokshin, G. B., Kuzovhov, A. D., Sheichenko, V. I., Rudoya, S. M., Veselova, S. I., and Rozynov, B. V., *Antibiotiki 19*, 486 (1974).
116. Tahano, S., Hasuda, K., Ito, A., Koide, Y., Ishii, F., Haneda, I., Chihara, S., and Koyama, Y., *J. Antibiot. 29*, 765 (1976).
117. Okazaki, T., Kitahara, T., and Okami, Y., *J. Antibiot. 28*, 176 (1975).
118. Kitahara, T., Naganawa, H., Okazaki, T., Okami, Y., and Umezawa, H., *J. Antibiot. 28*, 280 (1975).
119. Stroshane, R. M., Chan, J. A., Aszalos, A. A., Rubacalba, E. A., and Roller, P., 12th Middle Atlantic Reg. ACS Meeting April 5-7, 1978, Hunt Valley, Md. Available from A. A. Aszalos, P.O. Box B, Frederick, MD 21701.
120. Sasaki, K., Naito, T., and Satomi, T., *J. Antibiot. 29*, 147 (1976).
121. Fukuyama, T., Nakatsubo, F., Cocuzza, A. J., and Kishi, Y., *Tetrahedron Lett. 1977*, 4295.
122. Furukawa, M., Hayakawa, I., and Ohta, G., *Tetrahedron Lett. 1975*, 2989.
122a. Kondo, S., Migamoto, M., Nakagawa, H., Takeuchi, T., and Umezawa, H., *J. Antibiot. 30*, 1143 (1977).
123. Hornemann, U., Ho, Y. K., Mackey, J. H., and Srivastava, S. C., *J. Am. Chem. Soc. 98*, 7069 (1976).
124. Deshmulk, P. V., Kakinumia, K., Ameel, J. J., and Reinhart, K. L., Jr., *J. Am. Chem. Soc. 98*, 870 (1976).
125. Wagman, G. H., Marquez, J. A., Watkins, P. P., Gentile, F., Murewski, A., Patel, M., and Weinstein, M. J., *Antimicrob. Agents Chemother. 9*, 465 (1976).
126. Fujimori, M., Moriya, S., and Takahashi, N., *Meji Daigaku Nogakubu Kenkyu Hokoku 36*, 1 (1976).
127. Formica, J. V. and Apple, M. A., *Antimicrob. Agents Chemother. 9*, 214 (1976).

128. Formica, J. V. and Katz, E., *J. Biol. Chem. 248*, 2066 (1973).
129. May, W. S., Jr., and Formica, J. V., *Antimicrob. Agents Chemother. 5*, 296 (1974).
130. Katz, E., Williams, W. K., Mason, K. T., and Mauger, A. B., *Antimicrob. Agents Chemother. 11*, 1056 (1977).
131. Devan, M. L., Orlova, T. I., and Silaev, A. B., *Antibiotiki 20*, 243 (1975).
132. Kuznetsova, V. S., Orlova, T. I., and Silaev, A. B., *Antibiotiki 19*, 295 (1974).
133. Modest, E. and Sengupta, S. K., *Cancer Chemother. Rep. Part I 58*, 35 (1974).
134. Moore, S., Kondo, M., Copeland, M., and Meienhofer, J., *J. Med. Chem. 18*, 1098 (1975).
135. Moore, S., Patel, R. P., Atherton, Z., Kondo, M., Meienhofer, J., Blau, L., Bittman, R., and Johnson, R. K., *J. Med. Chem. 19*, 766 (1976).
136. Mortel, C. G., Schutt, A. J., Hahn, R. G., and Reitemeier, R. J., *J. Natl. Cancer Inst. 54*, 69 (1975).
137. Bogdansky, F. M., *J. Chromat. Sci. 13*, 567 (1975).
138. Aoyagi, T., Suda, H., Nagai, M., Ogawa, K., Suzuki, J., Takeuchi, T., and Umezawa, H., *Biochem. Biophys. Acta. 452*, 131 (1976).
139. Reich, E., *in* "Control of Proliferation in Animal Cells" (B. Clarkson and R. Beserga, eds.), p. 351. Cold Spring Harbor, NY (1974).
140. Umezawa, H. and Aoyagi, T., *in* "Proteases of Mammalian Cells and Tissues" (A. J. Barrett, ed.), p. 637. ASP Biological and Medical Press, Amsterdam (1977).
141. Umezawa, H., Ishizuka, M., Aoyagi, T., and Takeuchi, T., *J. Antibiot. 29*, 857 (1976).
142. Suda, H., Takita, T., Aoyagi, T., and Umezawa, H., *J. Antibiot. 29*, 100 (1976).
143. Nakamura, H., Suda, H., Kakita, T., Aoyagi, T., and Umezawa, H., *J. Antibiot. 29*, 102 (1976).
144. Suda, H., Takita, T., Aoyagi, T., and Umezawa, H., *J. Antibiot. 29*, 600 (1976).
145. Nishizawa, R., Saino, T., Takita, T., Suda, H., Aoyagi, T., and Umezawa, H., *J. Med. Chem. 20*, 510 (1977).
146. Fujimoto, K., Tetsuta, K., Tsuchiya, T., Umezawa, S., and Umezawa, H., *J. Antibiot. 27*, 685 (1974).
147. Martin, D. G., Childester, C. G., Mizsak, S. A., Duchamp, D. J., Baczyuskyi, L., Krueger, W. C., Wnuk, R. J., and Meulman, P. A., *J. Antibiot. 28*, 91 (1975).
148. Cooney, D. A., Jayaram, H. N., Ryan, J. A., and Bono, U. H., *Cancer Chemother. Rep. 58*, 793 (1974).
149. Argoudelis, A. D., Reusser, F., Miszak, S. A., and Bacynskyi, L., *J. Antibiot. 29*, 1007 (1976).
150. Arguoudelis, A. D., Mizsek, S. A., Baczynskyi, L., and Wnuk, R. J., *J. Antibiot. 29*, 1117 (1976).
151. Closse, A. and Hugnenin, R., *Helv. Chem. Acta 57*, 533 (1974).

152. Dreyfuss, M., Harri, E., Hoffmann, H., Kobel, H., Pache, W., and Tscherter, H., *Europ. J. Appl. Microbiol. 3*, 125 (1976).
153. Borel, J. F., Feurer, C., Hubler, H. U., and Stakelin, H., *Agents and Actions 6*, 432 (1976).
154. Ruegger, A., Kuhn, M., Lichti, H., Loosti, H. R., Huguemin, R., Quiquerez, C., and Wartburg, A., *Helv. Chem. Acta 59*, 1075 (1976).
155. Satoh, K., Komiyama, K., Kitao, C., Iwai, Y., Atsumi, K., Oiwa, R., Katagari, M., Umezawa, I., Omura, S., and Hata, T., *J. Antibiot. 27*, 620 (1974).
156. Perlman, D., Vlietinck, A. J., Matthews, H. W., and Lo, F. F., *J. Antibiot. 27*, 826 (1974).
157. Pettit, G. R., VonDreele, R. B., Harold, D. L., Edgar, M. T., and Wood, H. B., *J. Am. Chem. Soc. 98*, 6742 (1976).
158. Hozumi, M., Ogawa, M., and Sugimura, T., *Cancer Res. 32*, 1725 (1972).
159. Kakizoe, T., Esumi, H., Kawachi, T., Sugimura, T., Takeuchi, T., and Umezawa, H., *J. Natl. Cancer Inst. 59*, 1503 (1977).
160. Umezawa, H., Medea, K., Takeuchi, T., and Ohami, Y., *J. Antibiotic, Ser. A 19*, 200 (1966).
161. Umezawa, H., *Lloydia 40*, 67 (1977).
162. Umezawa, H., *Gann Monograph on Cancer 19*, 57 (1976).
163. Asakura, H., Hori, M., and Umezawa, H., *J. Antibiot. 28*, 537 (1975).
164. Umezawa, H., Asakura, H., and Hori, M., *J. Antibiot. 26*, 521 (1973).
165. Miyaki, M., Ono, T., Hori, S., and Umezawa, H., *Cancer Res. 35*, 2015 (1975).
166. Umezawa, H., *Prog. Biochem. Pharmacol. 11*, 18 (1976).
167. Kono, A., Matsushima, Y., Kojima, M., and Maeda, T., *Chem. and Pharmaceutical Bull. 25*, 1725 (1977).
168. Muller, W. E. G., Totsuka, A., Nusser, I., Zahn, R. K., and Umezawa, H., *Biochem. Pharmacol. 24*, 911 (1975).
169. Fujii, A., Takita, T., Shimada, N., and Umezawa, H., *J. Antibiot. 27*, 73 (1974).
170. Umezawa, H., *Prog. Biochem. Pharmacol. 11*, 18 (1976).
171. Umezawa, H., *Fed. Proc. 33*, 2296 (1974).
172. Umezawa, H., *Res. Mol. Biol. 4*, 171 (1974).
173. Yoshioha, T., Hara, T., Takita, T., and Umezawa, H., *J. Antibiot. 27*, 356 (1974).
174. Nakamura, H., Takita, T., Umezawa, H., Muraoka, Y., and Iitaka, Y., *J. Antibiot. 27*, 352 (1974).
175. Naganawa, H., Muraoka, Y., Takita, T., and Umezawa, H., *J. Antibiot. 30*, 388 (1977).
176. Muraoka, Y., Fujii, A., Yoshioka, T., Takita, T., and Umezawa, H., *J. Antibiot. 30*, 178 (1977).
177. Kawaguchi, H., Tsukiura, H., Tomita, K., Konishi, M., Saito, K., Kobaru, S., Numata, K., Fujisawa, K., Miyaki, T., Hatori, M., and Koshiyama, H., *J. Antibiot. 30*, 779 (1977).

178. Konishi, M., Saito, K., Numata, K., Tsuno, T., Asama, K., Tsukiura, H., Naito, T., and Kawaguchi, H., *J. Antibiotic.* *30*, 789 (1977).

179. Takasawa, S., Kawamoto, I., Sato, S., Yahashi, R., Okachi, R., Yamamoto, M., Sato, T., and Nora, T., *J. Antibiot.* *28*, 662 (1975).

180. Tahasawa, S., Kawamoto, I., Okachi, R., Kohakura, M., Yahashi, R., and Nara, T.,

181. Ohba, K., Shomura, T., Watanabe, H., Totsukawa, K., Kojima, M., Omoto, S., Tsuruoka, T., Inoue, S., Niida, T., German Patent 2,649,604 (1977).

182. Ooba, K., Kojima, M., Shomura, T., Watanabe, H., Tsuruoka, T., Inoue, S., Niida, T., Japan Patent 76 15694 (1976).

183. Bradner, W. T., Imaniski, H., Hirth, R. S., and Wodinsky, I., *Proc. Am. Assoc. Cancer Res.* *18*, 35 (1977).

184. Ross, S. L. and Moses, R. E., *Biochemistry* *17*, 581 (1978).

185. Yamashita, T., Naoi, N., Watanabe, K., Takeuchi, T., and Umezawa, H., *J. Antibiot.* *29*, 415 (1976).

186. Kumimoto, T., Hori, M., and Umezawa, H., *Cancer Res.* *32*, 1251 (1972).

187. Lippman, M. M. and Abbott, B. J., *Cancer Chemother. Rep.* *37*, 501 (1973).

188. Coronetti, M. and Lippman, M. M., *J. Natl. Cancer Inst.* *56*, 1275 (1976).

189. Lippman, M. M., *Cancer Chemother. Rep. Part I* *58*, 181 (1974).

190. Oki, T., Yoshimoto, A., Matsuzawa, Y., Hori, S., Tona, H., Takamatsu, A., Takeuchi, T., Ishizuka, M., Hamada, M., and Umezawa, H., *J. Antibiot.* *28*, 479 (1975).

191. Komiyama, K., Sugimoto, K., Takeshima, H., and Umezawa, I., *J. Antibiot.* *30*, 202 (1977).

192. Kihara, T., Takeuchi, S., and Yonekara, H., *J. Antibiot.* *27*, 994 (1974).

193. Sasaki, T. and Otake, N., *J. Antibiot.* *27*, 552 (1975).

194. Bogdanov. I. G., Dalev, P. G., Gurevick, A. I., Kolosov, M. N., Malkova, V. P., Plemyannikova, L. A., and Sorokina, I. B., *FEBS Lett.* *57*, 259 (1975).

195. Chan, J., Wei, T. T., Kalita, C. C., Warnick, D. J., Garretson, A. L., and Aszalos, A., *J. Antibiot.* *30*, 1140 (1977).

196. Karasaki, T., Hayashi, C., and Furuichi, E., German Patent 2,532,589 (1976).

197. Suniyama, H., Irie, D., Wada, M., and Tsukuni, H., German Patent 2,639,410 (1975).

198. Lin, H., Bruce, W. R., and Walcraft, M. J., *Cancer Chemother. Rep. Part I* *59*, 319 (1975).

199. Mizuno, S. and Umezawa, H., *J. Antibiot.* *29*, 309 (1976).

200. Zhigis, L. S., Stoyachenko, W. A., Cherches, B. Z., Reshetov, P. D., and Khokhlov, A. S., *Bioorganic Chem. (Russ.)* *2*, 506 (1976).

201. Maeda, H., Glaser, C. B., Kuromizu, K., and Meienhofer, J., *Arch. Biochem. Biophys.* *164*, 379 (1974).

202. Dell, A., Williams, D. H., Morris, H. R., Smith, G. A., Feeney, J., and Roberts, G. C. K., *J. Am. Chem. Soc.* **97**, 2497 (1975).
203. Martin, D. G., Mizak, S. A., Biles, C., Stewart, J. C., Baczynskyi, L., and Meulman, P. A., *J. Antibiot.* **28**, 332 (1975).
204. Samy, T. S. A., *Biochemistry 16*, 5573 (1977).
205. Elting, J. and Montgomery, R., *Biochem. Biophys. Res. Comm.* **71**, 871 (1976).
206. Miyamota, M., Kondo, S., Naganawa, H., Maeda, K., Ohno, M., and Umezawa, H., *J. Antibiot.* **30**, 340 (1977).
207. Takasawa, S., Kawamoto, I., Okachi, R., Machida, Y., and Nara, T., *J. Antibiot.* **27**, 502 (1974).
208. Ohazahi, H., Kishi, T., Beppu, T., and Ariwa, K., *J. Antibiotic.* **28**, 717 (1975).
209. Bergy, M. E., Hanka, L. J., and Herr, R. R., U.S. Patent 3,816,619 (1974).
210. Sono, K. I. and Suhadolnick, R. J., *Arch. Biochem. Biophys.* *173*, 141 (1976).
211. Fuska, J., Ivanitskaya, L., Horakova, K., and Kuhr, I., *J. Antibiot.* **27**, 141 (1974).
212. Fuska, J., Kuhr, I., Nemec, P., and Fuskova, A., *J. Antibiotic.* **27**, 123 (1974).
213. Arai, T., Yazama, K., Mikami, Y., Kulo, A., and Takahashi, K., *J. Antibiot.* **29**, 398 (1976).
214. Kitawa, F., Utsushikawa, K., Kohama, T., Saito, T., Kikuchi, M., and Ishida, N., *J. Antibiot.* **27**, 884 (1974).
215. Kubota, K., Hinok, H., Mayama, M., Motokawa, K., and Yasudo, Y., *J. Antibiot.* **28**, 931 (1975).
216. Umezawa, H., Aoyagi, T., Komiyama, T., Morishima, H., Hamada, M., and Takeuchi, T., *J. Antibiot.* **27**, 963 (1974).
217. Mesentsev, A. S., Kuliaeva, V. V., and Rubasheva, L. M., *J. Antibiot.* **27**, 866 (1974).
218. Petcher, T. J. and Weber, H. P., *J. Chem. Soc. Chem. Comm.* *1974*, 697.
219. Chin, Y. H. and Lipscomb, W. N., *J. Am. Chem. Soc.* **97**, 2525 (1975).
220. Saito, N., Kitame, F., Kikuchi, M., and Ishida, N., *J. Antibiot.* **27**, 206 (1974).
221. Nakanishi, T. M., Tomita, F., and Suzuki, T., *Agr. Biol. Chem.* **38**, 2465 (1974).
222. Minata, H., Katayama, T., and Tori, K., *Tetra. Lett.* **30**, 2579 (1975).
223. Ranieri, R. L. and Calton, G. J., *Tetra. Lett. 1978*, 499.
224. Takahashi, C., Yoshira, K., Natori, S., and Umeda, M., *Chem. Pharm. Bull.* **24**, 613 (1976).
225. Takahashi, C., Sekita, S., Yoshihira, K., and Natori, S., *Chem. Pharm. Bull.* **24**, 2317 (1976).
226. Marchalli, R. and Vining, L. C., *J. Antibiot.* **28**, 328 (1975).

227. Umezawa, H., Takeuchi, T., Iinuma, H., Ito, M., Ishizuka, M., Kurakata, Y., Umeda, Y., Nakanishi, Y., Nakamura, T., Obayashi, A., and Tanabe, O., *J. Antibiot. 28*, 87 (1975).

228. Gasco, A., Serafino, A., Mortarini, V., Meuziani, E., Blanco, M. A., and Scurti, J. C., *Tetra. Lett. 1974*, 3431.

229. Fleck, W., Strauss, D., Prauser, H., Jungstand, W., Heinicke, H., Gutsche, W., and Wohlrak, K., *Z. Allg. Microbiol. 16*, 521 (1976).

230. Szent-Györgyi, A., *Science 161*, 521 (1976).

231. Kurasawa, S., Takeuchi, T., and Umezawa, H., *Agr. Biol. Chem. 39*. 2003 (1975).

232. Kurasawo, S., Naganawa, H., Takeuchi, T. K., and Umezawa, H., *Agr. Biol. Chem. 39*, 2009 (1975).

233. Takeuchi, T., Chimura, H., Hamada, M., Umezawa, H., Yoshioka, O., Oguchi, N., Takahashi, Y., and Matsuda, A., *J. Antibiot. 28*, 737 (1975).

234. Wei, R., Schnoes, H. K., Hart, P. A., and Strong, F. M , *Tetrahedron 31*, 109 (1975).

234a. Jain, T. C., Dingerdissen, J. J., and Weisbach, J. A., *Heterocycles 7*, 341 (1977).

235. Umeda, M., Ohtsubo, K., Saito, M., Sekita, S., Yoshihira, K., Natori, S., Udagawa, S., Sakabe, F., and Kurata, H., *Experientia 31*, 435 (1975).

236. Sekita, S., Yoshihira, K., Natori, S., and Kuwano, H., *Tetrahedron Lett. 1976*, 1351.

237. Sekita, S., Yoshihira, K., Natori, S., and Kuwano, H., *Tetrahedron Lett. 1977*, 2771.

238. Cameron, A. F., Freer, A. A., Hesp, B., and Strawson, C. J., *J. Chem. Soc. Perkin II 1974*, 1741.

239. Pendse, G. S., *Experientia 30*, 107 (1974).

240. Patwardhan, S. A., Pandey, R. C., Dev, S., and Pendse, G. S., *Phytochemistry 13*, 1985 (1974).

241. Higashide, E., Asai, M., Ootsu, K., Tanida, S., Kozai, Y., Hasogawa, T., Kishi, T., Sugino, Y., and Yoneda, Y., *Nature 270*, 721 (1977).

242. Rosselet, J. P., Rowin, G. L., Ludwig, B. J., Gustafson, R. H., Spencer, H. J., and Berger, F. M., German Patent 2,527,626 (1976).

243. Fuska, J., Kuhr, I., and Koman, V., *Folia Microb. 19*, 301 (1974).

244. Anke, T., Oberwinkler, F., Steglich, W., and Schramm, G., *J. Antibiot. 30*, 806 (1977).

245. Hata, K., Japan Patent 75 36694 (1975).

246. Yabuuchi, E., Isagai, K., Sakai, J., Ikeda, Y., and Matsuki, H., Japan Patent 75 95492 (1975).

247. Okutani, K., Japan Patent 75 132189 (1975).

248. Minoda, Y. and Oomori, T., Japan Patent 76 151395 (1976).

249. Takatsu, M., Tabuchi, M., Sofue, S., Minami, J., and Otani, S., Japan Patent 75 12296 (1975).

250. Takatsu, M., Tabuchi, M., Sofue, S., Minami, J., Japan Patent 75 12295 (1975).
251. Takatsu, M., Tabuchi, M., Sofue, S., Minami, J., and Otani, S., Japan Patent 75 12295 (1975).
252. Hanka, L. J. and Dietz, A., *J. Antibiot.* *29*, 611 (1976).
253. Brazhnikova, M. G. and Konstantinova, N. V., *Antibiotiki 22*, 484 (1977).
254. Sakai, T. and Perlman, D., *J. Antibiot.* *28*, 749 (1975).

Index

Phosphonomycin, microbial transformation, 292

Piperacillin, 205, 206

Polyoxins, 319

Prednisolone, formed by immobilized cells, 116

Progesterone, transformation by immobilized spores, 115

Proteases

alkaline-serine protease from *Bacillus lichenformis*, 125, 126

Aspergillus oryzae, 128, 129

Aspergillus type for soy sauce, 125, 126

Bacillus cereus, 126

Bacillus sphaericus, 126

Bacillus subtilis, 127

Bacillus thuringiensis, 127

Candida lipolytica, 130

Cephalosporium species, 129

Endothia parasitica, 129

Mucor pusillus, 130

Mucor species, 130

Mucor type for cheese, 125

Neurospora crassa, 130

Neurospora sitophila, 129

penicillinase, 127

Penicillium caseicolum, 129, 131

Penicillium roqueforti, 129–131

Rhizopus chinensis, 129

takadiastase, 128

thermolysin, 126, 127

Protein supplements

from cellulose fermentation, 35–37

from cellulose fermentation via ethanol, 36, 33Pullulanase, 136, 137

Pyridoxine phosphate, formation by immobilized cells, 115

Q

Quadrone, 320

R

Red pigment from monascus, 134

Ribostamycin, methylation by biological system, 289

S

L-Serine production, by fermentation process, 156, 169, 171, 172

Sisomicin antibiotic group, 223, 224, 228

Sorbistins, 235

Steffimycinone, microbial transformation, 288

1,4-3-*keto*-Steroids, formed by immobilized microbial cells, 117

Sulfuric acid, as solvent for cellulose, 16–19

T

Tannase, 146

Thienemycins, 212, 213

Toyocamycins, microbial transformations, 288

L-Tryptophan, microbial production, 156, 159, 169, 171, 172

L-Tyrosine, production by immobilized cells, 106

U

Urocanic acid, conversion of histidine by immobilized cells, 110, 111

V

Validamycin, glycosylation, 286, 287, 291

L-Valine, microbial production, 156, 159, 169, 171

W

Wine, formation by immobilized cells, 116, 118

X

Xylanases, 139

Y

Yeast

propagation on worldwide basis, 1914ln194

process improvements

baker's yeast, 195

feed yeast, 197

food yeast, 196

Yeast-derived products

autolyzed yeast, 198

cell components

extractable components, 199

microbial protein, 199

RNA products, 199

ruptured cells, 198

Yogurt preparation, using immobilized cells, 112